Text and Context
Cross-Disciplinary Perspectives on Language Study

Series on
Foreign Language Acquisition
Research and Instruction

Barbara F. Freed, Carnegie Mellon University
General Editor

Volumes in the Series

Foreign Language Acquisition
Research and the Classroom

Barbara F. Freed, *Editor*

Text and Context
Cross-Disciplinary Perspectives on Language Study

Claire Kramsch and Sally McConnell-Ginet, *Editors*

Text and Context
Cross-Disciplinary Perspectives on Language Study

Claire Kramsch, Editor
University of California at Berkeley

Sally McConnell-Ginet, Editor
Cornell University

D. C. Heath and Company
Lexington, Massachusetts   Toronto

Published simultaneously in Canada.

Printed in the United States of America.

International Standard Book Number: 0–669–27024–5

Library of Congress Catalog Card Number: 91–72807

10 9 8 7 6 5 4 3 2 1

For
Vera and Louis
Anne and Charlie—
our parents.
They created our first cross-cultural contexts and gave us our first
pleasures in linguistic diversity.

Preface

Early in the spring of 1988, the two editors of this book first met and began talking about the convergence in different areas of language study of developments potentially important for the teaching and learning of foreign languages. Though we came from quite different disciplinary backgrounds, we discovered common interests in recent work on language in context. Claire Kramsch visited Cornell that spring and gave a talk for language teachers in the Department of Modern Languages and Linguistics (then chaired by Sally McConnell-Ginet) on the implications of some of this work for the theory and practice of language teaching. When she returned a few months later for a full year's visit, she found a very lively and engaged community of teachers who wanted to explore those ideas further. In a real sense, it was DMLL language teachers who inspired this project, and we both want to acknowledge our considerable debt to them.

It was a short step to the idea of a conference bringing together scholars from different disciplines working on basic questions about the functioning of language in social and cognitive experience. We wanted to introduce these scholars and researchers in foreign language education to one another, with the hope that hearing about and discussing one another's research might prove stimulating not only for the participating speakers but also for an audience consisting primarily of people engaged in or particularly concerned with university-level foreign language education. To our delight, Peter C. Patrikis, Executive Director of the Consortium for Language Teaching and Learning, responded enthusiastically to the suggestion that the Consortium's annual conference in 1990 be organized by us around the theme "Text and Context: Cross-Disciplinary and Cross-Cultural Perspectives on Language Study." Not only did the Consortium underwrite most of the direct conference expenses, but we also found Peter Patrikis and his staff enormously helpful and encouraging, and we are very grateful to him and to them.

We should also note that Cornell's College of Arts and Sciences, under the leadership of then Dean Geoffrey Chester and Associate Deans Philip Lewis and Don Randel, helped Sally McConnell-Ginet obtain funding from the Cornell President's Fund for the Improvement of Undergraduate Education in support of Claire Kramsch's year at Cornell, during which she not only taught and ran workshops for graduate students and language teachers but also did much of the basic planning for the conference, including lining up the distinguished roster of participants. Grants from the President's Fund are approved by Cornell's president, Frank H. T. Rhodes, with the help of Larry I. Palmer, Vice-President for

Academic Programs. And we also received both financial and administrative support from Cornell's Department of Modern Languages and Linguistics (currently chaired by John S. Bowers and administered by Ann VanDeMark) and the Western Societies Program (directed by Sander Gilman when we first began planning, with the capable help of assistant director Susan Tarrow and aide Tammy Gardner, who both continued their work with the conference when William Lesser became program director). To all these people, we offer our thanks for their part in making the conference possible. But there would have been no conference at all without the cheerful and capable assistance of Gunhild Lischke, DMLL Lecturer in German and the person who shouldered most of the responsibility for local arrangements, correspondence, and similar conference details as special assistant to the conference organizers, and we are especially grateful to her.

The 1990 Consortium Conference, "Text and Context: Cross-Disciplinary and Cross-Cultural Perspectives on Language Study," was held October 12–14, 1990 at Cornell University in Ithaca, New York. This volume does not completely reproduce the conference proceedings, but we think it does address many of the ideas raised there and conveys some sense of the "resonances" among the different voices heard. Charles Ferguson, Stanford University, gave closing comments at the conference, and Ralph B. Ginsberg, from the University of Pennsylvania, spoke on "Theories of Learning and the Design of Foreign Language Instruction"; unfortunately, their schedules precluded their preparing written versions of their comments for this volume. All the other invited speakers have contributed papers based (more or less closely) on the talks they gave; speakers Elinor Ochs and Barbara Freed have invited co-authors to join them. There would of course have been no conference without speakers, no book without authors; as editors, we are especially glad to have been able to work with such a distinguished group of thinkers, and we thank them all not only for their cooperation in dealing with the many details of conference organization (including preparing abstracts for advance distribution to conference participants) and book production but also for their willingness to engage with one another and with the conference participants in the audience (primarily language teachers, both from Cornell and from other Consortium and neighboring institutions) on many questions of interest for thinking about language study.

The conference lasted two full days, with four half-day sessions organized around a single theme. Each session included two presentations from outside the foreign language education field and two from within. Sessions concluded with a panel discussion among the speakers and the audience of 150, who addressed questions to the panelists either in writing or orally. Written questions, we found, were especially useful for bringing a wider range of participants into the discussion and for fostering candor and thoughtfulness. Sandra Savignon, University of Illinois, chaired Session I, Contexts of Communication; Nicolas Shumway, Yale University, chaired Session II, Textual Competence; James S. Noblitt, then of Cornell University and now at the University of North Carolina, chaired Session III, Contexts of Learning; Vijay Gambhir, University of Pennsylvania, chaired Session IV, Communication Across Cultures. The session chairs all contributed thoughtful comments of their own and moderated the subsequent panel discussions. Thanks to the assistance of Dominga Battista, then technician supporting the language and phonetics laboratory facilities at Cornell, and Slava Paperno, Senior Lecturer in Russian and DMLL Director of Technical Support Services, we were provided with excellent audio recording of the entire conference; the discussions were transcribed by Linda von Hoene, assistant to Claire Kramsch in the German Department, University of California at Berkeley. From these transcripts, Claire Kramsch has selected and arranged questions and comments to form a Conversational Epilogue at the end of this volume; the epilogue is organized in three parts to correspond to the organization of the book rather than that of the conference. We thank all these people and also the audience members for their contributions to this "conversation," which gives at least some flavor of the lively exchanges that characterized the conference weekend.

In preparing the book manuscript, Claire Kramsch was ably assisted by Linda von Hoene, who not only chased down references and called authors with queries but also raised general questions and comments for us to consider editorially. Both of us thank her for this important and demanding work. We are also appreciative of Barbara Freed's interest in having this volume as part of the series she is editing for D. C. Heath, and we are particularly grateful for the help and support of Denise St. Jean, Senior Acquisitions Editor, and Rosemary R. Jaffe, Senior Production Editor, at D. C. Heath.

Our own collaboration is emblematic of the cross-disciplinary scope of the book. Claire is trained in literary studies and has considerable experience as a specialist in the theory and practice of foreign language teaching, as a scholar-teacher, and as an administrator; Sally is a theoretical linguist specializing in formal semantics, pragmatics, and gender studies and also has some familiarity with the administrative and institutional side of foreign language programs. Claire drafted most of the introduction; Sally then suggested additions and emendations and drafted this preface. We discussed all the papers and our plans at each stage, and we are grateful for the technological context supporting our communications: the airlines that brought us face-to-face, the telephone cables that carried our voices across the continent, the electronic mail networks that linked our computers, the faxes and other ways to speed papers to one another. Finally, we each thank the other for the intellectual stimulus and pleasure this work has provided us, and we offer this book to the language teachers whose concrete experiences in actual classroom contexts will provide the ultimate test of the fruitfulness of this collaborative endeavor.

Claire Kramsch

Sally McConnell-Ginet

Contents

Foreword

Peter C. Patrikis

The Consortium for Language Teaching and Learning

The last decade has seen a variety of mixed blessings in the area of foreign language education. Dramatic changes in enrollments: increases overall, the missile-like rise of Japanese, steady increases in several of the so-called less commonly taught languages, such that we can no longer call them less commonly taught. Under different guises and names, many colleges and universities have created foreign language centers, offices, programs, or other structures to focus and bring together the diverse tasks of foreign language teaching and research. Proficiency-based testing swept many institutions into a fury of interviews and recordings, given an impetus by calls for accountability in the schools and by federal guidelines for Title VI funding. Many foundations opened their guidelines to foreign language projects, and we have seen an array of dazzling foreign language laboratories, rechristened foreign language resource centers, installed across the country. But foundations evolve and change their focuses, and there is some suggestion that those good times for foreign language projects may be drawing to a close. At the same time, the National Endowment for the Humanities has declared a special interest in foreign language proposals after several years of indecision. Last but not least, the Consortium for Language Teaching and Learning was created by a group of deans, language teachers, and fundraisers to address common issues among eleven private universities. Where all this activity will lead remains to be seen. The pessimists assert that things will get worse before they get better. The optimists see a light at the end of the tunnel.

The conference from which the papers in this volume are drawn was the fourth national symposium organized and sponsored by the Consortium for Language Teaching and Learning. Each of these conferences has, in its own manner, attempted to pose new or different questions. The Consortium has sought to reconfigure how we conceive of foreign language programs, to cause ourselves to reexamine our basic assumptions. The first conference on the governance of foreign language teaching and learning examined what is at the same time an intellectual and an administrative issue: how do we account for the aspirations of the foreign language teacher in terms of compensation, promotion, and allocation of resources and how are these aspirations to fit into departments that are essentially departments of literary or linguistic studies?[1] The second conference, on language learning and liberal education, asked whether there is an alternative to the paradigm of the adult native speaker for language learners and how language learning fits into undergraduate general education.[2] The third conference, on foreign language acquisition research and the classroom, examined the array of research questions that can enhance the work in the classroom.[3] As is evident, these three topics overlap and intersect in interesting ways.

What is clear in all these activities is that the task of the foreign language teacher is becoming increasingly complex. Each change brings along with it a new challenge that has to be met intellectually or administratively or financially. Gone are the days when the mere mastery of morphology, syntax, and lexical items constitutes language learning. Gone also are the days when mere communication suffices. The fourth conference, represented in this volume, was an attempt to view language study from a cross-disciplinary and cross-cultural perspective. As the adjacent disciplines bring more and more insights to bear upon teaching and learning and upon communication itself, the foreign language classroom becomes an open laboratory, a constant experiment for efficiency on the one hand and depth on the other.

The papers in this volume represent an ambitious endeavor. To attempt to cross disciplines and to cross cultures at this time in our state of knowledge is perhaps a bit like crossing a continent of quicksand. The redefinitions that many disciplines are now undergoing amount to the explosion of their boundaries. Analogously, the pace of change in the modern world can cause us to ponder the alterations of cultures right before our eyes. What are the strategies of cultural and intercultural representation that are fitting for an increasingly hybrid and mobile world community? Can we, as individuals, as teachers, and as students, understand our effort in terms of travel, instead of rootedness? These papers are explorations for a new conception of language teaching and learning. Let us recall the words of a poet: In his journals, Baudelaire notes, "*les seuls voyageurs sont ceux qui partent pour partir.*" As we say in American English, "The best part of the trip is getting there." It is our hope that these papers provoke discussions and reconsiderations of what it means to teach and learn another language.

Endnotes

1. Peter C. Patrikis, ed. 1988. *The Governance of Foreign Language Teaching and Learning: Proceedings of a Symposium, Princeton, New Jersey, 9–11 October 1987.* New Haven: Consortium for Language Teaching and Learning.
2. Peter C. Patrikis, ed. 1988. *Language Learning and Liberal Education: Proceedings of a Symposium, The University of Chicago, 15–17 April 1988.* New Haven: Consortium for Language Teaching and Learning.
3. Barbara F. Freed, ed. 1991. *Foreign Language Acquisition Research and the Classroom.* Lexington, Mass.: Heath.

Text and Context
Cross-Disciplinary Perspectives on Language Study

Section I

Introduction

Chapter 1

(Con)textual Knowledge in Language Education

Claire Kramsch

University of California
at Berkeley

Sally McConnell-Ginet

Cornell University

What they set out to do
They brought to pass;
All things hang like a drop of dew
Upon a blade of grass.

Gratitude to the Unknown Instructors
W. B. Yeats

HISTORICAL OVERVIEW

The terms *text* and *context* have an honorable tradition in American language education and its precursors. Their definition and the definition of their relationship to one another have varied with the theories of language itself and with the different methods for learning and teaching foreign languages proposed through the centuries in European countries and their one-time colonies.

At the time when education was primarily in the hands of the Catholic Church and when the only languages with any academic legitimation were classical Latin and Greek, the sacred texts or Scriptures formed the bedrock of language learning and teaching. Through them, learners acquired both literacy and religious education, they were initiated both to the rules of Latin grammar and to the mysteries of the Christian faith. The sacred text contained its own transcendental context of use. Associated in its etymological sense with such activities as weaving ("tessere"), crafting, manufacturing ("techne"), the term *text* referred to a crafted body of written words, interwoven so as to express truths intended as eternal. Church commentaries and religious practice helped to fix these "holy" truths, and they were often assumed to be readily translatable from one language to another (though see Miller, this volume). Even the secular texts of classical Greece and Rome were firmly embedded in historical and cultural traditions that assigned them singular meanings and quite rigidly prescribed uses as repositories of cultural values. For a long time in the study of classical languages, texts brought with them their own contexts.

As education became secularized and increasingly democratized, interest in classical languages declined and modern language study became more respectable. But the clarity of purpose associated with traditional language study was lost. Texts no longer came with a weighty tradition and narrowly defined interpretive uses. Those charged with teaching modern languages often wanted to share their own enthusiasm for particular literary works but typically filled the first years of language study with translation of written texts and exercises whose purpose was solely to instill knowledge of grammatical forms and dictionary entries. Few students could hope to achieve in this way enough linguistic facility to allow them to experience the pleasures of Goethe or Proust or Dostoevsky in their original tongues. Nor, of course, could they manage to converse in the foreign language. Not surprisingly, language study tended to function less as a meaningful enterprise than as a formal game, pursuit of a "linguistic skill" for its own sake.

As early as the mid-forties, there began to be a move away from the traditional exclusive focus on written texts and toward the acquisition of oral/aural facility. At Cornell, linguists who had helped train military personnel during World War II brought their methods to classroom teaching not only of "truly foreign" languages, the linguists' stock in trade, but also of the standard modern European languages that formed the core of foreign language curricula. Rather than translation of literary texts, the focus was on oral pattern drills and memorized dialogues. The approach adopted at Cornell spread and by the sixties audiolingual methods had largely replaced the more traditional grammar/translation methods. Students were still, however, isolated from communities of linguistic practice in which what they "learned" might actually be used meaningfully. What semantic sense they made of the newly acquired linguistic forms was at best limited, a pale shadow of the full-blooded communicative force that living people speaking a living language give to such forms as they use them in particular social contexts for varied social as well as informational purposes. Language students remained locked into the empty mouthing of decontextualized sentences or dialogues linked by shared formal features. These oral texts were really no more embedded in communicative contexts than the written texts they replaced.

In both religious and language education, "texts" or "textbooks" that became learning instruments tended to degenerate from fully meaningful discourses (e.g., the Scriptures as embedded in religious practices) to empty formal models— handbooks prescribing moral or linguistic behavior. Language course descriptions often still reflect the "handbook" approach, suggesting that the sole aim of language study is to "develop" and "sharpen" certain behavioral skills (speaking, reading, and writing), to lead the student to "master" a body of linguistic knowledge. The relation of such skills to any significant intellectual activity or content is at best unclear. Hence the recent proliferation of such initiatives as "content-based instruction" (Leaver and Stryker 1989), or "teaching language in context" (Omaggio 1986), which aim at restoring the earlier embedding of texts in contexts that endow them with real meaning.

The fact that, in language pedagogy, the term *text* refers to both an instance of meaning (a stretch of spoken or written language) and a program of action (a textbook), illustrates the basic dilemma of language teaching: we seek to achieve a certain competence, but we do not know whether we have achieved it unless that competence becomes performance, i.e., unless the learner knows how to transform this competence into social practice. This is what Fillmore calls the "Incarnation Theory" (1979: 13): Supposing that a "minor god . . . would wish to pass as a member of the human community," it would need to know much more than just the local grammar if it were to put enough constraints on its unlimited potential so as not to give away its divine origin. Indeed, it would need to know the whole social context of the "word made flesh." Of course no mere course can ever give the full, rich range of social and cultural context on which cultural natives draw as they speak with one another (see, e.g., Becker, this volume). Nonetheless, language study can and should help students go beyond static knowledge of linguistic forms to at least some kind of participation in socially embodied and meaningful linguistic practices beyond their classrooms.

Meaningful language use presupposes as well as develops social and cultural familiarity with communities using the target language. It does not require that the student "pass" as a cultural native (see Saville-Troike, this volume). Indeed, sometimes the language will not be used for access to the culture of those who speak it natively but will primarily serve for communication with other non-native speakers (this is true for many students of English around the world); in these cases too, however, students need to know that the forms of a language are only part of what is involved when people interact in the language. Part of learning a foreign language should include coming to appreciate that language use involves more than behavioral skills and some universal "common sense": language use is a social act, embedded in a web of social practices. Even native speakers from similar backgrounds do not always agree on the social meaning of what is said (or not said) and when (see Tannen, this volume): it would be highly unrealistic for learners to assume that they will some day never misunderstand or be misunderstood. Sociocultural contexts cannot be reduced to an inventory to be "mastered" like grammatical knowledge: they are not only too rich and various but also in constant flux as people reshape them through speaking and other forms of social action. Yet students can come to understand the centrality of context to linguistic communication and can develop some ethnographic skills to help them better understand the relevant contexts for their own uses of the target language.

In the early seventies, educators introduced a functional approach to language learning that acknowledged, rather than concealed, the fact that communication through language is a risky and painful process, and even more so if it takes place via an imperfectly acquired foreign language. Since then, communicative language teaching has, under various guises, attempted to embrace the gap between textual forms and contextual meanings. It has turned its attention to the *processes* at work in bridging this gap; it has tried to help learners *create* texts and *shape* contexts of use. This represents a radical departure from the traditional attitude toward texts as repositories of stable truths, be they religious or secular. Learners themselves are to weave together texts and contexts to make meanings and to give power to words: they can no longer passively recognize a transcendental realm of pre-made units of meaning associated with pre-built texts but must begin actively to engage in discursive practices that create spoken and written texts and endow them with meanings. Linguistic form does not disappear but assumes importance as a socially shared communicative resource.

We will briefly describe three aspects of such communicative approaches to language study, discussing both theoretical and pedagogical issues. We will then outline this volume and finally discuss some of its implications for current debates about the relationship of form and meaning in language education.

CREATION OF TEXTS IN DISCOURSE

One of the hallmarks of the communicative revolution was to move learners away from merely producing and deciphering isolated words and sentences and analyzing their formal links to other sentences; it channeled learners' energy instead into performing communicative acts in discourse. This represented a totally different way of viewing stretches of connected speech. For example, the traditional "explication de textes," or text analysis, inspired by philology and literary exegesis, had been interested in how linguistic features of a text were patterned so as to give the text structural cohesion. By contrast, discourse analysis, which derives its impetus from social anthropology and linguistic philosophy, explores the speech functions and speech acts performed by the textual features; it examines the communicative options available to the writer and the possible meanings conveyed; it makes the negotiation of meaning between text and reader a constitutive element of reading as a social practice (Widdowson 1975).

Widdowson captured this change in orientation in language study as follows:

> We may . . . use the label *discourse analysis* to refer to the investigation into the way sentences are put to communicative use in the performing of social actions, discourse being roughly defined, therefore, as *the use of sentences*. . . . If we are to teach language in use, we have to shift our attention from sentences in isolation to the manner in which they combine in text on the one hand, and to the manner in which they are used to perform communicative acts in discourse on the other. (1979: 93)

As Widdowson pointed out (1975), the same stretch of written language can be viewed either as text or as discourse, depending on how one views the relationship of text to context of use: On the one hand, as a static relationship between a finished product and stable, fixed contextual meanings, both to be discovered and analyzed by the reader/addressee; on the other hand, as a dynamic, interactive process of "interpretation, expression, and negotiation" (Breen and Candlin 1980: 92) between the producers and recipients of texts and the social context of communication. By both constraining and expanding one another, text and context constantly interact as they mutually construct each other and together construct meaning.

The main thrust of communicative or proficiency-oriented language teaching has been the creation of text as an "instance of the process and product of social meaning in a particular context of situation" (Halliday and Hasan 1989: 10). Much second language acquisition research has focused on the psycholinguistic conditions that facilitate or impede the creation of spoken and written texts in the classroom. Some of that research has been reported on in the previous volume in this series (Freed 1990). Similar issues are taken up in this volume: What kind of input do learners need (Ellis, Lightbown)? What type of interaction between native speakers and non-native speakers or among non-native speakers facilitates language acquisition (Wong Fillmore, Pica)? How do learners make sense of the cultural features of texts (Prince, Swaffar)? How can we introduce students in the somewhat artificial classroom community to the wealth of social meanings expressed by choice among informationally equivalent variants (Valdman)? Is adherence to some particular dominant sociocultural norms of verbal behavior possible, or even desirable (Saville-Troike)?

The pedagogical applications of the communicative approach have revolutionized language study. Learners now strive to create texts that derive their meaning from the situational context. Through role-plays (Kramsch and Crocker 1990), simulations (Omaggio 1986; di Pietro 1987) and interactive practices (see for example Grellet 1981; Kramsch 1984; Rivers 1987), they acquire the forms of the language *at the same time as* they choose to use one over the other in order to convey situationally appropriate meanings. Most textbooks now also present, besides formal features of speech, speech functions and gambits of social etiquette and of socially sanctioned conversational management.

However, the difficulty with any communicative approach has been how to constrain the context so as to make it teachable. After all, we know from Hymes that situational contexts are really a most complex affair: besides medium, topic, tone, register, and genre, they also include the physical setting, the purpose of the exchange, the relative roles and statuses of the participants, the socially acceptable norms of interaction (1974). To this list we have to add the variable perceptions of all these factors by the interlocutors. The disappointment experienced in Europe with functional-notional approaches (Coste 1980) and the misgivings voiced in this country with respect to the ACTFL Proficiency scale (Savignon 1985; Kramsch 1987) had the same concern: Which aspects of context can actually be taught in classrooms? Arguably, the possibly relevant contextual features cannot be enumerated in advance (see Levinson 1983 for some discussion) nor can contexts themselves ever be fully "teachable." Breen and Candlin's first programmatic statement, "Communicative curricula are essentially the means of capturing variability" (1980: 107), highlighted what has proved to be the Achilles heel of communicative approaches to language teaching. One way language pedagogy chose to respond to the challenge was to arbitrarily codify situational contexts and teach them as it had formerly done points of grammar. Thus in Europe, learners learned ten ways of excusing themselves rather than ten ways of conjugating verbs (Coste 1980); in the United States, proficiency-based instruction taught ten levels of functional and grammatical competence in fulfilling various individual tasks. Unfortunately, such strategies obscured the socially variable construction of contexts and their interactions with texts. They reduced contexts to items in a textbook and thus ignored the fact that people have considerable creative leeway in what they do and say, in how they construe and shape their sociolinguistic options.

We will first examine the variable nature of contexts in language learning. Then we will discuss what seem to us some promising alternatives for approaching the interaction of text and context in language study.

NEGOTIATION OF MEANING WITHIN SOCIAL CONTEXTS

To understand and help learners develop communicative competence in a language, one has to recognize the variable nature of context, both social and psychological. Sociolinguistics (Berns 1991; Preston 1989), conversation and discourse analysis (Goodwin 1981; Brown and Yule 1983; Schegloff 1988), and pragmatics (Levinson 1983; Blum-Kulka, House, and Kasper 1989) have emphasized the way in which social structure not only constrains but also is partly constituted by the choice of forms and functions in language use. The margin of individual creativity in the production of texts is not only limited by the way each language fulfills discourse tasks differently (Prince, this volume) but also by each language's idiosyncratic way of responding to the imperatives of sociopragmatic appropriateness (Thomas 1983). People (re)construct social classes, age categories, gender, and power relations as they talk with one another, but they typically operate within the bounds of appropriateness prevailing in some relevant group toward which their social practice is oriented (Duranti 1988; Goodwin 1991). The social dimensions of linguistic practice are much richer and more complex than is indicated by the common practice of observing correlations between a speaker's social characteristics (e.g., sex or status) and the forms which that speaker utters. Such correlational studies can be quite illuminating, however, and serve to draw attention to the interaction between linguistic and other social practices; at their best, they are complemented by detailed linguistic and ethnographic examination of discourses functioning in particular communities. There is now abundant evidence that linguistic form can be sensitive to and constitutive of such social relations as gender (Philips, Steele, and Tanz 1987; Coates and Cameron 1989; Gal 1990; Tannen 1990a,b, and this volume; Eckert and McConnell-Ginet, forthcoming), status and power (Kramarae, Schulz, and O'Barr 1984; Lakoff 1990), social class (Labov 1972a,b, 1980; Guy 1988; Eckert 1987, 1989), and, of course, nationality or ethnicity (Gumperz 1982a,b; Basham and Kwachka 1989; Fiksdal 1989). There has also been some success in trying to articulate certain general principles governing possible cross-linguistic and cross-cultural variation in the linguistic expression of social meaning (on politeness, e.g., see Brown and Levinson 1978, 1987), but scholars are only beginning to explore in detail the workings of language as social practice.

With regard to language learning, recent work in psycholinguistics has focused on variation in second language acquisition (Ellis 1987, 1989; Tarone 1988, 1989; Gass et al. 1989). Tarone lists the possible causes of systematic, i.e., predictable, variation in the interlanguage of language learners. They all have to do with context:

1. the linguistic context of the varying forms (referring to the phonetic, phonological, morphological, and syntactic context)

2. the "function" performed by the linguistic form in different sorts of discourse

3. psychological processing factors, identified variously as "attention to form," "automaticity," and "monitoring"

4. social factors, such as the speaker's relationship to the interlocutor, the topic of conversation, and social norms activated in the social setting

5. miscellaneous task-related factors, such as the form of the instructions given the speaker (Tarone 1989: 14).

Ellis (1989) shows how learners slowly build for themselves a network of sociolinguistic information about the use of forms in context. This accretion of information occurs in different ways, which account for different sources of variability in communicative competence:

1. linguistic context; i.e., the learner gradually learns which contexts the new form can be used in. (A student of English, e.g., must learn that the article *an* occurs before words that begin with a vowel sound or that adverbs like *passionately* cannot occur between the verb and its direct object.)

2. discourse context; i.e., the learner learns which topics or genres the new form belongs to. Initially, knowledge of a form may be restricted to that discourse context in which it was acquired. Subsequently, the learner begins to discover the discourse range of the new form. (So forms like English *mutant* and *mutation* might be first encountered in a biology lecture but only later extended to less technical discourses.)

3. social context; i.e., the learner discovers what social meanings the new form carries and learns to use it with the appropriate addressee. (Thus the learner becomes aware, e.g., that though *pee* or some other colloquial word would be appropriate for use in informal conversation with a good friend, a form like *urinate* or *void* would be expected in talking with a physician during a medical examination.)

4. interactional context; i.e., the learner learns to use the new form to perform an increasing range of communicative functions (not necessarily in accord with native-speaker use). (The English tag question, e.g., might first be used only to obtain confirmation ["We had an assignment due today, didn't we?"] and then later be extended to such functions as drawing others into a conversational exchange ["It's a beautiful day, isn't it?"]).

Increased appeals to include "culture" in language teaching represent one way in which language pedagogy has attempted to respond to the inadequacies of decontextualized language instruction. To develop appropriate interpretive schemata for understanding written texts (Swaffar, Arens, and Byrnes 1990) or to be able to produce and interpret spoken texts in socioculturally appropriate ways (Byrnes 1987), learners have to understand not only the institutional aspects of the target society, but the variable attitudes and perceptions that make up the social fabric of human relations in that society. And that is where, of course, much more research is needed from which the language teacher could draw. Even though he urges that teachers attend to the complexities of form-function interaction, Valdman admits that "the level of research in syntax and in pragmatics in this area is still very limited. . . . [It is] extremely difficult to try to draw any type of clear relationship between certain factors—either social or pragmatic or linguistic—and the use of certain features" (conversational epilogue, this volume). Indeed, unlike text, context cannot be taught directly; it can only be experienced, observed, and reflected upon. To sensitize learners to context, teachers need themselves to attend to cross-cultural comparisons and to ethnographic observations of language in use, not only in communities of the target culture but also within such settings as their own classrooms. Richer cultural and sociolinguistic education for language teachers may ultimately prove much more important than training in pedagogical methods.

The more light research sheds on the multiple aspects of context in language use, the greater the feelings of inadequacy of language teachers, who often find themselves yearning for the days when all they had to do was drill linguistic forms and retrieve them on fill-in-the-blanks tests. Now that attention has to be paid to language as socially signifying practice, they panic. How can they possibly teach all that has to be known in order to function effectively and appropriately in the society that speaks that language? They justly feel not only linguistically and culturally ill-suited to the task, but ill-prepared pedagogically. Can only native speakers with an intimate knowledge of the social context be effective language teachers? Or are fluent non-natives with an informed outsider's view of the target culture better able to help students enter new and different communities? Is a team required rather than a single individual for effective introduction to the variations of use in natural context? Is it not better to just teach the forms in class and for the rest, send the learners to the target country? But again, which forms should be taught in class: some arbitrary pedagogic norm or those forms actually used by native speakers? And even if the learners stay in the country long enough to acquire the appropriate behaviors, will they automatically gain an understanding of those behaviors? How can we most effectively educate language learners to approach cross-cultural contacts with sensitivity to the range of possible diversity and with respectful attention to alternative social practices?

Despite the theoretical injunctions of the early proponents of the communicative approach (Breen and Candlin 1980: 99; Breen 1985), the classroom context itself has been in practice devalued, fulfilling a mere service function for the real world to come. Pedagogic rhetoric reinforces the impression that the classroom is indeed, in time, space, use, and status, a transit place, a rehearsal studio for a later, more serious, performance. As the saying goes, "First you learn the forms, then you learn to use them in real contexts of communication."

Such a view of learning might be appropriate for developing technical skills; for learning a language, however, it can be alienating. It focuses all the energy of the learners on acquiring the surface features of sociolinguistically correct behavior and using them in the same unconscious manner as do native speakers in their respective society. It leaves no time or interest for a deeper critical understanding of cross-cultural contexts, beyond the satisfaction of "sounding native."

If, until the sixties, the pedagogic heritage of the classical languages had stifled modern language study and reduced it to dead translations or pattern drills, the pedagogic fallout of the economic migrations of the seventies made educational settings hostage to the questionable ideal of mainstream native speaker socialization (see Saville-Troike, this volume). Recent thought in various areas of the language sciences can help language teaching out of this dichotomy.

JOINT CONSTRUCTION OF CONTEXT THROUGH DIALOGUE

Recently the concept of communicative competence (see Habermas 1970) has been reexamined by those who had launched it in this country, notably by Dell Hymes. Habermas's concept, Hymes notes, was based on an ideal social consensus that could serve as a vantage point for critique and transformation of society. However, given the variability of the social context, how can there be social consensus? Hymes remarks:

> Habermas brings the efforts of many Marxists in this century to come to terms with cultural hegemony into direct connection with language and communication, but occludes particular existence and concrete individuality. His ideal of consensus through unlimited turntaking, whatever its difficulties as a theory of truth, is inadequate as a model of practical action, if the differential distribution of abilities in actual groups is not taken into account. (Hymes 1987: 225)

This criticism of Habermas echoes much recent unease in language teaching. Variability in context precludes the notion of a unitary foreign national culture of which every individual would be a reflection. Furthermore, communicative competence is not just the ability to take turns in conversation and negotiate meanings, but the capacity to exercise judgment as to when to speak and when to remain silent (see Becker and Saville-Troike, this volume.) "[A theory of communicative competence] will not be able to specify absolutely and in advance the character of communicative competence for a particular case, for that will be relative to the persons, activities, and needs involved, and perhaps, to judgments that have an ethical and political dimension" (ibidem).

Hymes's emphasis here on human judgment in communication has also been the focus of the work of the Soviet literary critic Bakhtin, co-opted by postmodern American literary theory, and made relevant for the first time to language education in this country by Cazden (1989). Like Hymes, Bakhtin rejects the Saussurean distinction between *langue,* this disembodied textual system, and *parole,* or language as social practice. "We know our native language—its lexical composition and grammatical structure—not from dictionaries and grammars but from concrete utterances which we hear and which we ourselves reproduce in live speech communication with people around us. We assimilate forms of language only in forms of utterances.... [They] enter our experience and consciousness together" (Bakhtin cited in Cazden 1989: 120). Stressing the extent to which all language is dialogic in nature, Bakhtin reminds students of language how much every word they utter contains the words of others, how much they unconsciously reproduce the speech, and with speech also the ideology of their environment. "We *are* the voices that inhabit us," writes a scholar from the Bakhtin circle (Morson 1986: 8). "Words in discourse always recall earlier contexts of usage, otherwise they could not mean at all. It follows that *every* utterance, covertly or overtly, is an act of indirect discourse" (ibidem: 24). For Bakhtin, context *is* text.

Now this view could be pretty discouraging for language teachers, whose task it is, after all, to have learners not just parrot a society's conventional discourse but find a voice of their own in the foreign language. Bakhtin explored precisely this dilemma. In the words of Morson, "[Bakhtin] questioned the extent to which we can be present in our own utterances, and he investigated our strategies for appropriating languages we have not made in contexts we have not chosen" (Morson 1986: 17). The solution, according to Bakhtin, is provided by language itself. It is the very property of language to mediate between conventionality and creativity. Not language as a closed system of dictionary entries, but language as dialogic interaction. Not talk as features in a textbook, as in "classroom activities to make students talk," which elicit often nothing more than display monologues, but talk as the joint construction of unfinished thoughts, the joint realization of potential meanings in conversation. This kind of dialogue, as van Lier noted, contains its own interactional momentum, its own "intrinsic motivation for listening" (1988: 106). Dialogue replaces individual performance as a measure of communicative competence.

From research in second language acquisition and applied linguistics, we are also hearing doubts about the feasibility and the educational validity of teaching social context without at the same time teaching the particular voices of texts. Valdman (this volume) advocates the elaboration of reasonable pedagogic norms of functional appropriateness, better suited to the particular voices of American learners of French; Nostrand (1989) calls for restraint in the euphoria surrounding the use of "authentic" texts for information retrieval. He pleads for a critical reading that would distinguish between societal and individual voices. Halliday and Hasan recommend linking context and text more closely:

> The notions of text and context are inseparable; text is language operative in a context of situation and contexts are ultimately construed by the range of texts produced within a community. . . . One commonsense conception is . . . that our ideas, our knowledge, our thoughts, our culture are all there—almost independent of language and just waiting to be expressed by it. This attitude is so deeply rooted that it finds its expression, for example, in our theoretical writings about language. Nothing makes us see the shortcomings of this approach so effectively as the study of text, for nowhere in the study of language is it so imperative that we clarify our ideas of the relationship between language and the so-called extra-linguistic reality. (1989: 117)

The voices of these and other major figures of foreign language education point, not to a retreat from the communicative ideals of the 1970s and 1980s, but to a rethinking of our educational mission. We are not retrenching into the isolation of the text; rather, we are giving more attention to how text shapes context. We are reaffirming the responsibility of the individual learner for his or her own particular choices. We don't have to drown in the endless relativity of contextual phenomena, impossible to capture in the classroom. If we take the privileged locus of the non-native speaker as a point of departure rather than the fixed linguistic rules of the text or the socially conventionalized patterns of the context, we can reinstate the power of the individual speaker to shape his or her environment in dialogue with other speakers. Interestingly enough, the renewed emphasis placed recently on the interpretation and production of written texts in foreign language instruction, and the comeback of literary texts into language syllabi indicate an opportunity for a critical language pedagogy that sees the role of education not only as a reflection of social order but as an instrument of social change.

OVERVIEW OF THE VOLUME

The perspectives discussed previously inform work in a diverse range of fields, including those represented in this volume: linguistics and its cross-disciplinary subfields of psycholinguistics, anthropological linguistics, and sociolinguistics; literary theory; education; language pedagogy; cognitive psychology. But of course each discipline has its own contexts of reference, spheres of influence, and intellectual traditions. We have tried not to impose schemata from our own disciplines, and we have also tried to situate these discussions in the context of the issues that face language teachers. There is not one uniform picture here, but there are striking patterns of recurrent themes that weave the diverse contributions into a richly textured set of essays and a "conversational epilogue," drawn from the give-and-take of discussion during the conference at which versions of these essays were presented.

We have grouped the papers in three sections, emphasizing certain of the strands connecting them. After briefly describing the contents of each paper, we will pick up again some of the other strands that cut across these divisions and that seem especially salient for thinking about language teaching and learning.

Section II, Creating Contexts of Communication, focuses on some of the social and linguistic practices that constitute communicative contexts. Section III, Negotiating Meaning Across Cultures, explores the problematics of interpretation, the insufficiency of linguistic or behavioral form to determine what is meant. Section IV, Shaping Contexts of Learning, examines both classroom practice and the larger institutional contexts in which language study is pursued. The volume concludes with the conversational epilogue. Though no written text is equivalent to the face-to-face communication of oral exchange, we offer these selected transcriptions of the informal discussions at the conference to allow further issues to be raised and more voices to be heard. By conveying something about the context from which the present volume emerged, we hope to help create new contexts for continuing discussions of language among language teachers and a wide range of disciplinary specialists.

Section II begins with "Science at Dinner," in which coauthors Elinor Ochs and Carolyn Taylor examine the social, linguistic, and cognitive dimensions of dinnertime talk in a number of middle-class Caucasian English-speaking families living in southern California. Their thesis poses a striking challenge to educators: what children need in order to acquire the cognitive skills crucial for doing the intellectual work of posing and exploring problems and hypotheses, of offering and revising explanations and theories, is the opportunity to participate in collaborative exchange with others who are their intimates. At the dinner table, the "problems" posed and explored centered on family members' experiences; the kind of collaborative thinking these families engaged in, however, manifested many of the features characteristic of scientific inquiry, where challenges and revisions are fundamentally important. We have suggested above that language learners must learn to attend to contexts, which requires developing a similar capacity to see alternative "versions" of what happens, to recognize different perspectives on events and their significance. Ochs and Taylor's work implies that such learning depends on collaboration by novices and experts in exploring the foreign language and culture. How then can language educators foster the intimacy that is both the condition for and the product of socially constructed understanding?

Lily Wong Fillmore's "Learning a Language from Learners" poses a dilemma, illustrated by the case of a Chinese-born teacher, Mrs. F. Mrs. F is an experienced and creative ESL teacher, who manages to create rapport and some sense of community even in her large classes, which are primarily populated by Chinese-American students whose home language is Cantonese. Mrs. F herself is quite fluent in English but not in mainstream "educated native" English; the English she provides as input for students bears many traces of Cantonese influence both in the way it sounds and in its grammatical structures. Since most of the school's students are also non-native English speakers, learners have little "standard" input and are likely to end up themselves speaking a "learner" variety of English much like Mrs. F's. Although skilled teachers like Mrs. F can do much to foster cognitive development and communicative facility in their students, drawing not only on general educational insights but also on insider knowledge of their students' linguistic and cultural backgrounds, learners in such situations are not adequately exposed to the kind of English they need to learn for full integration into mainstream educational and economic institutions. How can the talents of the many dedicated and capable teachers like Mrs. F be supplemented with educated native input and perhaps other instruction so that students have the opportunity to develop more standard varieties?

In "Performing Expository Texts in the Foreign Language Classroom," Courtney B. Cazden offers an exemplary case study of one approach to developing recognition of the complex perspectives, the alternative contexts, that can inform texts. In a writing course for teachers of writing (in English for native speakers of English), students used readers' theater techniques to give life to written texts by scripting and performing them orally in front of one another. Different voices highlight textual complexities: alternative viewpoints, shifts in level of abstraction, and a wealth of other textual features. Meaning, form, and their interconnections are highlighted, offering many potential benefits for foreign language classrooms. And, as Cazden emphasizes throughout, these activities are intrinsically social as well as cognitive, potentially useful for developing a more intimate community (or communities) in the classroom than is traditionally found.

In "Authenticity, Variation, and Communication in the Foreign Language Classroom," Albert Valdman directly confronts the issue of how foreign language teachers can cope with the sociolinguistic complexity of language use in foreign language communities. Valdman argues that for American foreign language students, unlike Mrs. F's American ESL students, full-fledged communicative competence—with the ultimate aim of communication with native speakers in a native-like way—is an unrealistic goal. Rather, he proposes, teachers can explicitly introduce students to some of the social dimensions of language use in foreign language communities, while also providing for learners attainable norms that will allow them to communicate acceptably (though clearly as foreigners) in target communities. Constructed pedagogical norms recognize the existence of variation in the forms available for particular communicative functions (e.g., the variety of interrogative constructions in French) and take account of not only the social meaning and discourse functions of native speakers' use of the variants but also their attitudes toward them.

As Ellen Prince shows in "On Syntax in Discourse in Language Contact Situations," informationally equivalent syntactic variants of the kind Valdman discusses may be essentially identical in their social meaning yet serve quite distinct discourse functions. Choice among such forms (e.g., "Kim saw this" vs. "What Kim saw was this" vs. "It was Kim who saw this") is central to construction of the discourse context. Prince has discovered from her work on Yiddish and on Yiddish-influenced varieties of English that in contact situations speakers attempt to "match" forms from the two languages and then extend discourse functions of the form in the source language to its (near) equivalent in the "borrowing" language; she hypothesizes that similar "matching" operates in other kinds of language learning situations as well. On the whole, assuming that forms do equivalent discourse work may be a useful learning heuristic; this strategy can, however, create a divergence between the learner's variety and the target when the L1 syntactic form has all the discourse functions of its target partner but more as well.

Section III opens with Alton L. Becker's "Silence Across Languages: An Essay." Meaning is built, Becker proposes, not only from what is said but from what has been said before and from what is not said, from silences. Shared memories and experience with prior texts inform interpretation: they help fill in some silences. Drawing on his own experiences with the Malay language during a recent stay in Malaysia, Becker develops the idea enunciated by José Ortega y Gasset that "some things [are left] unsaid in order to be able to say others. . . . Translation is a matter of saying in a language precisely what that language tends to pass over in silence." The cartography of silences for a particular group shows also what kinds of things they do not do with words, not only the language games they play but those that are avoided or even unknown.

J. Hillis Miller develops a similar theme in "Translation as the Double Pro-duction of Texts." As Miller demonstrates with the telling example of alternative English versions of Goethe's *Die Wahlverwandschaften,* translation is never a trans-parent simple map from one language to another. Rather, a translator (re)produces both the original and the target language text, illuminating multiple possibilities of meaning through the very divergence of the two distinct linguistic constructs. That translations of the German word *Bild* (which can mean both "picture" and "figure of speech") must use different words for what is expressed in German by a single word obscures the play of the German original on the connections and tensions between the different senses of *Bild;* at the same time, any translation is itself a reading of the original that highlights and emphasizes certain meanings. From translation, Miller argues, one learns something of each language and, more generally, of the nontransparent character of all (re)presentations of meaning.

As Deborah Tannen points out in "Rethinking Power and Solidarity in Gender and Dominance," the repertoire of language games and the silences they embrace may diverge even among those who speak what is in terms of formal resources essentially a single language. She focuses on the intrinsic "ambiguity" of the language of power and solidarity, drawing examples from English that could be paralleled in other languages. Again and again, a single linguistic strategy carries double messages, dominance and subordination being by their nature on the flip side of rapport and social distance. Interruptions, for example, can express dom-inance, wresting control of the conversation; interruptions also, however, can equally well express rapport, indicating involvement, interest, and empathy with the speaker. In some ethnic groups cultural norms seem to highlight expression of involvement, connections to others, through heavy use of interruption; others give greater importance to expressing consideration and respect for others as autonomous individuals, through a conversational structure where turntaking is important. Thinking about gender as parallel to such sociocultural divisions as ethnicity, Tannen points to the pitfalls of concluding that, e.g., men's interruptions of women indicate male dominance rather than different gender-based norms for preferred interactional styles.

Muriel Saville-Troike's "Cultural Maintenance and 'Vanishing' Languages" continues the theme of cultural difference in interactional style, especially in patterns of silence, and the consequences for negotiating meanings in cross-cultural communicative encounters. As Saville-Troike makes quite clear, a cultural group may acquire the full repertoire of a language's grammatical forms while at the same time maintaining in their uses of those forms norms for conversational interaction quite different from those prevalent among other speakers of the language. In many American Indian communities, for example, ancestral languages have virtually vanished and the basic linguistic resources of the community are English in vocabulary and grammar. Nonetheless, interactional norms remain much as they were before English forms became the community's linguistic currency, a fact that Saville-Troike convincingly demonstrates by comparing the significance of silence for Navajos and for Anglo-Americans. As in some of Tannen's cases of inter-ethnic communication, the distinct interactional norms lead each group to view the other very negatively. But Saville-Troike suggests that the possibility of sharing formal linguistic resources while retaining distinct interactional communicative cultures might be positively embraced as a healthy pluralism, with distinct cultural groups learning to respect each other's different ways of interacting.

Eleanor Harz Jorden addresses a distinct but related issue in "Culture in the Japanese Language Classroom: A Pedagogical Paradox." Americans do not need to "become" Japanese in order to learn Japanese (they could not do this) but they do need a deep appreciation of what Jorden calls "acquired" culture—the fundamental principles governing social interactions, self-definition, attitudes toward language and toward foreigners (including those trying to use the Japanese language). Acquired culture, Jorden argues, is mainly invisible to monocultural natives unlike "learned" culture (wrapping packages, origami, making sushi). Native Japanese instructors in American classrooms may offer their students inappropriate target language models to facilitate their eventual effective functioning to communicate in Japanese, leading not to sociolinguistically appropriate pedagogical norms of the sort Valdman argued for, but to a problematically American-style Japanese. What is needed, Jorden proposes, is understanding of the distinct communicative culture of the classroom as well as comparative analysis of predominant Japanese and American conversational cultures to help American students become "intercultural" communicators in Japanese.

Section IV continues the examination of classroom environments in "The Classroom Context: An Acquisition-Rich or an Acquisition-Poor Environment?" by Rod Ellis. Just what should go on in language classrooms to enhance acquisition of the target language? Reviewing a number of classroom-based studies, Ellis concludes that it is important to focus on providing opportunities for naturalistic communication in L2. At the same time, he cautions against eliminating pedagogic discourse and instructional activities altogether. Can such "learning" discourse be integrated with communicative discourse? What should be the relative emphasis in the classroom on naturalistic communication and formal learning? Most classrooms probably err by overemphasizing formal learning, treating the target language as an object of study rather than as a tool for genuine communication. Thus Ellis concludes that shifting the balance toward communication will almost certainly make classrooms acquisition richer environments; at the same time, he urges continuing exploration of how instructional discourse contexts contribute to language acquisition.

Patsy M. Lightbown's "Getting Quality Input in the Second/Foreign Language Classroom" discusses ways to provide learners with the "quality input" frequently missing from both communicative-oriented and structure-based classrooms. In one experimental ESL comprehension-based program, francophone children who listened to audiotaped readings by native speakers of English of books they chose were matched with children who spent the same amount of time in a conventional ESL classroom directed by a teacher who was a non-native English speaker. Tests showed not only that the first group had superior comprehension skills but also that their oral fluency exceeded that of the second group. Children in classrooms such as those described by Wong Fillmore might, Lightbown's results suggest, profit from similar listening opportunities. The other studies Lightbown reports bear on the question Ellis raised about how to integrate communicative and pedagogic discourse. Form-focused instruction added to an essentially comprehension-oriented intensive ESL course did indeed have long-term effects, Lightbown found, but only when the forms in question were important for students' communicative needs.

In "The Textual Outcome of Native Speaker–Non-native Speaker Negotiation: What Do They Reveal About Second Language Learning?" Teresa Pica examines the contributions to second language acquisition of native speaker–non-native speaker negotiation—exchanges that are aimed at clarifying a speaker's message for the listener. Communication tasks involving participants in such activities as mutual solution of a puzzle or exchange of opinions promote more negotiation than lessons or interviews. Pica's data show clearly that negotiation does indeed enhance learners' comprehension of L2 output and also that it provides learners with feedback on their own production as well as with information about formal and functional possibilities in L2. Longitudinal studies will be needed to see how well modifications in NNS production capacities achieved in negotiation are sustained over time. Nonetheless, negotiation between NS and NNS is certainly useful for promoting L2 development because it improves access to L2 input and, Pica proposes, it also offers invaluable insight into the acquisition process.

Janet Swaffar's "Written Texts and Cultural Readings" argues for developing insights into the target culture through use of extended "authentic" written texts—texts produced for native speaker audiences. As Swaffar notes, foreign language students fed an inventory of static cultural "features" will have no real comprehension of how such features connect to one another and emerge from patterned social practice. Her basic proposal is to train students to approach popular texts as ethnographers, using these texts as windows on the target culture's own normative views of social practices and values (and also secondarily using them to enrich target language input). Just what kind of "window" particular texts provide is, of course, a complex issue, and Swaffar's specific proposals for training students in "cultural reading" can also be debated. Her discussion should spark further exploration of just how teachers can help foreign language students become sensitive observers of cultural diversity and specificity in social practices and institutions.

In the final paper of the volume, "In and Around the Foreign Language Classroom," Barbara F. Freed and Elizabeth B. Bernhardt give a larger cultural perspective on the American foreign language classroom context. Classrooms may seem like discrete environments, but they are embedded in larger social and institutional contexts that have a profound effect on learning. Freed and Bernhardt discuss three features of American social life of special importance for understanding constraints on language classrooms: the continuing prevalence of monolingual attitudes, the "structural" orientation of education with its focus on efficient delivery of "practical" skills, and a tradition of foreign language education stressing "training" in "methods" rather than intellectual growth and reflection on the problematics of second language acquisition. The classroom's macro-context, Freed and Bernhardt argue, has meant that the language classroom is largely unaffected by the results of research in second language acquisition and related areas of linguistic and psychological investigation. American foreign language education will not really flourish until larger cultural and social issues are addressed: the micro-context inside the classroom should not be our only concern.

All the papers in the volume explore one or another aspect of the relationship between text and context, between form and meaning in language use. Their common strands are rethreaded in various ways across the loom of papers and the snatches of conversation transcribed in the epilogue. We comment in the following on those recurring educational issues that should be of particular interest to language teachers.

EDUCATIONAL ISSUES

Besides the psycholinguistic question of the optimal input conditions for the learners' cognitive and linguistic development, three themes emerge from the volume that are of crucial relevance for foreign language education.

The first is a complex one because linked to the freedom of the non-native speaker to abide by or flout social conventions is the issue of metalinguistic and metapragmatic consciousness in language use. Valdman makes a case for raising the epilinguistic and metalinguistic awareness of learners, i.e., both their attitude vis-à-vis language and language use, and their understanding of how language works in discourse. By advocating culturally appropriate pedagogic norms that combine sound pedagogy and sensitivity to the social uses of language, he reaffirms the healthy difference between competence and performance in language learning. Not all that is French needs to be actually performed by learners in the classroom. The multiple facets of the French language should be observed, analyzed, and interpreted in their multiple contexts of use with all the media and technology resources available; they don't need, however, to be produced by the learners themselves and tested on oral tests.

The competence acquired by these metalinguistic activities is akin to the kind of metapragmatic literacy advocated by Swaffar. In the same manner as isolated grammatical and lexical forms don't add up to discourse competence, "learned" cultural facts do not in themselves yield an understanding of what Jorden calls "acquired culture," i.e., the deep attitudes and beliefs about the world shared by native speakers—not to speak of the concomitant social behaviors. In order to help students discover the general cultural patterns of a society, Swaffar suggests taking as a point of departure possibly universal categories of human behavior as reflected in works of popular culture, and raising the learners' consciousness first about their own, then about the foreign culture. This approach does raise the question of whether there indeed exist such universal culture-free categories that can be filled with the particulars of each society; or whether we don't, right from the start, as Whorf said, "dissect nature along lines laid down by our native languages" (Whorf, cited in Schultz 1990: 38). Miller's meditation about the ultimate untranslatability of texts seems to cast doubt on the matter. So does Jorden's statement regarding the teaching of Japanese: "[T]here is no neutral culture or logic that can serve as a basis for comparison" (this volume: 167). Indeed, the case of Japanese and other so-called Less Commonly Taught Languages has always thrown a monkey wrench into any suggestion based on Western languages for teaching culture.

And so we're back, once again, to the realization that the form, or rather, the struggle with form, is the message. Many of the contributors to this volume stress this point. Cazden insists that the "abstraction" necessary to script stories should not be understood as disembodied generalization, but as "apprehension of form." It is by making apparent the different possible forms of a text that this text is given meaning. In a similar manner, Ochs's and Taylor's family conversations show that it is by working their way through different versions or incarnations of their respective stories that families give meaning to past experience.

A second deeper question discussed at length in the chapters by Ochs and Taylor, Ellis, Pica, and Cazden, has to do with the social foundations of cognition and learning. Research cannot, nor will it ever be able to, predict individual behavior from the social environment, but all the evidence adduced by the scholars mentioned above shows the strong links that exist between social dialogue, interaction, and conversation on the one hand and cognitive and linguistic growth on the other. As Elinor Ochs observed at the conference: "Intimacy is a breeding ground for metacognitive activity. Intimacy has a mind."

For language teachers, this observation is important, because it is often believed that the efforts to create an affectively congenial, "nonthreatening" climate in the classroom must be separate from the cognitive activities demanded from the students. The common belief of teachers and learners alike is that there are "fun" activities, such as songs and games, in which participants may forget about form and concentrate exclusively on content, and "boring" activities that focus on morphology and paragraph structure. One way of making the classroom non-threatening is to make learning a gamelike activity. There is, however, another way. Attention to form can be "fun" of a different, self-conscious kind, when linked to potentialities of meaning. Many of our students don't realize such an exploration of meaning through form can be fun until they have actually experienced it. Part of the role the study of language can play in education is precisely in the metacognitive intimacy it can create in communities of learning.

The final question refers to the ultimate mystery of human understanding and learning. Given the interaction of context and text, of the cultural and the particular, of social experience and individual learning, where do understanding and change take place? This is not a merely theoretical question, far removed from the lives of language teachers who have to teach day after day in the firm belief that what they teach has some causal relationship to what their students learn. In concrete terms, the question is: Where, and at what point, do the learners actually understand enough of what I, their teacher, am saying and doing in the classroom to change their way of being in the world? For example, Miller says that one can understand one's own and the foreign language only through experiencing the failure of translation or communication across languages. If indeed the capacity to understand is predicated on the failure to understand, then we have to realize what a unique paradox the teaching of foreign languages in classroom settings actually is.

Incapable of encompassing the whole variability of the foreign cultural context, the classroom can only offer a highly limited, and thus inauthentic, "text" of the foreign language and society. In addition, embedded as it is in the native educational context, it is constrained by the very culture of that context. Is then cross-linguistic and cross-cultural understanding in educational settings doomed from the start? We are dealing here with the well-known Pascalian paradox. In order to experience the failure of communication, one has to take up the challenge of communication. By doing "as if" it were possible to step out of one's usual frame of reference, to take on a different perspective, to enter into dialogue with a foreign speaker in a foreign language, by doing "as if" one could actually find answers to questions one wouldn't have even known could be asked, learners and teachers undergo an experience that does eventually change them and makes them see things differently. We have intentionally included teachers in that act of faith. For teachers are the catalysts that keep the dialogue going; as such they are also what learners make them to be.

This view of the teacher is both a much more modest and a much more ambitious view than that of the expert knower who transmits information in manageable increments, hoping that the sum will add up to its parts on the test. It calls, rather, for a kind of teaching that Chambers calls "palimpsestic," in reference to the old parchments that were scripted and rescripted by successive scribes, never erasing the past text, but just superimposing the new, as a permanent dialogue, permanently constructing its own context. Similarly, a palimpsestic pedagogy, writes Chambers, "appropriates the educational situation for its own purposes" (1990: 23).

Rather than making the classroom the artificial mirror of the external world, we apply the concept of communicative competence to the type of communication best suited for that setting. Talking and talking about talk are among the things the classroom does best (Edmondson and House 1981). This consciousness about language and the pleasure of dialogue for the here-and-now understanding it brings about creates a climate of complicity and intimacy that replicates the conversational intimacy families have around the dinner table. It provides both emotional support and a sense of power vis-à-vis social reality. By recognizing the unique role that classroom language learning can play in shaping that reality, we place *language study* in the central position it should have in education.

REFERENCES

Attinasi, J., and P. Friedrich. (Forthcoming). "Dialogic Breakthrough: Catalysis and Synthesis in Life-Changing Dialogue." *The Dialogic Emergence of Culture.* Eds. B. Mannheim and D. Tedlock. Philadelphia: U of Pennsylvania P.

Basham, C., and P. Kwachka. 1989. "Variation in Modal Use by Alaskan Eskimo Student Writers." *Variation in Second Language Acquisition.* Vol. 1. Eds. S. Gass et al. Clevedon, U. K.: Multilingual Matters. 129–43.

Berns, M. 1991. *Contexts of Competence: Social and Cultural Considerations in Communicative Language Teaching.* New York: Plenum.

Bialystok, E. 1981. "Some Evidence for the Integrity and Interaction of Two Knowledge Sources." *New Dimensions in Second Language Acquisition Research.* Ed. R. Andersen. Rowley, Mass.: Newbury. 62–74.

Blum-Kulka, S., J. House, and G. Kasper, eds. 1989. *Cross-Cultural Pragmatics: Requests and Apologies.* Vol. 31 of *Advances in Discourse Processes.* Series ed. Roy O. Freedle. Norwood, N.J.: Ablex.

Breen, M. P. 1985. "The Social Context for Language Learning—A Neglected Situation?" *Studies in Second Language Acquisition* 7: 135–58.

Breen, M. P., and C. Candlin. 1980. "The Essentials of a Communicative Curriculum in Language Teaching." *Applied Linguistics* 1: 89–112.

Brown, G., and G. Yule. 1983. *Discourse Analysis.* Cambridge: Cambridge UP.

Brown, P., and S. C. Levinson. 1987. *Politeness: Some Universals in Language Usage.* Cambridge: Cambridge UP.

Byrnes, H. 1987. "Features of Pragmatic and Sociolinguistic Competence in the Oral Proficiency Interview." *Proceedings of the Symposium on the Evaluation of Foreign Language Proficiency.* Ed. A. Valdman. Bloomington, Ind.: CREDLI. 167–78.

Cazden, C. B. 1989. "Contributions of the Bakhtin Circle to 'Communicative Competence.'" *Applied Linguistics* 10: 116–27.

Chambers, R. 1990. "Irony and the Canon." *Profession 90.* New York: MLA. 18–24.

Coates, J., and D. Cameron, eds. 1989. *Women in Their Speech Communities: New Perspectives on Language and Sex.* London and New York: Longman.

Coste, D. 1980. "Analyse de discours et pragmatique de la parole dans quelques usages d'une didactique des langues." *Applied Linguistics* 1: 244–52.

di Pietro, R. J. 1987. *Strategic Interaction. Learning Languages Through Scenarios.* Cambridge: Cambridge UP.

Duranti, A. 1988. "Ethnography of Speaking: Towards a Linguistics of the Praxis." *Linguistics: The Cambridge Survey.* Vol. 4. *Language: The Socio-Cultural Context.* Cambridge: Cambridge UP.

Eckert, P. 1987. "Adolescent Spread of Linguistic Change." *Language in Society* 17: 183–207.

Eckert, P. 1989. *Jocks and Burnouts.* New York: Teachers CP.

Eckert, P., and S. McConnell-Ginet. (Forthcoming.) "Gender Relations and Language Use as Social Practice. *Annual Reviews in Anthropology* 21.

Edmondson, W., and J. House. 1981. *Let's Talk and Talk About It: A Pedagogic Interactional Grammar of English.* Munich: Urban and Schwarzenberg.

Ellis, R., ed. 1987. *Second Language Acquisition in Context.* Englewood Cliffs, N.J.: Prentice.

Ellis, R. 1989. "Sources of Intra-Learner Variability in Language Use and Their Relationship to Second Language Acquisition." *Variation in Second Language Acquisition.* Vol. 2. Eds. S. Gass et al. Clevedon, U.K.: Multilingual Matters. 22–45.

Fiksdal, S. 1989. "Framing Uncomfortable Moments in Crosscultural Gatekeeping Interviews." *Variation in Second Language Acquisition.* Vol. 1. Eds. S. Gass et al. Clevedon, U.K.: Multilingual Matters. 190–207.

Fillmore, C. 1979. "A Grammarian Looks to Sociolinguistics." *Sociolinguistic Aspects of Language Learning and Teaching.* Ed. J. B. Pride. Oxford: Oxford UP. 2–16.

Freed, B., ed. 1991. *Foreign Language Research and the Classroom.* Lexington, Mass.: Heath.

Gal, S. 1990. "Between Speech and Silence: The Problematics of Research on Language and Gender." *Toward a New Anthropology of Gender.* Ed. M. DiLeonardo. Berkeley: U of California P.

Gass, S., C. Madden, D. Preston, and L. Selinker, eds. 1989. *Psycholinguistic Issues* and *Discourse and Pragmatics.* Vols. 1 and 2 of *Variation in Second Language Acquisition.* Clevedon, U.K.: Multilingual Matters.

Goodwin, C. 1981. *Conversational Organization.* New York: Academic.

Goodwin, M. H. 1991. *He-Said-She-Said: Talk as Social Organization in an Urban Black Peer Group.* Bloomington and Indianapolis: Indiana UP.

Grellet, F. 1981. *Developing Reading Skills.* Cambridge: Cambridge UP.

Gumperz, J. J. 1982a. *Discourse Strategies.* Cambridge: Cambridge UP.

———, ed. 1982b. *Language and Social Identity.* Cambridge: Cambridge UP.

Guy, G. 1988. "Language and Social Class." *Language: The Socio-Cultural Context.* Vol. 4 of *Linguistics: The Cambridge Survey.* Cambridge: Cambridge UP. 37–63.

Habermas, J. 1970. "Towards a Theory of Communicative Competence." *Inquiry* 13: 360–75.

Halliday, M. A. K., and R. Hasan. 1989. *Language, Context, and Text: Aspects of Language in a Social-Semiotic Perspective.* Oxford: Oxford UP.

Hymes, D. 1974. *Foundation of Sociolinguistics.* Philadelphia: U of Pennsylvania P.

———. 1987. "Communicative Competence." *Sociolinguistics—Soziolinguistik.* Eds. U. Ammon, N. Dittmar, and K. J. Mattheier. Berlin and New York: Walter de Gruyter. 219–30.

Kramarae, C., M. Schulz and W. O'Barr, eds. 1984. *Language and Power.* Beverly Hills: Sage.

Kramsch, C. 1984. *Interaction et discours dans la classe de langue.* Paris: Hatier-Credif.

———. 1987. "The Proficiency Movement: Second Language Acquisition Perspectives." Review article. *Studies in Second Language Acquisition* 9: 355–62.

Kramsch, C., and E. Crocker. 1990. *Reden, Mitreden, Dazwischenreden: Managing Conversations in German.* 2nd ed. Boston, Mass.: Heinle and Heinle.

Krashen, S. 1981. *Second Language Acquisition and Second Language Learning.* Oxford: Pergamon.

Labov, W. 1972a. *Sociolinguistic Patterns.* Philadelphia: U of Pennsylvania P.

———. 1972b. *Language in the Inner City.* Philadelphia: U of Pennsylvania P.

———. 1980. "The Social Origins of Sound Change." *Locating Language in Time and Space.* Ed. W. Labov. New York: Academic.

Lakoff, R. 1990. *Talking Power. The Politics of Language.* New York: Basic.

Leaver, B., and S. Stryker. 1989. "Content-based Instruction for Foreign Language Classrooms." *Foreign Language Annals* 22: 269–75.

Levinson, S. C. 1983. *Pragmatics.* Cambridge: Cambridge UP.

McLaughlin, B. 1978. "The Monitor Model: Some Methodological Considerations." *Language Learning* 28: 309–32.

Morson, G. S., ed. 1986. *Bakhtin: Essays and Dialogues on His Work.* Chicago and London: U of Chicago P.

Nostrand, H. L. 1989. "Authentic Texts and Cultural Authenticity: An Editorial." *Modern Language Journal* 73: 49–52.

Omaggio, A. H. 1986. *Teaching Language in Context. Proficiency-oriented Instruction.* Boston, Mass.: Heinle and Heinle.

Philips, S. U., S. Steele, and C. Tanz, eds. 1987. *Language, Gender and Sex in Comparative Perspective.* Cambridge: Cambridge UP.

Preston, D. R. 1989. *Sociolinguistics and Second Language Acquisition.* Oxford and New York: Basil Blackwell.

Rankin, J. 1989. "Revisiting 'Der Besuch der alten Dame': Strategies for Interpretation and Interaction at the Intermediate Level." *Die Unterrichtspraxis* 22(1): 24–34.

Rivers, W. M. 1987. *Interactive Language Teaching.* Cambridge: Cambridge UP.

Savignon, S. 1985. "Evaluation of Communicative Competence: The ACTFL Provisional Proficiency Guidelines." *Modern Language Journal* 69: 187–93.

Schegloff, E. 1988. "Discourse as an Interactional Achievement II: An Exercise in Conversation Analysis." *Linguistics in Context: Connecting Observation and Understanding.* Ed. D. Tannen. Vol. 29 of *Advances in Discourse Processes.* Series ed. Roy O. Freedle. Norwood, N.J.: Ablex. 135–58.

Schultz, E. A. 1990. *Dialogue at the Margins: Whorf, Bakhtin and Linguistic Relativity.* Madison, Wis.: U of Wisconsin P.

Sharwood-Smith, M. 1981. "Consciousness-raising and the Second Language Learner." *Applied Linguistics* 2: 159–69.

Swaffar, J. K., K. M. Arens, and H. Byrnes. 1990. *Reading for Meaning: An Integrated Approach to Language Learning.* Englewood Cliffs, N.J.: Prentice.

Tannen, D., ed. 1990a. Gender and Conversational Interaction. Special issue of *Discourse Processes* 13.1, January–March.

———. 1990b. *You Just Don't Understand: Women and Men in Conversation.* New York: Morrow.

Tarone, E. 1988. *Variation in Interlanguage.* London: Edward Arnold.

———. 1989. "Accounting for Style-Shifting in Interlanguage." *Variation in Second Language Acquisition.* Vol. 2. Eds. S. Gass et al. Clevedon, U.K.: Multilingual Matters. 13–21.

Thomas, J. A. 1983. "Cross Cultural Pragmatic Failure." *Applied Linguistics* 4: 91–112.

van Lier, L. 1988. *The Classroom and the Language Learner.* London and New York: Longman.

Widdowson, H. G. 1975. *Stylistics and the Teaching of Literature.* London: Longman.

———. 1979. *Explorations in Applied Linguistics.* Oxford: Oxford UP.

Section **II**

Creating Contexts
of Communication

Chapter 2

Science at Dinner

Elinor Ochs

University of California
at Los Angeles

Carolyn Taylor

University of Southern California

DINNER

In this discussion, we invite the reader to reflect with us on dinner, not as an epicurean event but as a social, linguistic, and cognitive event. Consider the social nature of dinner. During dinner, we consume food and imbibe liquids, yet these physical activities typically are conducted in a social space across the world's societies. They take place during socially specified times of the day and in socially acceptable spaces. For many people, dinners are also social in the sense that they involve the coordination of more than one person in their preparation, consumption, and cleanup. Meals, as every anthropologist knows, are rituals. We might think of ordinary, not-so-special meals as everyday rituals (Goffman 1959). Like grander ceremonial events, they are shaped in their own way by local social conventions and expectations and are critical to sustaining social institutions. Eating together is a universal modality for constituting domestic, political, religious, and economic forms of social order.*

In looking at the organization of meals across social groups, it is useful to examine the kinds of activities that help to constitute a 'meal' for a particular social group. Looking at meals in this way, we can think of them as complex composites of activities, or activity systems (Engeström 1987). While the activity of eating is a universal activity component of meals, what other activities also constitute meals will vary across family cultures and more widely across societies. For many families within the United States, talking is a critical activity component of family meals. In these families, ordinary meals are opportunities for verbal interaction regardless of whether families are eating around a single table or at separate TV tables and chatting during television programming. In this sense, for these families, talking is as important as eating in defining mealtimes.

Just as families and societies may vary in terms of whether or not talk activity characterizes their meals or perhaps more interestingly in terms of the kind and amount of talk activity that characterizes meals, so they will vary in terms of whether or not the cognitive activity of problem solving is characteristic or in terms of the kinds and amount of problem-solving activity characteristic of their eating ritual. In some of the world's societies, meals are not loci for collective problem solving; in others, participants problem-solve over everything from the logistics of food and children's expected comportment to family members' individual and collective dilemmas regarding work, school, and leisure-time activities. Our research examines family dinner meals among mainstream American English-speaking families across diverse socio-economic backgrounds. For these families, dinner is characterized by a high degree of problem-solving talk. These families use dinnertime to work out with one another family plans and/or problems that one or another family member has experienced during the course of the day or in the recent past. For these families, problem-solving talk is at the heart of what constitutes dinnertime.

Another potential function of the activities of eating and talking and problem solving beyond that of constituting dinnertime is that of constituting the family. For certain families, collaborative problem solving around some past or future event is at the heart of what it means to be a family. Kinds of cognition in this sense constitute kinds of social order. One of the most important points of this paper is that complex problem solving constitutes, for many social groups, familiarity. We are familiar either in a personal (e.g., a family member, a friend) or professional (e.g., a colleague, member of a seminar) sense because we problem-solve together. We sustain our familiarity in this way. And when we cease to problem-solve together or reduce the time devoted to problem solving with one another, we index to one another that we are no longer as familiar. We take social distance through cognitive distance. Or conversely, familiarity breeds problem solving, partly in this service of (re)constituting the familiarity. And this kind of familiarity-based problem solving is something we see as valued in domains that would seem far afield from the family dinner arena. This paper is entitled "Science at Dinner" because the kind of social, linguistic, and cognitive activity observed in American family dinners appears to have some affinity with the activity we refer to as science.

SOCIALIZATION OF SCIENTIFIC PRACTICES

When we think of the scientific community, we think of its members—scientists—as persons who devote their professional lives to isolating problems and proposing solutions. But we have recently learned that even amoeba problem-solve, so that this activity is hardly a distinctive characteristic of science. In the course of problem solving, however, scientists sometimes carry out an activity that is not shared by amoebas: they construct theories.

For purposes of this discussion, a theory is defined in terms of two properties:

1. A theory presents an explanation (causal, teleological, or otherwise) of a set of events.
2. The explanation posed by the theory is seen as challengeable, that is, as a *posited* explanation of actual or possible events.

In this definition, a theory is a *version* of events rather than a set of taken-for-granted 'facts' about events.

Observations of scientific activity within scientific laboratories challenge the position that scientific theories are constructed by an isolated researcher working out theorems in her or his wing of the laboratory (Latour and Woolgar 1986; Lynch 1985; Traweek 1988). Rather, theories are outcomes of more or less intense collaboration. Theories are 'co-constructed' in the course of ongoing scholarly dialogue, either through face-to-face conversation, electronic mail, preliminary tables and graphs representing experimental results of a group of researchers, or formal publications.

In the course of these oral or written dialogues, scientists not only collaboratively propose theories but challenge and transform theories as well. A hallmark of the scientific community is that it thrives on challenging matters of fact, procedures, and ideological tenets that are associated with a theoretical enterprise (Laudan 1984).

We suggest that, while theory building is highly elaborated in scientific settings, the activity is not exclusive to those settings. In particular, we propose here that family dinner interactions are also settings for complex theory construction in the course of problem solving. Like scientists, family members define problems and propose possible solutions to those problems. They offer theories of what did or could take place and theories of why some set of actions did or could occur. These theories revolve around *personal* experiences rather than the *impersonal* events of concern to scientists. Family members tend to talk about what did or could happen to them or people they know. Scientists tend to talk about physical events in the world or events that are generalizable beyond the individual events. Nonetheless, both social contexts are characterized by the practice of theory construction as integral to problem-solving talk.

If family dinnertime is a locus for theory construction, then this setting is an important milieu for the socialization of cognition. The family dinners we observed all involved young children as participants and all evidenced some degree of collaborative theory construction. Thus, while Vygotsky (1986) placed great emphasis on the school as a social environment that enhances the development of scientific thinking, our observations lead us to conclude that children are socialized into the rudiments of scientific communication and, by implication, the rudiments of scientific thinking, long before they enter formal school. The family dinner is potentially an opportunity space for involving children as interlocutors in and observers of the activity of collaborative problem solving.

DATA BASE

The generalizations presented in this discussion are based on observations of twenty families varying in socioeconomic status. The families are Caucasian, English-speaking Americans living in the southern California area. All the families in this study had at least two children—a five-year-old and at least one older sibling.

Each family was both video- and audiotaped on two evenings from about five o'clock in the afternoon until the five-year-old went to bed. During the dinner meal, the video camera was placed on a tripod near the eating area, and the researchers absented themselves from the immediate area. Two additional evenings were audiotaped by the families themselves. The data base for the present study consists of transcripts of twenty-four videotaped dinners drawn from twelve families.

PROBLEM SOLVING THROUGH NARRATIVE

While problem-solving talk takes many forms, the focus of our research has been on the relation of problem solving to narrative activity. We consider narrative activity to be the socially organized telling of temporally ordered past, present, or future events from a particular point of view. For example, reporting and storytelling focus on past events, whereas planning and setting up agendas focus on future events.

While all narratives have an element of temporal ordering and a point of view, some narratives center around events that are posed as problems. These problematic events are in turn seen as causing some set of psychological or external physical events. We refer to narratives that center around past problematic events as *story narratives*. We refer to narratives that center around present or future problematic events as *planning narratives*. To understand these narrative types, consider two narrative storytelling and planning interactions taken from our corpus of family dinner narratives:

1. Excerpt from First Week of School Story (round 2 of a 3-round story)

> M = mother
> J = Jacob (4 years, 4 months)
> L = Lily (5 years, 7 months)
> A = Martha (7 years, 10 months)
> R = Fred (10 years, 9 months)

> M: ((addressing Lily)) Miss (Green) said ((Lily looks up from her spaghetti, momentarily pausing in her eating)) you cried and cried at nap time?
>
> L: ((Lily nods her head yes several times))
>
> A: she did - she wanted (her) Mama

M: She said that was because - this was your first day to be at school without me?

((Lily is engaged in eating and spilling food))

M: but honey? - I only work - this - it was only this week that I worked there all week? because it was the first week? of school but -

          [

A: she *cried* at three o'clock too

M: but after this - it - I only work one day a week there and that's Tuesday

The central problematic event of this story narrative concerns Lily's first experience of a school day without the presence of her mother. Both mother and older sister Martha voice this problem ("She wanted her Mama"; "She said that was because - this was your first day to be at school without me?") This problematic event was first introduced by Lily herself earlier in the meal in the course of Lily's saying grace:

(Round 1)

L: = kay - Jesus? - plea:?se - um - help us to love and .hh um - thank you for letting it be a n:*ice* day and for taking a (fine/fun) nap? - a:nd - for (letting) Mommy go bye and I'm glad that I cried today? cuz I like crying .hh and =

          [

A?:   ((snicker))

L: = I'm glad (that anything/everything) =

          [

R?: ((snicker))

L: = happened today in Jesus name ((claps hands)) *A:*-MEN!

M?: amen

          [

J: amen

(pause)

((Lily dives in))

Embedded in this grace is a little story centered around the problematic event ("Mommy go bye") and the subsequent event it provoked ("I cried today"). This example is somewhat complex in that the problematic nature of the event "Mommy go bye" is at cross purposes with the conventional demeanor of thankfulness appropriate to saying grace. Thus at the same time as the narrated events show Lily to be sad ("I cried today") at her mother's absence, these events are reframed within the activity of saying grace as events for which Lily is thankful and glad.

Example 2 displays a planning narrative:

2. Eating Beets Plan

M = mother
S = Sharon (6 years, 2 months)

((Sharon tries to stuff a fork load of food into her mouth))

M: Those are *really* hard to stay on the fork aren't they?

S: ha ha - yeah:

       [

M: you want a spoon?

S: mhm?

M: You can use this spoon - it's right in the bowl if you need it

    ((Sharon stretches over to get spoon))

    (pause)

M: hhh ((deep sigh))

    (pause)

    ((Sharon eats beets directly out of bowl))

"Eating Beets" illustrates a plan for the immediate future and concerns a current central problematic event, namely that Sharon cannot seem to get the beets she is·attempting to eat to stay on her fork. This problem is initially voiced by her mother ("Those are *really* hard to stay on the fork") and subsequently confirmed by Sharon.

Although both storytelling and planning are problem-solving narrative activities, the present discussion will address only storytelling and its relation to the activity of constructing and evaluating theories.

STORIES AS THEORIES

Stories as Explanations

As defined earlier, a theory includes two properties: first, it constitutes an explanation and second it contains an element of challengeability. An explanation that is treated as God's truth or common sense or as an otherwise undisputed fact about the world is not a theory. Theories are posited. They are tentative and disputable. Let us consider how each of these properties applies to ordinary storytelling at family dinnertime.

Consider first the relation of explanation to storytelling. We have noted that stories are distinguished from other types of narrative in that they focus on a central problematic event. This central event is referred to as the "initiating event"

(Stein and Glenn 1979) in the psycholinguistic literature on storytelling and as the 'inciting event' among screenwriters. As these labels suggest, such central problematic events initiate or incite at least one and usually a series of subsequent events. In this sense, the relation of the initiating/inciting event to subsequent events is *causal*. For instance, in example 1, the initiating/inciting event of Lily's mother's absence from school is seen by the narrators as causing Lily to cry. Example 3 also displays a cause-effect explanation within a story narrative.

3. Amy's Shot Story

M = mother
F = father
J = Jason (7 years, 5 months)
A = Amy (5 years)

M: You know what Amy said that was really - I thought really smart? - and really good?

J: what

M: She said. - she couldn't stand to wait for the shot til the last thing

A: ((speaking straight at Jason)) so I - got it *first*

    (pause)

M: so she asked for her shot *first* - and that way she didn't have to wait - (and then) - I thought that was *really* - a terrific thing for her to do

F: ((nods yes)) I agree

M: (what do you think?)

    (pause)

J: ((nods yes)) If you let me go out then I think it's great

F: *no*

M: ((smiling)) And if we don't you think it's really dumb huh?

J: mhm?

M: unun that's interesting

This story concerns a problem that Amy faced that day, namely that she had to have a shot at the doctor's office and she hated waiting for it to happen. This problem is articulated by Amy's mother ("She said - she couldn't stand to wait for the shot til the last thing"). This problematic circumstance in turn provoked at least one subsequent event, namely that Amy asked for her shot first. These two events are related causally in that the earlier circumstance is the reason for the subsequent event. In other words, the earlier circumstance *explains* why Amy asked the doctor to give her the shot first.

The inciting/initiating event may cause not only an external event such as crying or asking the doctor to give a shot first thing. It may cause internal psychological responses as well. In example 1, the external event of crying implies an internal response of sadness. In example 3, the external event of asking for a shot first thing implies an internal response of anxiety.

Stories are full of cause-effect propositions beyond those involving the initiating/inciting event. For example, external events induced by an initiating/inciting event may in themselves cause psychological responses or other external action responses. Thus in example 3, Amy's external response to her problem in turn caused her mother's psychological response at the time the narrative events took place ("I thought [what Amy said was] really smart - and really good?"; "I thought that was *really* - a terrific thing for her to do") and a set of subsequent psychological responses at the time of the story's telling from father ("I agree") and from the ironic older brother ("If you let me go out then I think it's great").

Explanations, central to story narratives, are not the product of a single family member monologuing through a set of sequential events. Rather, as shown briefly above, different family members coauthor storytelling (Duranti and Brenneis 1986) and in so doing co-construct explanations dialogically.

Stories as Versions of Events

Theories are not only explanations; they are possible explanations, versions of what could or did or will occur. But not all storytellers treat their stories in this light. In some cases, the explanation within the story is taken for granted. Indeed that seems to be the case for the story related in example 1. In other cases, how someone sees the narrated problem and responds to the narrated problem is questioned. In some cases, the relation of problem to outcome is doubted because the problem is seen as incorrectly defined or because someone doubts that the problem provoked a particular set of responses. In these cases, the explanation is challenged because it does not match what at least one person considers to be the true state of the world. We can call such challenges *veridical challenges*. Examples 4 and 5 illustrate veridical challenges:

4. Excerpts from Jacob and David Story

   M = mother
   J = Jacob (4 years, 4 months)
   A = Martha (7 years, 10 months)

   A: Jacob ran out!

   M: *Jacob?*

   J: ((from dining room, seated)) *NO I DIDN'T!*

   M: Jacob - did you hit David . . .

      :

   A: all I know is Jacob *pushed?*

      :

J: *No* I *didn't*

     :

M: um? - Jacob? - David was crying and they said you hit him
     (pause)

J: No I *didn't*

          [

A: Mommy? - *all* I know is Jacob pushed him
     (pause)

M: WHY

     :

M: Why did you push him?

     :

J: I did no:::t

M: uh huh

     :

In this story narrative, Jacob is implicated in an inciting event that caused David
to cry. Among other actions, Jacob is said to have pushed David, an action that
for the mother seems to constitute hitting him. In this story, Jacob's older sister
Martha presents one version of the problematic event ("all I know is that Jacob
pushed") that explains why David was crying, and Jacob's mother elicits Jacob's
version, which turns out to directly contradict that of his sister. Here we have a
case of opposing views of the 'facts' of the situation. Eventually the mother adopts
Martha's version of the facts, as indicated in her question to Jacob "Why did you
push him?"

Example 5 also displays a veridical challenge. In this example, the spouses
disagree on the facts of the events which transpired when a friend of Mom's,
Susan, came by earlier:

5. Excerpt from Photo Negatives Story

     M = mother (Marie)
     F = father (Jon)
     J = Janie (5 years, 11 months)

M: Jon - do you have those negatives from the (pony?) pictures

F: Yeah - they're a:ll in your cabinet ((pointing))

M: ((clears throat)) I wish you woulda told (Janie) cuz that's why I sent her down (cuz Susan) wanted em - when she came? *so* (she could) go (if) she took my roll of film =

F: - Sorry - I told Janie I didn't have time to come in - Janie didn't ask me that - What Janie asked me was - Can *I* get the negative fo:r Susan's picture - That meant I had to go through all those negatives and I was - I said "Hey I - I don't - tell her I don't have *time* to do that right now"

In this story, the father and mother of the family have different versions of the initiating/inciting event involving their daughter Janie's relaying of the message from the mother to the father. (Janie is co-present to this narration but only listens.) The mother implies that she asked Janie to ask her father *where* the negative to Susan's picture was, whereas the father claims that Janie did not request information but rather requested the father's services ("What Janie asked me was - Can I get the negative fo:r Susan's picture"). In this way, the father challenges the mother's cause-effect account of what happened earlier in the day. Her account falls apart because the description of the problem is inaccurate, according to the father's experience. As the addressee of Janie's message, the father presents his alternative version as having the weight of an eyewitness 'factual' account of the events.

In scientific communities, a theory sometimes is challenged not because it does not match real world conditions but because the theory is in some way *inadequate* relative to some other theory. Let us call such challenges *adequacy challenges*. In storytelling among family members, one or another family member may similarly challenge a particular characterization of a story problem or story response because it is based on weak argumentation or entails a morally inadequate point of view. This is often the case in talking about cause-effect relations involving a psychological response. One party may feel that an event or set of events provokes or should provoke a particular psychological reaction whereas another party does not, as illustrated in 6 below:

6. Excerpt from Eating Chilies Story

   M = mother
   J = Jason (7 years, 5 months)

J: Wasn't it funny? when wa- wasn't it funny when - wasn't it funny when you - thought that thing was a pickle? and I ate it?

M: No that *wasn't* funny. - I thought it was uh um:: ((looks at father)) - a green bean

In this story excerpt, Jason begins to tell a story about a time when he mistakenly ate a hot chili pepper that his mother thought was a green bean (or a pickle). Jason's mother challenges not only veridical aspects of the story problem (correcting his version of the facts that she did not think the chili was a pickle but a green bean) but also the appropriateness of the psychological response Jason presents as the outcome of the whole set of events. Jason opens the story with a request for confirmation ("Wasn't it funny when . . .") concerning the resultant psychological response to eating a chili pepper. In response, Jason's mother flatly rejects Jason's attempt to see humor as the psychological outcome ("No that *wasn't* funny"). She is socializing Jason into her view that these kinds of events (where pain is involved) should not be seen as funny. Through her subsequent turn, Jason's mother reframes Jason's initial story as only a version of the events, one that is both inaccurate and inadequate. In this manner, Jason's mother is socializing him into the activity of building justifiable theories of the world. One socializing message is that, for a cause-effect explanation to hold up, it must match what others believe to be true about the world and must be ideologically acceptable as well. Jason is confronted with veridical and adequacy challenges that in turn may entail redrafting the initial story line.

Example 7 below represents another adequacy challenge. In this example, the mother, Marie, challenges her own responses to a problematic event. Marie runs a daycare center and the problematic event concerns Bev, mother of one of the daycare children. Bev has given Marie a sum of money beyond what she owes for her child. Marie voices her doubts to her husband as to whether or not her actions were legitimate.

7. Excerpts from Bev Story

    M = mother (Marie)
    F = father (Jon)

M: Bev walked up? and handed me three twenty?

F: mhm

    (0.6)

M: And I *thought* she only owed me eighty - and she said she didn't want a receipt - and I went in and got the receipt book (n:) she only owed me eighty

Here Bev's handing her the money is the initiating/inciting event that explains Marie's responses—checking her ledger and giving back what she determined was 'overpayment.'

However, the story is more complex in that Bev is pulling her child out of daycare without providing the required two weeks' notice. Marie relates this suddenly, several minutes later in the dinner:

M: Well, you know what - you know what though-
    ((points index finger to Jon, hand extended from elbow))

F: It's gone to even to the extreme?

    [   ]

M: I started questioning was the fact she gave me - no - notice - she just called up after the accident and said

F: Yeah "I'm not coming anymore"

          [

M: "That's it" - no -no two weeks' pay - not=

                                             [   ]

F: (Marie)

M: =no: consideration - (without ever   )

                     [

F: ((wiping mouth))   She did *a:ll that* when she paid you the three hundred and twenty dollars - she didn't do that=
((Marie with hand to mouth, reflective; daughter Janie gets up and goes to kitchen))
=by mistake - she wanted to see how *you* felt about it n she felt she *owed* you

[

M: No: way - no no no no - no ((shaking head and hand also to say 'No'))

Thus Marie *could* have seen the money as what was owed to her, but she chose not to do this. The challenge eventually is not to the *facts* of the events of handing over the money or Marie's response but to the *adequacy* of Marie's response. Should she have given the money back? Should she have kept the money and reminded Bev of the stipulated two weeks' notice? After several minutes of unrelated talk, Marie again probes this narrative:

M: ((head on hand, elbow on table))
You know Jon - I verbally *did* tell Bev two weeks' notice Do you think I shouldov stuck to that? or (to have) done what I did?

Jon takes issue with Marie's initial attitude that her response was morally justified and pushes her to accept a different moral framing of Bev's money in terms of 'contract ethics.'

F: When I say something I stick to it unless *she:* - s-brings it up. If *I* set a policy and I - and - they accept that policy - unless *they* have reason to change it and and say something? *I* do not *change* it . . . I should never have set the policy if I didn't believe in it . . .

Eventually Marie hesitantly accepts this ideological reworking of the story events:

M: I guess I just wish I would have said - I'm *not* upset with what happened - I just wanted - I think I *would* feel better if I had said something

In examples 1 through 7, the challenges to cause-effect explanations have involved opposing views of family members. One family member's explanation has been challenged by another family member. In other cases, however, it is not a co-present family member whose views are challenged but a non-present *third party* who is the target of the challenge. In these cases, family members sympathize with the version of the events presented by one of those present and collectively oppose an 'outsider,' as illustrated in 8 below:

8. Excerpt from Detention Story

   M = mother
   F = father
   L = Lucy (9 years, 7 months)

   L: I don't think Mrs. um Andrews is being fair because um

   M: ((high-pitched)) (?do you?) =

   F: = (about what?)

         [

   L: When we were back at school um - this girl? - she pulled um - Valerie's *dress* up t'here ((gestures to chest)) in front of the boys

   M: mhm?

   L: she only - all she did was get a *day* in de*ten*tion

   M: mhm? - *you* think she should have gotten suspended?

         (0.6)

   L: At *LEAST* - that's

         (0.4)

   M: mhm?

         [

   L: (it's) not allowed in *school*

In this story excerpt, Lucy challenges the response of the principal of her school, Mrs. Andrews, to a problematic event. Her challenge is not to Mrs. Andrews' rendering of the 'facts' of the problematic event, but to Mrs. Andrews' rendering of the seriousness of the problematic event. Mrs. Andrews' view of the problematic event is, from Lucy's point of view, inadequate, a view which her mother supports and extends ("*you* think she should have gotten suspended?"). When family members get together to challenge the moral adequacy of others' views of the problem or their responses to a problem, they collaboratively articulate family values and world views. Thus challenges to a third party's version of the events socialize children into local family culture.

Regardless of whether the challenge is to a co-present family member or some non-present third party, regardless of whether the challenge is to the facts or to the adequacy of the explanations, challenges are fundamental to scientific communication. In the world of science (which may not be so separate a world as we have tended to think), each scientific account can be thought of as a kind of story, not a story of personal events but a story of impersonal scientific events. And each story can potentially challenge and redraft another scientific 'story' and itself be subject to challenge.

This form of scholarly discourse has its roots in everyday storytelling in which interlocutors do not stand idly by, but actively question and modify how a story problem is characterized and assess the adequacy of protagonists' responses to it. Challenging and redrafting stories socializes children into metacognitive thinking in that interlocutors often step outside the narrated events to question and recontextualize them. These activities also socialize metalinguistic thinking in that interlocutors treat the telling of a personal experience as a *version* of experience. Both of these aspects of perspective taking are complex cognitive processes that are integral to scientific practice.

THE COGNITIVE CONSTITUTION OF DINNER

We began this paper with the argument that for many households, dinnertime is a moment in the social day not only for fueling bodies with calories but also for collaborative talk and collaborative thought. In the corpus we have collected, all the dinners were occasions for conversation and in each instance the conversation involved some degree of problem-solving narration. In all the dinners, the problem-solving narration was collaborative and involved challenging, defending, and reworking the facts and the moral stances of the problematic events narrated. Of course, some dinners and some narratives involved more of this sort of challenge and revision than others. Nonetheless dinners as we observed them are constituted by some measure of this complex cognitive activity. For those who regularly participate in these dinners, proposing and critiquing problems and responses is part of their cultural definition of dinnertime at home. Children as participants are socialized to varying degrees into this expectation, an expectation that serves them well as they enter scholarly activity systems.

THE COGNITIVE CONSTITUTION OF FAMILIARITY

We also began this discussion with the unusual proposal that familiarity has a cognitive underpinning. Collaborative problem solving is for the families in our study a constitutive activity carried out by families. For these people, to be a member of a family is to problem-solve together. Members of a family, within this cultural perspective, have the right and obligation to not just listen to a narrative account of some problematic event and the responses it incited but to question and probe and propose alternative versions. It is also the case that family members can become involved in the interpretation of the story events because they have at least some background knowledge about the story events and protagonists even if they did not directly experience the narrated events.

We think that families are not the only institutions that can be so constituted. For many people, friendships are also constituted by the kind of collaborative cognitive activity we have just been describing. Friends, within this cultural perspective, are persons who don't just listen to a narrative about a problematic event and its aftermath; friends help one another to understand those events in different lights and to weigh one view of the events over others. In this cultural framework, a friend can challenge another friend to a certain extent, because of the affective bond between them. Further, as with family members, a friend can challenge another friend because they have a communicative history together that gives each a data base for introducing information that may reinforce an existing perspective or trigger a shift in perspective.

Within this cultural framework, immediate family and friends are typically those whom we consider familiars or even intimates. We are used to them; we have shared time together; we are in communicative contact with them; they know a good deal about our lives and we know a good deal about theirs; they can count on us to help them and we can count on them; we can trust each other. When these features do not characterize family and friend relationships, then we say they are not or are no longer intimate. When one or more of these conditions weaken, it is an index that the parties are taking greater social distance.

Our hypothesis is that, in mainstream American society, it is precisely this sort of social familiarity that encourages complex collaborative problem solving. Where participants know one another well, they can rely on accumulated shared knowledge in telling a story and don't need to spell out the background details needed to understand the story's point. Where participants know one another well, they may be less hesitant to express uncertainty or perplexity over the problematic affairs in the narration and more open to invite the help of others in *explaining* the narrated events. Where participants know one another well, they are able within limits to enter into the other's telling of events and reconfigure the other's version without dissolving the relationship. They are able to do this in part because a familiar has elicited their involvement. If a familiar puts limits on the kind of narrative involvement, for example, by permitting only supportive involvement, then the familiar is defining the relationship in a certain light. If the "climate" is more "open," with familiars inviting others to help explain a set of events and helping others to explain some set of events they have drawn to their attention, then the familiars are defining their relation in a different light.

We suggest that these personal, familiar relationships establish the intellectual groundwork for collective problem solving. Following this suggestion, environments conducive to collaborative explaining and critiquing are those marked by *familiarity,* the very quality that most arenas of formal education lack. The large class size, the tendency to organize problem solving in terms of individuals rather than small, familiar groups, and the continual shift in class composition at least from year to year are some of the ingredients that sabotage a sense of mutual reliance and shared experience.

This suggestion that familiarity and complex cognition are linked is at odds with the suggestion that children learn critical cognitive skills such as decentering from interactions with strangers and unfamiliars in the context of writing and other school activities. We argue that *it is familiarity not social distance that best promotes cognitive decentering.* We are more willing to take on the perspective of others, even when that perspective contradicts our own, when we and the other have a relationship of trust and share some background and interest in one another's experiences. We are more willing to hear another's story version out or to invite another's participation in our story, to work on unresolved elements of a story if story collaborators have a solid background in the setting of the story events. It is exhausting to present and to wade through the background necessary to make sense of the story events, as writers and readers of theses and dissertations well know. The effort is so great that sometimes complex problem-centered stories don't get related among those who are not familiar. What schooling and literacy activities in particular ideally do is to train children and other novices to overcome this hurdle and relate/wade through the complex details of setting necessary to evaluate events and points of view. But this training hardly means that impersonal relationships promote cognitive decentering. Impersonal relationships may well inhibit decentering. Schooling ideally fortifies novices to break through the barrier of unfamiliarity and create some measure of familiarity from the ground up. Schooling trains novices to establish familiarity (at least in the sense of shared background knowledge) within the confines of a written or spoken text by laying out relevant history then and there. We should not lose sight of just how cumbersome a task *establishing* familiarity with unknown readers and audiences is and how different it is from the more complex forms of decentering displayed when familiars take another's point of view, work it through, challenge it, and transform it. These forms of complex cognition go on right under our noses in the most mundane environments, in the comfortable ambience of our homes, and even during hectic, seemingly chaotic family dinners.

ENDNOTE

*The research on which this paper is based was funded by two grants. The first research project "Discourse Processes in American Families" was funded (1986–89) by the NICHD (grant no. 1 ROH HD 2099201 A1). Members of the research team included E. Ochs and T. Weisner (co-P.I.s) and M. Bernstein, D. Rudolph, R. Smith, and C. Taylor (research assistants). The second project "Socialization of Scientific Discourse" is funded (1990–93) by the Spencer Foundation. Members of this research team include E. Ochs (P.I.) and P. Gonzales, S. Jacoby, and C. Taylor (research assistants).

REFERENCES

Duranti, A., and D. Brenneis. 1986. *The Audience as Co-author.* Special issue of *Text.* Vol. 6–3.

Engeström, Y. 1987. *Learning by Expanding.* Helsinki: Orienta-Konsultit Oy.

Goffman, E. 1959. *The Presentation of Self in Everyday Life.* Garden City, N.Y.: Doubleday-Anchor.

Latour, B., and S. Woolgar. (1986). *Laboratory Life: The Construction of Scientific Facts.* 2nd ed. Princeton, N.J.: Princeton UP.

Laudan, L. 1984. *Science and Values.* Berkeley: U of California P.

Lynch, M. 1985. *Art and Artifact in Laboratory Science: A Study of Shop Work and Shop Talk in a Research Laboratory.* London: Routledge & Kegan Paul.

Stein, N., and C. G. Glenn. 1979. "An Analysis of Story Comprehension in Elementary School Children." *New Directions in Discourse Processing.* Ed. R. O. Freedle. Vol. 2. Norwood, N.J.: Ablex. 53–120.

Traweek, S. 1988. *Beamtimes and Lifetimes: The World of High Energy Physics.* Cambridge, Mass.: Harvard UP.

Vygotsky, L. S. 1986. *Thought and Language.* Ed. A. Kozulin. Cambridge, Mass.: MIT P.

Chapter 3

Learning a Language
from Learners

Lily Wong Fillmore

University of California at Berkeley

THE PROBLEM

In this paper, I examine a second language learning situation that is rarely discussed or studied by language researchers. The situation I refer to is one in which *learners* of the target language far outnumber the *native speakers* who are available to provide access to the language. These situations are far from optimal for language learning, if we assume that contact and social interaction between learners and native speakers are necessary for language learning. For foreign language educators, what I am describing is hardly remarkable. These are precisely the conditions under which foreign languages are learned or not learned. Foreign languages have been taught and learned in situations where the only speaker of the language is the teacher. How successfully it is done depends on the instructor's teaching skills and knowledge of what is needed, the materials and pedagogical approach used, and the students' motivation and efforts to learn the language. The exposure they get to the target language through a formal course of study is hardly sufficient to keep them going. The students need special motivation to sustain the extraordinary expenditure of time and effort required in the study of a foreign language. Because the setting itself does not support the learning and use of the language, the learners have to invest special effort in study and practice in order to compensate for the inadequacies in the input.

But these are not the conditions under which *second languages* are learned ordinarily. In contrast to foreign language learning, a second language is learned in a societal context in which it is in everyday use, as is the case with English in the United States and in other English-speaking countries. How then can there be second language situations such as the one I have described? Where, say, in the United States are we likely to find learners of English who are not surrounded by native speakers of English and in constant contact with them?

In fact, one does not have to go far to find such situations. One has only to visit schools in any American city with a sizable immigrant or refugee population, such as San Francisco, New York City, Los Angeles, Seattle, Chicago, Boston, Houston, or Miami. In many schools in those cities, there are few native speakers of English among the students. Nearly everyone is a non-native speaker of English, and those who know the language well are greatly outnumbered by others whose knowledge of it is quite limited. In these schools, the teachers may be the only sure speakers of English, and it is up to them to provide access to the language and support for learning it to all of the students in the school. The teachers are not the only English speakers with whom the learners are in contact, however.

Because of the emphasis on English at school (and this is true whether we are considering students in bilingual or in English-only schools), newcomers become "English speakers" very quickly, often before they really know English well. Immigrant children encounter some powerful forces for assimilation as soon as they enter the English-speaking world of the American school. They discover that the languages they speak at home have no value or function at school. The language that is the medium of communication in that setting—English—is one they do not know, and not knowing it sets them apart from their classmates. (They have no way of knowing that few of their classmates actually know English all that well.) They come to believe that the only way they can take part in the social world of the school is by transforming themselves into English speakers. As soon as they learn a little English, they adopt it almost exclusively in their interactions with classmates at school.

Since they are novices in English, their knowledge of the language is incomplete. They nevertheless use what they know eagerly and frequently. This happens especially where the students come from different language backgrounds. When children share the same primary language, they can use it for talking to one another since it allows them to communicate far more easily and freely with one another than English does. However, the pressure to speak English is sufficiently great that it is often enough the language of choice even among children with a shared primary language. When children come from different language backgrounds, English is the only language they know in common: it is for them the default choice for wider communication. Either way, English is the language most frequently spoken by teachers and students alike in many, if not most, schools serving language minority students. Second language learners in such situations are indeed surrounded by people who speak English, but these are speakers of imperfect English. Because there are more students than there are teachers, the learners hear the English spoken by peers far more frequently than they do English spoken by teachers who, presumably, know the language well enough to serve as models. Thus the English of classmates is a major source of linguistic input for these children's language learning efforts, and since most of them are learners of English, the speech they produce, the language that serves as their English input, is imperfect and uncertain, as one might expect. But they have no way of knowing that. For them, English is English. They cannot judge what is grammatical and acceptable, and what is not.

LEARNERESE AS INPUT—
SITUATIONAL FACTORS

How imperfect is the language these children hear? Researchers who have studied the learning of English as a second language are familiar with "learnerese," the renditions of English produced by children who are in the process of learning it. The following speech samples produced by Asian background children from an urban second grade class are illustrative. There were Chinese, Cambodian, Vietnamese, and several Filipino children in the class. The children who produced these speech samples were average language learners: they were neither the most nor the least successful learners in their class. At age seven, they had been in school a little over two years (the samples were taken several months after the beginning of their third year in school). Most of the children in this class entered kindergarten knowing no English, and they learned the English seen in these samples in school. Their class was filled with children like them. Just two or perhaps three children in the class could be described as proficient speakers of English. Thus, aside from the English produced by the teachers in the course of the school day, what the children heard was speech like these samples they produced in response to my interview questions: "What does your mom tell you when you go to school? What does she say?"

JOANNA (Chinese)	She say, ah, I go a sko today a' you learn. Uh you learn. You s'pose to learn at sko every day.
LAM (Chinese)	Tell to work hard. Say have to make a good list'ner. She say has to 'pose to be have a good list'ner.
SAN (Chinese)	Ah, lissen to teacher. Don't playing. Don't bothering people. She tol' me Chinese. She tol' me to lissen to teacher.

When I asked the question of Nhue, he suggested that I interview his friend Ricardo, first:

NHUE (Vietnamese)	Him haat tran, get him a turn. (= It's his turn, give him a turn)
ADULT	Is it his turn? What do you want him to say?
NHUE	Him first. I say second. Give him first. (= Ask Ricardo first. I'll go second. Ask him first.)
ADULT	What does your mommy tell you to do when you go to school, Ricardo?
RICARDO (Filipino)	[No response]
ADULT	Can you tell me? What does she tell you?
RICARDO	[No response]
NHUE	[giggle-giggle] Him don' know speak in det.
ADULT	He doesn't speak English? What does he speak?
NHUE	Chinee. Him longk wan' to say. (= Chinese [Ricardo?!] He doesn't want to talk.)

It should be noted that except for Ricardo, none of these children appeared to have any trouble understanding me. Nor did they appear to have any trouble knowing how to respond to my questions in this interview. They had classmates like Ricardo who had not yet begun to speak English, but the four children whose speech is represented here were by no means "non–English speakers." They were limited, to be sure, but they were speaking English. They obviously had a long way to go, but for many of these children, English was apparently already their preferred language. Interviews with parents revealed that some of these children were speaking mostly English at home, and they were beginning to lose their primary language. What is the likely outcome of this kind of language learning situation? Will the children eventually achieve a full mastery of the standard forms of English? What happens when children base their learning of a second language largely on input provided by other learners?

The situations I have described are not uncommon. They are entirely familiar to educators and researchers who are concerned with the educational experiences of language minority students. Over the past decade and a half, I have spent a lot of time in schools, investigating sources of variability in second language learning. Many of the schools in which I have conducted research on language acquisition are ones with high concentrations of children who enter school speaking languages other than English. My purposes have been to identify and understand the conditions that affect the language and academic adjustment of these children. Some of them manage the difficult task of learning English more readily and successfully than others. What accounts for the differences we find across learners in how quickly and well they learn second languages? What accounts for the differences in academic outcome that will eventually be found among these children?

Over the years, my colleagues, students, and I have examined a variety of learner characteristics, situational factors, and target language speaker characteristics in our search for the sources of these differences. Through a series of studies, we have discovered the extent to which situational factors affected language learning (Wong Fillmore, McLaughlin, Ammon, and Ammon 1985; Wong Fillmore 1982, 1989). The relative proportion of language learners and English speakers in schools and classrooms constitutes a major situational factor affecting language learning outcomes, and it was found to interact with learner variables, with target language speaker variables, and with other situational factors such as class structure and organization to produce the variability in outcome that we have been interested in. Where English speakers were as numerous as language learners, or where they outnumbered the language learners, then individual learner characteristics such as sociability, talkativeness, self-confidence, and social skill played an important role in language learning (Wong Fillmore 1983, 1989). Learners who found it easy and desirable to interact with the English speakers were able to get more input and help in learning English, particularly if the class was structured in ways that permitted the children to interact more or less freely. In classes where the learners outnumbered the English speakers, however, such characteristics were not necessarily associated with rapid language learning. What was more important was the way the teachers structured their classes and how they used language for instructional purposes (Wong Fillmore 1985). Because teachers in those situations were the primary sources of English input, it was crucial that they spent enough time each day talking to everyone. They could not achieve this on a one-to-one basis, however, since in any four- or five-hour school day, they could at most offer each student five or six minutes of individual attention. This was simply not enough linguistic input to support any individual's language learning effort. The teachers had to organize their class around rather formal group instructional activities in which they could more efficiently provide input and practice for the children over the course of the day. In such situations, how well the children learned English depended on how well the teachers managed such instruction, on the opportunities they provided children to practice and hear English spoken, and on how well the language they used worked as input for language learning.

When the teachers know what to do (Lambert 1984; Wong Fillmore 1985), the children can learn both the language and the subject matter of school, as the Canadian immersion programs have amply demonstrated (Lambert and Tucker 1972; Swain 1974; Swain and Barik 1976; Swain and Lapkin 1982). In some respects, the conditions under which those programs have operated are quite similar to ones in the schools described in this paper, but they differ in several important ways. The aim of the Canadian immersion programs has been full bilingualism, whereas the aim in American school programs has been English transition. A second difference is that the Canadian programs are enrichment programs meant to teach a minority language, French, to majority group children, whereas the American programs are largely seen as compensatory programs designed to teach minority group students the majority group language. Although the Canadian programs are acknowledged successes, immersion students have also been affected by the situational factors discussed in this paper (Lapkin and Cummins 1984).

The earliest documentation of language learning problems attributable to situational factors was Selinker, Swain, and Dumas's study of fossilizing interlanguage forms in the speech of children who were in the Canadian immersion programs (1975). The children, they noted, were learning French from their teachers, but they were also getting it from one another as they used the language in their classes. Merrill Swain and her colleagues, in later studies of this phenomenon, found that a major problem for the immersion students was that the only native-speaker level French they heard was the language their teachers used in class (Swain 1985; Cummins, Harley, Swain, and Allen, in press). Thus, the language available to them as input did not contain the full range of forms and structures that are used when native speakers converse with other native speakers, but consisted instead of the more limited range that speakers would use in speaking to individuals who were not fully proficient in the language. A second problem Swain and her colleagues found was that the teachers tended not to offer the corrective feedback the learners needed to achieve mastery over the grammatical intricacies of the language. The teachers corrected pronunciation, but not errors in syntax or the pragmatic problems that the students were having.

TEACHERS AS SOURCES OF LEARNERESE INPUT

In the Canadian immersion programs studied by Swain and her colleagues, the teachers were native or near–native speakers of the language used in school. The speech they were providing their students as input for second language learning was a standard variety of Canadian or continental French. Whether or not they gave their students the corrective feedback they needed depended on their beliefs about the usefulness of such feedback. In many of the classrooms my colleagues and I have studied, the teachers were not native speakers of English. In fact, roughly a third of the teachers in whose classrooms we have studied second language learning were interlanguage speakers of English, and the language they produced as input for their learners was not a good representation of the standard variety. Consider, for example, this sample of speech taken from an interview with a teacher I will call Mrs. F. She was thirty-four at the time of the interview and had been living in the United States since she was eight years old. She knew a little English when she came from Hong Kong, she said, so it was not difficult for her to adjust to the American school system. She learned English quickly and did very well as a student in the urban Chinatown school where she now teaches as well as at the university later on. As we look at her speech, we will see that it is not quite standard. The deviations are not merely in pronunciation—evidence of an imperfect mastery of the English sound system—although there is plenty of that. Mrs. F's speech is entirely fluent and she is completely confident in her abilities in English. Her English is obviously mature and complete in the sense that she appears to have no difficulty saying the things she needs or wants to say, and in that it will probably not go much beyond its present state, at least not without a major effort on her part. However, if we examine this short sample of speech in response to interview questions concerning her methods for teaching the limited English speakers in her second grade class, we find numerous ways in which it varies from grammatical norms, as well as considerable grammatical variability.[1]

INTERVIEWER   Uh huh—what kind of special needs do those kids have then and how do you deal with them?

MRS. F   Well OK . . the special nee' ([spɛsəl ni']) is . . they they ([dɛy dɛy]) . . lota ([la:da]) stuff ([səf]). I like I tell you they never seen before. OK, and lota like games and s'uff like that and . . . uh they never see before and then we took . . and then . . they never been to lota places bef--like museums and . . you know pa:rks or . . you know . . s'uff like tha' ([dæ]) . . so I believe in lota wal:king trips and um bus trips to take them to places they haven't seen before like we went to the beach . . they don't know what **sea** shell is until we get there we **show** them what a seashell is . . and uh they really interested in it.

INTERVIEWER   OK now that was something I really wanted to ask you too . . now what are some of the **especially** effective ways that you have found for helping these kids. So trips would be one—

MRS. F   One . . and you know um . . trips . . you know . . . really . . trip is really a place to teach . . really . . I . . I . . I really enjoys it you know? . . . and um . . second thing is mani . . manipulative s'uff ([mːnIp . . mnIpIts:əf]) you know this ([dɛs])—

INTERVIEWER So things they can handle.

MRS. F   Jus haːndle you know like . . what we do is we have a little metal house you know? . . like . . . and we have **furnitures** in there ([dɛr]) . . . You know one a . . ([wənI']) toy playhouse. And . . they really enjoys a putting iːn . . and we tell 'em this a ([dIsəː]) **living** room . . and . . what we put in a living room. You see at firs' they don't even know what a living room is. You know? . . so we tell 'em that you know you put a TV in there and you put a couch and a coffee table you know s'uff like that . . and dining ([dayding]) room and . . you know I mean . . like things 'ay tha' ([sIngsay'dæ']) . . and they really enjoys it. I think that . . when you're teaching a . . **non** English kid or **any-bodys** as have no English . . . you know . . w'aː mean . . but if you do **action** with them . . you see? . . and so . . you don't have to even **taːlk** . . . mos' a time ([mosə taː ym]) . . you know like . . if you don-- . . you caːn't you know like . . certain teacher they don't **speak** Chinese and you have a Chinese kid in the classroom . . you don't even have to taːlk really . . you **shoːw** them . . what it is . . you know . . you show them . . then you teːll them what it is.

Grammatical variability in expressing essentially the same thing can be found in her speech. Commenting on her students' missing experiences, Mrs. F had earlier in the interview said:

They really have never gone to school before some of 'em.

In the excerpt from the interview we are looking at, she used several variants of the present perfect construction:

. . . lota s'uff like I tell you *they never seen* before.

OK, and lota like games and s'tuff like that and . . . uh *they never see* before and then we took . . and then . . *they never been* to lota places bef-- like museums . . .

and,

I believe in lota walːking trips and um bus trips to take them to places *they haven't seen* before . . .

Such variability is not, I believe, evidence of a system in flux, and her language is not likely to continue evolving grammatically. Her remarkably fluent speech is peppered with formulaic fillers, or speech habits such as "like," "see," "y'know"

"I mean," and other such forms that are typical of other speakers of English, and they function for her as they do for many native speakers—that is, as fluency preservers. She makes frequent use of left-dislocated subjects (e.g., *"Certain teacher they* don't speak Chinese"), as well as right-dislocated ones ("*They* really have never gone to school before *some of 'em*"), constructions that appear in other varieties of learner-based English that I have looked at. The word "teacher" in the example just cited was singular in form but plural in intention, and a close examination of the transcription will show that plural noun forms are in fact relatively rare in her speech, although there are instances of the plural morpheme being added redundantly to already pluralized forms and mass nouns as we see in "childrens" and "furnitures." In fact, for Mrs. F number agreement seems completely random at first sight, but in some cases, it seems clear that a verb has been learned with the agreement suffixes attached. "Enjoys" always occurs in that form apparently irrespective of its subject, as in "I really enjoys it" and "they really enjoys it."

Is Mrs. F a rarity? Not at all. She is a notable example only because she happens to be teaching in the same school she herself attended as a child. She is, above all else, a committed teacher who, despite her less than perfect command of English syntax and phonology, has gotten excellent results as a teacher of Asian immigrant children. She is well regarded by parents and students alike, and the students in her classes perform consistently above district and state norms in standardized achievement tests each year.[2] In schools everywhere with high concentrations of language minority children there are teachers who are speakers of varieties of English that vary to a greater or lesser degree from standard English. School administrators recognize the need for teachers who can provide linguistic minority children with cultural support if not native language support, and they try to hire teachers from the same ethnic background as the children's whether for bilingual or English-only programs. Most of these teachers speak English very well. Others, like Mrs. F, learned English in situations precisely like those they are now teaching in, and they learned it in much the same way their students are now learning it—based largely on input provided by other learners. Mrs. F happens to be a mature speaker of Cantonese, but she rarely uses it with the Cantonese speakers in her class because she is thoroughly committed to helping her students learn English. Her formula for teaching non–English speakers is simple. In fact, from her point of view, the ability to speak the student's primary language is really unnecessary since teachers can communicate with children nonverbally:

I think that . . when you're teaching a . . non–English kid or anybodys as have no English . . . you know . . w'a: mean . . but if you do action with them . . you see? . . and so . . you don't have to even ta:lk . . . mos' a time . . you know like . . if you don-- . . you ca:n't you know like . . certain teacher they don't speak Chinese and you have a Chinese kid in the classroom . . you don't even have to ta:lk really . . you sho:w them . . what it is . . you know . . you show them . . then you te:ll them what it is.

A PROBLEM OR NOT?

Should someone like Mrs. F be teaching at all, given her imperfect command of English? If she is the main source of English input for her students, can they possibly learn the standard forms of English required for academic development and for participation in this society?

This is an extremely controversial issue. Some people would say no to teachers like Mrs. F despite her successful performance as a teacher—they would argue that her English is not good enough for her to serve as a teacher of non-English-speaking children. Others would regard this entire discussion as inappropriate, a failure on my part to appreciate distinctive varieties of English: Mrs. F's speech is neither ungrammatical nor imperfect—it is just a different variety of English. Still others would regard even a discussion of this matter as a "problem" to be a betrayal of the minority groups of which these teachers are members. To document it, to bring it up at all, is tantamount to giving the critics of minority-oriented education programs ammunition to use against them—especially against bilingual education programs.

It is important to stress, however, that while Mrs. F was teaching in a school with a bilingual program, she was herself not a part of it by choice. Sad to say, she was philosophically opposed to bilingual education, and although she had a native-speaker command of Cantonese, she seldom used it in her teaching even though she might have expressed herself more effectively in it than she did in English. In this, Mrs. F is like many immigrants who have coped with the assimilative forces in the society by buying into the necessity of immediate and absolute assimilation. She regards bilingual education as a cop-out: she says she thinks it allows children not to take seriously the need to learn English as soon as possible and to use it in school. She makes her viewpoints known to her students and their parents. It is not surprising that many of her students are showing a marked preference for English even though they hardly know it well enough to use except for satisfying their most basic communicative needs. And therein lies a very great potential problem.

Mrs. F's knowledge of Cantonese, as far as we could tell, is mature and complete, although she was just eight when she immigrated to the United States with her family and was educated entirely in English from then on. She somehow managed to develop and maintain her primary language—despite her strong preference for English. Thus, she has at least one fully developed language in her linguistic repertory. But many of the children in her classes appeared not to be maintaining or further developing their native languages. Our interviews with their parents revealed a marked tendency for many of the children to speak English at home with siblings or with parents, even in homes where the parents speak no English at all. Over three-quarters of the parents of the students in this class whom we interviewed reported a substantial shift to English at home by their children since entering school two years earlier. They were not atypical. In an earlier study in which my students and I followed the course of English development in Latino and Chinese children over a three-year period, the effects of

English on language use in the homes of those children were evident within just one year. An interview with parents at the end of the kindergarten year revealed that 64 percent of the twenty-eight Chinese and 40 percent of the thirty Latino subjects were using English at home with their non-English-speaking parents. Over the past several years, I have been documenting patterns of language shift in children such as these. After a year or two in school, immigrant children are inclined, not only to favor English, but to abandon the use of their primary language (Wong Fillmore 1990, 1991). In time, their knowledge of their primary language erodes or is stunted. The learning of English as a second language for many of these children results, not in bilingualism, but in English monolingualism. In Wallace Lambert's terms, the process is subtractive rather than additive (1975, 1977, 1981).

How does this problem figure in our discussion of English language development? As I noted earlier, many of the children I have studied, including the ones in Mrs. F's class, were apparently giving up their primary language well before they were very far along in their learning of English. Given the conditions under which they were learning English, we might ask: What are the chances that they are going to learn a fully realized version of their second language? What happens when children do not learn a second language completely after deciding to give up their first language? One hesitates to suggest that the result may be what some people have described as "semilingualism" (Hansegård 1968; Skutnabb-Kangas and Toukamaa 1976; Skutnabb-Kangas 1978)—a condition many of us have been loath even to acknowledge as a potential outcome of second language learning (Ekstrand 1983). Nevertheless, it is a possible consequence of the phenomena discussed in this paper. In the case of children such as Joanna, Lam, San, Nhue, and Ricardo, it is too soon to say what the outcome of their language learning efforts will be. They may end up knowing and using English as well as Ted Koppel does, but again, they could end up with a version of it that is closer to Mrs. F's. As you might expect, the children in her class have been influenced by her speech.

Should people like Mrs. F teach? I would argue that she most certainly should. She does a better than adequate job imparting the substance of the second grade curriculum to her charges during the year they spend in her classroom. However, it is not without cost to them. Given her advocacy for English, her students' primary language skills suffer during the year they are with her. Her students would be better served if she were to encourage them to continue using their primary language at home even if she does not promote it at school. They would be even better served if she were willing to promote the children's use of their primary language at school, something she could do easily enough especially for the Cantonese speakers since she can speak their language. But she is not willing to do that. So what about Mrs. F as the main adult English model for the thirty or so language learners in her class each year? That, I believe, is a problem worthy of some attention. What can be done to compensate for her shortcomings as an English model for language learners?

POSSIBLE SOLUTIONS

Perhaps the most obvious and direct solution for teachers like Mrs. F would be to provide them with the formal English instruction they should have had much earlier, thereby enabling them to develop a more standard variety to use while teaching. During the sixties, while Mrs. F was learning English in grade school, there was little in the way of English as a second language (ESL) instruction in the public schools. She could not remember any special help given her or the other limited English speakers in her classes. There is an ESL program at the school now, and some of Mrs. F's students participate in it. The ESL program in the school where she teaches comprises forty-minute "pull-out classes,"[3] for groups of ten to fifteen students working with an ESL resource teacher three times each week. These classes turn out to be little more than tutoring sessions during which the students receive additional help with phonics, reading vocabulary, and other basic skills. We have observed virtually nothing that could be characterized as help in English grammar, in understanding its intricacies, or as opportunities to practice using it more effectively. In fact, the children spent much of their time working on workpages and little time using the language actively during these ESL classes. In other schools, ESL sometimes means formal language instruction, but more often than not, it is devoted to activities like those observed in Mrs. F's school. Much of what passes for ESL instruction in the public schools is inadequate or inappropriate. There are few ESL teachers in the public schools with formal training to do what they are doing. Most of them are regular classroom teachers who have been assigned to teach ESL often with little more than a workshop or two of special preparation.

The questions then are what can be done for teachers like Mrs. F, and what kind of ESL instruction is needed to help the students in their classes acquire a more standard variety of English? Can adults like Mrs. F benefit from ESL instruction? Can someone who has been speaking a fossilized interlanguage for as long as she has go back to being a language learner and acquire a more standard variety of English? The answer is obviously yes, adults can learn language—but it takes a special effort on their part to do so. And there are conditions.

First, adult learners must recognize the need to continue working on their version of the target language. This is not as simple a matter as it might appear to be. Adults who have functioned successfully as long as Mrs. F with their own version of English are not necessarily aware of the extent to which their language deviates from the varieties spoken by other speakers of the language. If they have communicated more or less successfully with others by means of the language they speak, they may be unaware that any real difference exists or that the differences matter much. Mrs. F, for example, appears to be largely unconcerned about any differences that she may recognize between her version of English and that spoken by others. At the very least, she does not give any evidence that it worries her. She talks confidently and unhesitatingly—she sometimes grapples with the content of her discourse but rarely with its form. Before she can go back to work on the grammar of the language she speaks so fluently, she will first have to be helped to see where her version differs from the standard version, and to be persuaded that the difference matters.

Second, adults like Mrs. F have to be especially motivated to do what is necessary to continue developing their second language. The motivation for learning a second language is usually simple and direct. Non-English-speaking immigrants arriving in most American communities, for example, quickly discover that they cannot get along without English. It is the language used by virtually everyone they have to deal with outside the home and in the immigrant community, if they happen to be in one. To buy food, to get medical care, to get a job, to get the children into school, to know what is going on in the community—all these tasks require English. The motivation to learn English is sufficiently great that most immigrants eventually do—however little it may be. But what about adult speakers of fossilized interlanguage varieties of English? If the variety spoken is not so greatly deviant that the speakers are able to communicate easily enough with people in the larger English-speaking community, what is the motivation to change it, to acquire a more standard variety of English? Why should these speakers work further to develop ther language if what they already have is serviceable? Perhaps the distinction in motivation drawn by Gardner and Lambert (1972) is critical here. They argued that "integrative motivation"—the desire to learn a language in order to participate in the life of the community that speaks it—leads to more successful second language learning than does "instrumental motivation"—the desire to learn a language because it would be useful to know it. However, the kind of motivation that gets adult immigrants started learning a second language is more likely instrumental than integrative. The practical reasons for learning English are sufficiently motivating that newcomers do what they must to survive. Eventually, integrative motivation is necessary as well. To get beyond the survival level, learners must see themselves as speakers of the language. They have to want to learn the language well enough not only to achieve their basic communicative goals, but to participate in the life of the larger community as well. We have seen that Mrs. F has clearly done that. She takes considerable pride in being an English speaker. What kind of motivation would it take for adults like her to go back to work on their knowledge of English? What it would take is a concern for form and rhetoric—an interest in those aspects of language that figure in effective communication: in structural detail, in expression, in words and their meanings, in turns of phrases, and in the effects of different ways of saying things. In short, I believe it takes an interest in the workings of language itself for adults like Mrs. F to get back to developing their knowledge of a language they already know.

The third condition for adults to further develop their second language skills is flexibility. How easily are language patterns changed? Can adults change lifelong patterns of speaking? Consider, for example, ridding oneself of speech habits such as the ubiquitous "y'know" or "like" or "y'know what I mean" that fill the interstices of so many English speakers' discourse. It is not easy. These phrases are like crabgrass in one's linguistic garden. Once the phrases take root in a person's lexical or phraseological terrain, they are devilishly difficult to control. The reader will recall that Mrs. F's speech was filled with such formulaic phrases.

But such speech habits are relatively trivial problems for the most part. The grammatical problems that interlanguage speakers have to work on are varied and oftentimes quite variable, as we have seen. The rules in a fossilized interlanguage (Selinker 1972) are like the rules in any grammar. The speaker is hardly conscious of them at all; they are thoroughly internalized and integrated into the speaker's grammatical system, and they can be applied without conscious effort, for the most part. Changing them may be even more difficult than dealing with the little speech habits represented by formulaic fillers such as "y'know." It takes not only effort to do so, but flexibility as well—and some people are more flexible than others.

One solution then, especially for individuals like Mrs. F, is adult ESL instruction designed to sharpen their knowledge of language, to enable them to analyze their current knowledge of English, to help them develop more effective and standard ways of using the language, and in general to get them to think more about the language they use. Such a course might not result in great changes in their speech behavior, but it would certainly make them become more aware of the language they speak and more knowledgeable about the standard variety. Mrs. F would not necessarily be a better model for her students' English language development, but if she knew English grammar better she might find it easier to recognize errors in their English and to offer help in the form of corrective feedback or in instruction designed to move them closer to standard forms.

Can teachers like Mrs. F provide their students with ESL instruction to help them develop a more standard variety of English than they are now learning? Lightbown (this volume) discusses teachers who were able to do just that using audio-recordings of books read aloud by native speakers. Written texts do offer teachers like Mrs. F a way to provide access to the standard variety of English even if they do not speak it themselves. Indeed, since Mrs. F's rendition of English is more standard sounding when she reads than when she converses spontaneously, she could read aloud to the children herself (something she seldom does) and thereby expose them to English as it is written, if not spoken, by native speakers.

In a sense, most children have to "learn" a different variety of language when they enter school. Studies of oral and written language differences (Chafe 1982; Rubin 1980; Tannen 1982; Olson 1977; O'Donnell 1974) have shown that rather considerable differences exist between the language used in talk and in written texts. Just how great the differences are can vary, of course, depending on the type of text and oral discourse being compared. Children whose parents have read to them come to the task with a familiarity with such language. Children whose parents have not done so are less familiar with the language of texts. For most children, however, learning to read involves learning the variety of language used in written texts. Few teachers recognize this, however, and fewer still do anything instructionally to facilitate the learning process. Reading instruction for the most part is directed at teaching children, first, the mechanics of decoding, and second, the process of making sense out of the text one is reading. The first is regarded by most teachers as basic and therefore prior to the second. Seldom do we find discussions of language itself in such instruction. Indeed, the earliest texts that children read in school do not lend themselves easily to a discussion of language since the language in them (e.g., "Look, look, look! See Spot run! Oh, oh, oh! Funny, funny Spot.") is hardly representative of the written language forms that children will encounter later on. Still, teachers can always find texts that are more natural and use them as the basis for familiarizing even the youngest children with the sounds, the feel, and the grammar of written English, if they realize how important it is to do so.

For interlanguage speaking teachers who work with limited English proficient (LEP) students, this kind of instructional effort is crucial. They can not easily provide students with models of standard English in their own speech, but they can through texts. They can read to the children and focus their attention on the grammatical, phraseological, and rhetorical aspects of the text. They can design language development activities around the texts to help the children practice using the structures they should be learning. Through the use of good children's literature and poetry, teachers can help LEP students develop an aesthetic feel for the language and for literature even as they are learning English as a second language. Giving LEP students opportunities to discuss these materials and encouraging them to write their own texts would help them make the language they are learning a part of their own developing grammatical system. In the course of learning to read and write, they will also develop more standard ways of speaking, I believe. That would be the most useful kind of ESL support teachers can provide language learners in situations such as the ones discussed in this paper.

In addition to the text-based ESL support their classroom teachers might offer, LEP students would also benefit from formal ESL instruction from teachers who have native-speaker level skills in the standard language. The instruction I have in mind is quite different from the kinds ordinarily found in schools, however. What is generally available to students, aside from mere tutorial assistance with basic skills, are programs of formal language instruction based on commercially produced materials or texts. Such materials are usually designed around some sort of a grammatical or functional syllabus. They are variously characterized and touted as "communicative," "cognitive," "natural," or "multicultural." Most programs call for students to be grouped for instruction by their ability in English, since they are all based largely on linear models of second language development. How the instructional syllabus is organized depends on the particular language teaching philosophy the designers of the materials adhere to, but in general, the students are taken through a preplanned presentation of forms and structures that may or may not meet their individual needs at the moment.

The ESL instruction I have in mind for children whose English is based largely on input from other LEP speakers is much more tailored to their special needs. Instead of following a course of study that is quite independent of what the learners need, this approach would target aspects of the grammar to work on based on errors that the children are making. Any effective instructional program would involve several major steps. The first is to identify a structure that needs developmental work. Interviews, such as the one I used for eliciting children's speech samples presented earlier in this paper, constitute one way of identifying problems in the children's speech. The children's knowledge of the language at the point of these interviews was rudimentary: there are numerous problems that might be targeted for special work and development. For example, Nhue could use some help with subject pronoun forms. ("Him don' know speak in dit.") All four children who were interviewed could use some work with verbal complement structures, as we could see in Joanna's and Lam's responses: "She say ah I go a sko today a you learn," and "She say has to 'pose to be have a good list'ner." The second step is to design some activities in which the children can practice using the targeted structures in meaningful ways. A game that calls for the children to direct one another in performing communicative tasks might give them practice in forming complement structures and using subject pronouns: for example, "Ask him to tie his shoes." "Tell him to give you a pencil." "He asked me to give him a pencil." The third step is to expand the students' use of these linguistic forms and link them to related structures: for example, "Tell him that you don't want that one. Ask him if he has another one."

Obviously, this kind of instructional program requires a lot of planning and a thorough knowledge of English. Teachers would be helped by having a good reference grammar of English in which they might look up the structures the learners are having difficulties with, especially if it offered suggestions for activities for teaching these structures to learners at different grade levels (see, e.g., Celce-Murcia and Hilles 1988; Celce-Murcia and Larsen-Freeman 1983; Ur 1988; Rin-volucri 1984).

CONCLUSION

The problem I have discussed in this paper is not a new one. The language learning conditions I have described can be found in nearly every immigrant community in the United States. They play an essential part of the development of societies with immigrant origins such as ours. What can we expect from them? The outcome, I believe, is the creation of "ethnic dialects"—namely, dialects of English that are spoken by many ethnic subgroups within the larger society. There are a great many of these in societies with diverse ethnic origins such as the United States or Canada. There are, for example, Chicano English—the Span-ish-substrate English spoken by Mexican Americans in places like East Los Angeles; Yiddish-influenced English that is associated with the Bronx in New York and with other Jewish communities in American cities; and, of course, Chinatown English. Such dialects develop in immigrant subcommunities, but they sometimes become community-wide or regional dialects, as happened with the Scandinavian-influenced variety of English spoken in the Minnesota–Wisconsin region.

What is clear is that these ethnic dialects are considerably closer to the target than is an interlanguage version such as Mrs. F's. She is a first-generation speaker of Chinatown English. As a near adolescent learner of English as a second language in the kind of situation that engenders the creation of such varieties, she helped to reinvent and revitalize the dialect, as it were. Hence we find the considerable variability in forms that we saw in her speech. If we compare her speech with that of some second-generation speakers of Chinatown English, we will find some of the features found in Mrs. F's speech, but their version of the dialect is far more regular. Consider, for example, the following speech samples drawn from a transcript of three ten-year-old girls, recorded while they were engaged in playing house.[4]

OPAL	We going to buy over here . . come on . . . we going to buy ah go to supermarket.
JADE	Buy a **ca:ke.**
PEARL	Come on. We'll find cake.
OPAL	Um--let's buy a cake. Where's cake?
JADE	I hope tomorrow is shi . . um . . shri . . got shun **shine.**
PEARL	Shining.
OPAL	(As "baby," in a singsong pretend-baby voice) OK . . I'm going. Oh . . look at the little cute puppy.
JADE?	No . . uh . . it's in the store . . let's go in the store and see if anybody is going to, uh, s--sell for us.
OPAL	How much is a ([ʹey]) puppy for?
PEARL	I think it's about **ten dollar.**
OPAL	Ten dollar? OK. Here.
PEARL	Wanna go to after we go to picnic you wanna go to uncle's house, and call uncle to go?
JADE	Oh here comes uncle. Oh hi, uncle.
PEARL	(As "uncle") Oh, baby? I never meet you.
OPAL	(As "baby") Hi. Are you going to picnic with us?
PEARL	OK let's go . . . let's go to picnic.
PEARL	(As "uncle," giggling) Let's go at twelve. Let's go to a restaurant and eat . . Uncle's hungry aren't you?
PEARL	Uncle wants to go to Jack in a Bo:x.
OPAL	**Wo:w** . . lookit! It's so many people in the car.
PEARL	OK let's go in . . . look at that **TV** let's open it watch . . hey there's a **book** . . look . . . I don't know what it's wri:ting (babbles) . . Let's open the TV. It doesn't go.

Busy, unhesitant, and completely fluent, these girls could compete well with other English-speaking preadolescents in their use of ready made formulas in their discourse. Their conversation was filled with expressions such as "Let's go," "come on," "wait a second," "wait a minute," and so on. Their speech offers some typical features of this variety of English. In contexts where standard English requires an article, this variety often does not. Auxiliary verbs *be* and *have* are sometimes omitted, as are the subject pronoun and *do* in yes-no questions:

> *We going* (buy ah) go *to supermarket.*
> Let's go *to picnic.*
> Where's *cake?*
> *Wanna* go to after we go *to picnic, you wanna* go to uncle's house and call uncle to go?
> *We never been to picnic.*

One also finds a distinctive use of prepositions:

> Let's go in the store and see if anybody is going to uh *sell for us.*
> How much is a *puppy for?*
> We go *to picnic.*

Another quite well known feature of this kind of English is the use of collocations such as *open* and *close* meaning *turn on* and *turn off* as in,

> Let's go in, look at that TV! Let's *open it* watch, Let's *open the TV!*

and the use of bare nouns such as *uncle* and *baby* as terms of reference:

> Wanna go to after we go to picnic you wanna go to *uncle's* house, and call *uncle* to go?
> Oh here comes *uncle.*

The three girls in this text are clearly operating with a stable grammatical system at the moment: it is a variety of English spoken by many second generation immigrant children in places like San Francisco's Chinatown. However, as children, they are still developing their linguistic resources. They may eventually pick up a more standard variety of English as they continue in school and as they come into greater contact with the larger community that surrounds the ethnic neighborhood they live in.

So what are the implications of all of this? It is clear that language changes in the mouths of learners, and it is precisely the language learning conditions discussed in this paper that invite the most rapid kind of change. But this is not a paper about language change. It is about language learning and about the problematic conditions under which some learners must operate. For the immigrant children who are learning English in schools and classrooms where nearly everyone they encounter is also a language learner, these conditions are a handicap. Language development is not easy when the target is a moving one. In order to do well in school, in order to take full advantage of the opportunities the society offers, these children have to learn a version of English that is more like the one used by others in the society than what they are currently learning. For some individuals—Mrs. F, for example—learning a variety that deviates considerably from the standard does not constitute a major handicap. Mrs. F's imperfect command of English has not held her back—perhaps because she has had the advantage of a well developed primary language that allowed her to develop her intellectual strengths and abilities. Others—perhaps some of the children she is now teaching—may find that that kind of English will create problems for them, especially if that is the only language they speak. The cost of subtractive bilingualism may be far greater than we realize.

ENDNOTES

1. *Transcription notes:* Consonants are represented by standard orthographic conventions, e.g., [ch, sh] = "ch, sh"; [j] as in "just." Vowels are sometimes represented phonetically, especially where standard spellings do not accurately represent the speaker's pronunciation: [æ] as in "cat"; [ɛ] as in "pet"; [ə] as in "the"; sometimes [a] represents an open "o." Ordinarily the consonant clusters are not shown as being reduced, although they are in Mrs. F's speech. Voiced initial interdentals are not shown as voiced alveolar stops, although they are most frequently stops in her speech. Words enclosed by double-asterisks are heavily stressed, and dots that are not periods represent notable pauses of varying lengths. Unusual lengthening of syllables is indicated by colons (:).

2. The Comprehensive Test of Basic Skills (CTBS) is the achievement test given to school children in California each year. Children in the second grade are tested on reading—the mechanics of reading, reading vocabulary, and the comprehension of sentences and short passages—and on math—basic computation and the application of math concepts in problems. Language minority children often do more poorly in the reading and language subtests in the third grade than they do in lower grades, perhaps because at that point the test requires them to go beyond the mechanics of language and reading to interpretation, which requires greater proficiency in English. It should also be noted that children are given this test in English irrespective of the language they have been instructed in. There is a Spanish version of the test (which is rarely given, even to children in Spanish bilingual programs), but none that I know of in Asian languages.

3. "Pull-out" refers to the practice of taking students from their regular classes for short periods of remedial instruction with special resource teachers.

4. Ten-year-olds Jade, Pearl, and Opal are Chinese-American children who live in an urban Chinatown. All three are bilinguals, having learned English and Cantonese from their parents before going to school. English is their preferred language: they use it exclusively with friends, and they use it more frequently with their parents than they do Cantonese. The quoted

lines are drawn from a much larger corpus of utterances produced during dramatic play.

REFERENCES

Celce-Murcia, M., and S. Hilles. 1988. *Techniques and Resources in Teaching Grammar.* Oxford: Oxford UP.

Celce-Murcia, M., and D. Larsen-Freeman. 1983. *The Grammar Book.* Rowley, Mass.: Newbury.

Chafe, W. L. 1982. "Integration and Involvement: Speaking, Writing and Oral Literature." *Spoken and Written Language.* Ed. D. Tannen. Norwood, N.J.: Ablex.

Cummins, J., B. Harley, M. Swain, and P. A. Allen. (In press.) "Social and Individual Factors in the Development of Bilingual Proficiency." *The Development of Second Language Proficiency.* Eds. B. Harley et al. Cambridge: Cambridge UP.

Ekstrand, L. H. 1983. "Maintenance or Transition—or Both? A Review of Swedish Ideologies and Empirical Research." *Multicultural and Multilingual Education in Immigrant Countries.* Ed. T. Husen. Oxford: Pergamon.

Gardner, R. C., and W. E. Lambert. 1972. *Attitudes and Motivation in Second Language Learning.* Rowley, Mass.: Newbury.

Hansegård, N. 1968. *Tvasprakighet eller halvsprakighet?* Stockholm: Aldus-Bonniers.

Lambert, W. E. 1975. "Culture and Language as Factors in Learning and Education." *Education of Immigrant Students.* Ed. A. Wolfgang. Toronto: Ontario Institute for Studies in Education.

———. 1977. "The Effects of Bilingualism on the Individual: Cognitive and Sociocultural Consequences." *Bilingualism: Psychological, Social, and Educational Implications.* Ed. P. A. Hornby. New York: Academic.

———. 1981. "Bilingualism and Language Acquisition." *Native Language and Foreign Language Acquisition.* Ed. H. Winitz. New York: New York Acad. of Sci.

———. 1984. "An Overview of Issues in Immersion Education." *Studies on Immersion Education.* Office of Bilingual-Bicultural Education. Sacramento: California State Dept. of Ed.

Lambert, W. E., and G. R. Tucker. 1972. *Bilingual Education of Children: The St. Lambert Experiment.* Rowley, Mass.: Newbury.

Lapkin, S., and J. Cummins. 1984. "Current Administrative Arrangements and Instructional Practices." *Studies on Immersion Education.* Office of Bilingual-Bicultural Education. Sacramento: California State Dept. of Ed.

O'Donnell, R. 1974. "Syntactic Differences Between Speech and Writing." *American Speech* 49: 102–10.

Olson, D. R. 1977. "From Utterance to Text: The Bias of Language in Speech and Writing." *Harvard Educational Review* 47: 257–81.

Rinvolucri, M. 1984. *Grammar Games: Cognitive, Affective and Drama Activities for ESL Students*. Cambridge: Cambridge UP.

Rubin, A. D. 1980. "A Theoretical Taxonomy of the Differences Between Oral and Written Language." *Theoretical Issues in Reading Comprehension*. Eds. R. J. Spiro et al. Hillsdale, N.J.: Erlbaum.

Selinker, L. 1972. "Interlanguage." *International Review of Applied Linguistics* 10: 209–31

Selinker, L., M. Swain, and G. Dumas. 1975. "The Interlanguage Hypothesis Extended to Children." *Language Learning* 25: 139–52.

Skuttnabb-Kangas, T. 1978. "Semilingualism and the Education of Migrant Children as a Means of Reproducing the Caste of Assembly Line Workers." Papers from the First Scandinavian-German Symposium on the Language of Immigrant Workers and Their Children. *Rolig Papir, 12*. Eds. N. Dittmar et al. Roskilde, Denmark: Roskilde Universitetcenter.

Skuttnabb-Kangas, T., and P. Toukomaa. 1976. "Teaching Migrant Children's Mother Tongue and Learning the Language of the Host Country in the Context of the Socio-Cultural Situation of the Migrant Family." Helsinki: Finnish National Comm. for UNESCO.

Swain, M. 1974. "French Immersion Programs across Canada: Research Findings." *Canadian Modern Language Review* 31: 117–29.

———. 1985. "Communicative Competence: Some Roles of Comprehensible Input and Comprehensible Output in Its Develoment." *Input in Second Language Acquisition*. Eds. S. Gass and C. Madden. Rowley, Mass.: Newbury.

Swain, M., and H. C. Barik. 1976. "A Large-Scale Program in French Immersion: The Ottawa Study Through Grade Three. *ITL, Review of Applied Linguistics* 33: 1–25.

Swain, M., and S. Lapkin. 1982. *Evaluating Bilingual Education: A Canadian Case Study*. Clevedon, U.K.: Multilingual Matters.

Tannen, D., ed. 1982. *Spoken and Written Language*. Norwood, N.J.: Ablex.

Ur, P. 1988. *Grammar Practice Activities: A Practical Guide for Teachers*. Cambridge: Cambridge UP.

Wong Fillmore, L. 1982. "Instructional Language as Linguistic Input: Second Language Learning in Classrooms." *Communicating in the Classroom*. Ed. L. C. Wilkinson. New York: Academic.

———. 1983. "The Language Learner as an Individual: Implications of Research on Individual Differences for the ESL Teacher." *On TESOL '82: Pacific Per-*

spectives on Language Learning and Teaching. Eds. M. A. Clarke and J. Hanscombe. Washington, D.C.: TESOL.

———. 1985. "Teacher Talk as Input." *Input in Second Language Acquisition.* Eds. S. Gass and C. Madden. Rowley, Mass.: Newbury.

———. 1989. "Language Learning in Social Context: The View from Research in Second Language Learning." *Language Processing in Social Context.* Eds. R. Dietrich and C. Graumann. Amsterdam: Elsevier.

———. 1990. "Now or Later? Issues Related to the Early Education of Minority Group Children." *Children at Risk.* Ed. C. Harris. New York: Harcourt.

———. 1991. "Language and Cultural Issues in Early Education." *The Care and Education of America's Young Children: Obstacles and Opportunities, The 90th Yearbook of the National Society for the Study of Education.* Ed. S. L. Kagan. Chicago: Chicago UP.

Wong Fillmore, L., B. McLaughlin, P. Ammon, and M. S. Ammon. 1985. *Learning English through Bilingual Instruction.* Final report to the National Institute for Studies in Education. Berkeley: U of California P.

Chapter 4

Performing Expository Texts in the Foreign Language Classroom

Courtney B. Cazden

Harvard Graduate School of Education

I write this paper as a teacher of English language arts who is trying to work with teachers, and thereby with their students, in ways consistent with cognitive and sociocultural perspectives on language learning.

The cognitive revolution of the last twenty-five years is familiar to all language teachers, although implications for teaching are still being explored. Applied to the foreign language classroom, the important question is: How do we design classroom instruction from which each learner can most easily construct an internal second language system?

During these same twenty-five years, the sociocultural aspects of this new view of learning have become more prominent. In part, this is due to ethnographic research on language acquisition in diverse cultures, represented for example by Elinor Ochs; in part, it is due to increased attention to the writings of Soviet psychologist Vygotsky (1962, 1978) and literary critic Bakhtin (1981; Cazden 1989). In the words of one psychologist, "Every human being has her or his subjectivity and mental life altered through the processes of seizing meanings and resources from some sociocultural environment and using them" (Shweder 1990: 2). Thus the important summary concept: "the social construction of knowledge." Human beings construct knowledge for themselves, but they do so with and through resources provided by their culture.[1]

Vygotsky and Bakhtin call our attention to particular cultural resources for this social construction, to two aspects of any sociocultural environment that become internalized and transformed into its citizens' mental life: first, social interactions from the moment of birth; and second, the semiotic systems, preeminently language, with all the structures of its oral and written forms, that are learned through those interactions and later from direct experience with written texts. While Vygotsky says little about sociocultural variation in either interactions or semiotic systems, Bakhtin calls our attention, as does the entire field of ethnography of communication, to what he calls the "heteroglossia" of language. Internalized, this heteroglossia brings what Wertsch, writing about both Vygotsky and Bakhtin, calls "voices of the mind" (1991).[2]

With that brief introduction, back to teaching: Given this view of the active learner, what should be the roles of the active teacher? One answer is to find ways to make the metaphor of "voices of the mind" more perceptible in both composition and interpretation. When classroom assignments in writing and reading are treated only as solitary activities, one unfortunate consequence is that mental processes are hidden from view. Performing texts in some kind of "readers' theater" externalizes some of those composing and interpreting processes and makes them more accessible for focal attention and discussion by the classroom group.

My examples come from classes of adults, mostly high school English teachers, at the Bread Loaf (summer) School of English at Middlebury College. For five summers, I have taught nonfiction writing under such titles as "Forms of talking, thinking, and writing" and "Writing, teaching, and the theater."

The Bread Loaf program has three interrelated parts: literature, writing, and theater. The theater work is unusual in both staff and function. There is an ensemble of professional actors (seven in 1990); and a director, Alan Mokler MacVey from Princeton, who works to integrate the ensemble into the life of the community outside the theater itself. So, in addition to playing major roles in dramatic productions (1989, Shakespeare's *Merchant of Venice;* 1990, Brecht's *Caucasian Chalk Circle),* the actors are available to participate in other classes. Over the last few years, members of the literature and writing faculties have worked with MacVey and the actors to develop innovative ways of bringing texts to life—giving them oral voice, often as dialogues, sometimes with dramatic actions as well—and helping the high school teachers learn to do likewise in their classes back home.[3]

EXAMPLES OF TEXT PERFORMANCE

The examples that follow (except Nadine Gordimer's essay) are from my classes in expository writing. As activities, they range on a continuum of enactment from reading aloud to readers' theater, and they will be given in that order. Each focuses attention on particular text features as they relate to meaning. At the end, I'll suggest possible benefits of such activities for the foreign language classroom.

Reading Aloud
and Making Observations

The first writing assignment in summer 1990 was a short piece (2–3 pages) on a literacy memory: some important experience as a reader, writer, or teacher. After two practice oral readings—to oneself to make sure that all the sentences were readable, and then to a roommate to develop confidence in one's public voice—the students read their pieces aloud in class. After each reading, there was a brief silence during which we (teacher included) each wrote down a one-sentence observation about something memorable heard in the piece. Neither criticisms nor suggestions were allowed, only observations. Then these observations were read aloud, around the circle, without further comment.

Here is the opening of "The KGB," written by a K–12 language arts specialist from Florida, about a small group of "bad guys" she worked with in one school:

> They named themselves the KGB. All but one of the eight were male. Some were discipline problems. Most went home to abusive, unemployed, or alcoholic parents, many of whom were single. Most of the KGB distinguished themselves with their black t-shirts, jeans with holes, long hair and earrings.
>
> All of the KGB were sophomores and juniors who were failing several subjects. The administration didn't want to add them to a list of dropouts. The counselor arranged for the group to meet with me for an hour once a week. The students were to find ways to stay in school.
>
> KGB stood for Kids Getting Better . . . (Susan Oestreicher).

And here is what the author wrote later in our class book (a group journal in looseleaf notebook form) about the observations she received from her peers:

> A couple of you mentioned word choices I'd used in the recollection of the KGB. You said they were appropriate for the topic. They included "tape recording," "approved," "manipulators," and "questioning." In an earlier draft I used "interrogation." I didn't choose those words consciously. I didn't say to myself, "Let's find words that come to mind with an image of the KGB." I never focused on the appropriateness of those particular words until you pointed them out. Listeners saw something in what I wrote that I didn't intentionally include, that I didn't know was there (Susan Oestreicher 7/10/90).

This is the minimum enactment: simply giving voice to one's own text so that others may hear and take note. Even so, for not-yet-confident writers, it is an initially scary and then rewarding experience. The author of "The KGB" also wrote, "In working with writers this fall, I need to remember how my palms perspired and my heart beat, not so much while I was reading, but while I waited for your comments."

Writing observations requires careful listening from everyone else and calls attention to features of a text that even the author may not have been aware of. Rather than singling out weaknesses, the observations focus on strengths and give the entire group of peers and teacher a chance to tell the writers, publicly, what they have done that works.

The rest of the examples are kinds of "readers' theater" (Smith 1984: 126–127) in which originally nonscripted texts are scripted for oral presentation by more than one voice. As an extension of the usual selection of narrative texts, our Bread Loaf version of readers' theater included expository texts in those courses where writing and teaching such texts was an important objective. In the scripting, small groups of students negotiate interpretations to the point of decisions about how to separate the text into voices, how to read it aloud, and (optionally) how to act. Scripting expository texts that are monologic in published format requires particularly interesting interpretive work.

The following examples show only some of the text features, or dimensions, that can become the basis for scripting.

Scripting for Shifts in Level of Abstraction

One important feature of expository writing that is difficult for many inexperienced writers is combining abstraction with vivid examples and detail. Books on expository writing agree that abstraction is a critical dimension for writers to control; but they discuss it in different terms. To Moffett, abstraction means generalization:

> The hinge between narrative and generalization may be the most crucial point in the thinking process, because it is then that the mind moves from once-upon-a-time to the timelessness of "recurring" events, from token to type (1985: 3).

To Ponsot and Deen, and to Berthoff, abstraction is the perception of structure or form:

> [One of five elemental skills is] writing both abstractly and concretely. . . The concrete is the perception of sense; the abstract is the perception of structure (Ponsot and Deen 1982: 5).

> [A]bstraction is not synonymous with generalization, . . . it is not the antithesis of "concrete." Abstraction is the apprehension of form and is accomplished in two different modes, by means of successive generalizations and by means of what Suzanne K. Langer calls "indirect, intensive insight" (Berthoff 1984: 38).

To dramatize this dimension of abstraction, I asked two Bread Loaf actors to script part of the chapter "Seeing" from Annie Dillard's *Tinker at Pilgrim's Creek*. I explained the task as a shift in mental distance, suggesting the metaphor of a camera shifting back and forth from wide-angle panorama to zoom lens. Here is their scripting, as they read it aloud in class, rewritten here to show one voice in lowercase, the other in CAPITALS:

> It was sunny one evening last summer at Tinker Creek; the sun was low in the sky, upstream. I was sitting on the sycamore log bridge with the sun at my back, watching the shiners THE SIZE OF MINNOWS who were feeding over the muddy sand in skittery schools. Again and again, one fish, then another, turned for a split second across the current and flash! . . . LIKE A SUDDEN DAZZLE OF THE THINNEST BLADE, A SPARKLING OVER A DUN AND OLIVE GROUND AT CHANCE INTERVALS FROM EVERY DIRECTION. Then I noticed white specks,

some sort of pale petals, small, floating from under my feet on the creek's surface, very slow and steady. So I blurred my eyes and gazed toward the brim of my hat and saw a new world. I saw the pale white circles roll up, roll up, LIKE THE WORLD'S TURNING, MUTE AND PERFECT, and I saw the linear flashes, gleaming silver, LIKE STARS BEING BORN AT RANDOM, DOWN A ROLLING SCROLL OF TIME. Something broke and something opened. I filled up LIKE A NEW WINESKIN. I breathed an air LIKE LIGHT; I saw a light LIKE WATER. I was THE LIP OF A FOUNTAIN THE CREEK FILLED FOREVER. I was ETHER, THE LEAF IN THE ZEPHER; I was FLESH-FLAKE, FEATHER, BONE (Dillard qtd. in Moffett 1985: 410).

In that moment of scripted reading, the actors' alternating voices dramatized Dillard's alternating perspective—between perceptions from the creek and metaphors from her mind (between "bottom-up" and "top-down" sources of knowledge, in cognitive psychology terms)—as the scene changed before her eyes. Although my metaphor of the changing camera lens fit better my initially limited meaning of abstraction as generalization, the actors gave back to us a vivid enactment of abstraction as apprehension of form. For the first time, we thought we understood what Berthoff had meant.

Professional writers like Dillard develop this shift along an abstraction dimension to a fine art. But I wanted also to demonstrate that such shifting is a basic cognitive process of the human mind, though expressed differently at different ages and in different cultures. Katherine Nelson's (1989) edited volume of analyses of the pre-sleep monologues of one little girl provided an example. Here is Emily, at 32 months, talking to herself in her crib about a race (presumably a marathon) that she wanted to watch her Daddy run. I scripted this for three voices:

normal type: remembering the past
italics: anticipating the future
CAPITALS: commenting on life in general

Today Daddy went, trying to get into the race but the people said no. *So he has to watch on television.* I DON'T KNOW WHY THAT IS, MAYBE CAUSE THERE'S TOO MANY PEOPLE. I THINK THAT'S WHY, WHY HE COULDN'T GO IN IT. *So he has to watch on television. On Halloween day, then he can run, run a race and I can watch him.* I WISH I COULD WATCH HIM. But they said no no no. *Daddy daddy daddy. No no no. Have to have to watch on television* (113).

Scripting for Points of View in an Essay

In a 1987 Bread Loaf class on "the essay," Shirley Brice Heath started scripting essays by essayists such as Virginia Woolf. One of her goals was to dramatize, literally and persuasively, the difference between the conversational voices of this originally British and French genre and the statement-support-restatement hour-glass structure of the five-paragraph themes required in school.

I tried it for myself as a heuristic strategy to understand better Nadine Gordimer's (1988) essay, "Who writes? Who reads? The rise of a people's literature in South Africa." In her last paragraph, Gordimer speaks of "the contradictions of a People's literature," and that would, I now think, be a more accurate subtitle for the complex argument of the whole piece. What does she consider the important qualities of a people's literature? What are the contradictions in achieving it? In this case, maybe scripting would illuminate not only structure but meaning.

Normally, in readers' theater it is against the rules of the game to change even one word. Here I have kept only the skeleton of the argument, not changing any words within the sentences quoted, but omitting freely between them. The following is about one-third of the entire essay, scripted for two voices that could be labeled as "Westerner" (perhaps the Radcliffe College Phi Beta Kappa audience to whom she first presented this talk, in lowercase) and "South African" (Gordimer herself, in CAPITALS):

> People's literature—what can the term connote for Westerners? The hero as tractor driver of early Soviet fiction? In most Western minds today, "People's Literature" is associated with boring, outdated propaganda.
> BUT WHERE I COME FROM THE SITUATION IS DIFFERENT. THE ILLIT-ERATE AND SEMILITERATE HAVE BEEN CALLED UP BY HISTORY. THEY HAVE BEEN CALLED UP BY JUSTICE. BEYOND THE OPPORTUNITIES TO ACQUIRE KNOWLEDGE OF MODERN SCIENCE, TECHNOLOGY, AND ADMINISTRATION, THERE IS THE MASSES' RIGHT TO ENJOY THE SELF-REALIZATION OF LITERATURE. THE DEMAND IS FOR A PARTICULAR FICTIONAL MODE. IT IS FORMULATED AS A CALL FOR A PEOPLE'S LIT-ERATURE.
> Do we recognize that tractor driver hero, now black, approaching over the veld? How does People's Literature differ from plain old Social Realism?
> IN SOUTH AFRICA, PEOPLE'S LITERATURE IS CONCEIVED AS THAT WRIT-TEN BY, NOT ABOUT, THE PEOPLE.
> Who are the people? Not whites, certainly. [And] not middle-class blacks either.
> A PEOPLE'S LITERATURE THEREFORE MEANS—TO PARAPHRASE WALTER BENJAMIN—LITERATURE CONCEIVED AS THESE PEOPLE'S "ABILITY TO RELATE" THEIR OWN LIVES.
> But Benjamin was speaking of the storyteller among the people—a title which in itself sets the relater aside . . . (1988: 2–3).

Only after doing this scripting could I understand the arguments, the contradictions, the dilemma, about where a South African people's literature that is better than the "propaganda" of early Soviet fiction can come from. On the one hand, the black "masses" have the right to literature written by, as well as about, themselves. On the other hand, aren't the "storytellers" of a people always set apart?

Details of the writing also became apparent: only the "Westerner" asked questions; only the "South African" used "I." These uncovered patterns then served to validate the scripting decisions.

Scripting for Social Voices

Native American writer N. Scott Momaday's (1969) autobiographical account of *The Way to Rainy Mountain* is separated by the author into untitled themes; each theme is written in three voices in distinct typefaces:

Elders retelling tribal myths
A historian/anthropologist commenting on tribal culture
Momaday narrating a journey back to his grandmother's grave

Here are the opening sentences of each of the three voices for the first theme in the book:

ELDER   You know, everything had to begin, and this is how it was: the Kiowas came one by one into the world through a hollow log.

HISTORIAN   They called themselves Kwuda and later Tepda, both of which mean "coming out."

MOMADAY   I remember coming out upon the northern Great Plains in the late spring (16–17).

As readers' theater, one can perform the three voices, one after the other, as they appear on each two facing pages. But it is also possible, as an interpretive activity, to change the sequencing within a single theme so that the voices speak to, clarify, or even interrupt each other. (The idea of doing this in the summer of 1989 was in part prompted by the acting ensemble's presentation of three plays by Samuel Beckett.)

For this activity, our class was divided into small groups, each of which prepared for performance the same two pages of the Momaday text, but spoke and acted them in very different ways. One group, for example, had the historian/anthropologist literally taking their words away from the elders. The result is functionally a very quick classroom version of producing and seeing multiple versions of a play: the search is no longer for one "correct" interpretation; instead, multiple interpretations are made visible for comparison and discussion.

Scripting One's Own Writing

As a last assignment, the students scripted a piece of their own writing—like a letter or an entry in the class book—something that had not been written with that purpose in mind and that had not been revised. The purpose of this assignment was self-awareness of their own mental processes as they "transcribed inner speech," as Moffett speaks of writing. Each student decided on the number of voices and then cast classmates as readers. Where the original had been written on a computer, it was easy to reformat into a script; and several people remarked on the additional meaning created by the white spaces in that process.

This assignment is best used after students have had experience in scripting texts for different text qualities. They will then be alert to more possibilities in their own writing. Unlike the other assignments, this one is carried out alone: each author selects the qualities that seem most important in the particular text.

Even though the following student had not been asked to script a piece of his own writing, he still made the mental transfer:

> Our younger readers don't make nearly as much mental drama in their heads as we do. [Readers' theater] . . . definitely helped ME understand how there could be in one sentence, two voices. Or how one voice can subtly, easily, change from line to line. And I even noticed after that exercise, in my own writing, that I use at least several voices in anything that I write. There's me the traveler, me the brought-up-middle-class-Jewish boy, there's me the academic, and there's me that hates this shit. There are very distinct voices right there, REALLY distinct (Low and Campbell 1989: 20).

USEFULNESS FOR THE FOREIGN LANGUAGE CLASSROOM

Some of the usefulness of these activities is not specific to either native language or foreign language classrooms. In suggesting such benefits, I draw not only on my subjective judgment as teacher or scripter (the latter for Emily's monologue and Gordimer's essay), but also on comments by some of the Bread Loaf students. From the 1989 class, these come from oral interviews included in a case study by two members of another class about the contributions of the actors to the literature and writing programs (Low and Campbell 1989). From the 1990 class, they come from written entries in our class book (such as Susan Oestreicher's reflections about what she learned from peer observations of "The KGB"). The 1989 interviews were quoted anonymously and are so reprinted here; the 1990 book entries were signed and names are used here with permission.

Following an examination of the value of this work for oral discussion and for understanding the structure of written texts, I will suggest one benefit more specific to second/foreign language classrooms: how repeated readings of written texts may reinforce subsidiary attention to well-formed syntax.

Oral Discussions

Performance activities stimulate discussion of two different kinds. First is the small group discussion in which enactments are planned and consensus reached on an interpretation. This planning not only stimulates discussion, but requires it. Small groups assigned to script and prepare a piece of text for performance will stay "on task" by the nature of the assignment; the next day they will be "on stage," and today's discussion must proceed to the point of decisions that will make that performance possible.

Second is the post-performance discussion in the whole class group in which the small groups' interpretive decisions are explained and compared. As each group explains their interpretation and answers questions from their peers, the investment of each student in this discussion becomes evident. As one student said:

> You get a certain closer look at literature by doing that. And by doing that it pulls everybody in. Everybody has that experience and that makes it somehow more relevant, that it's important that everybody gets a chance to comment on it. . . . It's just a more personal thing. . . . Mostly what we're talking about is our own personal experiences (Low and Campbell 1989: 16)

The result of such discussions is a richer classroom culture—a richer shared mental context of texts and activities involving them—that will make more likely not just more talk, but more talk of certain kinds. Even the first example of simply reading aloud one's own writing and then expressing observations on peer writing worked quickly to build a trusting community. After that class, one student wrote in the class book:

> I have, for some time, believed that writing classes create a unique intimacy among the class participants. Today, however, I experienced a greater sense of awe, intimacy, and appreciation for the members of this class than I have in my previous writing courses (Susan Fine, 7/4/90).

As Elinor Ochs showed from her analysis of language use in the very different situation of family meals (this volume), intimate relationships support and make more likely certain kinds of language use.

Understanding the Structure of Written Texts

In courses where the objective includes writing as well as speaking, assignments should require scripting of whatever kinds of texts the students are expected to read. In terms suggested by Janet Swaffar (this volume), the task gives students experience with one kind of "discovery procedure" for exploring text structure. Such procedures should be better ways of socializing students' attention to text structures than either immersion via reading by itself, or direct instruction of "rules" (such as for the five-paragraph essay). They are preferable to the latter for two reasons: they are ethnographically more valid (i.e., accountable to a wider set of texts as written in nonschool contexts) and are more likely to be internalized in a nonrigid, flexible way.

Here is one student's reflections on the experience of scripting and enacting part of an essay by Jamaican author Michelle Cliff, "A Journey into Speech," in three voices identified by their social origin: Jamaican, African, and the king's English Cliff learned at the University of London.

I think the first readers' theater that we did—the Michelle Cliff essay—I certainly got a much better understanding of the section that we read, because it was such a close analysis. At first I was pretty skeptical of the whole thing. . . . But once we started deciding how those voices were going to interact with one another, when we were trying to decide how we were going to block out the stage . . . then you started to get a really clear understanding of, you know, "Yeah . . . there are these different voices, but HOW do they interact?" (Low and Campbell 1989: 18).

Scripting may be especially useful in courses that require the reading of texts that express and organize meanings in culturally different ways.

Subsidiary Attention to Well-Formed Syntax

In Polanyi's discussion of personal knowledge, of which language is a prime example, he distinguishes between focal and subsidiary awareness:

> The most pregnant carriers of meaning are of course the words of a language, and it is interesting to recall that when we use words in speech or writing we are aware of them only in a subsidiary manner. This fact is usually described as the *transparency* of language (1964: 57).

In all the work of scripting and performing texts, focal attention is called to meaning: to voices and how they interact. Sentence-level syntax remains transparent, attended to only subsidiarily, as Polanyi describes.

In classrooms of native speakers of the language of the texts, this subsidiary attention has added value only as the language of literature is more complex than the language of conversation. But in foreign language classrooms, this subsidiary attention can be extremely important. The scripting activities motivate repeated readings and discussion of those readings. In the process, out-of-awareness, valid models of the target language are reinforced in each learner's mind. In classrooms where the teacher is not a native speaker of the target language (as in Wong Fillmore's paper, this volume), incorporating well-written texts into oral activities becomes even more critical.

While foreign language pedagogy may not be sure what conditions are necessary for "input" to become "intake," I assume that active involvement in hearing and reading must make a difference.

A POSTSCRIPT

It is important to make clear what these scripting activities are and are not designed for. First, they do not aim for emotional identification with any character or point of view, but for greater reflexivity about interpretive and composing processes;

in terms of dramatic theory, they are closer to Brecht than to Stanislavski (Bentley 1968). Second, all the words come from texts that preexist the acting situation; none are improvised on the spot. Dramatic activities based on other theories and requiring improvisation can also be useful in the foreign language classroom (Smith 1984).[4]

ENDNOTES

1. In his new book, *Acts of Meaning* (1990), Bruner argues against what he sees as the cognitive science distortion of the cognitive revolution in which he was one of the original players, and argues for the sociocultural view.

2. Schultz (1990) discusses her very interesting reinterpretation of Whorf's views on linguistic relativity in Bakhtinian terms:

   In his most successful artistic prose constructions (which are also his most controversial texts), Whorf fleshes out the dialogized voices, turning them into speakers of Amerindian and Standard Average European languages. . . . Put another way, Whorf's texts are polyphonic in the same way (according to Bakhtin) that Dostoevsky's novels are polyphonic. The images of the Hopi or the Shawnee or the Nootka which he constructs for his readers are, like Dostoevsky's characters, "capable of standing *alongside* their creator, capable of not agreeing with him and even of rebelling against him" (Bakhtin 1984 [1929], 6). . . . It is precisely this, Whorf's greatest accomplishment, that is, at the same time, the source of the greatest tension in his work. It is also the source of the many accusations of self-contradiction and inconsistency leveled at Whorf over the years (6–7).

3. I am especially grateful to one member of the ensemble, James Lobdell, an actor who has also been a high school English teacher and is now a doctoral student in the University of California at Berkeley School of Education, concentrating on the educational values of drama. He was the master teacher for most of these activities.

4. I am indebted to Sandra Savignon for this reference.

REFERENCES

Bakhtin, M. 1981. *The Dialogic Imagination*. Austin: U of Texas P.

Bentley, E., ed. 1968. *The Theory of the Modern Stage: An Introduction to Modern Theatre and Drama*. Harmondsworth (U.K.) and New York: Penguin.

Berthoff, A., ed. 1984. *Reclaiming the Imagination: Philosophical Perspectives for Writers and Teachers of Writing*. Portsmouth, N.H.: Boynton/Cook.

Bruner, J. 1990. *Acts of Meaning*. Cambridge: Harvard UP.

Cazden, C. B. 1989. "Contributions of the Bakhtin Circle to 'Communicative Competence.'" *Applied Linguistics* 10: 116–27.

Cliff, M. 1988. "A Journey into Speech." *The Graywolf Annual Five: Multi-Cultural Literacy*. Eds. R. Simonson and S. Walker. St. Paul: Graywolf. 57–62.

Dillard, A. 1985. "Seeing." *Points of Departure: An Anthology of Nonfiction*. Ed. J. Moffett. New York: NAL. 397–412.

Gordimer, N. 1988. "Who Writes? Who Reads? The Rise of a People's Literature in South Africa." *Radcliffe Quarterly* September: 2–4.

Low, R., and M. Campbell. 1989. "A Strange and Familiar Story. A Case Study: The Role of the Actor in Courtney Cazden's Class. Forms of Thinking, Talking and Writing." Middlebury College, Bread Loaf School of English, unpublished term paper.

Moffett, J. 1985. *Points of Departure: An Anthology of Nonfiction*. New York: NAL.

Momaday, N. S. 1969. *The Way to Rainy Mountain*. Albuquerque: U of New Mexico P.

Nelson, K. 1989. *Narratives in the Crib*. Cambridge: Harvard UP.

Polanyi, M. 1964. *Personal Knowledge: Towards a Post-Critical Philosophy*. New York: Harper.

Ponsot, M., and R. Deen. 1982. *Beat Not the Poor Desk: Writing: What to Teach. How to Teach It and Why*. Portsmouth, N.H.: Boynton/Cook.

Schultz, E. A. 1990. *Dialogue at the Margins: Whorf, Bakhtin, and Linguistic Relativity*. Madison: U of Wisconsin P.

Shweder, R. A. 1990. "Cultural Psychology: What Is it?" *Cultural Psychology: Essays on Comparative Human Development*. Eds. J. W. Stigler & G. Herdt. New York: Cambridge UP. 1–43.

Smith, S. M. 1984. *The Theater Arts and the Teaching of Second Languages*. Reading, Mass.: Addison.

Vygotsky, L. 1962. *Thought and Language*. Cambridge: MIT.

———. 1978. *Mind in Society*. Cambridge: Harvard UP.

Wertsch, J. 1991. *Voices of the Mind*. Cambridge: Harvard UP.

Chapter 5

Authenticity, Variation, and Communication in the Foreign Language Classroom

Albert Valdman

Indiana University

Even those who are dubious about the validity of the American Council on the Teaching of Foreign Languages (ACTFL) Proficiency Guidelines and the Oral Proficiency Interview concede that the so-called proficiency movement has led to a quantum leap in recognizing the achievement of communicative ability as a legitimate goal of foreign language (FL) teaching. Many FL teachers hold that only by setting our sights squarely on that goal, even in early stages of instruction, will we train young Americans who can interact effectively with peers from the target language (TL) community.*

Nonetheless, given the cultural and political context within which high school and college/university level FL instruction is imparted in the United States, communicative ability cannot realistically be the predominant objective. Instead FL instruction must be viewed as formative in nature, and it must aim to impart a substantive body of knowledge about the particular FL and the cultures of the communities that use it, as well as communicative skills. In proficiency-oriented instruction specifically, and in communicatively-oriented instruction in general, the attainment of communicative skills matching those of educated adult native speakers is set as the ultimate goal. As will be shown in this paper, this goal is both unrealistic and ill-founded, and more attainable objectives must be set. For beginning and intermediate university level instruction these objectives comprise, in addition to what I have termed a minimal communicative ability (as opposed to communicative competence) in the target language (TL), *metalinguistic* and *epilinguistic* outcomes. To recognize the importance of metalinguistic outcomes of foreign language (FL) instruction is not simply to revert to the traditional stress on knowledge of grammar rules that fell victim to the impact of structural linguistics on FL teaching in the 1960s. To impart metalinguistic awareness involves showing students how, in Michael Halliday's words (1990), "language is at the same time a part of reality, a shaper of reality, and a metaphor of reality." This is best effected indirectly by showing how linguistic forms carry both social and linguistic meaning, and how different languages, because they are the expression of different cultures, impose different views of the world on their speakers. Epilinguistics concerns attitudes toward language. In an unpublished paper delivered at the 1979 meeting of the American Association for Applied Linguistics, Charles A. Ferguson pointed out that in addition to their technical expertise, which allows for precision in the description of language behavior, linguists bring to language concerns two important attitudinal sets: reverence for language as a reflection of human intellectual capabilities and the willingness to suspend value judgments about societal aspects of language variation. The recognition that all forms of speech are worthy and that there are no "primitive languages" or "corrupted dialects," unsuited for the potential uses to which a given community may wish to put them, should be an important outcome of FL instruction. These attitudes will, it is hoped, guide the judgments of former FL students in their adulthood as they face the numerous language planning issues that confront today's complex multi-ethnic societies.

There are many reasons why a communicative competence matching that of adult native speakers cannot be attained by the tutored learning of an FL under ordinary classroom conditions. In its natural use language is deeply imbedded in the situational context. Coppieters (1987: 569) suggests that native speakers do not acquire such subtle semantic distinctions as the preterite versus the present perfect of English (*I lived/I have lived in England*) or the past definite (*passé composé*) versus the imperfect (*imparfait*) of French (*il a glissé/il glissait sur la glace*) in terms of context-free formal distinctions but by means of a set of richly contextualized exemplars that become associated with specific forms and that guide later context-embedded use. Even with the most ingenious simulated natural use of language it is impossible to create suitable conditions for the contextualized use of language among non-native speakers in a classroom environment. In its natural communicative use any language shows many different types of variation. Interactants from different regional areas or different social groups make use of variant features, and individual speakers will vary their linguistic behavior depending on numerous aspects of the situation in which the interaction takes place. The inseparable link that exists between linguistic variants and specific sociopragmatic situations makes it difficult for students to rehearse the appropriate use of these variants in the sociolinguistically impoverished context of the FL classroom. In the absence of opportunities to produce speech acts in authentic situational contexts, students should be given the opportunity to observe such speech acts. By guided observation they may gain an awareness of the role of language in constructing linguistic and social meaning and in symbolizing membership in social groups ranging from street gangs to nations. In the FL classroom many aspects of communicative ability can be learned without students actually producing FL discourse. But in addition to the constraints imposed by the classroom context itself, there are limits on the degree of sociopragmatic appropriateness and linguistic accuracy attainable by adult second language learners that stem from the very nature of second language acquisition and that are independent of the conditions under which learning takes place (Coppieters 1987).

I am not suggesting that no meaningful level of communicative ability can be attained in the FL classroom, and I am certainly not advocating that students be given no opportunities to communicate by means of a medium different from their primary language. By stating that there are limits to the communicative competence in an FL that can be imparted in the classroom, I am suggesting that the quixotic quest for this high level of accomplishment be replaced by a more realistic enterprise which is more likely to yield a product with higher surrender value. In the first section of this article I will identify one aspect of communicative competence where psychological factors impose upper limits on the level of achievement FL learners can realistically be expected to attain. But even if they stop well short of native communicative *competence,* learners can still reach a high level of communicative *ability* and interact successfully with members of the target language community. In the second section of the article I will describe an approach by means of which one may in the classroom deal with the variation that is inherent in any language. Although underlying this approach is the belief that foreign learners should not be expected to acquire the range of variation shown by certain types of target language native speakers, the goal proposed does include a significant range of target language variation. More importantly, this approach defines learner norms that are both acceptable to members of the target language community and attainable under classroom conditions. Finally, in the third section, I raise the issue of the better match between form, meaning, function, and context in devising grammatical syllabi. This better match may in fact lead to a higher level of communicative ability than is attainable with the aid of syllabi contained in so-called proficiency-oriented materials. In any case, it will lead to a higher level of awareness of how language is used to negotiate meaning in sociopragmatically embedded contexts.

UPPER LIMITS FOR FOREIGN LEARNERS

There is an extensive literature on the constraints imposed on the acquisition of speech (especially nativelike phonological perception and phonetic production) by neurolinguistic and psychological factors (see Long 1990 and Leather and James 1991 for broad reviews). Coppieters (1987) has also shown that highly proficient non-native users of French, many of whom had resided in France for more than ten years and most of whom could not be distinguished from native speakers of the same social level (highly educated middle class) on the basis of their linguistic performance, diverged markedly from native-speaker peers in their ability to make grammatical judgments.[1] Coppieters concludes that the lack of correspondence between advanced FL users' demonstrated proficiency and their imperfect control of the rules that underlie that proficiency and their differences from native-speaker behavior at the metalinguistic level reflects differences in the way grammatical knowledge about French is represented in the brain, that is, differences in linguistic competence between native speakers and highly proficient non-native speakers. For very advanced learners who interact with TL speakers *in situ* there are also powerful psychological factors that set upper limits on the acquisition of communicative skills, such as the organization of discourse and rules of conversational interaction. It is the latter type of constraint on linguistic behavior that will be treated in this section.

Collecting data very much as did Elinor Ochs and Carolyn Taylor (this volume), that is by staging and recording dinner table conversations, Molly Wieland (1990) compared the effect on cross-cultural understanding of differences in the elaboration and perception of politeness strategies on the part of native French speakers and highly competent American users of the language. One salient difference between American and French rules of conversation involves turntaking behavior. According to Wieland, in American culture conversation proceeds by consecutive turns; speakers have the right to hold the floor uninterrupted until they relinquish it. Interruptions or overlapping conversational turns are considered impolite, except when they are brief and consist of requests for clarification, information, or verification. In French conversation, on the other hand, turns overlap, and interruptions are generally viewed positively. Carroll (1987 qtd. in Wieland 1990: 14) claims that in French conversation, "interruptions are a sign of interest, warmth, spontaneity, and pleasure" and that "they encourage active participation in the conversation and create a feeling of solidarity among the participants."

In American conversation interruptions are clearly marked events. They tend to be short, they relate directly to what the turnholder is saying, and they cause the latter to stop in midutterance. In contrast, when French speakers are interrupted by a request for information, they will complete their utterance and then respond to the query. Interruption and overlapping speech turns are part of French turntaking norms. Interruptions are not considered to be dysfunctional; they signal a collaborative relationship between the interactants. The interrupter may provide additional information, clarify, verify, or correct facts, or even provide a prompt when the turnholder falters or gropes for the appropriate word. Typical of French conversation is example 1 below, in which Françoise provides support for Colette's statement about the prevalence of drug use in England; bracketed items indicate overlapping utterances at points of interruption (Wieland 1990: 73):

1. C: ce n'est qu'en regardant dans les yeux et tout ça, moi je pourrais presque faire un cours, quand j'étais en Angleterre on reconnaît les gens [qui se droguaient]

    simply by looking in people's eyes and all that, I could almost give a course, when I was in England you recognize the people who used drugs

    F: [et puis on les voit] se passer les drogues [dans les lieux publics]

    and then you see them giving each other drugs in public places

    C: [ah oui c'est sûr]

    ah yes that's for sure

F:	comme les gares ou les choses comme ça	*like in railway stations and things like that*
C:	c'est vrai	*that's true*

Interruptions allow listeners to voice disagreements with the turnholder, and French conversations can take a very interactive form, as shown in example 2, where Yvette questions Solange's rejection of the use of small electric kitchen appliances:

2. S:	installer ton robot ton truc euh pour raper trois carottes pour toi, après t'as beaucoup plus [d'assiettes à laver puis si tu les rapes]	*to install your robot your thinga-majig hm to grate three carrots for yourself, later you've got more dishes to wash than if you grate them.*
Y:	[non mais si si s'il est bien s'il est bien]	*no but if if if it's well if it's well*
S:	[euh tu pourrais le]	*hm you could it*
Y:	[fait non mais tu le] tu dépenses de l'huile de coude hein? Si tu les rapes	*constructed no but if you it you're using elbow grease right? If you grate them*

When faced with the French conversation style, Wieland's proficient American users of the language felt frustrated at times and uncomfortable. They could either adhere to their native rules of conversational interaction and remain silent as their French dinner companions talked out of turn, or they could assert their right to uninterrupted speech turns. Wieland reviewed the recorded dinner conversations with her American and French subjects, and she discussed with them the differences in conversational style. Although the Americans recognized the differences between the French and American conversational styles, they stated that they could not bring themselves to adopt the speech interaction behavior of the French because they consider interruptions, for example, impolite. Their own culture had conditioned them to show that one cares about what others have to say by listening attentively and not interrupting until one's turn comes up. Interestingly, when asked to comment on the recorded conversations, their French dinner companions indicated that the Americans' dogged attempts to hold the floor alone during their speech turn was impolite and uncooperative. Since the Americans could neither assume an equal role in conversational narratives without interrupting nor be viewed positively unless they behaved in a manner that was unacceptable according to their own rules, these Americans found themselves in a double-bind situation.[2]

Douglas Brown (1980) recommends that foreign learners be led to perceive and to follow the conversational rules of the target culture. But the behavior and reactions of Wieland's subjects, many of whom had lived among the French for many years, suggest that this goal might not be attainable, even under the best circumstances. These sociolinguistic aspects of language use appear to be too closely tied to the formation of the learners' personalities and to loyalty to their primary culture to be amenable to modification, at least for most adults (Littlewood 1975). More appropriate goals for the FL classroom would be to develop an awareness of these aspects of communicative competence, to gain an understanding of how they are integrated within the target culture and social structure as a whole, and to foster a tolerance for patterns that differ from those of the learners' primary speech community.

THE ILLUSIVE IDEAL NATIVE SPEAKER AND PEDAGOGICAL NORMS

At all levels of language, but more particularly at the phonological level, setting native-speaker performance as the ultimate objective is ill-advised since, at least for each of the three major FLs taught in the United States, there are several communities with their own speech norms. In the case of Spanish, for example, on what basis can the teacher choose between the peninsular accent and one of several Latin American variants? Even in a language such as French, where users from various parts of the world adhere to a single norm—Metropolitan Standard French—the norm allows considerable leeway, particularly at the phonological and lexical levels.[3]

Furthermore, native speakers do not always welcome foreigners who have acquired localized vernacular forms of speech that are closely linked to membership in closely knit, intimate social networks. Giles and Ryan (1982) remind us that accent serves as a powerful symbol of ethnicity and "psychological distinctiveness." Foreigners who closely conform to native forms may not be more favorably regarded by their hosts. They may instead be viewed with suspicion and be considered as having violated rules of hospitality. Leather and James (1991) cite Christophersen's (1973) description of the Englishman's reaction to an overperfect pronunciation in a foreign speaker as that of a host who sees an uninvited guest making free with his possessions.

Then should not the standard norm of the TL be imparted to classroom FL learners? No, for at least two reasons. First, that norm will seldom be evident in the samples of authentic oral texts to which they will be exposed. Second, to expose learners only to highly contrived materials that adhere to the standard norm will make it difficult for them to understand authentic texts or to have suitable models on the basis of which they may extract the rules that underlie vernacular speech. Precisely because they differ from the codified rules that characterize the standard norm, these rules do not appear in classroom materials. More compatible with tutored FL learning are dynamic *pedagogical norms* established on the basis of a variety of factors: (1) linguistic: the actual variable production of *targeted* native speakers in authentic communicative situations; (2) sociopsychological: native speakers' idealized views of their speech and the perceptions both native speakers and foreign learners have regarding expected behavior of foreign users; (3) psycholinguistic: relative ease of acquisition and use. I will illustrate the concept of pedagogical norm with a notoriously variable zone of French syntax, interrogative structures (Valdman 1975, 1976, 1983; Fox 1989). I will restrict my observations to WH-questions (Table 1).

Students of French are traditionally taught only two of the numerous WH-question constructions found in various geographical and social varieties of French: EST-CE QUE and INVERSION (see Table 1). As the data in Table 2 (Behnstedt 1973) show, these constructions are relatively rare in vernacular speech. Instead, metropolitan French speakers most frequently use syntactically less complex variants, FRONTING and WH-FINAL. However, these constructions are sociolinguistically stigmatized: Behnstedt's middle-class speakers underestimated their use while, on the other hand, they overestimated the proportion of INVERSION questions.

On the basis of the criteria of status and solidarity (Ryan 1983), one may assume that educated middle-class native speakers of French would expect foreign counterparts to favor INVERSION, which is the most highly valued construction in their own subjective norm and which they associate with planned discourse and the written medium. The second principle of pedagogical norm elaboration singles out INVERSION as the valorized variant from a sociolinguistic perspective and identifies it as the most suitable construction for foreign learners to use from the sociolinguistic and sociopsychological standpoints. On the other hand, IN-VERSION is subject to numerous constraints that render its handling difficult and prone to errors. Its sociolinguistically neutral status and the syntactic regularity of EST-CE QUE favor it as the choice for first-level approximation to authentic native speaker usage. However, from an acquisitional perspective

— Table 1

French WH-interrogative Variant Constructions

INVERSION	Quand pars-tu?	*When are you leaving?*
WH-FINAL	Tu pars quand?	
FRONTING	Quand tu pars?	
C'EST INSERTION	Quand c'est tu pars? Quand c'est que tu pars?	
EST-CE QUE INSERTION	Quand est-ce que tu pars?	
COMPLEMENT	Quand que tu pars?	
CLEFTING	C'est quand que tu pars?	

— *Table 2*

Relative Frequency of the Distribution of Interrogative Constructions in a Representative Corpus of Spoken French (Behnstedt 1973)

	Production			Perception
	Substandard French (Français populaire)	**Informal Standard French**	**Formal Standard French**	
PRONOMINALISATION Tu vas où?	12%	33%	25%	20%(−)
FRONTING Où tu vas?	36%	46%	10%	30%(−)
EST-CE QUE Où est-ce que tu vas?	8%	12%	3%	20%(+)
EST-CE QUE VARIANTS Où c'est que tu vas?	35%	4%	—	
INVERSION Où vas-tu?	9%	5%	62%	30%(+)
	N = 587	N = 446	N = 436	

FRONTING appears to be the most easily learnable construction, at least on the basis of the evidence provided by a study of American beginning university students (Valdman 1975, 1976). FRONTING occurred in high proportion in questions these students were made to produce, despite the fact that this variant was absent from the input to which they were exposed. This case of *creative construction* (Dulay et al. 1982) makes FRONTING a likely candidate for transitional use in early stages of learning. The ordering of French WH interrogative constructions as shown in Figure 1 represents a pedagogical norm. First, only four variants are selected from the larger set occurring in the full range of authentic native speech (see Table 1). Second, exposure of students to the four variants selected from the larger set of attested constructions (see Table 1) is carefully controlled. Because it appears easiest to process, FRONTING is presented as the initial target. But because it is stigmatized, it is progressively faded out in favor of the more neutral EST-CE QUE construction. Concurrently, INVERSION is introduced for written production and more formal oral discourse. In later stages of instruction all four variants are introduced for recognition and active control, but information is provided about the various sociolinguistic and syntactic restrictions that govern their use. At any one stage in this pedagogical progression students should be able to accurately formulate queries by using any one of the interrogative constructions to which they have been exposed. In this way, at the very least, they are able to match the performance of students who have followed the traditional approach in which the four variants are construed as synonymous. However, in addition, the longer they proceed in their study, the more likely they are to also use the variants in a sociopragmatically appropriate manner, in other words, to produce the variant that best matches the language medium (oral or written) and the various aspects of the situational context.

Associated with the notion of pedagogical norm is the rejection of a unidimensional model according to which language variation is determined by level of attention to speech and in which all social groups orient their behavior to that of a single dominant group (Labov 1966). Instead, linguistic behavior in complex societies is viewed as determined by competing norms. Speakers will shift their norm orientation depending on a variety of social and psychological factors, including the situational context and their communicative intent, and not only depending on various levels of discourse planning (Valdman 1989). This multinorm model accounts, for example, for the persistence of stigmatized forms in the speech of Harlem African-American youths studied by Labov (1972: 149). It is also consonant with Milroy's social network theory (1982). Within the framework of the multinorm model, interlinguistic continua may be viewed as vectors that are oriented toward a particular TL norm by filtering input and by controlling feedback. In naturalistic second language acquisition the types of communicative situations encountered by learners will determine in large part the norm orien-

— Figure 1

Progressive Ordering of WH-interrogative Variants

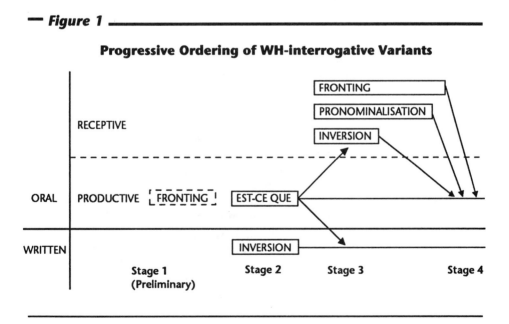

tation of their interlinguistic continua. In tutored learning, however, the norm orientation is controlled by the teacher. The notion of pedagogical norm can make this control more explicit.

The relationship between a pedagogical norm and the orientation of the learner's interlinguistic system toward competing native norms is illustrated in Figure 2. The large square delimited by solid lines and labelled TL_0 represents the totality of TL lects and subsumes all of the community's norms. The small circles included in TL_0 represent the various norms of the TL community. For the sake of convenience the model includes only the standard norm and two other competing norms, A and B. With regard to the French interrogative data displayed in Table 2, the norm that determines middle-class planned speech (formal) would be the standard norm, Norm C; the norm that determines working-class speech would be Norm B; and the norm that determines middle-class spontaneous speech (informal) would be Norm A. The large square delimited by broken lines represents the totality of deviant interlinguistic forms that fall outside of the overall system of the TL. In naturalistic second language acquisition, interlinguistic continua are oriented broadly and may include forms that fall outside of TL_0. In conventional instruction, interlinguistic systems are oriented toward the standard norm, but not explicitly. As was pointed out above, in the elaboration of a pedagogical norm the forms selected may be determined by any norm included in TL_0, including of course the standard norm.

INTEGRATING GRAMMAR AND SOCIOPRAGMATICS

The most paradoxical aspect of proficiency-oriented instruction is its continued reliance on static grammatical descriptions based on a highly restricted range of written text types. Communicative ability, both in its productive and receptive modes, can be attained only if learners are exposed to a variety of authentic oral and written texts illustrating a broad range of genres and pragmatic situations. (The term *authentic text* refers here to any type of text not constructed specifically for instructional purposes.) A pedagogical grammar compatible with communicatively oriented FL instruction must be solidly anchored in sociopragmatics; that is, it must reflect the functional use of language embedded in communicative situations. In other words it must be notional-functional in nature, and it must stress the meaning and function of linguistic features rather than their surface form. For the attainment of minimal communicative ability, which has been posited in the introductory section of this article as one of the outcomes of classroom FL, instruction does not require students to engage in interpersonal communication for its own sake. Rather its aim is to provide students with concrete examples of how this type of communication may be achieved with the use of an FL. Thus, accuracy in the use of the language cannot be subordinated to the achievement of success in communicating. As they engage in simulated speech acts, students must maintain a certain focus on form. But accuracy in the use of the FL must not be confused with purism or hypercorrection. For example, regarding the French variant WH-constructions presented in section 2, to eliminate FRONTING and WH-FINAL constructions from the syllabus because of their association with lower-class speech would constitute purism since these two constructions are the two most frequently used in the spontaneous speech of middle-class speakers; to recommend the use of INVERSION for neutral conversation because it is thought to elevate the style would constitute hypercorrection since targeted native speakers seldom use it in this type of speech.

In devising a communicatively-oriented syllabus, accuracy in the use of grammatical features does not become an independent objective. Rather, links must be traced between a specific grammatical feature and the semantic notions it represents or the pragmatic or sociolinguistic functions it serves. Also, it must be shown that the relationship between notions and functions on the one hand, and linguistic features on the other, is not bi-unique: a given grammatical feature may perform a variety of functions and, conversely, a given semantic notion or sociopragmatic function may be expressed by several linguistic features. In addition, a link must be established between linguistic features and the type of

---

— Figure 2 _____

Possible Orientations of Interlinguistic Continua
Toward Various TL Norms

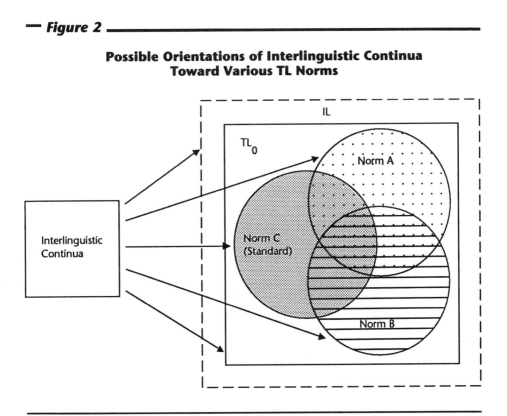

issues will be broached with reference to two central French grammatical features: WH-interrogative constructions and the *passé composé.*

The discussion of French variant WH-interrogative constructions in section 2 suggests that these correlate with social factors or the level of planning in discourse. Such a narrow view of the significance of language variation for linguistic communication reflects a reductionist determinism associated with early Labovian variationist research (Labov 1966). More recently sociolinguists, notably Romaine (1984), Milroy (1982), Le Page and Tabouret-Keller (1985), have stressed that the choices speakers make among variants signal identification with particular social groups and reflect communicative intent. There also has been among sociolinguists a lively debate concerning the applicability of the variationist methodology developed for the study of phonological variation to the syntactic level. Phonological variants are synonymous; the choice among variants can thus serve various indexical functions: to indicate membership in a particular social group or to mark degree of attention to speech form. For example, in Martha's Vineyard English centralizing vowel diphthongs (to pronounce *right* as [rÅjt] instead of [rajt], or *house* as [hÅws] instead of [haws] signals the fact that the speaker is a native of the island (Labov 1972: 36). Syntactic variants serve a broader range of functions in communication. Even though syntactic variants, such as the several French interrogative constructions, may have the same representational meaning (associated with truth value), they differ with regard to their textual or pragmatic value:

> . . . [I]t is just as reasonable to say that someone does not know the meaning of a word/expression if he cannot contextualize it as it is to say that he doesn't know the meaning if he doesn't know the truth conditions. . . . The problem with keeping a theory of language use projectionist, i.e., separate from an autonomous linguistic theory which deals with decontextualized or depragmatized system sentences, is that social context and meaning is relegated to a place of secondary importance. (Romaine 1984: 427)

The pedagogical grammars that underlie materials that are advertised as "proficiency based" or "communicatively oriented" persist in stating that WH- or *information* questions serve to elicit information, as the label suggests. Furthermore, with respect to French variant WH-question constructions specifically, except for the indication that INVERSION is associated with the formal register, most current teaching materials present them as synonymous free variants. But even early descriptions of French interrogatives (Foulet 1921; Fromaigeat 1938) commented on some of the rhetorical and pragmatic differences between the variants. For example, Foulet linked INVERSION to a high level of formality ("très correct mais abrupt") whereas he viewed EST-CE QUE as more neutral. Albeit in a very vague and impressionistic manner, he posited differences along a scale of communicative value; for example, he ranked variants according to what he termed "intensité interrogative," the degree of involvement of the questioner in the information elicited (Fox 1989). Although the polymorphism of French interrogative constructions has attracted the attention of many syntacticians and sociolinguists (see Fox 1989 for a comprehensive evaluative review of this research), the data base is still insufficient for an attempt at synthesis and, as a corollary, for the drafting of a comprehensive pedagogical grammar. Nonetheless, some preliminary links may be traced between particular variants and certain communicative functions and discourse contexts (Fox 1989; Coveney 1989):

1. INVERSION is excluded from confirmation questions: in example 3 both INVERSION and EST-CE QUE questions would be odd, since the intent of the speaker is not to query but to express disbelief and elicit a repetition of the seemingly outlandish name:

   3. Comment vous appelez-vous?   *What's your name?*

   —Jean Trucmachinchouette.   *—John Thingamajig.*

   Vous vous appelez comment?   *What's your name?*

   ?Comment est-ce que vous vous appelez?

   *Comment vous appelez-vous?

2. WH-FINAL is generally excluded from echo and rhetorical questions, as well as what may be termed *self questions*. In example 4 the interlocutor is repeating the query to reintroduce the topic that he or she will address. Although INVERSION could be used, WH-FINAL is excluded:

   4. Un bon professeur qu'est-ce qu'il désire?   *What does a good teacher want?*

   —Un bon professeur qu'est-ce qu'il désire? Et bien, il voudrait que ses élèves apprennent bien.   *What does a good teacher want? Well, s/he wants his/her students to learn well.*
   . . . que désire-t-il?
   * . . . il désire quoi?

Example 5 illustrates the exclusion of WH-FINAL from self-questions; the interrogative construction is used by the speaker to help retrieve some information from memory:

   5. Zut, où (est-ce qu'il) il habite?   *Darn, where does he live?*
   * . . . il habite où?

In example 6 the teenage Québecois girl is uttering the rhetorical question to deny the value of education for people who are interested in professions where talent is more important than knowledge:

| 6. | Quelqu'un qui veut, mettons, se diriger dans la musique, qu'est-ce que ça y sert l'école, d'apprendre deux plus deux égalent quatre?
—[ça y sert à rien] (Fox 1989)
* . . . ça y sert à quoi? | *Someone who wants to, say, go into music, what's s/he need to go to school for, to learn that two and two are four?*
[s/he doesn't need it at all] |

Not only do traditional pedagogical grammars limit themselves to linguistic forms abstracted from discourse and the situational context, but they posit an isomorphic relationship between linguistic features on the one hand, and semantic notions and speech acts on the other. For example, in an empirical study of the acquisition of French under classroom conditions. M. A. Kaplan (1986: 4) starts from the traditional view, which assigns unitary meaning to each of the two past tenses, the imperfect and the past definite (*passé composé*):

> Learners of French must distinguish two kinds of past tenses used in the everyday spoken language: the *passé composé* (compound past) and the *imparfait* (imperfect). According to the standard textbook explanations, the *passé composé* designates a completed past or change of state, and the imperfect designates a condition or habitual ongoing action in the past.

But in fact, both of these tenses express a variety of semantic notions and speech acts. For example, the imperfect may be used not only to express past progressive and durative, but to modulate actions. As shown in examples 7 and 8 this tense may modulate commands in the form of suggestions or show deference:

| 7. | suggestion:
Si on prenait le train? | *How about taking the train?* |
| 8. | deference/politeness:
Qu'est-ce que vous vouliez? | *What may I do for you?* |

The illustrative sentences in 9 and 10 (Bentolila 1973) show that the past definite expresses the completive aspect as well as the past punctual:

9.	Quoi, tu n'as pas encore rangé tes affaires?	*You mean to tell me you haven't yet straightened up your things?*
	Regarde Stéphane, il a rangé toutes ses affaires.	*Look at Stephane, he's straightened up his things.*
10.	A Noël mon père il est rentré à la maison avec plein de cadeaux qu'on lui avait donnés à son travail.	*At Christmas my father came back home with a lot of presents that they had given him at work.*
	Oui, il avait un chien, il a sauté à travers un cerceau avec du feu.	*Yes, he had a dog, it jumped through a flaming hoop.*

Some pedagogically oriented analyses of the French verbal system (for example, Matte 1989) do identify some of the different notions carried by the past definite. However, since they illustrate them with sentences abstracted from discourse, these traditional analyses fail to provide the learner guidance for the use of that linguistic feature to negotiate meaning in real communicative situations. Whether the past definite carries the meaning of completive or past punctual depends on the degree to which the speech act is embedded in situational context. Note that the syntax of the sentences in 9 and 10 differs markedly. In 9, which is abstracted from a dialogue, the sentences open up with shifters that refer to the situational context and link the two events to the present. The sentences in 10 are part of an oral narrative. The past definite carries the story line and the adverbial complements, which are lacking in 9, embed the events in a situational context.

CONCLUSION

This article has offered several variations on the theme of authenticity in FL teaching. First, characterizing a near-native mastery of the TL as including total sociopragmatic authenticity, interpreted as the display of rules of language use matching those of TL speakers, it has suggested that such mastery might not be attainable in tutored language learning. Citing a recent study on the acquisition of French conversational strategies on the part of Americans residing in France, it has shown that this ability may not even be achieved by advanced learners who interact naturally with TL speakers within the host community. A certain degree of variance must be tolerated, and in fact expected, between foreign learners and their TL models. This variance should not be viewed as dysfunctional, for an interlinguistic sociopragmatic system, even if it marks its user as an outsider, neither interferes with the transmission of meaning nor reflects negatively on the foreign user who otherwise shows a good mastery of the microlinguistic system.

The second variation on the theme of authenticity addressed the issue of choice of pedagogical norm. It was suggested that an invariant TL norm, based on the planned discourse of educated and cultivated TL speakers, is an illusory target for learners, especially at the beginning and intermediate levels. To speak like an educated native speaker requires the ability to select among several norms on the basis of the total situational context and in light of varying communicative intents. In addition, the norms for prestigious planned speech are usually complexified with respect to those that characterize vernacular unplanned speech. At the phonological level, they require finer discriminations; at the grammatical level, they involve numerous lower-level and highly specific constraints. Consequently, in trying to approximate these norms learners are likely to produce more deviant forms, both inaccurate from a linguistic perspective and inappropriate from a sociopragmatic one. A more realistic and satisfactory solution to reduce the variation inherent in language is to construct pedagogical norms. These norms are dynamic and offer learners changing targets that lead them progressively to the mastery of the full range of TL variants. This mastery is attained in two steps. First, learners develop an awareness of the relationship between variants and sociopragmatic factors. Second, they are able to produce variants that are appropriate in specific situational contexts.

The final variation on the common theme of authenticity concerns the relationship between traditional sentence-based grammars and the rules that underlie the performance of speech acts and the production of texts. The latter two aspects of the use of language for communication are closely bound to specific situations and communicative and expressive goals, as well as to identification with often varying social groups. Since the recognition of the concept of communicative competence two decades ago, we have seen a sort of additive progression rather than an integrative process. At early levels learners are introduced to monolithic morphosyntactic features: articles, noun phrase agreement, isolated verb tenses, disparate syntactic mechanisms. The order of introduction of these features often reflects that followed by grammatical treatments developed for mother tongue education. More advanced levels of FL teaching feature speech act taxonomies. Often, isomorphic relationships are established between linguistic forms and the textual and sociopragmatic uses they serve. What is needed is an integrative approach in which as more finely broken down linguistic features are presented, learners are introduced to the multifarious uses to which they can be put in negotiating meaning and in creating texts. Just as specialists of the language sciences need to develop an all-inclusive, rigorous theory that encompasses linguistic and communicative competence, so applied linguists and methodologists need to devise pedagogical grammars that help learners perceive how the TL links meaning and form, how its speakers construct whole messages that enable them to achieve communicative ends and texts that enable them to narrate events and to organize their experience.

The handling of linguistic variation within the TL and the integrative approach to syllabus design advocated here should contribute to the attainment of metalinguistic and epilinguistic outcomes to which we assign as high a value as to the achievement of a minimal communicative ability. The notion of pedagogical norm, formulated on the basis of native-speaker attitudes toward speech as well as on the basis of observable native-speaker performance, is concerned centrally with *epilinguistics*. The type of pedagogical grammar recommended, which shows explicitly the links existing between linguistic features and semantic notions and sociopragmatic functions, fosters the development of *metalinguistic* awareness, specifically an understanding of the way language functions to construct linguistic and sociopragmatic meaning.

ENDNOTES

*I would like to acknowledge, with gratitude, comments and suggestions made on various drafts of this article by graduate students and colleagues at Indiana University, especially Cheryl Engber, Laurel McLain, Cathy Pons, Deborah Piston-

Hatlen, and Charlie Pooser. Of course, this does not imply that they agree with all aspects of the position on classroom language instruction formulated here.

1. Coppieters compared judgments about the semantic differences between several basic French grammatical contrasts (past definite versus imperfect, pre-posed versus post-posed adjectives, *c'est* versus *il est,* etc.) elicited from a group of twenty-one non-native speakers and a comparable group of native speakers. The non-native speakers were mostly university professors or advanced graduate students whose residence in France averaged seventeen years. In judgments about the difference of meaning between the past definite and the imperfect, for example, deviations from prototypic judgments averaged 2 percent for the native speakers but 41.5 percent for the non-native speakers.

2. In order to reduce the number of social variables, Wieland assumed invariant French and American sets of conversational strategies. For American speakers, Deborah Tannen (this volume) has shown that significant differences exist in turntaking behavior between middle-class Californians and New York Jews; in fact, the latter's behavior resembles French behavior. It is no doubt the case that there are analogous differences correlating with geographical and social factors among the French.

3. For example, the midvowel system of MSF is affected by several types of neutralization of the opposition between high-mid and low-mid vowels. In the only pronunciation dictionary based on the observation of a particular group of speakers meeting widely accepted geographical and social characteristics of MSF (educated and cultivated middle-class Parisians), Martinet and Walter (1973) show that there are few words containing the "è" variable that will be pronounced the same by the sample of seventeen speakers.

REFERENCES

Behnstedt, P. 1973. *Viens-tu, est-ce que tu viens? Tu viens? Formen und Strukturen des direkten Fragesatzes im Französischen.* Tübingen: Gunter Narr.

Bentolila, A. 1983. *Temps et aspect en français: application au discours de l'enfant.* Port-au-Prince: Centre de Linguistique, l'Université d'Etat d'Haïti.

Brown, H. D. 1980. *Principles of Language Learning and Teaching.* Englewood Cliffs: Prentice.

Carroll, R. 1987. *Evidences invisibles: Américains et Français au quotidien.* Paris: Seuil.

Christophersen, P. 1973. *Second-Language Learning: Myth and Reality.* Harmondsworth (U.K.): Penguin.

Coppieters, R. 1987. "Competence Differences Between Native and Non-native Speakers." *Language* 63: 544–73.

Coveney, A. B. 1989. "Variability in Interrogation and Negation in Spoken French." Diss. U of Newcastle upon Tyne; U.K.

Dulay, H., M. Burt, and S. Krashen. 1982. *Language Two*. New York: Oxford P.

Ferguson, C. A. 1979. "Applied Linguistics." Paper presented at the 1979 annual meeting of American Association of Applied Linguistics, Boston.

Foulet, L. 1921. "Comment ont évolué les formes de l'interrogation." *Romania* 185: 243–348.

Fox, C. 1989. *Syntactic Variation and Interrogative Structures in Québecois*. Diss. Indiana University.

Fromaigeat, E. 1938. "Les formes de l'interrogation en français moderne." *Vox Romana* 3: 1–47.

Giles, H., and E. Ryan, eds. 1982. *Attitudes Towards Language Variation: Social and Applied Contexts*. London: Edward Arnold.

Halliday, M. 1990. "New Ways of Meaning: A Challenge to Applied Linguistics." *Journal of Applied Linguistics* 6: 7–36.

Kaplan, M. A. 1986. "Developmental Patterns of Past Tense Acquisition Among Foreign Learners of French." *Foreign Language Learning: A Research Perspective*. Eds. B. VanPatten, T. R. Dvorak, and J. F. Lee. Rowley, Mass.: Newbury. 52–60.

Labov, W. 1966. *The Social Stratification of English in New York City*. Washington, D. C.: Center for Applied Linguistics.

——1972. *Sociolinguistic Patterns*. Philadelphia: U of Pennsylvania P.

Leather, J., and A. James. 1991. "The Acquisition of Second Language Speech/ Pronunciation." *Studies in Second Language Acquisition* 13 (3): 305–41.

Le Page, R. B., and A. Tabouret-Keller. 1985. *Acts of Identity: Creole-based Approaches to Language and Ethnicity*. Cambridge: Cambridge UP.

Littlewood, T. 1975. "Role-Performances and Language Teaching." *International Review of Applied Linguistics* 13: 199–208.

Long, M. H. 1990. "Maturational Constraints on Language Development." *Studies in Second Language Acquisition* 12(3): 251–85.

Martinet, A., and H. Walter. 1973. *Dictionnaire de la prononciation française dans son usage réel*. Paris: France-Expansion.

Matte, E. J. 1989. *French and English Verbal Systems*. New York: Peter Lang.

Milroy, L. 1982. "Social Network and Linguistic Focusing." *Sociolinguistic Variation in Speech Communities*. Ed. S. Romaine. London: Edward Arnold. 141–52.

Romaine, S. 1984. "On the Problem of Syntactic Variation and Pragmatic Meaning in Sociolinguistic Theory." *Folia Linguistica* 18: 409–37.

Ryan, E. B. 1983. "Social Psychological Mechanisms Underlying Native Speaker Evaluations of Non-native Speech." *Studies in Second Language Acquisition* 5(2): 148–59.

Valdman, A. 1975. "Error Analysis and Pedagogical Variation." *Some Implications of Linguistic Theory for Applied Linguistics.* Eds. S. P. Corder and E. Roulet. Paris: Didier; Bruxelles: AIMAV. 105–26.

————. 1976. "Variation linguistique et norme pédagogique dans l'enseignement du Français langue étrangère." *Bulletin de la Fédération Internationale des Professeurs de Français* 12–13: 52–64.

————. 1983. "Language Variation and Foreign Language Teaching: Issues and Orientations." *Language Across Cultures, Proceedings of a Symposium Held at St. Patrick's College, Drumcondra, Dublin, 8–9 July 1983.* Eds. L. MacMathuna and D. M. Singleton. Dublin: Irish Association for Applied Linguistics. 171–84.

————. 1989. "The Problem of the Target Model in Proficiency-oriented Language Instruction." *Applied Language Learning* 1: 33–51.

Wieland, M. 1990. *Politeness-based Misunderstandings in Conversations Between Native Speakers of French and American Advanced Learners of French.* Diss. Indiana University.

Chapter 6

On Syntax in Discourse
in Language Contact Situations

Ellen F. Prince

University of Pennsylvania

INTRODUCTION

This paper will consider the discourse functions of syntactic form and will attempt to show that understanding that a particular form in a given language has a particular function is part of the linguistic knowledge of the speaker and must be learned with the language. Like other aspects of language-specific competence, this form-function correlation is a potential site for borrowing/transfer/interference in a language contact situation. This has implications not only for a theory of language but also for a theory of second language acquisition.*[1]

Every natural language has many ways of saying the same thing. Among these options are syntactic paraphrases. For example, whenever a speaker/writer (henceforth "speaker") says any one of the sentences in example 1 truthfully, she or he could have equally truthfully uttered any of the other sentences in 1:

1. a. Kim saw this.
   b. This was seen by Kim.
   c. This, Kim saw.
   d. It was this that Kim saw.
   e. What Kim did was see this.
   f. It was Kim who saw this.
   g. What Kim saw was this.
   h. Kim, she saw this.
   i. It was Kim that this was seen by.
   j. (They said Kim would see this and) see this, Kim did.
   k. She saw this, Kim.
   l. This it was that was seen by Kim . . .

Put differently, our syntactic competence permits us as English speakers to generate all the syntactic forms in 1 (and then some). A question then arises: what, if anything, tells us which of these to generate at a particular point in time during the creation of a text? Is the choice random or do the different syntactic forms in fact do different work?

First, note that the choice does not depend on the literal meaning that the speaker is trying to convey, since the different forms are truth-conditionally equivalent. That is, if any of the sentences in 1 is true, then all of the sentences in 1 are true. Likewise, if any of the sentences in 1 is false, then all of the sentences in 1 are false.

At the same time, a speaker who wishes to express the proposition shared by all the sentences of 1 is in fact not at liberty to choose the syntactic form randomly. For example, consider the coherent exchange in 2a, compared to the incoherent one in 2b:

2. a. A   What did Kim see?
        B   What Kim saw was this.
   b.   A   Who saw this?
        B   #What Kim saw was this.

Thus, we see that the choice is not random. As has been shown for an increasingly large number of languages (cf. the works of Bolinger, Kuno, Green, Gundel, Ward, Reinhart, Erteschik-Shir, *inter alia*), marked syntactic forms have discourse functions, which, while they do not alter the truth-conditional meaning of the proposition, tailor that proposition to the particular context.

More specifically, discourse functions of syntactic form turn out to involve primarily the marking of certain informational statuses of the referents of noun phrases (NPs) and the marking of certain information structures of the proposition conveyed. For example, the WH-cleft in examples 1e and 2a marks the variable-containing proposition represented by the WH-clause, here *Kim saw X,* as being already known to the hearer and already salient in the discourse model being constructed, and it marks the constituent following the copula, here *this,* as being the new-to-the-discourse instantiation of that variable. Thus 2a is felicitous because Kim's seeing something is already at issue; in 2b, however, what is at issue is not what Kim saw but who saw this and a response that marks what Kim saw as being the salient shared knowledge at that point in the discourse is infelicitous.

In what follows, we shall consider how the discourse functions associated with syntactic form may be affected when speakers are in a language contact situation. In particular, I shall try to show that discourse functions behave like every other linguistic phenomenon in that they may be a source of interference, or, more neutrally, in that they may be borrowed from one language into the other. We shall consider two cases reported in Prince 1989, one in which the discourse functions associated with a Slavic form apparently came to be associated with a somewhat modified Yiddish form, which has become part of Standard Yiddish, and another in which the discourse functions associated with a Yiddish form have come to be associated with an English form, in the speech of some Yiddish-English speakers and their offspring.

SLAVIC-TO-YIDDISH: YIDDISH *DOS*-SENTENCES

First, consider the Yiddish sentence in example 3:

3. Dos hot mayn bruder gešribn a briv.
   this has my   brother written a letter
   = 'It's my brother who wrote a letter.'

The *dos*-sentence in 3 is composed entirely of Germanic words; however, there is no analogous sentence in any other Germanic language that I know of. In fact, there is no correlate even in Old Yiddish, the Yiddish spoken in the Middle Ages by Jews living in German-speaking lands, before they migrated to the Slavic-speaking lands of Eastern Europe. Now consider the Russian sentence in example 4:

4. Eto moy brat   napisal pis'mo.
   this my brother wrote   letter
   = 'It's my brother who wrote a letter.'

The Russian *eto*-sentence in 4, which has analogues in other Slavic languages, has a great deal in common with the Yiddish sentence in 3: both are simple sentences (i.e., without subordinate clauses), each has a dummy NP in initial position, in both cases the dummy NP is the neuter demonstrative pronoun, and both are translated by the English *it*-cleft. One might conclude that perhaps we have here a case of so-called "syntactic borrowing." However, a closer look at the syntax of each sentence tells us that this is not a plausible account.

First, let us consider the syntax of the Yiddish *dos*-sentence in 3. Yiddish, like all other Germanic languages except English, is a Verb-Second language (Haider and Prinzhorn 1985; Santorini 1989, *inter alia*). That is, in Yiddish declarative sentences, the finite verb must occupy the second position in the sentence. In an ordinary canonical sentence—e.g., 5a—the subject occupies the first position. If something other than the subject—e.g., a topicalized adverbial—occupies the first position, then the subject moves rightward, either to the position right after the verb, as in 5b, or to the end of the Verb Phrase (VP), as in 5c. What cannot occur is a third-position finite verb, as in 5d:

5. **a. Mayn bruder** hot nextn   gešribn a briv.
      my   brother has yesterday written a letter
   b. Nextn   hot **mayn bruder** gešribn a briv.
      yesterday has my   brother written a letter
   c. Nextn   hot gešribn a briv **mayn bruder.**
      yesterday has written a letter my   brother
   d. *Nextn   **mayn bruder** hot gešribn a briv.
      yesterday my   brother has written a letter

Second, it is relevant to consider the nature of the first position occupied by the dummy NP *dos* in 3 above. The two most plausible possibilities are the complementizer position (COMP) or some "Topic" position. However, when we consider sentences like example 6, where the sentence is embedded and follows an overt complementizer, we see that the dummy NP cannot itself be in COMP:[2]

6. Zi veyst az   dos hot mayn bruder gešribn a briv.
   she knows that this has my   brother written a letter
   ='She knows that it's my brother who wrote a letter.'

Thus, we infer a structure on the order of 7 for the sentence in 3:[3]

7. [[dos] [hot] [mayn bruder] [gešribn a briv]]
   S XP   INFL NP   VP

Turning now to the syntax of the Russian *eto*-sentence in 4, we find two important differences. First, note that the finite verb is indeed in third position. That is, the subject, *moy brat,* appears to be in the same preverbal position that it would be in in the canonical variant of 4, given in example 8:[4]

8. Moy brat   napisal pis'mo.
   my   brother wrote   letter

This is not surprising, since Russian, unlike Yiddish, is not a Verb-Second language; note that the verb would be in third position if something—e.g., an adverb—were topicalized to first position, as in example 9:

9. Vtšera   moy brat   napisal pis'mo.
   yesterday my   brother wrote   letter

Second, if we check the occurrence of the *eto*-sentence in 4 in an embedded context, we find that it is ungrammatical, as shown in example 10, leading us to infer that the demonstrative dummy NP *eto* itself occupies COMP position:

10. *Ona znaet što eto   moy brat   napisal pis'mo.
    she knows that this my   brother wrote   letter
    ='She knows that it's my brother that wrote a letter.'

Thus, we infer a structure for the Russian *eto*-sentence in 4 on the order of 11:

11. [[eto]   [[moy brat] [napisal pis'mo]]]
    S' COMP S NP   VP

We may now return to the issue of whether the Yiddish *dos*-sentence is an instance of syntactic borrowing: clearly there has been no syntactic borrowing, since the syntax of the Yiddish *dos*-sentence is not at all the same as the syntax of the Russian *eto*-sentence. From where then did Yiddish get the syntax of the *dos*-sentence? In fact, the syntax of the *dos*-sentence is totally native. Consider another sentence form, the Yiddish *es*-sentence, cognate of English *there*-sentences and of even more similar German *es*-sentences, which is structurally identical to the *dos*-sentence (Prince 1988); this is exemplified in example 12 and in 13:

12. **a.** Es hot mayn bruder gešribn a briv.
     it has my brother written a letter
     = 'My brother wrote a letter,' 'There wrote my brother a letter.'
   b. Zi veyst az es hot mayn bruder gešribn a briv.
     she knows that it has my brother written a letter
13. [[es] [hot] [mayn bruder] [gešribn a briv]]
    S XP INFL NP VP

So what has Yiddish borrowed from Slavic to produce the *dos*-sentence, if not the syntax? Consider again the translations given in 3 and 4. Both the Russian *eto*-sentence and the Yiddish *dos*-sentence are translated by an English *it*-cleft. What *it*-clefts do is to structure the proposition they convey into two parts, which we may call the *focus* and the *presupposition* (Atlas and Levinson 1981; Bolinger 1972; Chafe 1976; Chomsky 1971; Clark and Haviland 1977; Delahunty 1982; Horn 1981; Prince 1978, *inter alia*). This is illustrated in example 14:

14. *Proposition:* wrote (my brother, a letter)
    Presupposition: wrote (X, a letter)
    Focus: X = my brother

The presupposition corresponds to information that the speaker takes to be salient, i.e., appropriately on the hearer's mind, at that point in the discourse. In other words, the speaker assumes the hearer is thinking "Someone wrote a letter." The focus instantiates the variable in the presupposition, in this case "The someone is the speaker's brother."

In view of what we have seen, I should like to propose that borrowing has indeed occurred but what Yiddish borrowed from Slavic is an association between a particular syntactic form and a particular discourse function. Of course, the actual details turn out to be fairly complex, but I should like to suggest the following story. First, the Slavic-Yiddish bilinguals responsible for the borrowing note the association between the Slavic *eto*-sentence and the focus-presupposition structuring of the proposition it conveys. Second, they search Yiddish for a way of approximating the string order of the Slavic *eto*-sentence, within the bounds of the grammar of Yiddish. This they find in the syntax of the Yiddish *es*-sentence: like the Slavic *eto*-sentence, it consists of a simple clause and it has a dummy NP in first position. The main difference between the two, in terms of string order, is the relative position of subject and finite verb, with the subject preceding the verb in Slavic and following it in Yiddish. This difference, I propose, would be "factored out" as irrelevant by the bilinguals, since they know that it follows from the independent fact that Yiddish obeys the Verb-Second Constraint whereas Slavic does not.

Once the syntax of the *es*-sentence is chosen as a way of producing a structure to be associated with the discourse function of the *eto*-sentence, one formal change is needed in Yiddish, but a change in the lexicon, not the syntax: the addition of the feature [+ dummy] to the demonstrative pronoun *dos*. Note that this in a sense parallels what we have already described: Yiddish did not borrow the Slavic demonstrative; rather, it adapted its own already existing demonstrative to do the work done by the Slavic one.

The exact details of the borrowing are, of course, beyond our ken.[5] What is, I believe, clear and what will be relevant in the case to be discussed is summarized in 15:

15. a. Speakers in a contact situation attempt to "match up" forms in a source language with forms in a borrowing language.

e.g. Russian *eto*-sentence with Yiddish *dos*-sentence

b. It is the string order that counts, not the hierarchical structure of those forms.

e.g. Dummy NP + clause

c. The matching is fairly sophisticated, with irrelevant, independently motivated differences being factored out.

e.g. The finite verb is in second position in Yiddish and in third position in Russian.

d. The lexical component of a language seems more easily modified than the syntax, which turns out to be a markedly robust and persistent system.

e.g. The Yiddish demonstrative *dos* acquires the feature [+ Dummy].

e. Once the matching/modifying is done, the discourse functions of the sentence form in the source language come to be associated with the sentence form in the borrowing language.

e.g. The Yiddish *dos*-sentence is a focus-presupposition construction, like the Russian *eto*-sentence and unlike the Yiddish *es*-sentence.

YIDDISH-TO-ENGLISH:
YINGLISH YIDDISH-MOVEMENT

We shall now consider another case of borrowing involving discourse functions, but where the borrowing has been from Yiddish into a dialect of English, "Yinglish," the English spoken by some Jews of Yiddish background.

The case we shall consider is "Yiddish-Movement," as it has been called in the syntax literature (Hankamer 1971; Jackendoff 1972; Postal 1971; Prince 1981; Ward 1988; *inter alia*). There are sentences of English that are impossible for standard speakers but that are acceptable among Yiddish-English bilinguals and their progeny. Examples are given in 16 and are marked with a six-pointed star, following Ross 1967:

16. a. "Look who's here," his wife shouted at him the moment he entered the door, the day's dirt still under his fingernails. "Sol's boy." The soldier popped up from his chair and extended his hand. "How do you do, Uncle Louis?" "✡A Gregory Peck," Epstein's wife said, "a Montgomery Clift your brother has. He's been here only 3 hours, already he has a date." (Roth 1963: 148)
    b. "You've got clean underwear?" "I'm washing it at night. I'm okay, Aunt Gladys." "By hand you can't get it clean." "It's clean enough. Look, Aunt Gladys, I'm having a wonderful time." "✡Shmutz he lives in and I shouldn't worry!" (Roth 1963: 54)
    c. That night, after dinner, I gave Aunt Gladys a kiss and told her she shouldn't work so hard. "In less than a week it's Rosh Hashana and he thinks I should take a vacation. ✡Ten people I'm having. What do you think, a chicken cleans itself?" (Roth 1963: 86)

Although such sentences are clearly unacceptable for standard speakers, it is not at first blush obvious why this should be so. Syntactically, they are identical to Focus-Movement sentences, which are part of every standard speaker's grammar of English, illustrated in 17:

17. a. Then this car drives up—**Caddie I think it was.** (*The Young Lions*)
    b. Yeah we did it. **Two or three times we did it.** (*Come Back to the 5 & Dime, Jimmy Dean Jimmy Dean*)
    c. Let's assume there's a device which can do it—**a parser let's call it.** (J. D. Fodor, lecture)

What is it that differentiates the Yiddish-Movements in 16 from the Focus-Movements in 17? The answer requires a consideration of the discourse functions of the two. Standard English Focus-Movement, in which some constituent has been preposed and receives tonic stress, has a very specific discourse function and thus a very constrained distribution. Briefly, it is a focus/presupposition-marking construction, in which the preposed constituent represents the focus and the rest of the clause, with a variable for that constituent, represents the presupposition. This is illustrated for a simplified version of 17a in 18:

18. *Proposition:*   was (it, a Caddie)
    Presupposition: was (it, X)
    Focus: X = a Caddie

As in the case of the *it*-cleft, *dos*-sentence, and *eto*-sentence discussed above, the presupposition must represent information that the speaker may believe is appropriately on the hearer's mind at that point in the discourse. What is specific to Focus-Movement, however, is that the focus, the new information, is constrained to represent a certain *type* of information, the value of some attribute that some entity has. That is, in the case of 17a, when the hearer has heard that some car has driven up, the speaker is warranted in believing that the hearer may well be wondering what make it was, the information in the presupposition in 18. What the Focus-Movement in 17a does is provide the value of the make-attribute, "Caddie." Likewise, in 17b, when the hearer has heard "We did it," he or she may appropriately be wondering how many times they did it, in other words, that they did it a number of times and what was the cardinality of that set of times. Thus the Focus-Movement in 17b supplies the cardinality of that set. Finally, in 17c, when the hearer has heard of the hypothesized device, he or she is warranted in thinking that devices are the sorts of entities that have a name-attribute and in wondering what the value of the name-attribute for that device is. Thus, the Focus-Movement in 17c supplies the name of the device.

If we turn back to the Yiddish-Movements in 16, we see that, while they are also focus/presupposition-marking constructions, they are far less constrained. For one thing, the focus need not represent the value of an attribute. In 16c, for example, the focus, "ten people," represents a set-entity, i.e., a set of participants in the discourse world, not the value of some attribute of some entity in that world. Second, there is no constraint that the presupposition be salient, i.e., be appropriately on the hearer's mind. Again, in 16c, there is no reason that the hearer, upon hearing that it's Rosh Hashana, should be thinking that Aunt Gladys is having company. As I've argued elsewhere, Yiddish-Movement presuppositions *are* constrained to be inferrable or plausible but *not* currently salient. That is, the variable-containing proposition represented by the presupposition of a Yiddish-Movement may not represent "brand-new" information, but it need not be currently salient. Consider example 19:

19. A   How's your son, Mrs. Goldberg?
    B1 Don't ask! °**A car he wants!**
    B2 Don't ask! ***A car he stole!**

In 19B1, we find a perfectly acceptable Yiddish-Movement, whereas, without a marked prior context, the response in 19B2 is unacceptable even for Yinglish speakers. Note that neither the presupposition of B1, *He wants X,* nor the presupposition of B2, *He stole X,* is salient in the discourse at that point in time.

The difference, I claim, is that the presupposition of B1 is inferrable/plausible within the Yinglish speech community, while the presupposition of B2 is not. Put differently, the sons of Yinglish speakers stereotypically want things but they do not stereotypically steal things.[6]

Thus we may summarize the difference between Standard English Focus-Movement and Yinglish Yiddish-Movement as follows. Both mark a focus and a presupposition. Yiddish-Movement foci are unconstrained, in particular they may represent entities as well as values of attributes, and Yiddish-Movement presuppositions are constrained only to represent information that is plausible or inferrable in the context. Focus-Movement foci are constrained to represent the value of an attribute of some entity and the presupposition, the fact that that entity has that attribute, must be salient in the context.

The question now arises as to why the two dialects differ in this way. The answer, I believe, lies in the discourse functions of Focus-Movement in Yiddish. Consider the naturally occurring Yiddish Focus-Movement in 20a and the translation of its discourse context in 20b:

20. a. A kopike git   er mir   nit
       a kopek gives he me-dat. not
    b. A poor man once went to a rich man's house . . . and asked for alms.
       The rich man . . . says, "Don't bother me, I have a brother with child-
       ren! Leave me alone, I don't give alms." The poor man heard this and
       it upset him, but he went away. What could he do? . . . So he went
       to the rich man's brother and said to him, "I've heard that you have
       a rich brother and that he gives you so much money." The other guy
       says to him, "What? My brother? A real pig! °A kopek he doesn't
       give me, he throws me out of his house." . . . (Olsvanger 1947: 164)

The Yiddish Focus-Movement in 20 is entirely standard and unexceptional, unlike the Yiddish-Movement translation of it, which is acceptable only in the speech of Yinglish speakers. The proposition conveyed by the Yiddish Focus-Movement in 20 and its Yinglish translation and its structuring into focus and presupposition are given in 21:

21. *Proposition:*   not(give(he, me, a kopek))
    Presupposition: not(give(he, me, X))
    Focus: X = a kopek

Note that the presupposition, *he doesn't give me X,* is certainly not salient in the discourse, there having been no discussion of what the rich man does not give his brother, but it is inferrable from the discussion of what he *does* give him. However, the focus, *X = a kopek,* may in fact represent the value of an attribute in that we may take the rich man's givings to have the attribute of having an amount and that amount is not even a kopek. To see that in general Yiddish-Movement foci are not constrained to represent the value of an attribute, consider 22 and 23:

22. a. A vertl   hot er gehat . . .
       a saying has he had . . .
    b. He was so cheap that, when one asked him what time it was, he would
       always say ten minutes less. And ⬦ a saying he had that whoever isn't
       cheap can't get rich in life. (Olsvanger 1947: 162)

23. *Proposition:*   had(he, a saying)
    Presupposition: had(he, X)
    Focus: X = a saying

In 22, the focus *a vertl,* "a saying," clearly represents an entity, something he
had. And note once again that the presupposition in 23, that he had something,
is generally inferrable but certainly not salient in the discourse context.

Note further that the Yinglish Yiddish-Movement translations in 20 and 22
are syntactically identical to the Standard English Focus-Movements in 17 but
that they are different from the Yiddish Focus-Movements in 20 and 22. That is,
in the Yiddish sentences, since the preposed NPs *a kopike* and *a vertl* occupy first
position and, since the finite verbs must occupy second position, the subjects are
moved rightward to the position following the finite verb. In the Yinglish translations, where there is no Verb-Second Constraint, the subjects stay in their
preverbal position, following the preposed NPs *a kopek* and *a saying.* A rough
approximation of the structure of the Yiddish Focus-Movement and the Yinglish
translation in 22 is presented in 24:

24. a. *Yiddish:* [[a vertl   [hot] [er] [gehat]]
                   S XP   INFL NP   VP
    b. *Yinglish:* [[a saying] [[he] [had]]]
                   S ?   S   NP   VP

Thus we see once again that no syntactic borrowing has occurred. Rather,
the Yiddish Focus-Movement has somehow been "matched up" with the English
Focus-Movement on the basis of string order and not hierarchical structure, where
independently motivated differences in the string order have been factored out
as irrelevant. Once this matching has been done, the English form becomes
associated with the discourse function of the Yiddish form, producing the di-
alectally marked Yiddish-Movement.

CONSTRAINTS ON THE BORROWING
OF DISCOURSE FUNCTIONS

At this point one must ask whether *any* discourse function at all associated with
a given form in one language may come to be associated with a given form in a
second language in a language contact situation. The answer, I claim, is no.

First, as noted above, the two syntactic forms must be "matched up" by the
speakers, following the string order of the constituents. This matching is highly

sophisticated in the sense that independently motivated differences between the two string orders are factored out as irrelevant, as the effects of the Verb-Second Constraint in Yiddish on string order were factored out in the two cases considered above.

Second, there must be a certain "consistency" between the discourse functions associated with the forms in the two languages before any borrowing takes place. More precisely, a discourse function associated with a form in the borrowing language is consistent with a discourse function associated with a form in the source language just in case there are no contexts where the borrowing language form is used that, *mutatis mutandis,* cannot be felicitous contexts for the source language form.

Let us illustrate this notion of consistency with the two cases discussed above. In the first case, Yiddish, the borrowing language, has created a new form, the *dos*-sentence. True, it is syntactically identical to an old form, the *es*-sentence, but it is in fact formally distinct from it by virtue of having a different dummy NP. Since it is a new form created as a result of the borrowing, it cannot be the case that, before the borrowing, speakers hear it used in contexts where the Russian *eto*-sentence cannot be used. Thus the criterion of consistency applies, vacuously as it were.

In the second case, English, the borrowing language, already has the relevant form, Focus-Movement. Although its discourse function is not identical to that of Focus-Movement in Yiddish, the source language, it is simply more constrained, not different in kind. That is, it is the case that, wherever English speakers can felicitously use English Focus-Movement, Yiddish speakers can felicitously use Yiddish Focus-Movement. Therefore, the Yiddish speakers in the contact situation hear nothing to contradict their hypothesis that the discourse function of English Focus-Movement is identical to the discourse function of Yiddish Focus-Movement. Of course, they are not hearing it used in many contexts in which they could utter a Yiddish Focus-Movement, but such negative evidence is not discernible—one hears only what is said and not what is not said. Thus the discourse function of English Focus-Movement is consistent with that of Yiddish Focus-Movement, permitting the association of the discourse function of the Yiddish form with the English form and producing English Yiddish-Movement.

To illustrate what I am predicting could not occur, let us consider a hypothetical situation in which English is the source language and Yiddish is the borrowing language. Could Yiddish borrow the discourse functions of English Focus-Movement, producing what we could then call English-Movement in Yiddish? That is, could speakers in a contact situation use Yiddish Focus-Movement in the highly restricted contexts in which they could use English Focus-Movement? I believe that they could perhaps, but only in the early stages of language contact. Eventually, they would hear enough counterevidence to the hypothesis that the Yiddish form was as constrained as the English form and would reject that hypothesis. That is, when they heard sentences like 22a, they would realize that it is not only values of attributes that may be focal and that the presupposition need not be salient, and they would realize that the Yiddish form had a somewhat different function from the English one.

While it is of course impossible to prove that something cannot occur, I can testify personally that, while Standard English speakers are aware that Yiddish-Movements like those in 16 are marked or strange, Yinglish speakers generally do not have the slightest idea that there is anything nonstandard about such sentences. This follows from the fact that English Focus-Movement is consistent with Yiddish Focus-Movement but not vice versa: the Standard English speaker is hearing Yiddish-Movements in contexts in which English Focus-Movements are impossible, whereas all the Standard English Focus-Movements the Yinglish speaker hears are fine for Yiddish-Movement.

IMPLICATIONS FOR SECOND LANGUAGE ACQUISITION

I believe there are a number of implications for second language acquisition. First, consider the phenomenon of "matching up" syntactic forms in two languages that we have seen here. This seems to follow from a more general fact about speakers in a language contact situation: they assume that a new language is like the old language in every respect, unless proven otherwise. I believe such metalinguistic reasoning is somehow inevitable: not only do language teachers and linguists think in terms of "relative clauses" and "passives" and the like cross-linguistically, whether they officially approve of that or not, but the naive speaker in a language contact situation does, too. Perhaps one might want to stop trying to ignore or stamp out such analogizing and instead put it to work. After all, the basic metalinguistic assumption that the new language is like the old language unless proven otherwise probably benefits the second language learner more than it leads him or her astray; in any event, it seems to be a fact of human linguistic behavior. Of course, I leave it to the language teaching specialists to decide how to deal with this fact; my suggestion is only that it must be dealt with.

Second, if I am right about the role of consistency, as defined above, then we would predict different "interference" effects depending on whether the discourse functions of the relevant syntactic form in the target language were consistent or not with the discourse functions of the relevant syntactic form in the source language, in that persistent interference should arise where consistency obtained but not where consistency did not obtain. This suggests that a differential treatment of syntactic forms in formal language teaching might be in order, following a close study of the consistency relations of the forms in question. For example, more explicit attention might profitably be paid by the language teacher to the use of English Focus-Movement for native Yiddish speakers than to the use of Yiddish Focus-Movement for native English speakers.

Third, an important difference emerges between strategies of first language acquisition and second language acquisition. Presumably, first language learners hear the "data" and hypothesize *the most restricted rule* that would generate that data. As an example from the data considered above, consider the acquisition of English Focus-Movement by children learning English as their native language.

In the data they hear, the focus is restricted to being the value of an attribute of some (known) entity. In principle, they could hypothesize a rule whereby anything can be the focus—that would surely generate the proper subset of possible Focus-Movements that they in fact hear, but it would also generate infinitely many impossible Focus-Movements, where items other than values of attributes are focused. Clearly, they do not hypothesize this less restricted rule. In sharp contrast, the second language learner appears to be taking a different route entirely. Instead of starting with the raw data and hypothesizing the most restricted rule to generate that data, the learner finds some "analogous" form in the first language and begins with that. In the event that the first language rule is more restricted than the second language rule, the difference should become obvious as "impossible" data are found. However, in the event that the first language rule is less restricted than the second language rule, the difference will go largely or entirely unnoticed, producing a marked dialect of the second language.[7] An important, though problematic, implication of this, as well as of the points mentioned above, is that second language teaching should be tailored to particular first languages, since each first language will trigger its own set of wrong hypotheses about each second language.

Finally, one is often tempted to think of grammatical competence as a micro-level phenomenon—nouns and verbs and prepositional phrases, etc.—and text competence as a macro-level phenomenon—higher-level reasoning and interactive skills and organizational ability, etc. However, a closer look at language shows us that the two are not quite so neatly divided and that text competence, at least the part of it that tells us in what contexts we may use a particular syntactic form, includes some extraordinarily micro-level stuff.

ENDNOTES

*I should like to thank Mascha Benya and Arkady Plotnitsky for their help with the Yiddish and Russian data, respectively.

1. Here and elsewhere I am not distinguishing between second language acquisition and foreign language acquisition.

2. Yiddish, like Icelandic but unlike the other Germanic languages obeying the Verb-Second Constraint, has generalized this constraint to subordinate clauses. See Santorini 1989.

3. There is of course nothing crucial to the present study about the particular syntactic framework used here or even the particular parses presented. What is crucial are the distributional differences between the sentences, differences that will have to be captured and accounted for regardless of the framework and parses adopted.

4. In fact, there is evidence that the subject of example 4 is topicalized; cf. i:

i. eto pismo moy brat   napisal.
   this letter my brother wrote
   = 'It's a letter that my brother wrote.'

This, however, does not affect the point being made here, that the syntax of the Russian *eto*-sentence is grossly different from the syntax of the Yiddish *dos*-sentence.

5. In fact, it is not even obvious when the borrowing can be said to have occurred. For the Slavic-to-Yiddish case, we do not know enough about the demography and sociolinguistics of the early Eastern European Yiddish speech community to speculate at all on what sorts of speakers were responsible for the borrowing. For the Yiddish-to-English case, we know a great deal about the demographic and sociolinguistic situation, but we still cannot answer the theoretical question of when the borrowing can be said to have occurred—when the first generation "interlanguage" speakers used it in their interlanguage, or when the next generation had it as a feature of their native dialect of English (i.e., Yinglish). I thank Charles Ferguson for raising this interesting question.

6. Obviously, if Mrs. Goldberg's son were known to be a thief, the Yiddish-Movement in 19B2 would be impeccable.

7. Perhaps this explains the "Chinglish" dialect of English of the totally fluent Chinese-American teacher discussed in Wong Fillmore's paper in this volume.

REFERENCES

Atlas, J. D., and S. Levinson. 1981. "It-clefts, Informativeness, and Logical Form." *Radical Pragmatics*. Ed. P. Cole. New York: Academic. 1–62.

Bolinger, D. 1972. "A Look at Equations and Cleft Sentences." *Studies for Einar Haugen*. Ed. E. Firchow. The Hague: Mouton. 96–114.

Chafe, W. 1976. "Givenness, Contrastiveness, Definiteness, Subjects, Topics, and Point of View." *Subject and Topic*. New York: Academic. 25–55.

Chomsky, N. 1971. "Deep Structure, Surface Structure, and Semantic Interpretation." *Semantics: An Interdisciplinary Reader in Philosophy, Linguistics, and Philosophy*. Eds. D. Steinberg and L. Jakobovits. New York: Cambridge UP. 183–216.

Clark, H., and S. Haviland. 1977. "Comprehension and the Given-new Contract." *Discourse Production and Comprehension*. Ed. R. Freedle. Hillsdale, N.J.: Erlbaum. 1–40.

Delahunty, G. P. 1982. Topics in the Syntax and Semantics of English Cleft Sentences. Bloomington, IN: Indiana University Linguistics Club.

Haider, H., and M. Prinzhorn, eds. 1985. *Verb Second Phenomena in Germanic Languages*. Dordrecht: Foris.

Hankamer, J. 1971. Constraints on Deletion in Syntax. Diss. Yale University.

Horn, L. 1981. "Exhaustiveness and the Semantics of Clefts." *Papers from Eleventh Annual Meeting of the North Eastern Linguistic Society*. Eds. V. Burke and J. Pustejovsky. Amherst: U Massachusetts, Dept. of Linguistics. 125–42.

Jackendoff, R. S. 1972. *Semantic Interpretation in Generative Grammar*. Cambridge, Mass.: MIT P.

Olsvanger, I. 1947. *Royte pomerantsn*. New York: Schocken.

Postal, P. 1971. *Crossover Phenomena*. New York: Holt.

Prince, E. F. 1978. "A Comparison of WH-clefts and IT-clefts in Discourse." *Language* 54: 883–906.

———. 1981. "Topicalization, Focus-Movement, and Yiddish-Movement: A Pragmatic Differentiation. *Proceedings of the Seventh Annual Meeting, Berkeley Linguistics Society*. Eds. D. Alford et al. 249–64.

———. 1988. The Discourse Functions of Yiddish Expletive ES + Subject-Postposing. *Papers in Pragmatics* 2: 176–94.

———. 1989. On Pragmatic Change: The Borrowing of Discourse Functions. In *Cognitive Aspects of Language Use*. Ed. A. Kasher. Amsterdam: Elsevier. 1–14.

Ross, J. R. 1967. Constraints on Variables in Syntax. Diss. Massachusetts Institute of Technology.

Roth, P. 1963. *Portnoy's Complaint*. New York: Random.

Santorini, B. 1989. The Generalization of the Verb-Second Constraint in the History of Yiddish. Diss. University of Pennsylvania.

Ward, G. 1988. *The Semantics and Pragmatics of Preposing*. New York and London: Garland.

Negotiating Meaning
Across Cultures

Chapter 7

Silence Across Languages: An Essay

A. L. Becker

The University of Michigan

It has long seemed to me that the experience of writing an essay and the experience of learning a new language *in situ* have much in common. In the rhetoric book I wrote years ago with Richard Young and Kenneth Pike, fieldwork was very much in our minds—the work of discovery and emerging understanding within a strange and distant language. When we finished *Rhetoric: Discovery and Change,* I was in Java, trying to attune myself to a strange wordscape. Pike had done it many times.

EXOTIC WORDSCAPES

I have just returned once again from an episode of fieldwork, five months in Malaysia where I was living again in a very different culture, speaking a very different language, feeling my identity eroding and reshaping once again, as it had before in Burma and Java—each time no less painfully. This last time, in fact, I was not there in Malaysia to gather information or to seek instruction but rather just to have this experience once again.

I was teaching semantics in Malay at a Malaysian university, and so I had a forum, my class, in which reflections on the experience of entering a new language were appropriate. In Malaysia a lot of things happened to me just because I could understand Malay pretty well, even though I expressed myself very awkwardly. But few of the people I met during long weekend walks through the countryside knew that I could understand them: they would say things to each other on the assumption I could not understand, and some of the things they said they would be far too polite to say if they thought I could understand. For instance, I would sometimes be referred to by children as Mat Salleh, a common Malay name frequently used in colonial times to refer indirectly to an Englishman. It sounds like "mad sailor," for only a mad dog, Englishman, or drunk would walk around so fast in the noonday sun, but I am not sure where the name comes from. They wouldn't have used that name if they thought I could understand it. It triggered elaborate verbal play and a flurry of jokes among children, as I walked by not letting on I understood—but taking it all back to class as the raw material for studying semantics.

Gradually, as one becomes more and more attuned to the unfamiliar word-scape, a context different from the context of English emerges. Some very exotic things, like food and dress for instance, become familiar rather rapidly—even rotten fish (Burma) and bare bellies (Bali)—and very familiar things become more and more exotic—like modes of verification or courtesy. When we confront a distant language, we are compelled to give full attention to the fact that saying, for instance, "I am" is something we do with words in English, for in that distant language there is no "I" like our "I," and no "am" at all. To put one's speaking self into words in Burmese, Javanese, or Malay is to make claims of status (high or low) that alienate our very selves, and in none of those languages is there either a verb like *be* (a copula) or a distinction between present and past tense.

And so, in these exotic wordscapes, there is always an exuberance of meaning that comes of reading English into the wordscape (seeing "I" and "being" and "present tense" in the world, not in my language). And there is a simultaneous deficiency of meaning that comes of not bringing the distinctions of Burmese, Javanese, or Malay into play. Fieldwork is where these things get sorted out, slowly, over generations.

SILENCES

At the center of fieldwork one confronts silence—a silence beyond language. The great Spanish philologist, José Ortega y Gasset, described it clearly and succinctly when he wrote:

> The stupendous reality that is language cannot be understood unless we begin by observing that speech consists above all in silences. . . .

We think first of the little pauses between words and sentences—the silences between sounds—but Ortega means something more basic. He continues:

> A being who could not renounce saying many things would be incapable of speaking. . . .

Such is clearly the case for us all, even in monolingual settings, but Ortega carries the idea further to the interaction across languages, to translation:

> And each language represents a different equation between manifestations and silences. Each people leaves some things unsaid *in order to* be able to say others. Because *everything* would be unsayable. Hence the immense difficulty of trans-

lation: translation is a matter of saying in a language precisely what that language tends to pass over in silence. A "theory of saying, of languages," would also have to be a theory of the particular silences observed by different peoples.

PRIOR TEXT

Let's think about these silences across languages. Silence is more than the fact that in Malay or Burmese there isn't a word for something (like "I"), and silence is also not just about having or not having a grammatical distinction (like tense) or having or not having a syntactic figure (like the copula figures); silence is something far more pervasive and difficult to cope with than these—the silence of memory. My hearing of Malay, reinforced by many grammars and many dictionaries, is almost entirely one-dimensional. I do not know, when I hear something in Malay, whether it is an original utterance or a cliché or a proverb. Suppose I said to you, "Seek and ye shall find," and you took that sentence as an original act of language shaping by me. In just that way, I often did not know whether a Malay was saying something new and original or old and well known. It was the same a few years ago when my written account of the power and originality of the Javanese shadow play struck my Javanese friends as we might be struck if someone said the obvious, like "The interesting thing about TV is the way stories are interrupted by commercials." What was fresh for me was obvious for them.

When one considers that everything anyone says or writes both speaks the past (says something old) and speaks the present (says something new), to use Maurice Bloch's terms, then the importance of not being able to tell old from new and past from present gets serious.

In my failure to recognize quotations or clichés, I began to sense the pervasiveness of a kind of indirect quotation in all of our languaging. *Everything* anyone says has a history and hence is, in part, a quotation. *Everything* anyone says is also partly new, too, and part of anyone's ability in a language is the ability to tell the difference between the new and the old. But when you speak a foreign language, everything is contemporary, for outsiders have very little memory in that new language and its past is silent. It seems to me that grammars and dictionaries are attempts to remedy this deficiency of memory.

One can have a similar experience in one's own language, experiencing lingual exclusion nearer to home. I once found myself, a small-town midwesterner, at a rather prestigious East Coast institution. At lunch, I was repeatedly intimidated by the power and originality of the conversation, so much so that I stopped having lunch at all after a few weeks, for I felt my confidence as a teacher and writer slipping away, and that seemed, just then, more essential than good food. A friendly local native finally told me that the problem was only a deficiency of prior text, which could be overcome if every morning I read, as they did, the "agenda," *The New York Times*. I did, and it worked. I now shared with them a daily prior text, an aggregate of memories, and I heard now the pervasiveness of prior text in all they said. They were not intimidating and I could speak, now, with confidence and originality. Language intimidates until, like Dorothy with the Wizard, you find out how it all works.

All that we know has an agenda, an aggregate of remembered and half-remembered prior texts which are there to be evoked. And most of what we say about sports, politics, war, science, philosophy, health, law—in fact, almost everything—has come to us from prior texts. It comes to us already in words, already languaged. When we speak, we adjust this old language to new situations, but our originality, of social necessity, is minimal. In Malay I had no memory to speak from. What prior texts Malay evoked for me were all English, except for a very few literary texts: the *Hikayat Hang Tuah,* the *Sejarah Melayu,* a few Malay poems by a friend, and a few Malay proverbs I had memorized once from a book. Essentially Malay was and remains one-dimensional to me.

I believe that it is this one-dimensionality, the absence of memory, which creates the basic need for grammars and dictionaries. In the absence of a lingual memory to draw upon in Malay, I try to formulate tactical generalizations about how to shape utterances in Malay and to establish equivalences between Malay and English words. This is, of course, not something I do alone, for it is part of a long, historical process, begun when the first unknown Anglophone met the first unknown Malayophone. They probably met in mutual fear and it was an act of bravery for the one who first spoke of herself or himself as "I" or "aku" in the other's language.

The only way I can verify any of this is to point to these experiences, tell these stories, and hope that they evoke resonant memories in you, for there is no human Language of Truth beyond individual human languages. If there were a Language of Truth (Sanskrit? Latin? Arabic? English? Malay?), I could describe Malay in it for you and you would see that what I say is true or false. But there is no Language of Truth—only many languages in which people try to tell the truth, and these languages are very different. Each language is a different equation between manifestation and silence. If these deep differences between languages are not real, then there is no reason, as too many now believe, not to strive for a world in which only English remains. But I doubt that any Malay or Burmese or Javanese wants that, for it entails a loss of all but English memories. One senses that the important battles of the twenty-first century will be over the noosphere, the realm in which we shape, store, retrieve, and communicate our knowledge.

The silence of the fieldworker is a silence of memory. Silence here is a negative thing: something is missing. Prior text. It is worth noting, I think, that there is this same silence in all structural linguistics—an absence of time, of memory. The dominant metaphor in most current linguistics sees language as a timeless code, encoding timeless, universal "thought" or "concepts" in different ways. An alternative to this is to think of languaging as an endless social process of orienting and reorienting ourselves and each other to a constantly changing environment. The Javanese call this process *jarwa dhosok,* pressing old texts into the present situation. Here we do well to replace the word "language" as an accomplished system or structure with the word "languaging" as the performance of a repertoire of games or *orientations,* à la Wittgenstein or Goffman or Maturana (e.g., greetings, lectures, last words, messages on answering machines, little signs in the rear windows of cars, etc.), all of them changing over time, driven by their own pasts. Language in this view is not denotational but orientational; in other words, languaging is one means by which we continually attune ourselves to context. In a distant language, we have to relearn to attune ourselves, which means primarily building new memories.

A fieldworker learns, it seems to me, that we have a common language to the extent we have common prior texts.

THAT REMINDS ME OF A STORY

On the first day of the semantics class in Malaysia, I told a story, translating it unrehearsed from English to Malay. I wanted to make a point about stories, shifting the focus of these advanced Malay students of linguistics away from words and sentences examined out of context, toward stories in context. "Storying-in-context" is a basic way people understand things and hence the appropriate basis for this course in semantics I was to teach there. Thinking about stories this way—as *orienting* people, not denotating "concepts"—was something I had first learned from the work of Gregory Bateson and so I felt it was appropriate to begin the study of semantics in Malaysia with homage to him. Telling this story of his would, in my plan, lead into discussion of Bateson and his way of thinking. And also, one learns in Southeast Asia that it is far better to speak the past in statements concerning basic truths than it is to speak the present. It is a matter of both politeness and verification. It is seemly to praise one's teachers and it lends validity to what one says.

Here is Gregory Bateson's little story about stories, in his words:

> There is a story which I have used before and shall use again: A man wanted to know about mind, not in nature, but in his private large computer. He asked it (no doubt in his best Fortran), "Do you compute that you will ever think like a human being?" The machine then set to work to analyze its own computational habits. Finally, the machine printed its answer on a piece of paper, as such machines do. The man ran to get the answer and found, neatly typed, the words:
>
> THAT REMINDS ME OF A STORY

In the silence that followed my retelling of this story in Malay, I finally laughed, out of the awkward self-consciousness of speaking a new language. Nobody in the class understood the story. It struck me that my Malay was completely inadequate, and so in a panic that I hoped was concealed, I asked a Malay professor, Dr. Azhar Simin, who had finished his Ph.D. in linguistics at Michigan and had read Bateson, if he would tell the story. He agreed, and as I listened to his Malay it seemed beautifully lucid. But still, nobody in the class laughed, nobody understood. And so we tried to explain, Dr. Simin and I, and it all got more and more complex. Trying to translate that story into Malay consumed the class period and left it tangled like knotted string.

That night I tried to put my finger on why it had been so difficult to explain Gregory's little story. It was not that my Malay students didn't know computers, for there was a room full of computers down the hall and I had seen these students working there. They knew what the words meant, even Fortran. It was the silences that gave them trouble: why did the man want to know about mind? they had asked, and why did it remind the computer of a story? And I had answered that it didn't matter why the man wanted to know, only that he was the kind who might . . . and it dawned on me that one never said in Malay, "That reminds me of a story." That sentence, translated into Malay, evoked no memory. If you haven't heard that sentence many, many times, Gregory's story has no point, for it rests on the ordinariness, the vernacularity of "That reminds me of a story." The point of the story is the way the answer to the man's question *demonstrates* the computer's understanding. It takes real effort for us to see how much prior text that story rests upon.

In my room that night in Malaysia I tried to list the silences a Malay might face in understanding that story—the prior texts it requires to be both funny (a joke) and serious (an insight) at the same time. The next day I would check my list with the class. I would use the story as an example of silence across languages, and I got out my Ortega, another voice from the past I wanted to share. Then it occurred to me that I couldn't think of a Malay word for "silence." How would I talk about the English word *silence* in Malay?

I got out some dictionaries, but there was no Malay word for *silence* that didn't also entail too many other things, like loneliness or motionlessness. For the rest of my stay in Malaysia I asked the help of poets and scholars, but we found no useful Malay word for the English word *silence*. And even if we had found one in the end, the difficulty of the search suggests that the word would have evoked little memory in my undergraduates.

Now, it is very important that you, the reader, not see this as a description of any inadequacy of Malay or Malays. I fear to tell these stories because they are so often taken as instances of cross-cultural condescension, particularly English-language condescension to Malay. Every human language must appear deficient from the point of view of another language. Every human language is a way that people have developed of orienting themselves to each other and to nature, and each is a different equation, in Ortega's terms, between utterance and silence. There is no competition between English and Malay to eliminate all silences, and I leave it to others to point out all the silences of English. It just seemed to be a fortuitous coincidence that Malay should be silent about *silence.*

And I hope the reader is careful in the way a fieldworker must be, reminding ourselves continually that *silence* is not a transcendental, universal concept, but a word in our language with a history. And the difficulty of translation I experienced did not uncover a hole in Malay, but rather a hint of a significant difference between the languages. Each language, from the point of view of another, appears full of holes. Forgive me for repeating this point, but it is crucial—and for a fieldworker who has returned home and re-entered Plato's Cave, it is a persistent point of misunderstanding.

FIELDWORK AND WRITING

Before going any further with these reflections of a semantics teacher in Malaysia, I want to turn to some of the reasons I think that these matters are relevant to someone writing an essay.

The silences we all face in writing are very much like those I confronted in Malaysia. Our differences of memory are just as troublesome right at home as they are across the world in Southeast Asia. I can only guess, reader, what prior texts these words and stories evoke for you. I count on enough similarity so that you can recognize what I am trying to do and enough charity that you will help in supplying the similarities from your own repertoire of stories. A writer counts on that in a reader. But the difficulty of writing, like the difficulty of reading, is that across two different minds there is so much exuberance and so much deficiency in the understanding of each. Contemplating the experiences of fieldwork, you come to see this not as a special problem but as the normal situation of languaging. Ortega called these two conditions (*exuberance* and *deficiency*) the first two axioms of modern philology. Everything anyone says or writes is always, to another, both exuberant (i.e., says more than it plans) and deficient (i.e., says less than it intended). Across distant cultures or between husband and wife, these can be and frequently are intolerable.

In return for the reader's filling in of silences, a writer promises useful or at least amusing stories.

ANOTHER STORY: YOU CAN'T ASK QUESTIONS LIKE THAT

Here is another story about Ortega's kind of silence. (I am convinced that if I tell the right story the right way you will believe me.) This story too is about absence of prior text. It is from *The New York Times* (i.e., the "agenda"), Sunday, November 13, 1977; it is titled "They Call Him the Baryshnikov of Bali." The article is written by Allen Hughes, paraphrased and condensed here by me.

The Baryshnikov of Bali was Wayan Pasek Yusabawa, a young Balinese dancer in a troupe touring in the West who was evoking very laudatory reviews in the London and New York press. He was called "a boy prodigy," a "star." Mr. Hughes interviewed him in New York via a translator:

> The first question was, "How old are you?" Wayan looked perplexed. The translator explained that the matter of age in years has little meaning in Bali.
>
> Wayan's passport says 17, which is clearly impossible, and a recent press release mentioned 12. Somebody at the interview said he was 13, which seemed not unreasonable since he is in the equivalent of our first year of junior high school.
>
> That was only the beginning of all those questions about age and time.

"How old were you when you began to dance?" Shoulder shrug and doubtful look. "Ten?" The answer was something of a question.

"And how long have you studied dance?" Answer: "Study?"

The company administrator says not more than six months, adding, "In Bali, six months can be too long for a child."

Then, "Do you practice dance every day?" Answer: "Every day? Why would anyone do that? No, only when we have to dance somewhere."

There are many more exchanges in Mr. Hughes's very perceptive story of this interview, but I will quote just one more, near the end:

"What do you want to be when you are an adult? A dancer?" Silence.

Translator: "You can't ask Indonesians questions like that."

What the translator meant, I think, in explaining the silence of the Baryshnikov of Bali was not just that it is impolite to ask an Indonesian questions like that, but that you are putting the boy in real jeopardy if you expect him to make an utterance only a God could utter. Not every being can utter every "I."

It is not just that a particular story, like Gregory's computer story, may never have been told in another language but also that what you do with words in one language is not the same as what you do with words in another. The language games are different—not all but most. What do you do in an interview? What do you not do?

The silences across languages involve not only things one is not able to say, but also things one *should* not say or *must* not say, for one reason or another. An act of languaging, a language game, has a past but it also has some essential silences: things you do not do with words without changing the game. Howsoever the Balinese translator might describe what happened to evoke that boy's silence, he declared the question outside the game of interviewing.

PUTTING AN EDGE ON IT

So far this essay has been a string of stories (walking roads in Malaysia, teaching semantics there, reading *The New York Times,* telling Gregory's story about the computer, the Baryshnikov of Bali, among others) oriented around silence. I have served you if you find any of them retellable—reoriented to your own memories. To give them point, I have added commentary and some quotations, with the hope these also are useful. But there is something more, something elusive.

I think maybe it is restrained aggression. Anger, maybe. Against what? Disrespect for silence. Each people—and each person—leaves some things unsaid in order to be able to say others. Each language—and each person—represents a different equation between manifestations and silences.

And "anger" is a word for a rhetorical motive, a reason for doing something with words. With anger, the breath gets a little rough and strong. Try to breathe in and out heavily and speak at the same time. You will sound angry. Why would anyone want to sound like that? Silence. Discretion suggests keeping silent what should be kept silent, but I would like to have an edge of anger to push these words a little harder, a little anger like a barely perceived motion, seen out of the corner of the eye, alongside a road in Malaysia.

ACKNOWLEDGMENTS _____

The references to Ortega y Gasset are primarily to Chapter 11 ("What People Say: Language. Toward a New Linguistics") in *Man and People* (translated by Willard R. Trask), New York: Norton, 1957. The references to Bateson are to the introduction of *Mind and Nature: A Necessary Unity*, New York: Dutton, 1979. The references to Wittgenstein are to *Philosophical Investigations*, New York: Macmillan, 1953. References to Goffman are to his last book, *Forms of Talk*, Philadelphia: University of Pennsylvania Press, 1981. References to Maturana are to *The Tree of Knowledge: The Biological Roots of Human Understanding*, Boston: New Science Library, 1987. The references to Bloch are to "Symbols, Song, Dance and Features of Articulation," in *European Journal of Sociology*, 15, 1974 and to the introduction of his *Political Language and Oratory in Traditional Society*, New York: Academic Press, 1975.

On silence, see particularly Bernard P. Dauenhauer, *Silence: The Phenomenon and Its Ontological Significance*, Bloomington: Indiana University Press, 1980; and Deborah Tannen and Muriel Saville-Troike, editors, *Perspectives on Silence*, Norwood, N.J.: Ablex, 1985.

I must also acknowledge the help of my students and colleagues in Malaysia and Indonesia, particularly Mohd. haji Salleh, Azhar Simin, Ariel Heryanto, and Bamabang Kaswanti. In America, I am grateful to The English Department of Carnegie Mellon University, particularly Richard Young; the Law and Culture Club, particularly James B. White, Kenneth DeWoskin, and Joseph Vining; and the English Composition Board, University of Michigan, particularly Barbra Morris, for useful reactions to previous versions of this essay.

Chapter 8

Translation as the Double Production of Texts

J. Hillis Miller

University of California at Irvine

Translation produces two texts. As translators move from word to word and from sentence to sentence through the text they produce bit by bit replicas of the original in a different language. At the same time, as I shall demonstrate by way of an example, an original text is also produced. A different translation produces a different original, by emphasizing different faultlines in the original, that is, by traducing the original in one way rather than another. The original is led out into the open where the translator is obliged to see hitherto hidden features. These features are both semantic and syntactical. To encounter them is to encounter what is, strictly speaking, untranslatable in the original. Sometimes a way of putting words together has no equivalent in the other language. Sometimes a univocal word in the source text has no exact equivalent in the other language, as it has been argued that German *Brot* is not accurately translated by either English *bread* or French *pain.*[1] Sometimes a complex word in the original has many different meanings not corresponding to the multiple meanings in any single word in the language of translation. Sometimes a word is used figuratively that cannot be used figuratively in that way in the target language. Anyone who has translated will know the odd experience of being able to read and understand the original perfectly, as well as having native mastery of the target language, but of running constantly into unexpected and perhaps even insuperable difficulties in trying to turn the source text into the target language. The arrow keeps going awry and missing the target.

Encountering these difficulties the translator learns something hitherto unnoticed about the source language. The translator also learns something about the target language: that there are certain things that "cannot be said" in that language. The translator encounters the material level of both languages, the places where fortuitous homonyms or paranomasias interfere with the ideal transparency and therefore translatability of meaning. To encounter these obstacles in the double production of texts in translation is to discover two things at once about language. One is the way each language falls short of that ideal quality of translatability whose original model is a sacred text like the Bible. The worldwide diffusion of Christianity depended on the assumption that the Bible could be translated without loss into any language. The other is the way any text in any language, both the "original" and the translation, are idiomatic, timebound, marked by their places in history. The paradox of translation as the double production of texts is that the more fluent, readable, and transparent a translation is—the more readers say, "It sounds as if it had been written in English"—the worse it is. It is worse because it has left out those material and historical elements that are essential in the original. It has substituted for these, probably unwittingly, forms of language that betray the historical placement and ideology of the translator. No translation, however, can be free of these historical and ideological marks.

It would follow that the best translation may be the least readable. The paradigmatic example of the latter is those translations of Sophocles done by Hölderlin just before he went mad. By translating literally the word order and syntax of the Greek, Hölderlin produced a translation that is notoriously unreadable. In these translations, as Benjamin (1969a: 69) puts it in "The Task of the Translator": *In ihnen stürzt der Sinn von Abgrund zu Abgrund, bis er droht, in bodenlosen Sprachtiefen sich zu verlieren* ("In them meaning falls from abyss to abyss, until it threatens to become lost in the groundless depths of language").[2]

I shall try to give these generalizations substance through the example of one word and group of related words in Goethe's *Die Wahlverwandtschaften*, the word *Bild* and its compounds. *Die Wahlverwandtschaften* is a good example for two reasons. No less than three different English translations are now in print, so it is a good test case for comparing different renderings and for identifying losses and gains in choosing one English word or phrase rather than another.[3] Moreover, *Die Wahlverwandtschaften* is in a multitude of ways *about* translation as well as posing challenge to translators. As I have argued in another essay,[4] the issue of translation, carrying over, transference, displacement, or *Bild* in the double sense of representation in another medium and metaphorical transposition, is present everywhere in *Die Wahlverwandtschaften*. It is not too much to say that the novel is not only difficult to translate but that it is *about* translation, in the broad understanding of that term. In this sense the novel contains its own oblique commentary, before the fact, on the problems that will be encountered in translating it or commenting on it, that is, in creating a new text in a different language that will be grafted on the original and will draw its life from that original, while being as different from it as a grafted tree is from the rootstock on which it grows.

A list of the diverse examples in *Die Wahlverwandtschaften* would almost be a recapitulation of all the thematic and linguistic material that makes up the novel. The novel opens with a scene in which Edward is grafting new shoots on his trees, carrying the life of the old trunk into the new growth, just as Ottilie's diary and the interpolated novella are grafted within the normal third-person narration of the text. They translate its concerns into other languages, as do the two scenes of *tableaux vivants* that occur at crucial moments in the action. The apparently irrelevant attention to landscape design and to the question of portraits and gravestones translates the central concern of the main action into other thematic domains. That action, finally, along with its fundamental interpretative figure, the image in the title, has to do with the question of what is involved in the transfer of affections from one person to another and with what is involved in the use of a terminology (*Wahlverwandtschaften,* "elective affinities") to name such displacements that is carried over from the necessitarian realm of the natural sciences (which borrowed it in the first place from the human realm) to personify the irresistible affinities of one person for another as if they were "elective" or willfully "chosen" (*gewählt*).

I have already introduced the German word *Bild* and have commented on its double meaning: it means both "picture" and "figure of speech." The word and other German words compounded from *Bild* are crucial in that sequence of passages discussing portraits and gravestones. I shall concentrate my discussion on the difficulties of translating that word and its cognates and on the way the effort to do so produces the double *Die Wahlverwandtschaften* I have defined, drawing it out in both German and English. For Benjamin (1969a) the notion of translatability always implicitly involves the metaphysical or religious notion of a lost, pure sacred language of which both original and translation are impure and fallen renditions. This is parallel to (a "translation" of) Goethe's concern in the passages having to do with the relation of pictures or figures (*Bilder*) to the absent or dead. Translation as the double production of texts, it may be, always encounters the relation between the material, historical, and contingent aspects of language, on the one hand, and the ideal transparency of sign to meaning, one form of which is the proper representation of the dead, on the other. In German *Bild* is a focus for this issue.

The passages in question are splendid examples of the subtlety of *Die Wahlverwandtschaften*. In this novel, apparently casual passages almost always function as signs of something else. In one episode of the novel, Charlotte, as she lays out new paths and walkways around the estate, moves all the old gravestones from the little churchyard and has them set in a neat row against the church. She does this so she can make the churchyard into a green lawn with a path going through it. This desecration of holy ground is part of the topographical theme of estate planning and estate making that runs all through the novel. One family whose members have for generations been buried in the churchyard sends its lawyer to explain that the family is withdrawing its annual gift to the church to protest the moving of the gravestones. This becomes the occasion of a discussion about the relation between external signs, in this case gravestones with their pictures and inscriptions, and the buried reality that these signs mark, in this case the bodies of the beloved dead. For the lawyer, a gravestone with its inscription should be the sign of the direct and immediate presence of the body, and even of the person, of the beloved dead.

> Yet this stone it is not which attracts us; it is that which is contained beneath it, which is entrusted, where it stands, to the earth. It is not the memorial so much of which we speak, as of the person himself; not of what once was, but

of what is [*nicht von der Erinnerung, sondern von der Gegenwart*]. Far better, far more closely, can I embrace some dear departed one in the mound which rises over his bed, than in a monumental writing which only tells us that once he was. In itself, indeed, it is but little; but around it, as around a central mark [*Markstein*], the wife, the husband, the kinsman, the friend, after their departure, shall gather in again. (Goethe 1967: 132; Goethe 1975: 110)

The lawyer here assumes the immediate and living presence of the signified to the sign. In the case of graves, he assumes the presence of the person himself, not just his body, to the central mark that indicates him. This mark is not only the gravestone with its inscription, but the actual mound of earth (*Grabhügel*).

Charlotte and the Architect, on the other hand, hold to an alternative semiotic theory. For them a sign is a memorial, the indication of an absence. There is therefore no need for the sign to be in physical proximity to what it signifies. A dead body melts, so to speak, into the earth in which it is buried, and one need not remember exactly where it was put. "[T]he pure feeling of a universal equality [*Gleichheit*] at last, after death," says Charlotte, "seems to me more composing than this hard determined persistence in our personalities, and in the conditions and circumstances of our lives [*Anhänglichkeiten und Lebensverhältnisse*]" (Goethe 1967: 133; Goethe 1975: 110). Since Charlotte feels this way, it has seemed no desecration to her to move all the gravestones of the little churchyard. The Architect supports her in this and articulates the theory of memorial monuments that justifies her action. "[I]t is not from remembrance," he says, "it is from *place* that man should be set free [*nicht vom Andenken, nur vom Platze soll man sich lossagen*]" (Goethe 1967: 134; Goethe 1975: 111). If this is the case, then the mounds of earth should be allowed to disappear. The ground may be smoothed over, and the monuments and inscriptions may be placed anywhere, "not sown up and down by themselves at random, but erected all in a single spot [*an einem Orte*], where they can promise themselves endurance" (Goethe 1967: 134; Goethe 1975: 111).

In accordance with this theory the Architect redecorates the side chapel of the church with all sorts of earthly and angelic figures taken as he needs them from his copies of such figures. He has made a collection, neatly compartmentalized, of weapons, implements, and artifacts taken from old Germanic barrow-graves, wrested, like the pictures he paints on the chapel wall, from their proper places and made into purely aesthetic signs: "[T]hese solemn old things, in the way he treated them, had a smart dressy appearance, and it was like looking into the box of a trinket merchant" (Goethe 1967: 137; Goethe 1975: 114).

The two theories of inscription and of grave-markers here are versions of the two semiotic theories and the two associated theories of interpersonal relations between which *Die Wahlverwandtschaften* remains poised. In one case the sign is grounded in a phenomenally available nonlinguistic reality, the reality of a physical object or the reality of a person. The sign gives immediate access to this. In the other theory, the sign is free-floating. It has nothing behind it. Therefore it is not tied to any particular place. It creates the reality to which it seems to refer out of its own aesthetic surface, out of its relation to other signs, and out of the activity of reading (or "reading into") by which the spectator interprets it. This reading projects into the sign a ground that it does not have. The novel everywhere indicates, most subtly in its central story, that men and women are continually beguiled into living according to the first theory of signs whereas in fact the human condition is defined by its subjection to the second.

A discussion of portraits (*Bilder*) grows out of this disagreement between Charlotte and the lawyer about the proper relation of gravestones and monuments to the bodies of the dead. The word *Bild* is crucial in this discussion. Related to the problem of the relation between sign and body (*sema* and *soma*, in the old Greek play on words) is the question of the function of portraits, particularly portraits of the dead. The Architect says, apropos of his claim that a funeral monument need not be placed next to the corpse of the person it commemorates, that "at all times the fairest memorial of a man remains some likeness [*eigenes Bildnis*] of himself. This better than anything else, will give a notion of what he was; it is the best text for many or for few notes [*er ist der beste Text zu vielen oder wenigen Noten*]" (Goethe 1967: 134–135; Goethe 1975: 111). The image here is apparently of a musical score set to a verbal text, another form of "translation." Charlotte responds that this supports her claim that a gravestone does not need to be contiguous to the body it commemorates, but that a portrait also generates in her an odd sense of guilt that arises from the absence of the pictured from the picture: "The likeness [*Bild*] of a man is quite independent [*unabhängig*]; everywhere that it stands, it stands for itself [*überall wo es steht, steht es für sich*], and we do not require it to mark the site of a particular grave. But I must acknowledge to you to having a strange feeling; even to likenesses [*die Bildnisse*] I have a kind of disinclination. Whenever I see them they seem to be silently reproaching me. They point to [*deuten auf*] something far away from us—gone from us; and they remind me how difficult it is to pay right honor to the present [*die Gegenwart*]" (Goethe 1967: 135; Goethe 1975: 112).

Ottilie in her diary also discusses the function of portraits. This occurs in the first diary entry the narrator gives the reader. These entries are Ottilie's self-portrait, outlined by that red thread of attachment and affection that characterizes her life. The text manifests the issues it discusses: it presents a portrait, and then it identifies the problematic of portraits. Made up of aphorisms, quotations, and general reflections, Ottilie's diary is strangely impersonal. These function, the narrator tells the reader, as an indirect expression of Ottilie's love for Edward and as an analysis of the quality of that love. It is an unwitting self-portrait, a translation of what Ottilie is into a picture in words.

Ottilie's diary begins with an entry in which she imagines how good it is to think of resting in death beside the body of the one we love. Her ultimate "destiny" is to lie in death beside Edward in the little chapel, but Ottilie's thought also tells the reader something about the nature of her love while she is alive. The image of fulfillment of love in the contiguity of two corpses leads directly to Ottilie's reflections on pictures, reflections that are more than a little odd. "Of the various memorials and tokens [*Denkmale und Merkzeichen*] which bring nearer to us the distant and the separated," writes Ottilie, "—none is so satisfactory as a picture [*Bild*]" (Goethe 1967: 139; Goethe 1975: 115). Ottilie then suggests what seems, if one thinks of it, a peculiar figure for this bringing together of the distant by means of a figure or picture, a representation. The German word *Bild,* the reader will remember, means "figure" in the sense of figure of speech as well as in the sense of picture. Goethe is unostentatiously exploiting this play in the word in all this section of the novel. The problem for a translator is that the play disappears in an accurate and fluent translation. The translation says "picture" or "portrait"; "figure" or "metaphor," while the German says only *Bild* and so connects to one another all the passages in which these words appear. And the association of *Bild* with the cognate *Bildung* ("education") are altogether lost in translation. The effort to translate brings these losses into the open, develops it, as a photographic film is developed, though the finished translation obscures it again when it is read by someone who does not know German. Froude and Boylan, for example, translate *Keins ist von der Bedeutung des Bildes,* in the passage just cited, as "none is so satisfactory as a picture," while Hollingdale translates it as "none is more meaningful than the portrait" (Goethe 1983: 164), and Ryan, in the most recent translation, renders it: "None has as much significance as does a picture" (Goethe 1988: 181). Each translation has a slightly different nuance of meaning in English, though each is accurate enough. All lose the association of *Bild* with "metaphor," and *von der Bedeutung* is a German idiom that has no easy English equivalent, though it seems clear enough in German.

"To sit and talk to a beloved picture [*Die Unterhaltung mit einem geliebten Bilde*]," Ottilie writes, "even though it be unlike [*unähnlich*], has a charm in it, like the charm which there sometimes is in quarreling with a friend. We feel, in a strange sweet way, that we are divided and yet cannot separate" (Goethe 1967: 139; Goethe 1975: 115). What an odd idea! Few people, I think, sit and talk to a picture, loved or hated. A picture or portrait (which is it?), according to Ottilie, brings together and keeps separate. It is a mediation, like a quarrel, a channel, which at the same time marks the permanent distinction between the two vessels that it joins. All portraits are unlike in the sense that they are not the same thing as what they represent, just as all translations are unlike the original. What Froude and Boylan translate as "To sit and talk to a beloved picture" is given by Hollingdale as "being with a much-loved portrait" (Goethe 1983: 164), and by Ryan as "To converse with the portrait of a loved one" (Goethe 1988: 181). Hollingdale suppresses the strange idea of a conversation with a portrait in favor of the much tamer "being with." Which is correct, or is each of the three renderings an "unlike" portrait of the original?

In the next diary entry Ottilie shifts again, this time to a surprisingly different figure and to a different theory of figures or *Bilder.* The actual encounter with "a present person [*einem gegenwärtigen Menschen*]," without intermediary, is, writes Ottilie, often like an encounter with a picture (*als mit einem Bilde* [Goethe 1975: 115]). In moving from the intermediary to the immediate, we remain still with the intermediate, as if we were confronting a representation, or to put this another way, as Charlotte has already put it, a picture stands for itself as a person's face does. Neither is a representation of anything else. This, the reader may remember, is just what Ludwig Wittgenstein says about pictures in "The Brown Book" (Wittgenstein 1965: 162–163). Our relations to a picture and to a person are the same.

They mix presence and absence, the immediate and the mediate, in a way whose peculiarity lies in the fact that there is never any possibility of measuring the validity of the representation by setting it against what it represents. The relation always remains one between spectator and picture, image, figure, *Bild*. "[W]e look at him [a present person], we feel the relation [*Verhältnis*] in which we stand to him; such relation can even grow without his doing anything toward it, without his having any feeling of it: he is to us exactly as a picture [*ohne daß er etwas davon empfindet, daß er sich eben bloß zu uns wie ein Bild verhält*]" (Goethe 1967: 139; Goethe 1975: 115–116). Hollingdale translates this as "without his realizing in any way that his relationship with you is merely that of a portrait" (Goethe 1983: 164), while Ryan gives it as "without his noticing that we are treating him as if he were a picture" (Goethe 1988: 181); Froude and Boylan drop the syntactical connection between *empfindet* and the concluding phrase and thereby give the sentence quite a different meaning.

Ottilie then goes on to observe that the impossible difficulty of portrait paint- ing lies in the fact that the painter must paint not the person but the relation of the spectator to the person, and not just his own relation, but that of everyone else too: "[T]hey [portrait painters] must gather up into their picture the relation [*Verhältnis*] of every body [*sic*] to its subject, all their likings and all dislikings" (Goethe 1967: 140; Goethe 1975: 116). A person's face is not what it is. It exists as its relations to all who know the person. It is analogous in this to a sign. A sign also is a configuration of matter that is not what it is, since it includes its interpretation as part of itself, as well as its differential relations to all the other words in the same code, even its relations to all the languages into which it may be translated.

At the end of this first section from her diary Ottilie returns to the relation between pictures and the dead. If a portrait preserves a person after death, the picture too is mortal. It too eventually will crumble. With its crumbling will crumble also the signified of which it was the sign, since the portrait brings its reference into existence rather than merely pointing to something that could and does exist without it: "[W]e may fancy the life after death to be as a second life, into which a man enters in the figure, or the picture, or the inscription, and lives longer there than when he was really alive [*in das man nun im Bilde, in der Überschrift eintritt und länger darin verweilt als in dem eigentlichen lebendigen Leben*]. But this figure [*Bild*] also, this second existence, dies out too, sooner or later" (Goethe 1967: 140; Goethe 1975: 116). The phrase *im Bilde* is translated here as "in the figure or the picture." Froude and Boylan for once acknowledge the fact that *Bild* may mean "figure" as well as "picture." Hollingdale gives this as "which you enter as a portrait or an inscription, and in which you remain longer than you do in your actual living life" (Goethe 1983: 165), while Ryan translates it as "entered into as if into a picture whose inscription lingers longer than in the real life we live" (Goethe 1988: 181). Hollingdale adds an "or" where the German has a comma of apposition, while Ryan produces the odd notion that the picture disappears while its inscription remains. But surely Goethe is referring here to the funeral portrait with its inscription, together at once a portrait and a figure of the dead person. Both meanings of *Bild* are required, as Froude and Boylan recognize, though with the reservation of an "or": "in the figure, or the picture." But though no English sentence may render in one word the significance of *im Bilde* in German, the effort to translate this apprently simple phrase brings something important about both languages into the open.

The quietness of Ottilie's diary may obscure the genuinely radical nature of what she often says there, as in this case. The afterlife, in her picture of it, is not the dead person's entry into a transcendent realm sustained by God. It is an entry into a second existence generated and kept in being by the figures of that person, portraits or epitaphs, pictures or writings, which other men and women have made as memorials of the dead. Since these signs, support of the person's second life, are made of the same fragile matter as the body was when the person was alive, they are subject to the same mortality. They too will die and in their death, for example in the crumbling of a tombstone, the person dies again, this time for good and all. But the specificity of the sign generates a particular signified, and a change in the sign, for example by translation, will generate a different signified. The spiritual immortality promised in the New Testament is, it seems, only a figure for the transient immortality created by the figure, *Bild,* in all its senses, that universal prosopopoeia whereby a man sees his countenance in the face of another and then projects elsewhere figures of that mask. I am thinking here of that important passage in *Die Wahlverwandtschaften* in which Goethe has Edward say: "But man is a true Narcissus; he delights to see his own image everywhere; and he spreads himself underneath the universe, like the amalgam behind the glass [*Aber der Mensch ist ein wahrer Narziß; er bespiegelt sich überall gern selbst; er legt sich als Folie der ganzen Welt unter*] (Goethe 1967: 31; Goethe 1975: 29).[5] The corresponding text in English literature is Wordsworth's great lament for the fragility of books at the opening of Book Five of *The Prelude:*

> . . . Thou also, man! hast wrought,
> For commerce of thy nature with herself,
> Things that aspire to unconquerable life;
> And we feel—we cannot choose but feel—
> That they must perish . . .
> . . . Oh! why hath not the Mind
> Some element to stamp her image on
> In nature somewhat nearer to her own?
> Why, gifted with such powers to send abroad
> Her spirit, must it lodge in shrines so frail?
>   (ll. 18–22; 43–49)

In the admirable sequence in *Die Wahlverwandtschaften* from the lawyer's remarks to those of the Architect, to those of Charlotte, to those of Ottilie, Goethe has presented in intertwined complexity several different theories of figure. He has in addition made for the reader the application to interpersonal relations of the notion that man is a true Narcissus that is essential to the interpretation of the main story. There are at least three different notions of figure here, with a number of intermediate positions also indicated. For the lawyer, the value of a sign, a picture, a figure, or an inscription lies in its proximity to what is signified. The gravestone should be above the body because only the presence of that body, dead though it is, gives validity to the sign. This is a mimetic, representational, or phenomenal theory of signs. For the Architect, Charlotte, and Ottilie, in slightly different ways and in only part of what they say, a sign brings near the distant, the absent. Its functioning depends on the absence of what it signifies. It is free of place, need not be, and indeed should not be, near what it represents. It makes what it signifies present in its absence, though it still depends for its meaning and function on the independent existence of that signified. On the other hand, in what Charlotte says about the picture standing for itself, therefore being entirely free not only of the location but even of the existence or nonexistence of what is signified, the sign is seen as creating what it signifies, rather than as merely pointing to it either close at hand or out of sight. What Ottilie says of our relation to a real person being like our relation to a picture carries this a step further. Our relation to "real people" is like our relation to a sign, but a sign of the odd sort that has no preexisting reference. The person is created in our response to his or her face or figure. We read a personality into the face that confronts us. This reading into is like the interpretation of a *Bild* in the sense of figure of speech, as well as in the sense of likeness, portrait. It is, however, a figure of speech of that odd sort called *catachresis*. A catachresis is a figure or *Bild* that is neither figurative nor literal, since its referent cannot be brought forth from the unknown to be compared to the sign for it. If a person's face is like a picture in this sense, then interpersonal relations are necessarily narcissistic, my reading of my own face in the mirror of other people. We can never encounter another person face to face in that person's otherness or enter into a direct relation with that otherness, though indirect relations to the unreachable otherness of other people may obscurely determine our fate.

These contradictory concepts of *Bild* are essential to the meaning of Goethe's novel, as could be shown by a more extensive reading of it. But this complexity is obscured by translations that use different English words for what is expressed in German by a single word. Or it might be said that the novel is a *Bild* of its meaning, while the translation is a *Bild* of a *Bild,* in all the senses of that word. Those senses are doubly produced by the failure of the translation to be adequate to the original, not through some contingent and remediable error of the translation but through an intrinsic recalcitrance of the two languages. The original text is a catachresis generating a meaning that depends on the material complexity of the word *Bild,* while the translation in its inadequacy is like a portrait (*Bild*) that in its unlikeness to the original expresses more our relation to the meaning gestured toward by the original than that original in itself.

I began this paper by saying that translation is a double production of texts, the original and the translation, and that one learns something about both languages through experiencing the failures of translation, something that cannot easily be learned in any other way. I claim to have shown this through an example that is also a profound and troubling meditation about (or one might almost say "allegory of") the problems of translation, under the figure of the transfer of the absent or dead into figurative (*bildlich*) memorials.

1. See Benjamin (1969a: 61):

   In "Brot" und "pain" ist das Gemeinte zwar dasselbe, die Art, es zu meinen, dagegen nicht. In der Art des Meinens nämlich liegt es, daß beide Worte dem Deutschen und Franzosen je etwas Verschiedenes bedeuten, daß sie für beide nicht vertauschbar sind, ja sich letzten Endes auszuschließen streben: am Gemeinten aber, daß sie, absolut genommen, das Selbe und Identische bedeuten.

   This is translated by Harry Zohn as:

   The words *Brot* and *pain* "intend" the same object, but the modes of this intention are not the same. It is owing to these modes that the word *Brot* means something different to a German from the word *pain* to a Frenchman, that these words are not interchangeable for them, that, in fact, they strive to exclude each other. As to the intended object, however, the two words mean the very same thing (Benjamin 1969a: 74).

   See also the discussion of this passage in de Man (1986: 87–88, 95–97).

2. I have used here the translation by Tom McCall (1990) in a distinguished unpublished essay. I have been much helped in thinking through my own arguments here by McCall's essay.

3. I have discussed these in a review essay of the newest of these translations, that by Judith Ryan (Miller 1990).

4. Forthcoming in the *Goethe Yearbook*.

5. I have written (Miller 1990) about the difficulties of translating this passage and of the multiple meanings of *Folie*.

REFERENCES _____

Benjamin, Walter. 1969a. "Die Aufgabe des Übersetzers." *Illuminationen*. Frankfurt am Main: Suhrkamp. 56–69.

———. 1969b. *Illuminations*. Trans. Harry Zohn. New York: Schocken. 69–82.

de Man, Paul. 1986. "Conclusions: Walter Benjamin, 'The Task of the Translator.'" *The Resistance to Theory*, Minneapolis: U of Minnesota P.

Goethe, J. W. von. 1967. *Elective Affinities*. Trans. James Anthony Froude and R. Dillon Boylan. New York: Ungar.

———. 1975. *Die Wahlverwandtschaften*. Munich: Deutscher Taschenbuch Verlag.

———. 1983. *Elective Affinities*. Trans. R. J. Hollingdale. Harmondsworth, U.K.: Penguin.

———. 1988. *Elective Affinities* (with *The Sorrows of Young Werther* and *Novella*). Trans. Judith Ryan. New York: Suhrkamp.

McCall, Tom. 1990. "Benjamin's 'Writing That Agitates' and the Question of History." Unpublished.

Miller, J. Hillis. 1990. "Translating the Untranslatable." *Goethe Yearbook*. Ed. Thomas Saine. Vol. 5. Columbia, S.C.: Camden House. 269–78.

Wittgenstein, Ludwig. 1965. "The Brown Book." *The Blue and Brown Books*. New York: Harper. 77–185.

Wordsworth, William. 1959. *The Prelude*. Ed. Ernest de Semcourt. Oxford: Oxford UP.

Chapter 9

Rethinking Power and Solidarity in Gender and Dominance

Deborah Tannen

Georgetown University
and
Princeton University

In analyzing discourse, many researchers assume that all speakers proceed along similar lines of interpretation. But Gumperz (1982) makes clear that this is so only to the extent that cultural background is shared. To the extent that cultural backgrounds differ, lines of interpretation are likely to diverge. My own research shows that cultural difference is not limited to the gross and apparent levels of country of origin and native language, but also exists at the subcultural levels of ethnic heritage, class, geographic region, age, and gender. My earlier work focused on ethnic and regional style; my most recent work focuses on gender. I draw on this work here to demonstrate that utterances have widely divergent potential implicatures, because of the ambiguity of power and solidarity.

POWER AND SOLIDARITY

Since Brown and Gilman's 1960 pioneering study, and the subsequent contributions of Friedrich (1972) and Brown and Levinson ([1978] 1987), the concepts of power and solidarity have been fundamental to sociolinguistic theory. (Fasold [1990] provides an overview.) Power is associated with nonreciprocal forms of address: a speaker addresses another by title-last name but is addressed by first name. Solidarity is associated with reciprocal forms of address: both speakers address each other by title-last name or by first name. Power governs asymmetrical relationships where one is subordinate to another; solidarity governs symmetrical relationships characterized by social equality and similarity. In my own work (Tannen 1984, 1986) exploring the relationship between power and solidarity as it emerges in conversational discourse, I argue that although power and solidarity, closeness and distance, seem at first to be opposites, they also entail each other. Any show of solidarity necessarily entails power, in that claiming similarity and closeness limits freedom and independence. At the same time, any show of power entails solidarity by involving participants in relation to each other.

I once entitled a lecture "The Paradox of Power and Solidarity." The respondent to my talk appeared wearing a three-piece suit and a knapsack on his back. On one level, the suit represented power, the knapsack solidarity. Now, wearing a knapsack would also mark solidarity at, say, a protest demonstration. And wearing a three-piece suit to the demonstration might mark power by differentiating the wearer from the demonstrators, perhaps even reminding them of his superordinate position in an institutional hierarchy. But wearing a three-piece suit to the board meeting of a corporation would mark solidarity, and wearing a knapsack in that setting would connote not solidarity but disrespect, a move in the power dynamic.

This ambiguity gives rise to what has been a major thrust in my previous decade's work analyzing conversation: what appear as attempts to dominate a conversation (an exercise of power) may actually be intended to establish rapport (an exercise of solidarity). This occurs because power and solidarity are bought with the same currency: the same linguistic means can be used to create either or both. The paradigm example from my analysis of a two-and-a-half-hour dinner table conversation (Tannen 1984) involves interruption, or, more accurately, overlap, which can be interpreted as interruption. For some, speaking along with another is a show of enthusiastic participation in the conversation (solidarity); for others, only one voice should be heard at a time, so any overlap is an interruption (power). The result was that enthusiastic listeners who overlapped cooperatively, talking along to establish rapport, were perceived as interrupting. This doubtless contributed to the impression reported by the other speakers that the overlappers had "dominated" the conversation. Indeed, the tape and transcript also give the impression that they had dominated, because their overlap-aversant friends tended to stop speaking as soon as another voice began.

The key to solving the puzzle of whether power or solidarity is primary is symmetry. If Speaker A repeatedly overlaps and Speaker B repeatedly gives way, the resulting communication is asymmetrical, and the effect is domination. But if both speakers avoid overlaps, or if both speakers overlap each other and win out equally, there is symmetry and no domination.

The dynamics of power and solidarity are also seen in the tension between similarity and difference. Scollon (1982: 344–345) explains that all communication is a double bind because of the conflicting needs to be left alone (negative face) and to be accepted as a member of society (positive face). Becker (1982: 125) expresses this double bind as "a matter of continual self-correction between exuberance (i.e., friendliness: you are like me) and deficiency (i.e., respect: you are not me)." I (Tannen 1984: 17) have described this double bind as inherent in communication in that we send and receive the simultaneous and conflicting messages, "Don't assume I'm the same as you" and "Don't assume I'm different from you." All these formulations elaborate on the tension between similarity and difference, or what Becker and Oka (1974) call "the cline of person," a semantic dimension they suggest may be the one most basic to language; that is, one deals with the world and the objects and people in it in terms of how similar, or close, they are to oneself.

In my most recent work (Tannen 1990c) I have continued to explore the paradoxical and mutually entailing relationship between power and solidarity by examining how conflict is negotiated in conversational interaction. This involves exploring how what appears as dominance may not be intended as such, but also how what seems like cooperation may actually be intended to dominate. Throughout, I demonstrate that the linguistic strategies by which power and solidarity are achieved and expressed can be the same, so intentions such as dominance cannot be correlated with linguistic strategies. Rather, the "meaning" of any strategy depends on context, the conversational styles of participants, and the interaction of their styles and strategies with each other.

SIMILARITY AND DIFFERENCE

Harold Pinter's most recent play *Mountain Language* (1988), composed of four brief scenes, is set in a prison in the capital city of an unnamed country. In the second scene, an old mountain woman is finally allowed to visit her son across a table as a guard stands over them. But whenever she tries to speak to her son, the guard silences her, ordering the prisoner to tell his mother that their mountain language is forbidden. Then he continues:

> GUARD   And I'll tell you another thing. I've got a wife and three kids. And you're a pile of shit.
> *Silence.*
>
> PRISONER   I've got a wife and three kids.
>
> GUARD   You've what?
> *Silence.*
> You've got what?
> *Silence.*
> What did you say to me? You've got what?
> *Silence.*
> You've got *what?*
> [*He picks up the telephone and dials one digit.*]
> Sergeant? I'm in the Blue Room . . . yes . . . I thought I should report, Sergeant . . . I think I've got a joker in here (31, 33).

The Sergeant soon enters and asks, "What joker?" The stage darkens and the scene ends. The final scene opens on the same setting, with the prisoner bloody and shaking, his mother shocked into speechlessness. The prisoner was beaten for saying, "I've got a wife and three kids." This quotidian statement, which would be unremarkable in casual conversation, was insubordinate in this hierarchical and oppressive context because the guard had just made the same statement.

When the guard said, "I've got a wife and three kids. And you're a pile of shit," he was claiming, "I am different from you." By repeating the guard's words verbatim, the prisoner was saying, "I am the same as you." (I have demonstrated at length [Tannen 1987, 1989a] that repeating another's words creates rapport on a meta-level.) The guard was asserting his own humanity and denying the prisoner's; by claiming *his* humanity and implicitly denying the guard's assertion that he is "a pile of shit," the prisoner challenged the guard's right to dominate him. Similarity is antithetical to hierarchy.[1]

The ambiguity of closeness, a spatial metaphor representing similarity or involvement, emerges in a nonverbal aspect of this scene. In the performance I saw, the guard repeated the question "You've got what?" while moving steadily closer to the prisoner, until he was bending over him, nose to nose. The guard's moving closer is a nonverbal analogue to the prisoner's statement, but with opposite effect: he was "closing in." The guard moved closer and brought his face into contact with the prisoner's not as a sign of affection (which such actions could signify in another context) but as a threat. Closeness, then, can mean aggression rather than affiliation in the context of a hierarchical rather than symmetrical relationship.

THE AMBIGUITY OF LINGUISTIC STRATEGIES

The potential ambiguity of linguistic strategies to mark both power and solidarity in face-to-face interaction has made mischief in language and gender research, wherein it is tempting to assume that whatever women do results from their powerlessness. But all the linguistic strategies that have been taken by analysts to be evidence of dominance can under certain circumstances be instruments of affiliation. These include indirectness, interruption, silence versus volubility, topic raising, and conflict and verbal aggression. For the remainder of this paper, I demonstrate the ambiguity of each of these strategies in turn.

Indirectness

Lakoff (1975) identifies two benefits of indirectness: defensiveness and rapport. Defensively, a speaker can later disclaim or rescind an indirect communication that does not meet with a positive response. At the same time, indirectness yields the pleasant experience of getting one's way not because one demanded it (power) but because the other wanted the same thing (solidarity). Many researchers have focused on the defensive or power benefit of indirectness and ignored the payoff in rapport or solidarity. Conley, O'Barr, and Lind's (1979) claim that indirectness is the language of the powerless has been particularly influential. Women are then seen as indirect because they don't feel entitled to make demands. Yet those who feel entitled to make demands may prefer not to, seeking the payoff in rapport. Furthermore, there are circumstances in which a party is so powerful that it is unnecessary to make a demand. For example, an employer who says, "It's cold in here," may expect a servant to close a window, but a servant who says the same thing is not likely to see the employer rise to correct the situation. This may explain the otherwise surprising finding of Bellinger and Gleason (1982; reported in Gleason 1987) that fathers' speech to their young children had a higher incidence than mothers' of both direct imperatives ("Turn the bolt with the wrench") *and* implied indirect imperatives ("The wheel is going to fall off").

Cultural relativity sheds crucial light on the use of indirectness. Keenan (1974) found that in a Malagasy-speaking village on the island of Madagascar, women are direct and men indirect, although the men are socially dominant and their indirect style more highly valued. My own research (Tannen 1981) found that whereas American women were more likely to take an indirect interpretation of a sample conversation, Greek men were as likely as Greek women, and more likely than American men *or women,* to take the indirect interpretation. Indirectness, then, is not in itself a strategy of subordination.

Interruption

That interruption is a sign of dominance has been as widespread an assumption in research (for example, Leet-Pellegrini 1980) as in conventional wisdom. A frequent finding (for example, West and Zimmerman 1983) is that men dominate women by interrupting them in conversation. Tellingly, however, Deborah James and Sandra Clarke (forthcoming), reviewing research on gender and interruption, discovered that studies comparing amount of interruption in all-female versus all-male conversations find more interruption, not less, in the all-female ones. Though initially surprising, this finding reinforces the need to distinguish linguistic strategies by their interactional purpose. Does the overlap show support for the speaker, or does it contradict or change the topic? Elsewhere (Tannen 1989b, 1990c) I explore at length the problems inherent in the claim that interruption can be identified by mechanical means, and I give examples of conversation in which there is overlap but no interruption and interruption but no overlap.

This is not, however, to say that interruption never constitutes dominance nor that men never interrupt or dominate women. Fictional discourse provides an example of a situation in which it is and one does. In the short story "You're Ugly, Too" by Lorrie Moore (1989), Zoë is talking to a man she has just met at a party. He asks, "What's your favorite joke?" When she begins, "A man goes to a doctor," he interrupts: "I think I know this one. A guy goes into a doctor's office, and the doctor tells him he's got some good news and some bad news—that one, right?" It is obvious that this is not right, because Zoë's joke is "about the guy who visits his doctor and the doctor says, 'Well, I'm sorry to say, you've got six weeks to live.'" But instead of saying "No," Zoë says, "I'm not sure. This might be a different version," leaving open the door for him to tell his joke, which turns out to be not only different but offensively obscene. This interruption does seem dominating because it comes as Zoë is about to tell a joke, so the man is usurping the floor to tell it for her.

The point, then, is that in order to understand the "meaning" of an interruption, or, indeed, whether an overlap is an interruption, one must consider the context, both speakers' styles, and the interactive frame—that is, what the speakers are trying to do by their communication.

Silence versus Volubility

The excerpt from Pinter's *Mountain Language* dramatizes the assumption that powerful people do the talking and that powerless people are silenced. This is the trope that underlies the play's title and its central theme: by outlawing their language, the oppressors silence the mountain people, rob them of their ability to speak and hence of their humanity. In the same spirit, many scholars (for example, Spender 1980) have claimed that men dominate women by silencing them. Again, there are surely circumstances in which this is accurate. Coates (1986) notes numerous proverbs that instruct women, like children, to be silent.

Silence in itself, however, is not a sign of powerlessness, nor volubility a self-evident sign of domination. A theme running through Komarovsky's 1962 classic study *Blue Collar Marriage* is that many of the wives interviewed said they talked more than their husbands: "He's tongue-tied," one woman said; "My husband has a great habit of not talking," said another; "He doesn't say much but he means what he says and the children mind him," said a third. Yet there is no question but that these husbands are dominant in their marriages.

Indeed taciturnity itself can be an instrument of power. This is precisely the claim of Sattel (1983), who argues that men use silence to exercise power over women. He illustrates with a scene from Erica Jong's novel *Fear of Flying*, only a brief part of which is presented here. The first line of dialogue is spoken by Isadora, the second by her husband Bennett. (Spaced dots indicate omitted text; unspaced dots show a pause included in the original text.)

> "Why do you turn on me? What did I do?"
> Silence.
> "What did I do?"
> He looks at her as if her not knowing were another injury.
> "Look, let's just go to sleep now. Let's just forget it."
> "Forget what?"
> He says nothing.
>
> . . .
> "It was something in the movie, wasn't it?"
> "What, in the movie?"
> ". . . It was the funeral scene. . . . The little boy looking at his dead mother. Something got you there. That was when you got depressed."
> Silence.
> "Well, *wasn't* it?"

Silence.

"Oh come on, Bennett, you're making me *furious*. Please tell me. Please"
(Jong qtd. in Sattel 1983: 120–21).

The painful scene continues in this vein until Bennett tries to leave the room and Isadora tries to detain him. It certainly seems to support Sattel's claim that Bennett's silence subjugates his wife, as the scene ends with her literally lowered to the floor, clinging to his pajama leg. But the reason his silence is an effective weapon is her insistence that he tell her what's wrong. If she too receded into silence, his silence would be disarmed. The devastation results not from his silence in itself but from the interaction of their differing styles.

Volubility and taciturnity, too, can result from style differences rather than speakers' intentions. As I (Tannen 1984, 1985) and others (Scollon and Scollon 1981; Scollon 1985) have discussed at length, there are cultural and subcultural differences in the length of pauses expected between and within speaking turns. In my study of dinner table conversation, those who expected shorter pauses between conversational turns began to feel an uncomfortable silence ensuing while their longer-pausing friends were simply waiting for what they regarded as the appropriate time to take a turn. The result was that the shorter pausers ended up doing most of the talking, another sign interpreted by their interlocutors as dominating the conversation. But their intentions had been to fill in what to them were potentially uncomfortable silences, that is, to grease the conversational wheels and ensure the success of the conversation. In their view, the taciturn participants were uncooperative, failing to do their part to maintain the conversation. So silence and volubility, too, may imply either power or solidarity.

Topic Raising

Shuy (1982) is typical in assuming that the speaker who raises the most topics is dominating a conversation. However, in a study I conducted (Tannen 1990a, 1990b) of videotaped conversations among friends of varying ages recorded by Dorval (1990), it emerged that the speaker who raised the topics was not always dominant, as judged by other criteria (for example, who took the lead in addressing the investigator when he entered the room). To illustrate: in a twenty-minute conversation between a pair of sixth-grade girls who identified themselves as best friends, Shannon raised the topic of Julia's relationship with Mary by saying, "Too bad you and Mary are not good friends anymore." The conversation proceeded and continued to focus almost exclusively on Julia.

Similarly, most of the conversation between two tenth-grade girls was about Nancy, but Sally raised the topic of Nancy's problems. In response to Nancy's question, "Well, what do you want to talk about?" Sally said, "Your mama. Did you talk to your mama?" Overall, Sally raised nine topics, Nancy seven. However, all but one of the topics Sally raised were questions focused on Nancy. If raising more topics is a sign of dominance, Sally controlled the conversation when she raised topics, although even this was subject to Nancy's collaboration by picking them up. It may or may not be the case that Sally controlled the conversation, but the nature of her dominance is surely other than what is normally assumed by that term if the topics she raised were almost all about Nancy.

Finally, the effect of raising topics may also be an effect of differences in pacing and pausing, as discussed above with regard to my study of dinner table conversation. A speaker who thinks the other has no more to say on a given topic may try to contribute to the conversation by raising another one. But a speaker who was intending to say more and was simply waiting for the appropriate turn-exchange pause, will feel that the floor was taken away and the topic aggressively switched. Yet again, the impression of dominance might simply result from style differences.

Conflict and Verbal Aggression

Research on gender and language (see Maltz and Borker [1982] for a review) has consistently found male speakers to be competitive and more likely to engage in conflict (for example, by arguing, issuing commands, and taking opposing stands) and females to be cooperative and more likely to avoid conflict (for example, by agreeing, supporting, and making suggestions rather than commands). Ong (1981: 51) argues that "adversativeness" is universal, but "conspicuous or expressed adversativeness is a larger element in the lives of males than of females."

In my analysis of videotapes of male and female friends talking to each other (Tannen 1990b, 1990c), I have begun to investigate how male adversativeness and female cooperation are played out, complicated, and contradicted in conversational discourse. In analyzing Dorval's videotapes of friends talking, for example, I found a sixth-grade boy saying to his best friend, "Seems like, if there's a fight, me and you are automatically in it. And everyone else wants to go against you and everything. It's hard to agree without someone saying something to you." In contrast, girls of the same age (and also of most other ages whose talk I examined) spent a great deal of time discussing the dangers of anger and contention. In affirming their own friendship, one girl told her friend, "Me and you *never* get in fights hardly," and "I mean like if I try to talk to you, you'll say, 'Talk to *me!*' And if you try to talk to me, I'll *talk* to you."

These examples of gendered styles of interaction are illuminated by the insight that power and solidarity are mutually evocative. As seen in the statement of the sixth-grade boy, opposing other boys in teams entails affiliation within the team. (The most dramatic instance of male affiliation resulting from conflict with others is bonding among soldiers, a phenomenon explored by Norman [1990].) By the same token, girls' efforts to support their friends necessarily entail exclusion of or opposition to other girls. This emerges in Hughes's 1988 study of girls playing the game foursquare. The social injunction to be "nice" and not "mean" was at odds with the object of the game, to eliminate players who are then replaced by waiting players. The girls resolved the conflict, and formed "incipient teams" composed of friends, by claiming that their motivation in eliminating some players was to enable others (their friends) to enter the game. In their terms, this was "nice-mean." This dynamic is also supported by my analysis of the sixth-grade girls' conversation: most of their talk was devoted to allying themselves with each other in opposition to another girl who was not present. So their cooperation (solidarity) also entails opposition (power).

For boys, power entails solidarity not only by opposition to another team, but by opposition to each other. In the videotapes of friends talking, I found that all the conversation between young boys (and none between young girls) had numerous examples of teasing and mock attack. In examining preschool conversations transcribed and analyzed by Corsaro and Rizzo (1990), I was amazed to discover that a fight can be a way of initiating rather than precluding friendship. In one episode, a little boy intrudes on two others and an angry fight ensues in which they threaten to punch and shoot poop at each other, and to snap a Slinky in each other's faces. By the end of the episode, however, the three boys are playing together amicably. Picking a fight was the third boy's way of joining the play of the other two.

These examples call into question the correlation of aggression and power on one hand, and cooperation and solidarity on the other. Doubt is also cast by a cross-cultural perspective. For example, many cultures of the world see arguing as a pleasurable sign of intimacy. Schiffrin (1984) shows that among working class men *and women* of East European Jewish background, friendly argument is a means of being sociable. Frank (1988) shows a Jewish couple who tend to polarize and take argumentative positions, but they are not fighting; they are staging a kind of public sparring, where both fighters are on the same team. Byrnes (1986) claims that Germans find American students uninformed and uncommitted because they are reluctant to argue politics with new acquaintances. For their part, Americans find German students belligerent because they start arguments about American foreign policy with Americans they have just met.

Greek conversation provides an example of a cultural style that places more positive value, for women and men, on dynamic opposition. Kakava (1989) replicates Schiffrin's findings by showing how a Greek family enjoys opposing each other in dinner table conversation. In another study of modern Greek conversation, Tannen and Kakava (1989) find speakers routinely disagreeing when they actually agree, and using diminutive name forms and other terms of endearment—markers of closeness—just when they are opposing each other. In the following excerpt, for example, I express agreement with my interlocutor, an older Greek woman who has just told me that she complained to the police about a construction crew that illegally continued drilling and pounding through the siesta hours:

DEBORAH   Echete dikio.

STELLA   Ego *echo* dikio. Kopella mou, den xero an echo dikio i den echo dikio. Alla ego yperaspizomai ta symferonta mou kai ta dikaiomata mou.

DEBORAH   You're right.

STELLA   I *am* right. My (dear) girl, I don't know if I'm right or I'm not right. But I am watching out for my interests and my rights.

Stella disagrees with my agreement with her by reframing my agreement in her own terms rather than simply accepting it by stopping after "I *am* right." She also marks her divergence from my frame with the endearment *kopella mou* (literally, "my girl" but idiomatically "my dear girl").

In another conversation, presented by Kakava as typical of her family's sociable argument, the younger sister has said that she cannot understand why the attractive young woman who is Prime Minister Papandreou's girlfriend would have an affair with such an old man. The older sister, Christina, argues that the woman may have felt that in having an affair with the prime minister she was doing something notable. Her sister replied, "Poly megalo timima re Christinaki na pliroseis pantos" ("It's a very high price to pay, Chrissie, anyway"). I am using the English diminutive form "Chrissie" to reflect the Greek diminutive ending *-aki,* but the particle *re* cannot really be translated; it is simply a marker of closeness that is typically used when disagreeing, as in the ubiquitously heard "Ochi, re" ("No, *re*").

CONCLUSION

The intersection of language and gender provides a rich site for analyzing how power and solidarity are created in discourse. But prior research in this area evidences the danger of linking linguistic forms with interactional intentions such as dominance. In trying to understand how speakers use language, we must consider the context (in every sense, including at least textual, relational, and institutional constraints), speakers' conversational styles, and, most crucially, the interaction of their styles with each other.

Attempts to understand what goes on between women and men in conversation are muddled by the ambiguity of power and solidarity. The same linguistic means can accomplish either, and every utterance combines elements of both. Scholars, however, like individuals in interaction, are likely to see only one and not the other, like the frequently cited picture that cannot be seen for what it is—simultaneously a chalice and two faces—but can only be seen alternatively as one or the other. In attempting the impossible task of keeping both images in focus at once, we may at least succeed in switching from one to the other fast enough to deepen our understanding of power and solidarity as well as communication between women and men.

ENDNOTE

1. Following the oral presentation of this paper, both Gary Holland and Michael Chandler pointed out that the prisoner may be heard as implying the second part of the guard's statement: "and you're a pile of shit."

REFERENCES

Becker, A. L. 1982. "Beyond Translation: Esthetics and Language Description." *Contemporary Perceptions of Language: Interdisciplinary Dimensions. Georgetown University Round Table on Languages and Linguistics 1982.* Ed. H. Byrnes. Washington, D.C.: Georgetown UP. 124–38.

Becker, A. L., and I. Oka. 1974. "Person in Kawi: Exploration of an Elementary Semantic Dimension." *Oceanic Linguistics* 13: 229–55.

Bellinger, D., and J. Berko Gleason. 1982. "Sex Differences in Parental Directives to Young Children." *Sex Roles* 8: 1123–39.

Brown, P., and S. Levinson. [1978]1987. *Politeness: Some Universals in Language Usage.* Cambridge: Cambridge UP.

Brown, R., and A. Gilman. 1960. "The Pronouns of Power and Solidarity." *Style in Language.* Ed. T. Sebeok. Cambridge, Mass.: MIT P. 253–76.

Byrnes, H. 1986. "Interactional Style in German and American Conversations." *Text* 6: 189–206.

Coates, J. 1986. *Women, Men and Language.* London: Longman.

Conley, J. M., W. M. O'Barr, and E. A. Lind. 1979. "The Power of Language: Presentational Style in the Courtroom." *Duke Law Journal* 6: 1375–99.

Corsaro, W., and T. Rizzo. 1990. "Disputes in the Peer Culture of American and Italian Nursery School Children." *Conflict Talk.* Ed. A. Grimshaw. Cambridge: Cambridge UP. 21–65.

Dorval, B., ed. 1990. *Conversational Coherence and Its Development.* Norwood, N.J.: Ablex.

Fasold, R. W. 1990. *The Sociolinguistics of Language.* Oxford: Basil Blackwell.

Frank, J. 1988. "Communicating 'by Pairs': Agreeing and Disagreeing Among Married Couples." Unpublished ms. Georgetown University.

Friedrich, P. 1972. "Social Context and Semantic Feature: The Russian Pronominal Usage." *Directions in Sociolinguistics.* Eds. J. J. Gumperz and D. Hymes. New York: Holt; Oxford: Basil Blackwell. 270–300.

Gleason, J. B. 1987. "Sex Differences in Parent-Child Interaction." *Language, Gender, and Sex in Comparative Perspective.* Eds. S. U. Philips, S. Steele, and C. Tanz. Cambridge: Cambridge UP. 189–99.

Gumperz, J. J. 1982. *Discourse Strategies.* Cambridge: Cambridge UP.

Hughes, L. A. 1988. " 'But That's Not *Really* Mean': Competing in a Cooperative Mode." *Sex Roles* 19: 669–87.

James, D. and S. Clarke. Forthcoming. "Women, Men and Interruptions: A Critical Review." *Gender and Conversational Interaction.* Ed. D. Tannen.

Kakava, C. 1989. "Argumentative Conversation in a Greek Family." Paper presented at the Annual Meeting of the Linguistic Society of America, Washington, D.C., December 29, 1989.

Keenan, E. 1974. "Norm-Makers, Norm-Breakers: Uses of Speech by Men and Women in a Malagasy Community." *Explorations in the Ethnography of Speaking.* Eds. R. Bauman and J. Sherzer. Cambridge: Cambridge UP. 125–43.

Komarovsky, M. 1962. *Blue Collar Marriage.* New York: Vintage.

Lakoff, R. 1975. *Language and Woman's Place.* New York: Harper.

Leet-Pellegrini, H. M. 1980. "Conversational Dominance as a Function of Gender and Expertise." *Language: Social Psychological Perspectives.* Eds. H. Giles, W. P. Robinson, and P. M. Smith. Oxford: Pergamon. 97–104.

Maltz, D. N., and R. A. Borker. 1982. "A Cultural Approach to Male-Female Miscommunication." *Language and Social Identity.* Ed. J. Gumperz. Cambridge: Cambridge UP. 196–216.

Moore, L. 1989. "You're Ugly, Too." *The New Yorker.* July 3, 1989. 30–40.

Norman, M. 1990. *These Good Men: Friendships Forged from War.* New York: Crown.

Ong, W. J. 1981. *Fighting for Life: Contest, Sexuality, and Consciousness.* Ithaca: Cornell UP; Amherst: U of Massachusetts P.

Pinter, H. 1988. *Mountain Language.* New York: Grove.

Sattel, J. W. 1983. "Men, Inexpressiveness, and Power." *Language, Gender and Society.* Eds. B. Thorne, C. Kramarae, and N. Henley. Rowley, Mass.: Newbury. 119–24.

Schiffrin, D. 1984. "Jewish Argument as Sociability." *Language in Society* 13: 311–35.

Scollon, R. 1982. "The Rhythmic Integration of Ordinary Talk." *Analyzing Discourse: Text and Talk. Georgetown University Round Table on Languages and Linguistics 1981.* Ed. D. Tannen. Washington, D.C.: Georgetown UP. 335–49.

————. 1985. "The Machine Stops: Silence in the Metaphor of Malfunction." *Perspectives on Silence.* Eds. D. Tannen and M. Saville-Troike. Norwood, N.J.: Ablex. 21–30.

Scollon, R., and S. B. K. Scollon. 1981. *Narrative, Literacy and Face in Interethnic Communication.* Norwood, N.J.: Ablex.

Shuy, R. W. 1982. "Topic as the Unit of Analysis in a Criminal Law Case." *Analyzing Discourse: Text and Talk. Georgetown University Round Table on Languages and Linguistics 1981.* Ed. D. Tannen. Washington, D.C.: Georgetown UP. 113–26.

Spender, D. 1980. *Man Made Language.* London: Routledge.

Tannen, D. 1981. "Indirectness in Discourse: Ethnicity as Conversational Style." *Discourse Processes* 4: 221–38.

————. 1984. *Conversational Style: Analyzing Talk Among Friends.* Norwood, N.J.: Ablex.

———. 1985. "Silence: Anything But." *Perspectives on Silence*. Eds. D. Tannen and M. Saville-Troike. Norwood, N.J.: Ablex. 93–111.

———. 1986. *That's Not What I Meant!: How Conversational Style Makes or Breaks Your Relations with Others*. New York: Morrow, Ballantine.

———. 1987. "Repetition in Conversation: Toward a Poetics of Talk." *Language* 63: 574–605.

———. 1989a. *Talking Voices: Repetition, Dialogue and Imagery in Conversational Discourse*. Cambridge: Cambridge UP.

———. 1989b. "Interpreting Interruption in Conversation." *Papers from the 25th Annual Regional Meeting of the Chicago Linguistic Society*. Eds. B. Music, R. Graczyk, and C. Wiltshire. Chicago: Dept. of Linguistics, U of Chicago. 266–87.

———. 1990a. "Gender Differences in Conversational Coherence: Physical Alignment and Topical Cohesion." *Conversational Coherence and Its Development*. Ed. B. Dorval. Norwood, N.J.: Ablex.

———. 1990b. "Gender Differences in Topical Coherence: Creating Involvement in Best Friends' Talk." *Discourse Processes* 13: 73–90.

———. 1990c. *You Just Don't Understand: Women and Men in Conversation*. New York: Morrow, Ballantine.

Tannen, D., and C. Kakava. Forthcoming. "Power and Solidarity in Men's and Women's Conversations in Modern Greek." *Journal of Modern Greek Studies*.

West, C., and D. H. Zimmerman. 1983. "Small Insults: A Study of Interruptions in Cross-Sex Conversations Between Unacquainted Persons." *Language, Gender and Society*. Eds. B. Thorne, C. Kramarae, and N. Henley. Rowley, Mass.: Newbury. 103–17.

Chapter 10

Cultural Maintenance and "Vanishing" Languages

Muriel Saville-Troike
University of Arizona

INTRODUCTION

It has been a central tenet of anthropology since the days of Franz Boas that the relationship between language and other aspects of culture is an essentially arbitrary one, a point repeatedly demonstrated by the great cultural differences found between speakers of closely related languages or by instances of cultural similarity among speakers of unrelated languages. While the recognition of this fundamental point is a commonplace among anthropologists and linguists, it is less familiar to teachers and curriculum developers who are engaged in the international marketing of English or other "world languages," or to those involved in the education of national linguistic and/or cultural minorities. Failure to recognize the arbitrariness of the language-culture link has serious consequences, however, for it can foster cultural imperialism and mask important issues of ethnic identity and cross-cultural (mis)communication.

My main point is that, although language is unquestionably an integral part of culture, teachers and textbook writers—in common with much of the lay public—often mistakenly assume that specific cultural experiences and rules of behavior must be invariable correlates of specific linguistic skills. But there is certainly no intrinsic reason why the structures and vocabulary of one language cannot be used by diverse speech communities to express the different cultures of those communities, and in ways in keeping with their rules of appropriate behavior. Thus, for example, as English is developed and used creatively as an auxiliary language in Nigeria, India, and elsewhere in the world, it becomes "Englishes" in the enactment of different cultural values and beliefs.

My concern for this point stems in part from the discovery that many of my own teacher trainees in ESL do not understand the notion of relativity in the attachment of culture to language, or at least find it a "novel" idea. The concept of the interdependence of language and culture has been well learned before students reach us at the graduate level—perhaps overlearned, to the point of rigidity. All "know," for instance, about the three, or six, or fifty terms Eskimo has for "snow," depending on which version of that academic myth they have heard (convincingly discredited by Martin [1986]). Some of them see the teaching of English as promoting learning about culture, as though the two were inextricably linked (this is certainly an underlying motivation for USIA support for English teaching around the world). Others display surprise or annoyance, or propose remedial treatment, if they find English being used in an "un-American" way. I am sure this observation could be generalized to teachers of most foreign languages.

LANGUAGE AND CULTURE:
A RELATIVISTIC PERSPECTIVE

The more arbitrary aspect of the relationship of language and culture that I wish to highlight in this context has been discussed at length by Braj Kachru, director of the Division of English as an International Language at the University of Illinois. He writes that "in Third World countries . . . the English language is not taught as a vehicle to introduce British or American culture, [but] is used to teach and maintain the indigenous patterns of life and culture" (1986: 100). Referring to the formal distinctiveness of English in India, Kachru attributes this to the fact that it "functions in the Indian sociocultural context in order to perform those roles which are relevant and appropriate to the social, educational and administrative network of India." The use of English for these indigenous purposes is, of course, the legacy of colonialism and empire building, but it has ceased to serve those original functions and has been adapted to the postcolonial needs of groups that have adopted it.

A partially analogous situation has taken place within the United States, where "internal colonialism" decreed the imposition of English on Native American populations. One major difference is that for the vast majority of American Indians, English was not merely added to the repertoire of these communities as an auxiliary language. In virtually all cases, ancestral languages have given way to monolingual "competence" in English, or at best, traditional linguistic resources have been seriously depleted. However, the analogy with Third World colonialism continues to the extent that many American Indian groups, in spite of using linguistic forms that are superficially very similar to those spoken by the dominant society, still constitute distinct speech communities. I am of course not meaning to generalize to all American Indians, and certainly not to those that have fully assimilated both linguistically and culturally. But significant numbers do not share the dominant society's norms of speaking and interpretation of speech performance, its attitudes and values regarding language forms and use, nor its sociocultural understandings and presuppositions with regard to speech (see definitions of "speech communities" in Saville-Troike 1989: 16–20; Hudson 1980: 25–30).

In these cases, as well as in the Third World contexts described by Kachru, English has been adopted—but also adapted to the transmission and maintenance of indigenous patterns of culture. The result is that a number of so-called "vanishing" languages are still "spoken," just using English vocabulary and grammar.

EDUCATIONAL ISSUES

A number of rather sensitive topics might be addressed at this point in relation to second language instruction, and to language policy more generally. The situation just described illustrates what Lambert (1975) termed "subtractive bilingualism." Some educators claim that many students from the communities I am talking about come to school speaking neither their "native" language nor English fluently—a condition unfortunately labeled "semilingualism" (cf. Cummins 1979). Others argue that the students do have adequate linguistic skills for their own communicative purposes, but lack those required for academic competence. All agree that the situation has resulted in major educational problems—poor achievement and high dropout rates. Efforts at remediation range from early childhood programs designed to "get children into English" earlier (which has in general hastened the demise of extant languages without enhancing the desired English skills) to native language recovery programs designed to reintroduce or revitalize "dead" or "dying" languages. The latter programs have met with very little success, in large part because the English that has been adopted and adapted by the communities has already replaced the ancestral languages for most social functions (see St. Clair and Leap 1982).

While these vital and emotional issues clearly deserve attention, addressing them first requires considering the nature of the diversity we are dealing with, and that is my primary aim here. For, while according to Kachru, recognition and tolerance of diversity within "World Englishes" is spreading, recognition and acceptance of the multiple "Englishes" that have developed within the United States is much less widespread. I believe many of the educational problems with American Indian students are not the result of linguistic factors per se, but are due to lack of recognition and provision for this substratal communicative diversity.

The charge I was given for this paper was at least in part to relate issues of language and culture that concern *foreign* language instruction. In speaking only about English, I am taking the position that what is "foreign" in such contexts need not be the linguistic code. Sharing grammar and vocabulary does not ensure peoples' sharing the same language. These are but the tip of a communicative iceberg. Not recognizing the differences that lie below surface-level similarities holds serious potential for misunderstanding. In the case of English-medium instruction for minority group students in the United States, this lack of recognition has additional important implications for identity and achievement.

COMMUNICATION DIFFERENCES

Many examples of cultural differences in the use of English, and their consequences, concern the patterning of sounds and silences, to continue a theme introduced in other papers in this collection. Such differences include what is and what is not voiced, as Becker has shown, and norms for interaction, as discussed by Tannen (both this volume). I will briefly describe two events to illustrate what I have in mind.

The first occurred several years ago when I was visiting a kindergarten class on the Navajo reservation. A Navajo man opened the door to the classroom and stood silently, looking at the floor. The Anglo teacher said, "Good morning," and waited expectantly, but the man did not respond. The teacher then said, "My name is Mrs. Jones," and again waited for a response. There was none. In the meantime, a child in the room put away his crayons and got his coat from the rack. The teacher, noting this, said to the man, "Oh, are you taking Billy now?" The man uttered his only word to her, "Yes." The teacher continued to talk to the man while Billy got ready to leave, saying, "Billy is such a good boy," "I'm so happy to have him in class," etc. Billy joined his father and the man left in silence. The teacher shrugged her shoulders at me, conveying helplessness and frustration.

From a Navajo perspective, the man's silence was appropriate and respectful. The teacher, on the other hand, expected not only to have the man return her greeting, but to have him identify himself and state his reason for being there. This would have required the man to break not only Navajo rules of politeness but also a traditional religious taboo that prohibits individuals from saying their own name. The teacher engaged in small talk in an attempt to be friendly and to cover her discomfort in the situation, as appropriate in her own speech community, while the man continued to maintain the silence appropriate in his.

Two aspects of this encounter are worthy of further note. One is that it undoubtedly reinforced the teacher's stereotype that Navajos are "impolite" and "unresponsive," and the man's stereotype that Anglo-Americans are "impolite" and "talk too much." These same attitudes are widely held between teachers in that region and many of their students, clearly to the detriment of teaching and learning. The second point of interest involves a historical note. One of the earliest sociolinguistic descriptions I have found concerns greeting and leavetaking behavior among White Mountain Apaches, who are closely related to the Navajo. The report was prepared by a physician who was serving with the U.S. cavalry in the nineteenth century. In part it reads:

> Apaches . . . seem to have no form of salute or of greeting—when meeting or of taking leave of each other. . . . [In the instance I observed, where a man was returning home after an absence of several weeks], the Indian simply rode up to his little brush dwelling and dismounted. . . . There he stood motionless and speechless for some ten to fifteen minutes when at last he took a seat on the ground and engaged in ordinary conversation without having observed any form of greeting (White c. 1880).

This occurred early in the period of Indian contact with English speakers, so of course that conversation was in an Apache language, but the same sociolinguistic behavior can be observed today between Apaches and Navajos who converse in English, and it reflects the same norms of interaction that the Navajo man was following in the kindergarten class. Such rules appear to be more resistant to "foreign" influence than do grammar and lexicon.

The second event occurred at a conference in Albuquerque, New Mexico, on American Indian education. I visited with some Navajo teachers after one of the small group sessions. The session was supposed to have been a "discussion" about educational problems in their schools, and an important goal of the organizers had been to get those teachers' input. But none of the teachers had talked. The difference that led to this breakdown was the temporal pattern of silence in turntaking between questions and answers, which occupies a significantly longer time-space for Navajos than is generally used by non-Navajo English speakers. The non-Navajo participants in the conference session had answered questions that had been addressed to Navajos, and the discussion leader had repeated or rephrased the questions, because the period of silence following them had gone beyond her own limit of tolerance. At the same time, the Navajo teachers were effectively kept out of the discussion because not enough time-space was ever allowed to reach an appropriate extent for them to respond. The teachers recognized what the problem was and discussed it afterward. There was obviously cross-cultural conflict involved. They considered the non-Navajo timing pattern quite impolite, and the short time between questions and answers a sure sign that those who did speak had no sincere concern for the issues that were being addressed. Although all were fluent English speakers, the Navajos obviously did not wish to add such impolite behavior to their communicative repertoire.

These events illustrate differences in rules for speaking held by members of different speech communities that have been maintained across the shift to English. They are probably so persistent largely because the affective meaning carried by rules for speaking is so strong. Adopting those requires violations of culture—of values and beliefs—that merely using English surface structure does not.

Other general areas where there may be culturally-based differences include the possible aftereffects of speaking, expectation of who may or may not speak in certain settings, to whom one may speak, whether one may speak on behalf of others, and how one may talk to persons of different status and roles. Violations of any of these norms clearly constitute far more serious but less visible "errors" in communication than would deviations from normative rules of pronunciation or grammatical structure.

EFFECTS ON LITERACY

Cultural conflicts in the use of English are not limited to speech, nor to personal interaction. English teachers at the high school and college level report that even students who do achieve a high level of decoding skill may have difficulty with British and nineteenth-century American literary texts, for instance. Although vocabulary and grammar may be familiar, the lack of shared experiences and knowledge representations constitute a major cultural barrier. Most inaccessible appears to be interpretation of metaphor. I have found that middle-class foreign students from Europe sometimes have a better understanding of the same text, even with much more limited knowledge of the grammar and vocabulary, probably because the cultural information and patterns of inference are shared to a greater degree.

Different dimensions of this conflict are addressed by Scollon and Scollon (1979), who describe how the discourse properties of the essayist prose style, which is a common model for learning to read and write in this society, are perceived as foreign to Athabaskan Indians in Alaska. Reading and writing in English require a different way of organizing knowledge, and above all, decontextualizing text. Differences in discourse organization have also been described for monolingual English-speaking students from the Kiowa, Creek, and Cherokee tribes in Oklahoma (Cooley and Lujan 1982). Teachers judged the texts those students produced to be incoherent and rambling, although ironically the model of discourse organization they were following came from speeches by elders in these tribes who were renowned for their rhetorical skills.

Further, "with the heightened emphasis on truth value rather than social or rhetorical conditions comes a necessity to be explicit about logical implications" (Scollon and Scollon 1979: 9). The decontextualized essayist prose style and content are in violation of Athabaskan norms in being monologic, in speaking to unknown audiences, in displaying knowledge and dominance, in creating their own contexts of interpretation, and in speaking to the future and other situations inappropriate to Athabaskan practice.

In the Scollons' words, essayist literacy is essentially "inter-ethnic" communication, and producing such written text requires Athabaskans to adopt discourse strategies they have been socialized in their communities to consider arrogant and irrelevant—or else they must undergo cultural change and become bicultural or perhaps even estranged from their community culture.

Other dimensions of conflict may arise from generalizable differences between oral and literate traditions. St. Clair (1980) found, for instance, that American Indian students in the Northwest used visual metaphors extensively in their written compositions, following oral rhetorical practice. Such differences in oral versus literate style may in part account for the fact that there has been only minimal acceptance of literacy in the native language in those communities where the spoken language remains in use for at least some domains. More importantly, perhaps, resistance to native language literacy may be seen as a means of protecting traditional culture from the modernizing (and more public) influence of writing (see Spolsky and Irvine 1982).

CONSEQUENCES AND CONCLUSION

Some aspects of culture are lost when a language dies, to be sure, and I do not mean to diminish the profound sense of loss many groups of American Indians, as well as others, feel. Consequences may be particularly serious when language loss results in a group's inability to maintain certain critical cohesive rituals.

But, as I emphasized at the outset of this discussion, the relationship between language and culture is largely an arbitrary one, and as illustrated above, many aspects of native culture may survive in communicative behaviors even if an ancestral language is lost. For those who have adopted, and adapted, English surface structure, but who have maintained culturally-based "ways of speaking," what are the consequences?

On one side, whether intentionally or not, they are maintaining at least part of their cultural heritage, along with their group identity. To paraphrase Braj Kachru, they are using English as a vehicle to teach and maintain indigenous patterns of life and culture. English thus comes to function in their sociocultural context as a medium for performing those roles that are relevant and appropriate to that medium. In a sense, their languages have not totally "vanished," but in part have merely gone underground.

On the other side, the educational and administrative systems of the larger society are assuming that the adoption of English entails the adoption of the dominant culture as well. This, after all, was the motivation for the U.S. government mandating English in Indian education in the first place. In the words of the commissioner of the Bureau of Indian Affairs in the 1880s:

> The first step to be taken toward civilization, toward teaching the Indian the mischief and folly of continuing in their barbarous practices, is to teach him the English language. . . . We must remove the stumbling-blocks of hereditary customs and manners, and of those language is one of the most important (Atkins 1887).

This language policy was only partially successful, but the consequence of cultural maintenance for many has been poor educational achievement, misunderstanding and stereotyping in cross-cultural communication, and widespread discrimination. Thus, there is a dilemma.

What is the answer? I do not pretend to propose a panacea, but important first steps would be to break the grip of the one language:one culture fallacy, and to sensitize teachers and other educational personnel to the fact that the use of the "same" surface linguistic code may conceal significant cultural differences in communicative intentions and understandings. Further, I would hope that recognition and acceptance of such diversity by educators might lead to greater opportunities for minority group members in this society who adopt and adapt English as a native language, without demands that they abandon their traditional/ancestral identities.

REFERENCES

Atkins, J. D. C. 1887. "Annual Report of the Commissioner of Indian Affairs." *House Executive Document* No. 1, 50th Cong., 1st sess., ser. 2542. 19–21.

Cooley, R., and P. Lujan. 1982. "A Structural Analysis of Speeches by Native American Students." *Bilingualism and Language Contact.* Eds. F. Barkin, E. A. Brandt, and J. Ornstein-Galicia. New York: Teachers College Press. 80–92.

Cummins, J. 1979. "Linguistic Interdependence and the Educational Development of Bilingual Children." *Review of Educational Research* 49(2): 222–51.

Hudson, R. A. 1980. *Sociolinguistics.* Cambridge: Cambridge UP.

Kachru, B. B. 1986. *The Alchemy of English: The Spread, Functions and Models of Non-Native Englishes.* Oxford: Pergamon.

Lambert, W. E. 1975. "Culture and Language as Factors in Learning and Education." *Education of Immigrant Students.* Ed. A. Wolfgang. Toronto: Ontario Inst. for Studies in Ed. 55–83.

Martin, L. 1986. " 'Eskimo Words for Snow': A Case Study in the Genesis and Decay of an Anthropological Example." *American Anthropologist* 88(2): 418–23.

St. Clair, R. 1980. *Visual Metaphor in Native American Rhetoric.* Paper presented at the meeting of the Midwest Modern Language Association, Minneapolis. Cited in I. C. Siler and D. Labadie-Wondergem. 1982. "Cultural Factors in the Organization of Speeches by Native Americans." *Bilingualism and Language Contact.* Eds. F. Barkin, E. A. Brandt, and J. Ornstein-Galicia. New York: Teachers College Press. 93–100.

St. Clair, R., and W. Leap, eds. 1982. *Language Renewal Among American Indian Tribes.* Rosslyn, Va.: Nat. Clearinghouse for Bilingual Ed.

Saville-Troike, M. 1989. *The Ethnography of Communication.* 2nd ed. Oxford: Basil Blackwell.

Scollon, R., and S. B. K. Scollon. 1979. *Literacy as Interethnic Communication: An Athabaskan Case.* Sociolinguistic Working Paper No. 59. Austin, Tex.: Southwest Ed. Dev. Lab.

Spolsky, B., and P. Irvine. 1982. "Sociolinguistic Aspects of the Acceptance of Literacy in the Vernacular." *Bilingualism and Language Contact.* Eds. F. Barkin, E. A. Brandt, and J. Ornstein-Galicia. New York: Teachers College Press. 73–79.

White, J. B. [c. 1880.] *A History of the Apache Indians of Arizona Territory.* Unpublished ms. Archives of the Smithsonian Institution. Bureau of American Ethnography. 179.

Chapter 11

Culture in the Japanese Language Classroom: A Pedagogical Paradox

Eleanor Harz Jorden
Cornell University

INTRODUCTION

For the first time in American foreign language education, a noncognate language is being mainstreamed. It is being taught not only at our large colleges and universities that offer a broadly diversified curriculum, but also at smaller institutions whose curricula include no related area courses. At an increasing number of schools at the K–12 level, programs in this language are springing up everywhere: by the latest count it is taught at approximately 800 precollege institutions scattered throughout the country. Several thousands of students receive instruction in this language in teledistance programs via satellite. It is even possible for kindergarten pupils to sign up for intensive instruction that occupies most of their school day. The language is, of course, Japanese—for the past decade the fastest growing foreign language in the American educational system.

An enrollment explosion of this magnitude has resulted not surprisingly in a critical shortage of trained instructors at every level. On that point alone the field is agreed. But the question as to what constitutes a trained instructor of Japanese, to say nothing of the ideal methodology of training—these are matters that divide the field into factions with seemingly irreconcilable differences.

CULTURE IN THE CLASSROOM

Discussions on the advisability or viability of including instruction in culture in the foreign language classroom bring to mind immediately the countless Japanese courses entitled "Japanese Language and Culture." Invariably within the high school curriculum the culture portion consists of facts and activities related to Japan—folding paper cranes, practicing the martial arts, making sushi, playing games, taking field trips to museums, and the like—all conducted in English and having no direct relation to the learning of the language. Significantly, the cultural component itself lacks the particular type of cultural instruction without which the Japanese language will never be interpreted accurately by the foreigner.

Moving on to college level instruction, the number of so-called "Language and Culture" courses diminishes, but a "cultural component" may continue nevertheless. The use of the Japanese language increases during extracurricular sushi making, and the advanced student may begin viewing Japanese films with reduced dependence on subtitles, but even at this level there is a tendency to assume an extremely limited definition of culture.

LEARNED CULTURE AND ACQUIRED CULTURE

Using as a model the distinction made by some linguists between "learned language" (i.e., language known through conscious and deliberate study) and "acquired language" (i.e., language competence gained unconsciously and out of awareness, as native speakers become proficient in their native spoken language), a distinction can be made between "learned culture" and "acquired culture." The learned variety, learned, that is, by cultural natives and foreigners alike through conscious study or imitation, can be roughly divided into three varieties: aesthetic (including the study of literature, art, music, etc.), informational (facts about the culture, such as population, form of government, dates in history, etc.), and skill (how to cook, wrap packages, saw wood, etc.). Acquired culture, in contrast, is the deep culture of the native, the mindset, the behavioral and attitudinal framework that underlies daily conduct. How individuals interact and interrelate, how they define the self, how they view time and space, their attitudes toward foreigners, their attitudes toward language—foreign and native—all these are part of acquired culture, the driving force that is omnipresent. We can all expect to be totally under the influence of this kind of culture. Within the boundaries of an acquired culture system, we find variation among individuals at the surface level, and it is the surface level that may change as a result of extended contact with other cultures, but the deepest level, acquired during early socialization, can be expected to remain constant and persistent.

Thus, in studying a foreign language, emphasis should be placed not on language *and* culture but rather on language *in* culture—acquired culture, that is, of which language is but one manifestation. The former is a pairing that represents an optional combination based on a deliberate selection; the latter is unavoidable and essential. For those with elementary-level proficiency in the foreign language, any connection with learned culture depends on the use of the learners' native language and in no way improves proficiency in the target language. It would be better to divide a language *and* culture course into two separate courses, and give each topic the kind of attention it deserves.

THE DIFFICULTY OF JAPANESE

The Linguistic Code

On the basis of all available evidence, Japanese (spoken and written) is the most difficult of all the languages offered in regular foreign language programs for Americans to learn. Its difficulty stems first from its contrast with English: what the American with foreign language experience in only cognate Indo-European languages assumes to be universals of language—distinctions of number, person, and tense, for example—are lacking, whereas structures and patterns totally lacking in English—inflection of adjectives, infixes that represent potentiality, causation, and passivization, and the like—are common. Another difficulty arises from the countless examples of partial overlap with English on every level: just when it appears that Japanese vocabulary item (or pattern or structure) X resembles an English Y, further investigation proves that the resemblance obtains only in certain contexts; elsewhere, the occurrence of X in Japanese and of Y in English may show no relationship whatsoever.

The Japanese writing system is of staggering complexity. It uses 1,945 currently approved characters (*kanji*), originally borrowed from the Chinese, each of which (with only rare exceptions) has at least two completely different pronunciations, usually representing similar or related meanings; one pronunciation is native Japanese and the other a Japanese adaptation of an original borrowing from Chinese. The appropriate pronunciation of each occurrence of a *kanji* is determined by context. These *kanji* occur in combination with two syllabaries (*kana*) of about fifty symbols, each representing a syllable-like unit. One set (*hiragana*) is used for the representation of grammatical signals (postpositions, inflectional endings, infixes, etc.) and of uninflected words and roots of inflected words for which there is no *kanji* or no approved *kanji*. The other set (*katakana*) is used principally for writing the japanized version of words recently borrowed from foreign languages, notably English. Thus *kanji* characters represent morphs (sound + meaning) whereas *kana* symbols represent sound only, that is, syllable-like units that have no reference to meaning.

If English used a comparable writing system, we might imagine a *kanji* # representing "big" and "magn-" or "magni-": the appropriate reading of a particular occurrence of # would depend on context. As an independent word, # would always be read "big," as it would in the combination # + "-er," # + "-est," # + "-hearted," # + "-wig," and # + "-mouth"; but # + "-animous" would be read "magnanimous," # + "-fy" "magnify," # + "-ate" "magnate," and # + "-um" "magnum." The items added to # in the preceding examples would be written in *kana* (in the case of units like "-er," "-est," "-ed," etc.); but "-heart," "-mouth," "animous" would be written with other *kanji*, each of which would also have multiple readings, thereby requiring a decision as to which one of those the context requires. A further complication of the writing system in general is the fact that no spaces divide words or mark any linguistic division within a clause or sentence. In fact, there is no word in Japanese that corresponds exactly with "word" in English; the concept, as Americans know it, is missing. Needless to say, preknowledge of the language prior to reading—a skill regularly acquired by native speakers of every language before beginning to learn to read—is a tremendous asset.

The Cultural Code

However, all these complexities of the Japanese language and of its writing system are features of the linguistic code. It is even more difficult for the American learner to understand the acquired cultural matrix within which the Japanese language is used and to handle with accuracy the sociopragmatics. Unquestionably the most difficult feature is the choice of appropriate politeness and distancing forms, determined by context. In Japanese there are no stylistically neutral utterances, spoken or written. There is no neutral equivalent of an English statement like "I am studying French." Depending on who is addressing whom, third person(s) present, occasion, general topic of conversation—the salient features of context are many—the Japanese equivalent takes on very different forms. An important determinant, particularly difficult for a foreigner, is the identification of ingroup/outgroup distinctions in a given setting. When A talks to B in reference to C, A may use an honorific form or a humble form or a plain form, depending on the hierarchical relationship among A, B, and C. Another factor that must be considered is the degree of closeness between A and B. All these features are represented overtly in Japanese in terms of roots, prefixes, and infixes, as well as by choice of vocabulary in general, and they depend on a classification of society that is foreign to Americans.

Consider, as another example of "foreignness," the use of the imperative mode. Forms that express direct commands are in conflict with the Japanese avoidance of direct confrontation, a frequently cited characteristic of the society. The language does indeed have an imperative form, but its use is severely constrained as to the contexts in which it occurs: direct imperatives of most verbs are characteristic of markedly abrupt, aggressive, blunt style, unless embedded as indirect quotations. The only really commonly occurring imperatives are of verbs of giving, which can be used in combination with another verb or verb derivative that expresses the action to be performed. Thus the direct English "Come in!," which has no inherent connotation of abruptness, has as one type of Japanese equivalent a sequence meaning literally "Give me entering!" Predictably there are multiple verbs expressing the act of giving, differentiating the direction of the act (toward or away from the giver/ingroup and upward toward a superior, downward toward an inferior, or level toward one of similar rank). By expressing the directive in terms of something *given* to the speaker—particularly if a polite verb of giving is selected—the stigma of the command is counteracted. Of course, request forms that avoid the use of imperatives entirely are even more common in Japanese. There are in all about thirty different patterns for asking an addressee to perform a particular action, distinguished by level of politeness and degree of distancing, but the actual contextual occurrence of these differing patterns is a question of sociopragmatics.

However, in countless situations, no request form at all, much less a command, turns up in contexts in which an imperative is the English norm. 'Reduce speed!' 'Stop!' 'Yield!' 'Keep left!' order typical American traffic signs. In Japan, a feeling of togetherness is promoted by the suggestion, 'Let's drive slowly.' From the Japanese point of view, 'Drink Coca Cola!' is hardly conducive to increased consumption; 'Let's drink Coca Cola' does the job better. 'Let's turn off our stoves when we leave our apartments' is the warning in the elevator of a Tokyo apartment house. Examples are everywhere.

Some requests are even more indirect: Play over here! is the directive an American mother might give to her child. From the Japanese mother, we might hear a conditional verb with question intonation: (literally) If there were playing here? This strange English equivalent without any direct reference to the addressee matches the Japanese, which would normally include an addressee referent only if it were occurring in a pattern of contrast ("you" in contrast with someone else) or exclusivity ("you" as the indicator of who was to do the playing). The comparative infrequency with which speaker and addressee referents occur in Japanese contrasts with the multiplicity of possibilities. There is a long list of equivalents for "I" and "you," differentiated once again by contextual relationships. It is as if the identity of the ego and the addressee changed, depending on the conversation partners and the occasion.

What feature of acquired culture, then, accounts for the marked infrequency of the occurrence of these words, compared to the use of their closest equivalents in English? Japanese society consists of interacting groups, the makeup of which is constantly shifting depending on the relationships of those involved in any given situation. There is a constant division into ingroup and outgroup. An individual is ingroup with fellow employees when speaking with employees of another company (the outgroup), but fellow employees become the outgroup when speaking with members of one's family (the ingroup). The ego is probably best viewed as the minimal ingroup. Contrast this "groupiness" with the individualism stressed in American society, reflected in the constant use of "I," "me," "my," "mine," and "you," "your." The unmarked Japanese equivalent of an English exchange like 'Do you understand? . . . No, I don't' includes no overt mention of the addressee or speaker. It is as if the question referred simply to an occurrence of understanding, with the addressee expected to determine any referent intended by the speaker through context. To claim that a *particular* linguistic item has been deleted or is understood in this kind of exchange is to give evidence of the workings of an English-based acquired culture. This can only be an obstacle to the analysis and understanding of a foreign language, particularly one as "truly foreign" as Japanese.

THE NATIVE SPEAKER/CULTURAL
NATIVE INSTRUCTOR

What many see as the best pedagogical solution for handling these difficulties generated by a different linguistic code and a different acquired culture is to engage a native speaker/cultural native instructor, born, raised, and educated in Japan, who will be able to impart not only linguistic guidance—how to construct grammatically accurate Japanese and how to read and write—but also the main features of Japanese acquired culture, specifically in terms of its reflection in the language. The potential benefit of native speakers as models of a target language has long been recognized, but what about their value as models of their acquired culture?

THE PARADOX OF THE JAPANESE
LANGUAGE CLASSROOM

We now confront a double Japanese paradox. Acquired culture is the deeply embedded mindset acquired by cultural natives outside of awareness. That mindset determines our everyday normal behavior, often mistakenly assumed by us to be normal *human* behavior. Contact with other cultures may lead to culture shock, and when there is a serious clash, a common reaction is anger, resentment, or confusion, with the blame placed on what is foreign. But some more subtle differences are not noticed by one side or the other or identified as intercultural mismatches. Do Japanese know their stereotypical image among Americans, and do Americans know how they appear to Japanese? One thing is clear: the identification and analysis of differences in acquired culture, particularly in terms of their interrelation with sociopragmatics, require specialized training and knowledge. Target language native instructors trained only as classroom technicians are not equipped to analyze their own behavior and values beyond the level of casual observation. Thus cultural natives, serving as cultural models, are often unaware of the behavioral features they are modeling. Clearly such individuals must not be assumed to be cultural analysts unless they are academically trained.

This brings us to the second portion of the paradox. Do instructors who are natives of the target language/culture in fact serve as recognizable models of their acquired culture? Is classroom interaction between native instructors and learners sufficient to introduce learners to the target acquired culture?

Unfortunately learners often forget that, while they may indeed be observing a manifestation of that culture, they are more specifically in contact with the target acquired culture of the foreign language classroom, with all the special features that influence that environment. It is not an exaggeration to say that many features of the acquired culture of the Japanese classroom are in direct conflict with the practices of recommended American foreign language instruction. What works well for the Japanese learner may not always be as successful for Americans.

Traditionally, the Japanese have identified with their language to a degree that amazes foreigners. To be Japanese means that one knows Japanese, and to know Japanese is to be Japanese. The recent influx of Americans with varying levels of Japanese language competence is having some effect on the second part of that conviction, but it is significant that praise for foreigners' competence in Japanese tends to be in inverse proportion to the actual level of proficiency: the stumbling beginner is warmly flattered but the minor errors made by a highly competent foreigner are often noted in detail.

Japanese/American Contrasts in the Classroom

Native Japanese who become instructors in already established language programs in the United States typically adjust in accordance with whatever procedures have been established. But when the new, inexperienced instructor acts independently, we are apt to find a very different approach. Learner-centered instruction is not a feature of the Japanese education system, for the teacher is supreme in the classroom. In the foreign language setting, decisions as to what will be taught and the methodology that will be used are made on the basis of the Japanese teacher's own background—totally different from that of the American students. Misunderstandings often arise when these teachers interact with their American students, many of whom seem lacking in commitment and seriousness. Particularly at the high school level, when Japanese students are obsessed with competing for admission to prestigious colleges, commitment to one's studies is all-important in Japan. The presence in some American high schools of casual, "laid back" students who resist any out-of-class assignments is baffling. And in this context, imagine the reaction of Japanese instructors to the American system of student evaluation, used in many academic situations. It is not only unpleasant; it is incomprehensible.

The background of native Japanese instructors reminds them that their class time relating to the Japanese language was devoted to written Japanese, not the spoken language. Even in American high schools, where most students study Japanese for two years at the most, sometimes with no plans to continue later, the emphasis tends to be on reading and writing. What is forgotten or ignored is the fact that students coming out of such programs will not be able to read any authentic materials beyond loanwords adapted from English and some advertisements, no matter what percentage of the program is devoted to reading. American students in foreign language classes like to learn to speak the language, a classroom activity unusual for many Japanese students of foreign languages. An American student's plea, overheard recently in a Japanese language class, that the group be taught to *speak* Japanese, elicited the surprised instructor's reply, "Speak!? You don't even know how to read!" Recall that the native speaker of Japanese is still learning basic *kanji* throughout *twelve years* of precollege education. An approach to pedagogy that asks that Japanese teachers recognize the special goals of foreigners who are studying Japanese as a foreign language and the special methodology that is accordingly required in pursuing those goals has not been a feature of Japanese attitudes toward their language and its instruction.

American learners usually assume that they are being taught authentic Japanese, provided their instructor is a native speaker of Japanese. But the Japanese mindset, on the basis of its belief that true mastery of a language as unique as Japanese is impossible for Americans, favors Japanese that has been adjusted to resemble English. I am reminded of a textbook attributed to a group of Japan's pretigious linguistic scholars in which countless examples in the introductory lessons begin with *watakusi,* the polite equivalent of English "I." The emphasis is on adjusting Japanese in the interest of making it more like English and therefore easier for the American learner. The assumption that true mastery of one's native language is impossible for foreigners is, of course, not limited to the Japanese. What is of special interest to us is their reactive behavior.

Exerting a strong influence is the underlying requirement for comparatively greater politeness to—and consideration for—the outgroup, to which foreigners as a category belong, combined with the widespread layman's conviction that Japanese cannot really be analyzed in foreigners' terms. This leads to grammatical explanations that are no more than context-dependent translations into English, adjustment of the language itself to make it more like English, and a reluctance to correct the foreign learner. Countless Americans in the United States and Japan begin most of their utterances with an equivalent for "I" without the slightest notion of how that word is actually used. Desiderative adjectives derived from verbs, equivalent in their basic form to English "want to X," "would like to X," occur in the speech of many Americans in contexts appropriate to English only, but are not corrected. American-style Japanese may soon become a special dialect of the language, best understood and tolerated by those Japanese who have taught their language to Americans, and after extended exposure to it, have begun to adopt features of it as their own.

The question of stylistic levels, relevant to every Japanese utterance, is often avoided by teaching just one level, as if it were neutral, with only rare excursions into others as if only they were linguistically marked. The danger of such an approach is obvious: this crucially important feature of the language, so revealing of the acquired culture of the Japanese, is insufficiently analyzed and woefully misunderstood by the foreign student.

A JAPANESE DIALECT FOR FOREIGNERS

The ultimate in distorted-for-foreigners Japanese came, several years ago, in the form of a special dialect, *kanyaku nihongo,* developed at the prestigious Japanese National Language Research Institute, to be taught to foreigners studying Japanese. Surprisingly the director of the institute and the principal advocate of the dialect defended its creation and use in an article in which he supported the study of a foreign language as the best way to learn its culture—how its speakers think and act and interact (Nomoto 1989). The most striking characteristic of the new dialect is its constant use of a single stylistic form even in contexts in which such forms do not ever occur in the authentic use of the language. How can one learn anything of the culture from language that has been stripped of the feature that is most revealing of the culture? This dialect offers only the derived benefit that comes from consideration of why it was created. It should be pointed out that quite a linguistic furor arose in Japan; language teachers in particular resented having to learn a new dialect of their own language that made use of abnormal speech patterns.

THE IMPORTANCE OF HIERARCHY

The importance of hierarchy is everywhere apparent in Japanese society, but its relevance to the classroom is not always identified. It is this feature that accounts for the lack of learner-centered instruction and the opposition to the evaluation of teachers by students. It also exerts a strong influence on the workings of a staff. A young, extremely well-trained, competent instructor, hired to improve a program staffed by older, less-well-trained staff members, can hope to effect little change in this setting, even if assigned a supervisory position. And there are still those Japanese male instructors who resist supervision by Japanese women, regardless of their credentials.

THE INGROUP/OUTGROUP DICHOTOMY

The ingroup/outgroup dichotomy is exemplified by the class situation in that all foreign learners form an outgroup of Japanese society as a whole, while native Japanese instructors are members of the ingroup. However, there are times when the two will come together as an ingroup vis-à-vis a different outgroup (for example, members of Japanese programs from another institution). Language practice reflecting such changing relationships should be emphasized, but their importance is usually overlooked in the classroom. All too often the native Japanese instructor, who has acquired competence in this complex feature of Japanese without any conscious effort, assumes it cannot be analyzed or explained in terms that will produce competence in a foreign language.

The numerous features of the culture of the classroom tend to go unexplained, overlooked, or avoided by target native instructors and unnoticed or misinterpreted by the learners. But recognition and understanding of an acquired culture, in all its facets, are required for effective interaction with a target society and for reading and writing with perception.

If situations that call for complaining, criticizing, disagreeing, complimenting, or joking in American settings are handled by learners of Japanese on the basis of translation of the English that is appropriate, the learners are doing little to achieve accurate intercultural communication. They will find out that Japanese acquired culture is different, it is hoped, before too much damage is done. Did an American student compliment a senior professor on his lecture? This violates the principles of hierarchy by suggesting that a subordinate is in a position to judge a senior or that the latter's lectures might be anything but good in the eyes of a student. Did an American complain directly to the person in question? This constitutes confrontation, which should be avoided by the use of a go-between in order to prevent the breakdown of smooth relations between the principal participants. Did an American engage in direct criticism without including a face-saving feature for the person being criticized? Again this means confrontation, with the added problem of causing loss of face. Did an American openly and categorically disagree with a Japanese, allowing for no medial, neutral area? This suggests the necessity to dichotomize between a right and a wrong, which in turn leads to loss of face for someone.

Cross-Cultural Resemblances with Different Meanings

Another pitfall derives from the fact that, in some situations, the two cultures give rise to similar behavior and parallel language use that is seriously misinterpreted when its meaning in one is applied as its meaning in the other. When engaged in conversation, the honest, upright American is expected to look the addressee straight in the eye. Avoidance of direct eye contact is regarded as a sign of shiftiness, but for the Japanese, casting one's eyes downward and looking away from the addressee are signs of humility and politeness. A linguistic example is furnished by the American mother complaining about the scholastic performance of her child (she means it) and the Japanese mother expressing similar concerns (she is being modest about a child who is excelling). In other words, the meaning of patterns of behavior and language is culture-specific, and when two societies are as divergent as Japan and the United States, the possibilities for misunderstanding are legion.

High-Context and Low-Context Cultures

Edward Hall (1983) has described Japanese culture as high context, one in which the context exerts strong influence on behavior including language. The United States, on the other hand, is low context, with stress on individualism—individualistic behavior including language usage and individualistic decision making. There is much in both societies that contradicts these generalizations, but there is no question of the contrasting emphases. The clash is ironically exemplified by the number of American students of Japanese who, in order to "be different" and not conform to the usual in American foreign language study, have elected to study the language of a society that stresses conformity and requires linguistic and behavioral "knuckling under."

BILINGUALISM AND BICULTURALISM

In the light of such major differences between Japanese and American society—cultural including linguistic—are bilingualism and biculturalism possible? Bilingualism, even if it is interpreted according to its strictest definition (i.e., proficiency in two languages that is equivalent to that of a monolingual native speaker of each language) is undoubtedly achievable. Individuals who have been raised in households where two languages are used natively and who have extensive experience, starting in early childhood, living and attending schools in the societies where each language is native, have been able to acquire two spoken languages and learn two writing systems to the level of a native speaker.

Japanese/American biculturalism is another matter. There is no question that there are individuals able to function smoothly in both societies, but if biculturalism is defined as the equivalent of two types of monoculturalism, it becomes impossible. When confronting a situation to which the reactions are exactly opposite in American and Japanese society, the attitude toward a type of behavior is inevitably reflected in actual behavior. True monoculturals, when interacting with members of the foreign culture, are called on repeatedly to play roles that conflict with the dictates of their native acquired culture and that, in some cases, they find annoying or strange or repugnant or amusing. Sometimes they cannot bring themselves to make a particular cultural adjustment. But there are those who, through upbringing during their early socialization or long experience in the foreign culture, function relatively effortlessly and nonjudgmentally in both societies without conscious role-playing, but who nonetheless, in the eyes of a monocultural, on occasion exhibit dominant cultural characteristics stemming from the other culture. I prefer to call such individuals "interculturals," to indicate that they are not double monoculturals in the sense in which bilinguals are double monolinguals.

CONCLUSION

The mainstreaming of a "truly foreign" language, particularly one as different from English as Japanese, indicates expanding horizons on the foreign language front. But as long as the true nature of the language and its differences are avoided, and as long as instructors attempt to force it into categories familiar to the learners, it will never be truly understood. And while it is said that to know another language is to know another culture, that knowledge will be distorted if the language is distorted. What then becomes significant is only the analysis of the distortion itself.

The degree to which we are influenced by our acquired culture goes unrecognized. Consider, for example, the case of the recent interest in the connection between gender-related language and power. A direct connection apparently obtains in many languages, but for Japanese, the link becomes more questionable. Wetzel (1990) has pointed out that descriptions of Japanese speech in general coincide remarkably with descriptions of female speech in English, regularly described as lacking power. To move from this discovery to the conclusion that all Japanese speech is powerless depends on the mistaken assumption that "power" in English can be closely matched with a parallel concept in Japanese. Actually, as Wetzel points out, "powerful speech" and "powerless speech" in the American sense seem to be totally lacking in Japanese.

Significantly all the comments made in this study, including the emphasis on learner-centered instruction, are manifestations of an American mindset. Unquestionably foreign language pedagogy that is most effective and efficient develops in its students competence in authentic foreign language through methodology that is compatible with *their* native mindset. Unfortunately there is no neutral culture or logic that can serve as a basis for comparison of all acquired cultures. Thus the challenge is not only to identify the features of a particular foreign acquired culture but also to recognize the ever-present cultural biases and assumptions that stem from one's own, through which everything foreign is inevitably filtered.

Kore de owarasete itadakimasu. "Being this, in an already realized state (as of the realization of what is expressed in what follows), the ingroup does or will accept in a politely humble way the causation of closure." In other words, as an American would say, "At this point I'll close."

REFERENCES

Hall, E. T. 1983. *The Dance of Life: The Other Dimension of Time.* Garden City, N.Y.: Anchor Doubleday.

Nomoto, K. 1989. "Simplified Japanese for Language Education." *Japan Echo.* Special Issue 16: 55–57.

Wetzel, P. J. 1990. "Are 'Powerless' Communication Strategies the Japanese Norm?" *Aspects of Japanese Women's Language.* Eds. I. Sachiko and N. Hanaoka McGloin. Tokyo: Kurosio. 117–28.

Section IV

Shaping Contexts of Learning

— Chapter *12* ——————

The Classroom Context: An Acquisition-Rich or an Acquisition-Poor Environment?

Rod Ellis

Temple University, Japan

INTRODUCTION

During the last thirty or so years we have seen a major change in how we approach foreign language pedagogy. The starting point, which once was "What does the target language consist of and how do I teach it?" has become "How do learners acquire a second language and what do I have to do to facilitate it?" As Corder (1976) put it:

> Efficient foreign language teaching must work with rather than against natural processes, facilitate rather than impede learning. Teachers and teaching materials must adapt to the learner rather than vice-versa.

This change in perspective has led to researchers seeing the classroom not so much as a place where the language is taught but as one where opportunities for learning of various kinds are provided through the interactions that take place between the participants. One of the key questions has become "What kinds of interaction promote L2 learning?" In this paper, I want to consider research that has examined a number of interactional features of language classrooms that bear on this question. I also want to examine critically the assumption that underlies much of this research, namely that acquisition is best promoted by providing opportunities for authentic communication, and to give some consideration to the role formal instruction plays in helping to create an acquisition-rich classroom.

CLASSROOM VERSUS
NATURALISTIC DISCOURSE

Much of the research that has taken place has been motivated by the assumption that classroom second language acquisition will be most successful if the environment conditions found in naturalistic acquisition prevail. According to this view, all that is needed to create an acquisition-rich environment is to stop interfering in the learning process (Newmark 1966) and to create opportunities for learners to engage in interactions of the kind experienced by children acquiring their L1 or by child and adult learners acquiring an L2 naturalistically.

It is common to emphasize the differences that exist between pedagogic and naturalistic discourse. A good example of this is to be found in work on turntaking. In ordinary conversations in English, turntaking is characterized by self-regulated competition and initiative (Sacks, Schegloff, and Jefferson 1974), whereas in classroom discourse there is frequently a rigid allocation of turns. Who speaks to whom at what time about what topics is subject to strict control with the result that competition and individual learner initiative are discouraged. Lörscher (1986), for instance, found that English lessons involving learners aged between eleven and eighteen in different types of German schools involved little opportunity for the negotiation of openings and closings. Turns were allocated by the teacher, the right to speak always returned to the teacher when a student turn was completed, and the teacher had the right to stop and interrupt a student turn. These characteristics, Lörscher argues, are determined by the nature of the school as a public institution and by the teaching-learning process.

In general, the differences between pedagogic and naturalistic discourse are viewed negatively. Riley (1977), for instance, speaks of the "falsification of behaviour" and "distortion" that occur in pedagogic discourse. Pedagogic discourse is seen as constituting an acquisition-poor environment.

We need to examine such a conclusion critically, however. First, there is evidence to suggest that classroom discourse is not invariably different from naturalistic discourse. Van Lier (1988), for instance, reports that in the lessons he examined learners frequently do self-select and that "schismatic talk" (i.e., talk that deviates from some predetermined plan) occurs quite often. Faerch (1985) gives examples in classroom data of the same kind of vertical structures that have been reported in conversations with beginner learners in naturalistic settings. Mitchell (1988) provides evidence to show that classrooms can provide opportunities for real communication—as, for instance, when the L2 serves as the medium for classroom organization. Classroom interaction is probably best viewed as a continuum, reflecting at one pole instructional discourse and at the other natural discourse (cf. Kramsch 1985). The kind of discourse that arises will depend on the nature of the roles adopted by the teacher and learners, the teaching-learning tasks employed, and whether the knowledge focus is on content and accuracy or on process and fluency.

Second, we need to consider the theoretical grounds for the claim that naturalistic discourse is necessary for an acquisition-rich environment. On what basis can we claim that having L2 learners communicate in a natural manner constitutes the most efficient way of promoting L2 acquisition? This is the central question, for we need to be certain that the kind of pedagogic discourse that results from traditional language teaching is not as restrictive as has been claimed. We will begin, then, by examining a number of features of classroom discourse that have attracted the attention of researchers on the grounds that they constitute the key to the relationship between communication and acquisition.

INTERACTION IN THE L2 CLASSROOM AND L2 ACQUISITION

Simplified Input

The language that teachers address to language learners is often simplified. Furthermore, the degree of simplification that takes place relates to the learners' level of proficiency. Chaudron (1988), in a review of studies examining the rate of teachers' speech, concluded that "the absolute values of speech to beginning learners are around 100 w.p.m.," while intermediate and advanced learners receive speech that is 30–40 w.p.m. faster. Henzl (1979) and Kleifgen (1985), among others, found evidence of lexical simplifications, with lower type-token ratios with less proficient learners. Gaies (1977) and Hakansson (1986) have found marked differences in the syntactic complexity of speech that teachers address to learners as opposed to native speakers, although other researchers (e.g., Wesche and Ready 1985) have failed to find any difference. In some instances, although rarely, teacher-talk can result in ungrammatical input (cf. Hatch, Shapira, and Gough 1978).

Teachers, it seems, do much the same as the caretakers of young children. Their speech is characteristically well formed and they ensure that the general level of their language is tuned to their learners' level. There is, however, no clear evidence that these formal adjustments promote language acquisition. No studies of L2 acquisition have directly addressed the effect of simplified input on learning. L1 acquisition studies (e.g., Wells 1985) report that all children get simplified input so the presence or absence of such input does not account for differences in the rate of acquisition by children.

It does not follow, however, that simplified input is unimportant. Indeed, it is almost certainly crucial in helping learners to segment the speech flow into phonological and grammatical units. Schmidt (1990) has argued that acquisition depends on learners being able to "notice" linguistic features in the input. Access to simplified input may in fact be a necessary condition for "noticing" to take place. As anyone who has tried to learn a language knows, acquisition depends on the ability to identify words and phrases, and this is almost impossible in the early stages if the only source of input is "authentic" native-speaker speech—one reason why listening to the radio or watching television is of little use in the early stages.

Teachers, then, need to simplify their speech but they do not need to be aware of the precise state of their students' L2 knowledge or to have an exact idea of gradations in linguistic complexity. All that is required is an intuitive feel for what makes input simple or complex for a given group of learners. Many teachers have an intuitive ability to simplify their speech, aiming perhaps at some hypothetical learner (Hakansson 1986). They are able to establish a "threshold level" by means of "rough tuning" and so ensure that the majority of their learners receive input which they can process. Both Wong Fillmore (1985) and Kleifgen (1985) characterize the expert teacher as one who is able to adjust her language in accordance with the feedback supplied by learners. But there are some teachers who, in my experience, do not possess this ability (or, alternatively, do not act on it) and whose input, as a result, is often pitched at an inappropriate level.

Interactional Modifications

The interactional hypothesis, as propounded by Long (1983), states that:

1. interactional modifications that are directed at solving a communication difficulty help to make input comprehensible, and

2. comprehensible input promotes acquisition.

According to the interactional hypothesis, an acquisition-rich environment is one that is characterized by high frequencies of such interpersonal functions as clarification requests, confirmation checks, comprehension checks, and self- and other-repetitions. These constitute the overt signs of attempts to negotiate meaning. Long hypothesizes that interactional modifications are much more important than input modifications of the kind examined in studies of teacher-talk.

There is some support for the first part of the hypothesis. Pica, Young, and Doughty (1987), for instance, compared the effects of premodified input in instructions with those of interactionally modified input that arose in two-way exchanges during similar instructions with no premodified input. They found that interactional modifications assisted comprehension, whereas the reduction of linguistic complexity in the premodified input had no such effect.

There is, however, very little evidence to support the second part of the interactional hypothesis. I know of only one attempt to demonstrate that classroom discourse rich in interactional modifications results in accelerated L2 acquisition. Loschky (1989) studied the effects of premodified input (involving input modifications) and negotiated interaction (involving conversational modifications) on the acquisition of locative patterns by beginner learners of L2 Japanese. Loschky found that the group that experienced opportunities to negotiate meaning did better in comprehension of test sentences containing the locative patterns, but that there was no evidence of improved retention of the grammatical structure. In other words, Loschky's study provides support for the claim that negotiated interaction facilitates comprehension but *not* for the claim that it promotes acquisition.

The interactional hypothesis, despite the very limited empirical support it has received, has motivated a number of classroom studies. Pica and Long (1986) compared the frequency of the kind of conversational adjustments involved in the negotiation of meaning in noninstructional and ESL classroom conversations and found significant differences. Confirmation checks and clarification requests were much more frequent in noninstructional conversation, while comprehension checks were more frequent in the ESL classroom. They concluded that overall the amount of negotiation of meaning that occurs in the classroom setting is much smaller. Other studies have examined the effects of task type on the amount of modified interaction (e.g., Duff 1986) and differences in the amount of negotiated interaction found in teacher-class lessons as opposed to small groups (e.g., Doughty and Pica 1986). These studies have sought to identify the conditions under which maximum conversational modifications will occur.

The interactional hypothesis as currently stated, however, may be of limited value. First, there seems to be no clear empirical basis for the claim that negotiated interaction results in acquisition. Second, the theoretical rationale is of doubtful validity. Sato (1986), for instance, points out that conversational modifications may facilitate communicative performance without facilitating the acquisition of new linguistic features. Loschky comes to a similar conclusion, citing Sharwood-Smith's (1986) claim that the processes of using input for comprehension are different from those involved in using input for acquisition. Third, the categories used to measure modified interaction may be far less watertight than the existing literature leads us to believe. Kitazawa (1990) attempted to replicate Doughty and Pica's study of interaction in small group work with conversations in L2 Japanese but found their classification system "difficult and sometimes impossible to use." The faith that has been placed in the identification of such a limited set of interactional features, on the grounds that these hold the secret to an acquisition-rich environment, seems unwarranted and, in retrospect, perhaps even a little naive. It would be wrong to conclude, however, that interaction is not of central importance for acquisition. Brown (1968: 287) is surely right when he comments:

> It may be as difficult to derive a grammar from unconnected sentences as it would be to derive the invariance of quantity and number from the simple look of liquids in containers and objects in space. The changes produced by pouring back and forth, by gathering together and spreading apart, are the data that most strongly suggest the conservation of number and quantity.

We need to develop the tools to measure the "pouring back and forth" and the "gathering together and spreading apart" that take place in interaction. It is doubtful whether the categories of modified interaction that Long and Pica have proposed achieve this. Far more promising is the kind of qualitative analysis that Bygate (1988) has undertaken. Bygate shows how oral communication in group work involves the learners in "accessing chunks, constituting them correctly, combining them and modifying them efficiently" (1988: 65). His work shows how learners manipulate discourse, using it to negotiate their way to the construction of full clauses. Recent work undertaken by Pica and associates (cf. Pica, this volume) is also promising in that it attempts to show how particular kinds of interaction help to make semantic and structural relationships in the L2 more transparent and, therefore, more noticeable to the learner.

Teachers' Questions

Teachers—and, in particular, language teachers—ask large numbers of questions. There would appear to be two reasons for this. First, questions require responses and, therefore, they serve as a means of obliging learners to contribute to the interaction. Learners' responses also provide the teacher with feedback that can be used to adjust content and expression in subsequent teacher-talk. Second, questions serve as a device for controlling the progress of the interaction through which a lesson is enacted. It is for this reason that many teacher questions are of the display variety (i.e., designed to test and, therefore, having predetermined answers) rather than of the referential kind (i.e., truly information seeking and, therefore, permitting "open" answers).

In language lessons where the focus is on form, display questions are likely to predominate. Long and Sato (1983), in a study of six ESL teachers, found that 79 percent of their questions were display and pointed out that this contrasts with the use of questions in naturalistic discourse, where referential questions predominate. In lessons using a content-based approach to teaching, display questions also predominate. Johnson (1990) found that 60 percent of the questions asked by three teachers in content classrooms were display. However, a careful study of the detailed results provided by both studies shows that there is considerable individual variation among teachers. Thus, in the Long and Sato study one teacher asked more referential than display questions, while in Johnson's study one teacher divided her questions more or less equally between referential and display. The teachers in these studies also varied greatly in the total number of questions they asked. Thus the predominance of display features is only a probable and not a necessary feature of language classrooms.

The general assumption underlying these studies of questioning behavior is that display questions are less likely to contribute to an acquisition-rich environment than are referential questions. There would appear to be a number of grounds for such an assumption. First, educational arguments can be advanced for encouraging a less transmission-oriented approach to teaching (Barnes 1976). Referential questions allow the learner more opportunity to take part in her own learning. Second, referential questions are more compatible with a focus on meaning exchange (as opposed to form), which has been hypothesized to be necessary for acquisition to take place (Krashen 1981). Third, referential questions are more likely to result in extended learner responses. Brock (1986) found that learners' responses to referential questions were significantly longer and more syntactically complex and also contained more connectives than their responses to display questions. It should be noted once again, though, that a causative relationship between referential questions and acquisition has not been demonstrated. It may be that teacher questions of any kind are not especially facilitative in that they are topic-controlling (see next section).

The questioning behavior of teachers has proven amenable to change through training. Long et al. (1984) and Brock (1986) have shown that teachers can be successfully trained to increase the number of referential questions they ask and that the effects of such training appear to last. A simpler way to ensure questions that contribute to a more "communicative" classroom environment, however, might be to have the learners ask the questions. Midorikawa (1990) found that when the responsibility for questioning was handed over to students, they invariably asked referential questions. When this occurs, the learner also achieves control of the topic.

Topic Control

The issue of topic control has attracted somewhat less attention from L2 classroom researchers than other issues. This is surprising given that it has been shown to be a significant factor in naturalistic acquisition. Wells (1985) contrasts the interactional styles of mothers who are "supportive"—that is, who allow their children the opportunity to both initiate and control topics—and those who are "tutorial"—that is, who control the discourse through the use of display questions and evaluative feedback. He argues that the supportive style results in faster L1 learning. Hatch (1978) also provides evidence to show that allowing L2 learners the opportunity to nominate topics provides an effective basis for building conversations.

One study that has examined the effects of topic control in L2 classrooms is that of Slimani (1989). This study is also unique in that it seeks to establish a direct relationship between aspects of classroom interaction and acquisition. The method that Slimani used involved requesting students to record on "uptake charts" any item that they thought they had learned from a lesson and then checking through transcriptions of the lesson to identify where the items they listed occurred. Slimani found that "whatever is topicalized by the learners rather than the teacher, has a better chance of being claimed to have been learnt." Also, learners appeared to benefit from topics nominated by other learners rather than from topics they themselves had initiated. This suggests that learners might benefit more from listening to exchanges in which other students are involved than in participating themselves.

Topic control may be important for L2 acquisition in several ways. It is very likely that learners will be more motivated to attend to input if they are involved in choosing and developing the topics that are talked about. Having control over the topic is also one way of ensuring that the linguistic complexity of the input is tailored to the learner's own level. Better opportunities for negotiating meaning when a communication problem arises are likely to occur. Topic control may also stimulate more extensive and more complex production on the part of the learners.

It is no easy task to give learners control over the topics of conversation in large classrooms, however. One reason for the predominance of the tutorial style in the classroom is the need to ensure that the interaction is orderly. Another reason may be the teacher's desire or need to cover the syllabus. In such large-group situations, which are much more common than those in which classes are small and teachers are free to devise their own curriculum, handing over topic control to the students may seem methodologically very difficult and even undesirable. One way of ensuring at least some opportunities for learner topic control is through small-group work.

Learner Participation

The role of learner participation in L2 acquisition is one of the more controversial issues. On the one hand there are those like Krashen (1985) who argue that "speaking is the result of acquisition, not its cause." On the other hand, a strong case has been made for learner output as a contributory factor to successful L2 acquisition. Swain (1985), for instance, has proposed the comprehensible output hypothesis as an addition rather than replacement for Krashen's input hypothesis. Swain argues that producing output that is precise, coherent, and appropriate encourages learners to develop the necessary grammatical resources; provides the learner with opportunities to test hypotheses; and may force the learner to move from the kind of semantic processing that is possible in reception to the syntactic processing required in production.

According to Swain, it is not just any kind of output that is needed but rather "pushed language use." Allen, Harley, and Swain (1989) provide evidence to suggest that even in immersion classrooms, which might be expected to foster pushed language use, there are in fact relatively few opportunities. Less than 15 percent of student turns in French immersion classrooms were "sustained" (i.e., more than a clause in length). It is likely that the opportunities for pushed language use are even rarer in more traditional language classrooms.

Once again, however, there is an absence of clear, direct evidence to show that learner participation is crucial for successful L2 acquisition. Ellis (1988) reviewed a number of studies that have investigated the relationship between learner participation and learning and showed that the results are very mixed. Some studies (e.g., Seliger 1977; Naiman et al. 1978) reported a positive correlation between measures of participation in class and learner proficiency, while others found no such relationship (e.g., Day 1984). Even in those studies reporting a positive relationship it is not possible to claim that participation *causes* learning, for it is quite possible that learners with higher proficiency elect or are nominated to participate more frequently than those with lower proficiency. In other words, an "acquisition-causes-participation" explanation is just as tenable if not more so than a "participation-causes-acquisition" explanation.

Other evidence is available to cast doubts on the value of learner participation. Slimani, in the study referred to above, found that listening to other learners was most strongly related to uptake. Reiss (1985) found that "silent speaking" (i.e., silently rehearsing answers to questions addressed to other learners) was one classroom strategy that good language learners used. Ellis and Rathbone (1987) found that some learners responded negatively when they were required to participate. Performing "in public" in the classroom can result in a high level of learner anxiety.

These studies, however, have examined participation in general, not "pushed language use." Thus, they do not address the comprehensible output hypothesis directly. Although they enable us to query the faith in learner production that underlies much language teaching, they do not provide a basis for rejecting learner participation as an important feature of an acquisition-rich classroom. It is likely that the relationship between learner participation and acquisition is a complex one depending on a host of factors to do with the personality of the learner, the learner's level of proficiency (participation may be much more important for more advanced learners than for beginners), whether the production is volunteered or requested, how sustained the production is, and to what extent learners need to express themselves precisely and coherently. The kind of participation needed to foster acquisition may be difficult to achieve in lockstep teaching. As Allen, Harley, and Swain (1989) suggest, the kind of talk needed may be best encouraged through small-group work.

Use of the L1

The extent to which the use of the L1 is desirable and the particular uses for which it is legitimate are issues of real importance to many foreign language teachers. Surprisingly, although there is no shortage of methodological advice, little research has addressed the use of the L1 and its effect on acquisition.

There is even a paucity of descriptive research on what use of the L1 teachers typically make. There are likely to be marked differences even in classrooms where the teacher knows the learners' L1. Kaneko (1990) found that in a classroom where both teacher and learners were Japanese, nearly 40 percent of the total speaking time was conducted in the L1, whereas in a similar classroom where the teacher was an American who spoke fluent Japanese, only 18 percent of the speaking time was in the learners' L1. The nature of the activity also affects what language is used. Thus, in Kaneko's study, the Japanese teacher was more likely to use English in interactions where there was an explicit pedagogic purpose than in interactions dealing with the organizational requirements of the lesson or in social interactions, where L1 Japanese predominated. In contrast, the American teacher used L2 English frequently in organizational and social interactions as well as pedagogic interactions. Mitchell (1988) found that teachers of elementary French in Scottish secondary schools also used the L2 in organizational instructions, but preferred the L1 when it came to giving instructions relating to the performance of a pedagogic activity.

When it comes to the relationship between L1 use and acquisition we know even less. Wong Fillmore (1985), in a study of classrooms in American schools containing children with limited proficiency in English, argues that a clear separation of languages is desirable. She comments: "In the bilingual classes that worked well for learning, the two languages of instruction were kept quite separate." Translation obviated the need for students to figure out what was being said. Also if teaching took place in both languages, the L2 version was unlikely to contain the necessary modifications to aid comprehension and the students tuned out. Kaneko examined the effects of language use on learner uptake (using Slimani's method of measuring this). She found that students reported learning L2 items that occurred in topic sequences conducted entirely or mainly in the L2 to a much greater extent than they did in topic sequences conducted mainly or entirely in the L1. This proved to be the case in the lessons conducted by both the Japanese and American teachers.

There is little information on which to base any firm conclusions regarding the use of the L1. Clearly learners learn from L2 input and if they have little of this, they will not learn much. Some methodologists (e.g., Prabhu 1987) have rejected extensive use of small-group work in monolingual classrooms on the grounds that the learners will communicate together using their shared L1 and the opportunities for uptake will be reduced. But there may be some legitimate uses of the L1—such as translating unknown lexical items or explaining grammar rules.

CONCLUSION

Hatch (1986) has characterized the task of applied linguistics as that of discovering the links between experience and learning. The problem is that we still know very little about the relationship between experience and acquisition—a point that Hatch herself acknowledges and that is clear from the research reviewed in the previous section.

We do know that learners—first and second—can acquire a language successfully without the benefit of formal instruction. L2 learners, both children and adults, are able to use the experiences provided by participating in face-to-face interaction with native speakers or other learners to build a knowledge structure of the L2. One way of creating an acquisition-rich environment in the classroom, therefore, is by replicating these natural learning experiences. As Hatch (1986: 20) has put it:

> For both the teacher and the teacher trainer, the task is to find those experiences that contribute most to learning and to work out ways to bring reasonable copies of those experiences, and the ways of dealing with them.

The following are some of the features which we examined in the previous section and which have been hypothesized important for creating the kind of naturalistic environment which is believed to contribute to successful language acquisition.

1. Teacher-talk is simplified to a level that makes it possible for the learners to process input for comprehension.

2. Classroom interaction provides opportunities for learners to observe the way utterances are constructed in the process of building discourse and to manipulate chunks of language in the expression of meaning content.

3. Referential questions that encourage learners to express their own content in their own way in extended responses are used.

4. Learners have opportunities to nominate their own topics and to control the development of these topics.

5. Learners are given opportunities to participate actively in the classroom communication but are not required to produce until they are ready to do so. Advanced learners may need opportunities for extended production.

6. The use of the L2 is not restricted to pedagogic functions but is also used for organizational and social functions.

It is probably true to say that most L2 classrooms do not manifest these characteristics and, therefore, might be said to constitute acquisition-poor environments. One reason for this is what Edmondson (1985: 162) has called "the teacher's paradox": "We seek in the classroom to teach people how to talk when they are not being taught." The paradox results in a tension between discourse appropriate to pedagogic goals and discourse appropriate to pedagogic settings. The classroom affords "coexisting discourse worlds," depending on whether the participants are engaged in trying to learn or trying to communicate. In many classrooms, pedagogic discourse is predominant.

The question we need to ask is whether classrooms that offer only pedagogic discourse constitute acquisition-poor environments. Clearly, if a strong "natural learning" position is adopted, the answer is yes. This is Krashen's position and, somewhat less clearly, also Long's. The thrust of their theoretical and empirical work and their advice to teachers is that classrooms should concentrate on creating the conditions needed for authentic communication to take place. However, if, like Edmondson, we take up a less absolutist position and accept that formal language instruction can contribute to learning, we will also have to accept that pedagogic discourse, even though it displays very different characteristics from those listed above, can provide experiences that contribute to learning.

There is sufficient evidence now available to refute a strong natural learning position (cf. Long [1988] and Ellis [1990] for detailed reviews of research that has investigated the effects of formal instruction on L2 acquisition). Although there are clear restrictions that govern whether formal instruction directed at a specific linguistic feature results in its acquisition, learners who receive formal instruction do appear to learn more rapidly and to develop higher levels of proficiency. Also, some adult naturalistic learners, such as the Japanese painter Wes whom Schmidt (1983) investigated, fail to develop much in the way of linguistic competence even though their overall communicative abilities develop considerably. One explanation Schmidt provides for this in Wes's case is that he did not receive any formal instruction. It would seem, therefore, that activities that require the learner to behave as a "learner" rather than as a "communicator" may be desirable.

An acquisition-rich classroom, therefore, is best characterized as one that provides both those experiences associated with communication in natural discourse and those experiences derived from cognitive activities designed to raise the learner's consciousness about the formal properties of the L2 and their function in language use (see Valdman, this volume). Spada (1987) in a comparative study of learner groups exposed to different types of instruction found that "attention to both form and meaning works best" and that both are required in the development of oral communication skills. This is, of course, nothing new. The need for some kind of mixture of opportunities for communicating and learning has long been recognized and is reflected in mainstream language pedagogy. There are still important questions to be answered, however. One concerns the nature of the relationship between the two discourse worlds that result from attempts at communicating and at learning. To what extent can these worlds be linked through activities that require the learner to transfer what has been studied formally into authentic language behavior? Are the worlds so incompatible that trying to integrate them is like mixing oil and water? What are the ideal proportions of the two types of discourse in an instructional program?

Finally, we need to acknowledge the difficulties that teachers in many parts of the world face in creating the conditions in which genuinely communicative experiences can occur in a classroom context. Creating an acquisition-rich communicative environment in the classroom represents a major challenge. It involves not only access to the methodological techniques of a communicative methodology but also, more crucially, the attitudes of both teacher and learners. In many teaching contexts, the target language continues to be viewed as an object to be studied rather than as a tool for communication. If the focus of attention in the last decade has been on how to create opportunities for communicative experiences in the classroom, this is surely because these have often been missing. Thus, even though we still know very little about how communication shapes acquisition, this focus is probably the right one, providing that it does not result in the exclusion of opportunities for formal learning.

REFERENCES

Allen, P., B. Harley, and M. Swain. 1989. "Analytic and Experiential Aspects of Second Language Teaching." *RELC Journal* 20: 1–19.

Barnes, D. 1976. *From Communication to Curriculum*. Harmondsworth, U.K.: Penguin.

Brock, C. 1986. "The Effects of Referential Questions on ESL Discourse." *TESOL Quarterly* 20: 47–59.

Brown, R. 1968. "The Development of WH Questions in Child Speech." *Journal of Verbal Learning and Behavior* 7: 279–90.

Bygate, M. 1988. "Units of Oral Expression and Language Learning in Small Group Interaction." *Applied Linguistics* 9: 59–82.

Chaudron, C. 1988. *Second Language Classrooms.* Cambridge: Cambridge UP.

Corder, P. 1976. "The Study of Interlanguage." *Proceedings of the Fourth International Conference of Applied Linguistics.* Munich: Hochschulverlag.

Day, R. 1984. "Student Participation in the ESL Classroom." *Language Learning* 34: 69–98.

———, ed. 1986. *Talking to Learn: Conversation in Second Language Acquisition.* Rowley, Mass.: Newbury.

Doughty, C., and T. Pica. 1986. "Information Gap Tasks: Do They Facilitate Second Language Acquisition?" *TESOL Quarterly* 7: 305–25.

Duff, P. 1986. "Another Look at Interlanguage Talk: Taking Task to Task." *Talking to Learn: Conversation in Second Language Acquisition.* Ed. R. Day. Rowley, Mass.: Newbury. 147–81.

Edmondson, W. 1985. "Discourse Worlds in the Classroom and in Foreign Language Learning." *Studies in Second Language Acquisition* 7: 159–68.

Ellis, R. 1988. "The Role of Practice in Classroom Language Learning." *Teanga* 8: 1–25.

———. 1990. *Instructed Second Language Acquisition.* Oxford: Basil Blackwell.

Ellis, R., and M. Rathbone. 1987. *The Acquisition of German in a Classroom Context.* London: Ealing Coll. of Higher Ed.

Faerch, C. 1985. "Metatalk in FL Classroom Discourse." *Studies in Second Language* ✓ *Acquisition* 7: 184–99.

Gaies, S. 1977. "The Nature of Linguistic Input in Formal Second Language Learning: Linguistic and Communicative Strategies." *On TESOL '77.* Eds. H. Brown, C. Yorio, and R. Crymes. Washington, D.C.: TESOL. 204–12.

Hakansson, G. 1986. "Quantitative Studies of Teacher Talk." *Learning, Teaching and Communication in the Foreign Language Classroom.* Ed. G. Kaspar. Aarhus: Aarhus UP.

Hatch, E. 1978. "Discourse Analysis and Second Language Acquisition." *Second Language Acquisition.* Ed. E. Hatch. Rowley, Mass.: Newbury. 401–35.

———. 1986. "The Experience Model and Language Teaching." *Talking to Learn: Conversation in Second Language Acquisition.* Ed. R. Day. Rowley, Mass.: Newbury. 5–22.

Hatch, E., R. Shapira, and J. Gough. 1978. " 'Foreigner-Talk' Discourse." *ITL Review of Applied Linguistics* 39/40: 39–59.

Henzl, V. 1979. "Foreign Talk in the Classroom." *IRAL* 17: 159–67.

Johnson, S. 1990. "Teacher Questions in the Academic Language-Content Classroom." Unpublished paper, Temple University, Japan.

Kaneko, T. 1990. "L1 Use in Foreign Language Classrooms." Unpublished paper, Temple University, Japan.

Kitazawa, M. 1990. "Is Pica and Doughty's System of Interaction Classification Applicable to a Japanese Language Classroom?" Unpublished paper, Temple University, Japan.

Kleifgen, J. 1985. "Skilled Variation in a Kindergarten Teacher's Use of Foreigner Talk." *Input in Second Language Acquisition.* Eds. S. Gass and C. Madden. Rowley, Mass.: Newbury. 59–68.

Kramsch, C. 1985. "Classroom Interaction and Discourse Options." *Studies in Second Language Acquisition* 7: 169–83. ✓

Krashen, S. 1981. *Second Language Acquisition and Second Language Learning.* Oxford: Pergamon.

———. 1985. *The Input Hypothesis.* London: Longman.

Long, M. 1983. "Native Speaker/Non-Native Speaker Conversation in the Second Language Classroom." *On TESOL '82: Pacific Perspectives on Language and Teaching.* Eds. M. Clarke and J. Handscombe. Washington, D.C.: TESOL. 339–54.

———. 1988. "Instructed Interlanguage Development." *Issues in Second Language Acquisition: Multiple Perspectives.* Ed. L. Beebe. Rowley, Mass.: Newbury. 115–41.

Long, M., C. Brock, G. Crookes, C. Deicke, L. Potter, and S. Zhang. 1984. *The Effect of Teachers' Questioning Patterns and Wait Time on Pupil Participation in a Public High School in Hawaii for Students of Limited English Proficiency.* Technical Report 1. Manoa: U of Hawaii P.

Long, M., and C. Sato. 1983. "Classroom Foreigner Talk Discourse: Forms and Functions of Teachers' Questions." *Classroom Oriented Research in Second Language Acquisition.* Eds. H. Seliger and M. Long. Rowley, Mass.: Newbury. 268–86.

Lörscher, W. 1986. "Conversational Structures in the Foreign Language Classroom." *Learning, Teaching and Communication in the Foreign Language Classroom.* Ed. G. Kasper. Aarhus: Aarhus UP. 11–22.

Loschky, L. 1989. "The Effect of Negotiated Interaction and Premodified Input on Second Language Comprehension and Retention." Master's thesis, University of Hawaii, Manoa.

Midorikawa, H. 1990. "The Effects of Questions on Japanese EFL Discourse." Unpublished paper, Temple University, Japan.

Mitchell, R. 1988. *Communicative Language Teaching in Practice.* London: Centre for Information on Language Teaching.

Naiman, N., M. Fröhlich, H. Stern, and A. Todesco. 1978. *The Good Language Learner.* Research in Education 7. Ontario: U of Ontario Inst. for Studies in Ed.

Newmark, L. 1966. "How Not to Interfere in Language Learning." *International Journal of American Linguistics* 32: 77–83.

Pica, T., and M. Long. 1986. "The Linguistic and Conversational Performance of Experienced and Inexperienced Teachers." *Talking to Learn: Conversation in Second Language Acquisition.* Ed. R. Day. Rowley, Mass.: Newbury. 85–98.

Pica, T., R. Young, and C. Doughty. 1987. "The Impact of Interaction on Comprehension." *TESOL Quarterly* 21: 737–58.

Prabhu, N. 1987. *Second Language Pedagogy.* Oxford: Oxford UP.

Reiss, M. 1985. "The Good Language Learner: Another Look." *Canadian Modern Language Review* 41: 511–23.

Riley, P. 1977. "Discourse Networks in Classroom Interaction: Some Problems in Communicative Language Teaching." *Melanges Pedagogiques.* Nancy: U of Nancy. 109–20.

Sacks, H., E. Schegloff, and G. Jefferson. 1974. "A Simplest Systematics for the Organization of Turn-Taking in Conversation." *Language* 50: 696–735.

Sato, C. 1986. "Conversation and Interlanguage Development: Rethinking the Connection." *Talking to Learn: Conversation in Second Language Acquisition.* Ed. R. Day. Rowley, Mass.: Newbury. 23–45.

Schmidt, R. 1983. "Interaction, Acculturation, and the Acquisition of Communicative Competence." *Sociolinguistics and Language Acquisition.* Eds. N. Wolfson and E. Judd. Rowley, Mass. 137–74.

———. 1990. "The Role of Consciousness in Second Language Learning." *Applied Linguistics* 11: 129–58.

Seliger, H. 1977. "Does Practice Make Perfect? A Study of Interaction Patterns and L2 Competence." *Language Learning* 27: 263–75.

Sharwood-Smith, M. 1986. "Comprehension vs. Acquisition: Two Ways of Processing Input." *Applied Linguistics* 7: 239–56.

Slimani, A. 1989. "The Role of Topicalization in Classroom Language Learning." *System* 17: 223–34.

Spada, N. 1987. "Relationships Between Instructional Differences and Learning Outcomes: A Process-Product Study of Communicative Language Teaching." *Applied Linguistics* 8: 137–55.

Swain, M. 1985. "Communicative Competence: Some Roles of Comprehensible Input and Comprehensible Output in Its Development." *Input in Second Language Acquisition.* Eds. S. Gass and C. Madden. Rowley, Mass.: Newbury. 235–53.

Van Lier, L. 1988. *The Classroom and the Language Learner.* London: Longman.

Wells, G. 1985. *Language Development in the Pre-School Years.* Cambridge: Cambridge UP.

Wesche, M., and D. Ready. 1985. "Foreigner Talk in the University Classroom." *Input in Second Language Acquisition.* Eds. S. Gass and C. Madden. Rowley, Mass.: Newbury. 89–114.

Wong Fillmore, L. 1985. "When Does Teacher Talk Work as Input?" *Input in Second Language Acquisition.* Eds. S. Gass and C. Madden. Rowley, Mass.: Newbury. 17–50.

— Chapter *13*

Getting Quality Input in the Second/Foreign Language Classroom

Patsy M. Lightbown

Concordia University, Montreal

For about twenty-five years, second language acquisition researchers have been accumulating evidence that second language acquisition proceeds in systematic ways and that characteristics of the input, and particularly formal instruction, have only a limited effect on the patterns of development. This research has challenged the assumption that syllabus and teacher and learners' efforts were the determining factors in the development of the target language. It was important to challenge this assumption. When I first became involved in the study of second language acquisition in classroom settings, the classes I observed were organized within a very strict audiolingual framework. Structures were presented one by one and practiced carefully until learners could perform nearly perfectly in classroom drill. Only when the class had mastered one structure did the teacher feel justified in going to the next. Longitudinal observations showed, however, that this apparent mastery was often misleading. Learners of English as a second language who appeared to have reached high levels of accuracy in their use of some structure or other would show declines in that accuracy when they ceased to practice the structure regularly or when they learned another related one. Learners also seemed to learn rules that did not correspond to the English language as it is spoken ordinarily, but rather to the pseudo-English to which they had been exposed in the classroom (Lightbown 1983, 1984).*

On the basis of that research (and that which others reported at about the same time), I argued that restricting learners to a limited diet of structure-by-structure teaching led to the development of knowledge that eventually had to be unlearned if the students were to move toward more native-like knowledge and use of English (Lightbown 1985). My argument was that second language acquisition is a process that is carried out largely without the learner's awareness. That is, in being exposed to comprehensible samples of the language, the learner (whether in a classroom or elsewhere) inevitably forms some idea of what the patterns of that language are. If the language to which the learner is exposed is not the real target language but a distorted and incomplete sample of sentences from it (inevitably the case in strictly audiolingual or grammar-translation approaches), the learners' developing knowledge of the language will reflect the inadequacy of the input. If learners are to develop a knowledge of the target language that accurately reflects the realities of that language, they must have opportunities to be exposed to the language in its authentic form.

The notion of "interlanguage"—a systematic, rule-governed, transitional linguistic competence developed by the learner in the presence of meaningful interaction and/or comprehensible input—is now well established (Corder 1967; Selinker 1972). Changes in second language pedagogy have, in fact, altered the kind of input available to learners. The advent of communicative language teaching has led to more student-student interaction in pair and group work, more task-based rather than structure-based language, more student-initiated talk and fewer teacher-centered activities, and above all, more focus on meaning than focus on form. Such an instructional approach is potentially far more motivating than the more traditional ones, and there is good evidence that students in these classes develop greater confidence in their ability to understand and use the target language (see, for example, Spada and Lightbown 1989).

In research that we are currently carrying out in communicative classrooms, however, the evidence is that students are still having difficulty getting "quality input" for second language acquisition. It may be argued that the notion of the learner's "built-in syllabus" has become too powerful and that the role of instruction has been diminished too much. This is probably much less true of university-level foreign language instruction contexts, but in other contexts, there has been a dramatic shift away from the assumption of teacher/syllabus control to an assumption that all that is necessary for second language acquisition to proceed is for learners to get "comprehensible input" (Krashen 1985) or to be involved in meaningful interaction (Long 1981).

In many second language classes, teachers show their conviction that their responsibility is to provide opportunities for interesting activities which will get students involved in using language. They have been convinced not only that it is not necessary to focus on formal aspects of the language but that it is in fact harmful for them to do so, that such behavior on their part will have a negative impact on learners' motivation and will potentially interfere with the unfolding of the natural sequences of development. If we look back at the extremes of form-focused instruction of previous approaches, we know that such effects were present in language teaching that was primarily form focused. However, it is my view that in classes based exclusively on an interpretation of communicative language teaching that excludes form-focused activity and error correction, learners will also have difficulty getting quality input. Through extensive student-student interaction, learners are exposed to input that is not a sample of the authentic target language, but of other learners' interlanguage. The problem is especially acute in classes where students share the same native language. The errors and inaccuracies students hear will reinforce their own misanalyses of the target language, creating a circle out of which it is difficult to escape. This may be partly because such interlanguage input will not tend to cause any breakdown in communication that might lead learners to adjust their language. Even when communication difficulties do arise, learners may not have the resources to enable them to get the correct information about the aspect of the language that has caused the breakdown.

In this paper, I will draw on a study of a comprehension-based program for ESL and on some recent experimental work in intensive, communicative ESL classes in suggesting two quite different ways to provide quality input in foreign language classrooms. Both these experimental programs are in French-speaking areas of Canada where students rarely hear English outside their second language instruction in school. These are contexts in which the objective is not native-like mastery of the target language, but a level of communicative facility and confidence that will enable learners to continue using and learning English on their own outside the classroom (through reading, television, personal contacts, further study) if they wish to do so.

COMPREHENSION-BASED ESL

In a few small-town and rural schools in northwestern New Brunswick, a radical experiment in second language teaching has been going on for about five years (Forsyth 1990: Lightbown, forthcoming). New Brunswick is the only officially bilingual province in Canada, but in these French-speaking areas of the province, both trained ESL teachers and native speakers of English are rare. Nevertheless, English is a required subject in school from grade three (when students are approximately eight years old), and parents and educators believe that English is an important part of the education of Canadian francophones.

The experimental program is based on a number of general pedagogical principles as well as some assumptions about second language acquisition: that comprehension, not practice, is the driving force in language development; that learning takes place best when learners are positively motivated and not stressed or threatened; and that students (even at age eight, nine, or ten) can be responsible in large measure for their own learning. The experimental program consists entirely of one half-hour a day during which students read and listen to cassette recordings of illustrated storybooks, songbooks, picture dictionaries, ESL textbooks, simple science books, biographies of famous people, and the like. Students work entirely on their own, reading the book(s) of their choice at the beginning of each class period, and sitting at individual tape recorders with earphones to listen to the tapes. They keep their own records of what they have read by checking off items in an individual log book. Apart from a general recommendation that students read a good number of the books in Menu 1 before proceeding to Menu 2, there is little structural grading. Materials in the twelve menus do tend to become progressively more difficult (particularly in the sense that the vocabulary size increases), but there is a great deal of variety within each menu.

During the experimental period of the project, while a formal evaluation was being carried out, there was no interaction with the teacher, no checking of comprehension by the teacher, no testing. The regular classroom teacher helped out if students had a problem with a tape recorder or could not find the material they were looking for. But the teacher's role was not that of a typical language teacher.

At the end of three years of participation in the experimental program, these children who had never practiced spoken English were able to understand written and spoken English as well as a comparison group that had been taught according to an interactive audiolingual program for the same amount of time per day (plus some homework outside that half-hour a day). Furthermore, they had developed a larger vocabulary and, the biggest surprise perhaps, they could speak English with greater fluency and accuracy than the audiolingual program students (Lightbown forthcoming).

Lest I seem here to be saying that language acquisition can be accomplished entirely without interaction, without feedback, without focused instruction, it must be recalled that both the experimental group and the audiolingual group were still at quite basic levels of English development. At the end of three years of instruction they would have accumulated a total of about 270 hours of exposure to English. Add to that the small amount of English they may get from television and it is clear that they are still early stage learners. Thus no claim is made for a comprehension-based program as a sufficient basis for reaching high levels of language mastery. No such hypothesis was tested. What is striking, however, is that in the samples of spoken language we collected, the experimental students were more capable of using some of the aspects of the English language than students whose instruction had emphasized oral practice. More research is certainly called for, but I believe it is at least a reasonable hypothesis that the experimental students' greater ability to produce, for example, the English plural marker, the progressive -ing marker, more elaborated noun phrases and longer sentences, comes from the students' greater exposure to quality input: listening to tapes of native speakers reading interesting texts and following the written versions of those texts.

INTENSIVE ESL: EXPERIMENTAL STUDIES

In another school-based second language acquisition context, we have been studying the development of English by francophone students in the province of Quebec. Ordinarily, students in Quebec elementary schools receive two hours a week of ESL instruction, beginning in grade four. However, a small number of school boards have begun to offer "intensive" ESL, that is, a one-time five-month program which may be offered in either grade five or grade six. In these programs, regular subject matter instruction (French, math, social science) is suspended and English is the only subject matter taught. In this sense, the intensive ESL programs are different from French immersion programs where French is used as the medium of subject matter instruction rather than as the declared subject of instruction itself. They are similar to French immersion, however, in the sense that all students share the same native language and the instructional model emphasizes language as a vehicle of communication rather than as the focus of instruction.

The instructional style that characterizes these intensive courses is based on the curriculum for ESL that was implemented by the Ministry of Education of Quebec for regular two-hour-a-week courses. The syllabus is principally notional-functional and the pedagogical approach is strictly "communicative." That is, the emphasis in the classroom is on creating meaningful activities in which students will have opportunities to interact with each other and with samples of authentic English (newspaper ads, menus, train schedules, etc.). There is little or no focus on language form in most of the classes, and teachers tend to be unusually dynamic and energetic. French, the students' shared first language, is rigidly excluded—at least until after the first week or two of the five-month program.

Findings from these programs have been very positive. Students develop very dramatically in their comprehension of English over the five-month period, and they also develop confidence in their ability to use English for communication in a variety of settings. Their oral production is fluent, marked by the liberal and unapologetic use of such communication strategies as gesture, circumlocution, and word coinage. Their ability to use English communicatively places them above the level of students five years older who have accumulated the same total number of hours of English, but over a much longer period of "drip-feed" (Spada and Lightbown 1989).

Students who participate in these intensive ESL courses rarely have an appropriate follow-up course. They usually return to the "regular" stream with students who have not had any special English program. Nevertheless, there is evidence that the level of English they have acquired in the intensive course enables them to keep on learning on their own. Contrary to what one might have predicted on the basis of previous experiments in early second language instruction (for example, Burstall et al. 1974), students' ability to use English five years later is better than that of students just completing the intensive program (they have continued to learn), and their performance is superior to that of students who have never had the intensive experience (the regular students don't "catch up") (Lightbown and Spada 1989).

Even though students speak fluently and confidently, however, their oral English is marked by numerous errors, errors common to virtually all students (Lightbown and Spada 1990). Research in French immersion settings has provided similar evidence from students who have had many more hours of exposure to their second language (Swain 1985). In these contexts, where learners share the same native language and are at similar levels of second language acquisition, they provide each other with the principal comprehensible input that drives the acquisition mechanism. Incorrect hypotheses about the target language find massive confirmation in the interlanguage-based speech of their classmates (see also White 1990; Wong Fillmore, this volume).

We have found, in a series of both observational and experimental studies, that when some focus on form is provided—within a communicative frame-work—students can realize both short- and long-term gains in the accuracy with which they use certain structures. A problem typical of French speakers' learning (and of other learners of English as well, of course) is the confusion of *be* and *have* in a variety of sentence types—expressions of age, hunger, heat, and cold, but also presentational forms such as "There *is* a boy playing ball" as opposed to "You *have* (or "it *has*") a boy playing ball." In an observational study of franco-phone students in intensive ESL, students whose teacher provided spontaneous immediate feedback on this error—but no other group of students—overcame the tendency to substitute *have* for *be* and, most important, one year later, even though they had not continued to have focused attention or feedback on this point, they had not forgotten it. Furthermore, their counterparts from other intensive ESL classes had not acquired it in the meantime (Lightbown 1991).

It is essential to point out that in earlier research in audiolingual classrooms we had observed students who also reached a very high level of accuracy on the use of this structure. These students, however, did not have the advantage of knowing or using *have* in other contexts. That is, they had not learned the verb *have* at all in two or three years of structure-based instruction. As soon as they learned *have*, they began to use it in all the places where for two years they had correctly used *be* (Lightbown 1984). This suggests strongly that focus on form is most effective, not in advance of communicative contexts, but at the moment when learners *know* what they want to say, indeed are trying to say something, and the means to say it more correctly are offered to them. This may be seen as related to Tomasello and Herron's (1988, 1989) research on the "garden path" technique. In this procedure, learners in university French classes who were led to overgeneralize on the basis of the general rules they had been taught eventually performed better on the particular structures in question than students who had been warned *in advance* about the exceptions to the general rules. Although the learning contexts of these university students and the young adolescents referred to previously are quite different, both suggest that contrary to the old adage even a pound of prevention may not be worth an ounce of cure administered at the right moment.

In two experimental studies, we provided teachers in the intensive ESL classes with teaching materials focusing on two aspects of English that the learners were far from mastering. The aim of these studies was to explore the effect of intro-ducing more correct examples of target language structures together with some focused instruction and corrective feedback so that learners could see how their interlanguage differed from target language rules.

In the first, we asked some intensive program teachers to teach students that, even though adverb placement in English is relatively free, there is one position where English does not normally allow adverbs in simple sentences: between the verb and the direct object. Note that this is not the case in French, where this position is allowed.

*Mary buys often flowers for her mother.
Marie achète souvent des fleurs pour sa mère.

After two weeks (approximately nine hours of instruction), of relatively brief daily activities involving both "consciousness raising" (through the presentation of examples, corrective feedback on error), and communicative activities where adverbs were used, students in the experimental group were dramatically better than a control group who had not had these lessons. The control group had been taught another structure using similar techniques to control for the effects of familiarity with the testing instruments. Five weeks later they were still performing with a high level of accuracy. One year later, however, they had slipped back to a level not significantly different from their pretest performance (White 1991a).

Our classroom observations confirmed that adverbs were exceedingly rare in the classroom speech these learners were exposed to. With the exception of a few adverbs of frequency, neither teacher nor students use adverbs very often.[1] The fact that students appear to learn the restriction on the placement of adverbs between the verb and the object, and then forget it, may be attributable to its infrequency and relative lack of importance in their communicative use of English. The finding that students fail to retain the restriction also points to the difficulty of discovering from "positive evidence" (simple exposure to samples of the target language) that a particular structure is *not* permitted (see White 1990).

In the second experimental study we prepared instructional packages for the teachers on the formation of English questions, both *yes/no* and *wh* types. French has a large variety of ways to form grammatical questions (see Valdman, this volume). French-speaking learners of English might be expected to assume, once they identify some of the English question forms that both French and English permit, that English has the same range of questions (with the same pragmatic force) as French.

The design of the study was similar to that of the adverb study reported above. The instruction included consciousness raising and communicative activities with opportunities for teachers to provide corrective feedback. And the results of the study were somewhat similar. That is, students performed significantly better after instruction than before instruction on a variety of tasks—oral and written—in which they either produced questions or indicated which of two questions was more correct (or whether both were equally correct or incorrect). The difference was that, six months later, the students were still improving. Their accuracy in using questions and in judging the grammaticality of questions had not slipped back to preinstruction levels (Lightbown, Spada, and Ranta 1991; White et al. forthcoming).

There are several possible explanations for the difference between the adverb results and the question results. One is that questions, unlike adverbs, are always available with high frequency in the input. The adverb placement lessons involved the somewhat contrived creation of situations requiring the use of adverbs during the instructional period. Once that instructional period was over, the frequency of adverbs in classroom talk dropped to near zero again. Questions, on the other hand, are very frequent in these classrooms. Teachers ask scores of questions every day, providing a steady stream of correct models for students to hear. Furthermore, unlike many second language classes (see Long and Sato 1983; White and Lightbown 1984), these are classes where students themselves ask many questions. Thus there were possibilities, if the teacher chose to take them, for learners to get feedback on the accuracy of their questions. This feedback did not necessarily come in the form of intentional correction of error by the teacher, but rather in the adjustments that are often made to speech as meaning is negotiated (see Pica, this volume). Questions, that is, usually occurred in activities with considerable communicative content, when students had a genuine interest in saying something and in being understood.

Another factor contributing to the difference might be couched in terms of Meisel, Clahsen, and Pienemann's (1981) "multidimensional model" of language acquisition. According to this model, some features of second language acquisition are *developmental,* that is, acquired in a predictable "natural" sequence, in spite of differences in motivation, salience or frequency in the input, or focused instruction. Other features are considered to be *variational,* that is, acquired and used at various times by different individuals on the basis of motivational or environmental differences. There is substantial evidence that question formation is a developmental structure (Pienemann, Johnston, and Brindley 1988), and it may be that adverb placement is a variational feature.[2] In these terms, one may hypothesize that once learners have reached a certain developmental stage, they are not likely to revert to earlier stages. Variational features, on the other hand, may be learnable at any time, but easier to forget as well. In any case, learners appeared able to retain the gains made in question formation and in fact to continue to improve even when focused instruction was discontinued and contact with English was substantially reduced. In contrast, gains made in adverb placement were lost after months of no instruction and little contact with English.

The findings of these experimental studies add to the evidence from previous research that when form-focused instruction is introduced in a way that is divorced from the communicative needs and activities of the students, only short-term effects are obtained. Our findings give further support to Long's (1988) claim that what makes a difference in classroom instruction is not "focus on forms" but "focus on form." When learners are involved in meaningful and interesting activities, when they are trying to express themselves and know what they wish to say, when the sentence type comes up frequently in the input they are exposed to and the interaction they engage in, then drawing their attention to the way in which their utterances need to be restructured can have lasting effects. Such focus on form is another way for students to get quality input in the foreign language classroom.

CONCLUSION

The two instructional environments discussed in this paper are contexts in which learners have difficulty getting quality input. Two different solutions have been tried by teachers, program developers, and researchers seeking to overcome this difficulty. The two solutions are not mutually exclusive, nor are they by any means the only ways in which the problem might be dealt with. In the current atmosphere of emphasis on communicative language teaching that involves learners in activities focusing primarily on meaning, the quality of the input available to the students must be given serious attention. For even if it proved to be true that, as Krashen (1985) has argued, the necessary and sufficient conditions for second language acquisition are found in exposure to comprehensible input, that input must be truly representative of the target language that learners are seeking to learn, not a misleading and distorted sample of it.

ENDNOTES

*Research reported in this paper was funded by the Ministère de l'Education du Québec through its grant program (Formation des chercheurs et l'aide à la recherche) and through the Direction générale du développement des programmes, by the Social Science and Humanities Research Council of Canada, and by the Ministry of Education of New Brunswick. Principal research assistant for the New Brunswick research is Randall Halter.

1. These adverbs of frequency often come between subject and verb in English, the one position from which French excludes adverbs:

   John often does his homework.
   *Jean souvent fait ses devoirs.

   Interestingly, exposure to the relatively infrequent occurrence of English sentences such as these seems to have been sufficient to inform students even before instruction that English, unlike French, *does* permit adverbs in this position. In the various tasks, students showed that they accepted these sentences as correct and even constructed such sentences themselves. Furthermore, when their accuracy in adverb placement declined over the months following the instructional period, this particular form remained acceptable to them and was indeed the first word order arrangement many of them proposed in a task in which they constructed sentences using sets of word cards. This is a good example of how positive input seems sufficient to help learners discover what the target language permits that their own does not, but does not help them discover what the target language will *not* allow (White 1990).

2. But see White et al. (1991b) for a discussion of how adverbs are hypothesized to be related to other linguistic features through the "verb-raising" parameter.

REFERENCES

Burstall, C., M. Jamieson, S. Cohen, and M. Hargreaves. 1974. *Primary French in the Balance*. Slough: NFER.

Corder, S. P. 1967. "The Significance of Learners' Errors." *IRAL* 5(4): 161–70.

Forsyth, A. 1990. Projet Expérimental en Anglais Langue Seconde à l'Elémentaire, au Nouveau-Brunswick. *Education Canada.* Summer: 23–29.

Krashen, S. 1985. *The Input Hypothesis: Issues and Implications.* New York: Longman.

Lightbown, P. M. 1983. "Exploring Relationships Between Development and Instructional Sequences in L2 Acquisition." *Classroom-oriented Research in Second Language Acquisition.* Eds. H. Seliger and M. Long. Rowley, Mass.: Newbury. 217–43.

———. 1984. "Input and Acquisition in Second Language Classrooms." *TESL Canada Journal* 1(2): 55–67.

———. 1985. "Input and Acquisition for Second-Language Learners in and out of Classrooms. *Applied Linguistics* 6(3): 263–73.

———. 1991. "What Have We Here? Some Observations of the Influence of Instruction on L2 Learning." *Foreign Language Pedagogy Research: A Commemorative Volume for Claus Faerch.* Eds. R. Phillipson, E. Kellerman, L. Selinker, M. Sharwood-Smith, and M. Swain. Clevedon, U.K.: Multilingual Matters.

———. Forthcoming. "Can They Do It Themselves? A Comprehension-based ESL Course for Young Children." *Comprehension-based Language Teaching: Current Trends.* Eds. R. Courchêne, J. St. John, C. Therrien, and J. Glidden. Ottawa: Ottawa P.

Lightbown, P. M., and N. Spada. 1989. *A Secondary V Follow-up Study of Learners from Primary-level Intensive ESL Programs.* Research report. Available from SPEAQ (la Société pour la promotion de l'enseignement de l'anglais, langue seconde, au Québec), 600 Fullum, Montreal, Quebec, H2K 4L1, Canada.

———. 1990. "Focus-on-form and Corrective Feedback in Communicative Language Teaching: Effects on Second Language Learning." *Studies in Second Language Acquisition* 12(4): 429–48.

Lightbown, P. M., N. Spada, and L. Ranta. 1991. "The Effect of Instruction on 'IL-Formed' Questions." Paper presented at the Second Language Research Forum, Los Angeles, March 2.

Long, M. 1981. "Input, Interaction and Second Language Acquisition Theory." *Native Language and Foreign Language Acquisition.* Ed. H. Winitz. *Annals of the New York Academy of Sciences* 379: 259–78.

———. 1991. "Focus on Form: A Design Feature in Language Teaching Methodology." *Foreign Language Research in Cross-Cultural Perspective.* Eds. K. de Boot, R. Ginsberg, C. Kramsch. Amsterdam: John Benjamins. 39–52.

Long, M. H., and C. Sato. 1983. "Classroom Foreigner Talk Discourse: Forms and Functions of Teachers' Questions." *Classroom-oriented Research in Second Language Acquisition.* Eds. H. Seliger and M. Long. Rowley, Mass.: Newbury.

Meisel, J., H. Clahsen, and M. Pienemann. 1981. "On Determining Developmental Stages in Natural Second Language Acquisition." *Studies in Second Language Acquisition* 3(2): 109–35.

Pienemann, M., M. Johnston, and G. Brindley. 1988. "Constructing an Acquisition-based Procedure for Second Language Assessment." *Studies in Second Language Acquisition* 10(2): 217–44.

Selinker, L. 1972. "Interlanguage." *IRAL* 10(3): 201–31.

Sharwood-Smith, M. 1991. "Speaking to Many Minds." *Second Language Research* 7(2): 118–32.

Spada, N., and P. M. Lightbown. 1989. "Intensive ESL Programmes in Québec Primary Schools." *TESL Canada Journal* 7(2): 11–28.

Swain, M. 1985. "Communicative Competence: Some Roles of Comprehensible Input and Comprehensible Output in Its Development." *Input in Second Language Acquisition.* Eds. S. Gass and C. Madden. Rowley, Mass.: Newbury. 235–53.

Tomasello, M., and C. Herron. 1988. "Down the Garden Path: Inducing and Correcting Overgeneralization Errors in the Foreign Language Classroom." *Applied Psycholinguistics* 9(3): 237–46.

———. 1989. "Feedback for Language Transfer Errors." *Studies in Second Language Acquisition* 11(4): 385–95.

White, L. 1990. "Implications of Learnability Theories for Second Language Learning and Teaching." *Learning, Keeping and Using Language.* Vol. 1. Eds. M. A. K. Halliday, J. Gibbons, and H. Nicholas. Amsterdam: John Benjamins.

———. 1991a. "Adverb Placement in Second Language Acquisition: Some Effects of Positive and Negative Evidence in the Classroom." *Second Language Research* 7(2): 133–61.

———. 1991b. "The Verb-Raising Parameter in Second Language Acquisition." *Language Acquisition* 1(4).

White, J., and P. M. Lightbown. 1984. "Asking and Answering in ESL Classes." *Canadian Modern Language Review* 40(2): 228–44.

White, L., N. Spada, P. M. Lightbown, and L. Ranta. Forthcoming. "Input Enhancement and L2 Question Formation." *Applied Linguistics* 12(4).

Chapter 14

The Textual Outcomes of Native Speaker–Non-Native Speaker Negotiation: What Do They Reveal About Second Language Learning?

Teresa Pica

University of Pennsylvania

FAY	TANAKA
next	next house have uh chimney . . .
	there are two window uh in
	front door
ok	and uh there is uh there is uh
	[zɛbrə]
	you know [zɛbrə]
	[zɛbrə] . . . horse [zɛbrə]
[dɛbrə]?	[zɛbrə] . . . [zɛbrə] horse
a horse?	[zɛbrə] . . . how say uh
I don't know what that word is	[zɛbrə] [zɛbrə] is uh Z
G?	E
G E?	B
B	U . . . R . . . R . . . A . . . [zɛbrə]
[j l b]?	[zɛd]
with a G? G?	[z] . . . [z] . . . [zɛt] [zit]
oh /zibrə/	[zibrə] that's a roof
the roof oh /zibrə/ . . . yeah ok	
(laughs)	ok? [zibrə] next?

This opening text of native speaker–non-native speaker (NS-NNS) interaction occurred during a communication task in which the participants were given different portions of a picture sequence of houses, hidden from their view, and attempted to reproduce the unseen sequence by exchanging information on their own uniquely held portions. Here, Tanaka, the NNS, tried to describe the roof of his house to Fay, the NS. Since it was striped, he referred to it in terms of a zebra, which he repeatedly pronounced as [zɛbrə]. Fay indicated in a variety of ways that she could not understand what Tanaka meant by [zɛbrə]. As shown in the text, both Tanaka and Fay worked together linguistically, until they came to a mutual understanding of what Tanaka was trying to say. Tanaka attempted different pronunciations, even spelled the word for Fay. Fay signaled her lack of understanding explicitly and also attempted different pronunciations, eventually providing [zibrə], which best matched the referent Tanaka intended. This, in turn, served as a model that Tanaka himself produced before moving on to the next house in the task.

From the perspective of interactionist theories of second language acquisition (SLA), learners' participation in this type of interaction, known as *negotiation,* is believed to provide conditions necessary for them to advance beyond their current level of second language (L2) development. Specifically, what has been claimed is that as learners and their interlocutors work together in negotiation to resolve communication breakdowns and/or to reach mutual understanding, they experience opportunities to comprehend initially unfamiliar L2 input, be given feedback on their interlanguage comprehensibility, and manipulate and modify their interlanguage output. Such comprehension, feedback, and production opportunities, as acted upon separately or collectively by the learner, are believed to represent conditions for successful SLA. Research has begun to identify the ways in which negotiation with NSs offers learners opportunities for comprehension, feedback, and modified production and, in turn, also promotes development and internalization of their interlanguage system.

In light of this work, this paper will address some of the possible contributions of negotiation to SLA, documented through quantitative and qualitative analyses of linguistic features of NS-NNS negotiation during communication tasks. Texts extracted from NS-NNS negotiation will be used to reveal how negotiation provides learners with: (1) L2 input adjusted or modified for their comprehension needs, serving as another, more comprehensible version of what was initially unfamiliar; (2) feedback on semantic and structural features of their interlanguage; (3) opportunities to adjust, manipulate, or modify their interlanguage semantically and structurally; and (4) a source of L2 data that segments linguistic units, highlights L2 semantic and structural relationships, and thereby reveals to learners how the L2 can be manipulated to express what Prince (this volume) has called discourse functions.

WHAT IS NEGOTIATION?

In order to illustrate how learners' participation in negotiation can provide them with an effective context for language learning, it is important first to define negotiation operationally and to situate it within current theoretical claims about SLA. The term "negotiation" is neither original nor unique to SLA but has been used in a variety of contexts, including those pertaining to business and politics. It has been used extensively throughout the fields of ethnomethodology and conversational analysis to refer to the ways in which interlocutors communicate meaning and structure their social relationships through interaction (see, e.g., Garfinkel 1967). In SLA literature, the term has been subject to varying interpretations among both writers and readers and often interchanged with more general labels such as *interaction* and *interactional modification* (see, e.g., Long 1980; Pica, Doughty, and Young 1986; and Pica, Young, and Doughty 1987).

Increasingly, in theoretical and empirical literature on SLA, the label *negotiation* has been applied to those interactions in which learners and their interlocutors adjust their speech phonologically, lexically, and morphosyntactically to resolve difficulties in mutual understanding that impede the course of their communication. (See, e.g., studies by Doughty and Pica 1986; Gass and Varonis 1984, 1985, 1986, 1989; Hatch 1978; Long 1980, 1981, 1983, 1985; Pica 1987a, 1987b; and Varonis and Gass 1982, 1985a, 1985b, and articles in the collection edited by Day 1986).

This work was used as a basis in analyzing data and selecting texts from the research reviewed in this paper. Negotiation was defined as an activity that occurs when a listener signals to a speaker that the speaker's message is not clear, and listener and speaker work linguistically to resolve this impasse. Signals can take the form of open requests for clarification such as "What?" or as in Fay's case above, "I don't know what that word means." Or signals can repeat or reword and seek confirmation of the input, as when Fay responded, "a horse?" As illustrated in the text of Tanaka and Fay, negotiation is a mutual activity, as both interlocutors modified and adjusted Tanaka's message toward comprehensibility in their signals and responses to each other.

NEGOTIATION AND CONDITIONS FOR SLA: A BRIEF REVIEW

Characteristics that serve to define negotiation such as NS and NNS attempts at improving message comprehensibility, their striving toward mutual comprehension, production of clarification signals, and modification of speech, make it an especially attractive learning context since, in several recent theories of SLA, learners' L2 comprehension and production are emphasized as essential conditions for their internalization of L2 rules and structures. First proposed by Long (1980, 1983, 1985) as essential to comprehension of L2 input, negotiation has since been claimed to provide a theoretical framework for feedback and modified production as well.

Briefly, what has been claimed theoretically about SLA is that, first, before learners can internalize new L2 forms and structures, they must understand the meaning of messages that these forms and structures encode. Exposure to L2 input is not sufficient for the learner to be able to internalize an L2 system. L2 input must be made comprehensible if it is to assist the acquisition process (see, e.g., Krashen 1980, 1985; Long 1980, 1981, 1983, 1985). However, L2 comprehension in itself may not be sufficient for acquisition, since, as argued by Long (1983, 1985), learners can experience comprehension of L2 input but fail to incorporate into their interlanguage the forms and structures that had encoded the input.

In light of the necessity but insufficiency of input comprehension to SLA, two possible contributions to SLA made by learner production have been proposed. Schachter, for instance, has looked to production as a way for learners to gain interlocutor feedback on the clarity and precision of their interlanguage (Schachter 1983, 1984, 1986). Schachter refers to this feedback as "negative input," which provides learners with metalinguistic information about their interlanguage and the L2 variety of their interlocutor.

Further, Swain (1985) has made the point that comprehension of L2 input is necessary throughout the acquisition process, but that production is also important, especially with regard to learners' ultimate L2 attainment. She argues that it is possible to understand the meaning of an utterance without reliance on or recognition of its morphology or syntax; to master an L2, however, learners must be given opportunities to produce "comprehensible output," that is, to organize and structure their output syntactically.

Each of these theoretical claims provides compelling arguments about the contributions of comprehension, feedback, and interlanguage modification to language learning. However, each has also been questioned in terms of its sufficiency for explaining the learning process.

What has been lacking from claims about the necessity for L2 input comprehension, for example, is a theoretical link between learners' comprehension of L2 input and its incorporation into their interlanguage system, retention in memory, and retrieval during subsequent communication. (These concerns have been expressed in Chaudron 1985, Faerch and Kasper 1987, and Sharwood-Smith 1987.) On an even more basic level, moreover, the precise role of L2 input as data in the learning process is as yet unclear. As demonstrated through Prince's findings (this volume), learners can induce L2 rules from their input, yet fail to figure out precisely the appropriate distribution of and constraints on these rules in L2 discourse.

Theories differ in their views on the nature and sufficiency of L2 data, and on whether and how the data must be organized for learners in order for SLA to proceed. From a nativist perspective—such as that expressed in Cook (1988), for example—sufficient L2 data would be that which allowed learners to reset the parameters of innate principles of language structure and to recognize restrictions on L2 lexis (e.g., which verbs allow both prepositional phrase and dative constructions for indirect objects and which verbs allow only prepositional phrase constructions). From a theoretical perspective which assumes a more active language learner (see Faerch and Kasper 1984), sufficient L2 data would be that which enabled learners to discover and induce L2 rules and structures through application of their own cognitive processing procedures.

Regardless of the view taken on input sufficiency, as has been argued as far back as Corder (1967, 1973) and as recently as White (1987), no theory has yet to emerge as to how L2 input interacts with the learner's existing grammar to bring about interlanguage development (but see Meisel, Clahsen, and Pienemann 1981 and Pienemann 1984 for an exception). Without a theory as to how input is used to destabilize and change the current state of the learner's grammar, it is impossible to specify what is meant by input that is "sufficient" for language learning.

Joining these concerns about input are differing views on the role of feedback in the learning process. Schachter's views on feedback have been questioned on both theoretical and empirical grounds related to theoretical claims that individuals come to the language learning experience with an innate endowment for language learning. One feature of this endowment is that it places constraints on the interlanguage grammar, thereby reducing the learner's need for the kinds of negative evidence that feedback would supply (see., e.g., White 1987).

As Prince's research (this volume) has brought out, however, one of the problems with L2 learning is that learners often overgenerate L2 rules, as in the case of her bilinguals, who overgenerate and overapply an L2 discourse function. Further, what Prince has pointed out is that it is difficult for learners to determine what does not belong in the L2, since many of their hypotheses about a particular L2 feature are readily confirmed through the L2 input they actually hear. This may be where correction can help learners. However, as research has shown, the problem is that when learners' production is comprehensible, their listeners, even their teachers, let these imprecisions go, seldom interrupting a conversation or even a classroom discussion to provide correction of grammatical accuracy. Thus, the role of corrective feedback in L2 learning has been minimized in light of research that has found that, even when made available to learners, it often has little impact on their production (see Brock et al. 1986 and Schachter herself 1986 for a review).

Finally the role of modified output in the learning process has also been called into question. Initially, this was because there had been no research directed toward Swain's position (1985) that learners need to produce modified output. Her arguments had been based on inference rather than direct evidence, namely, on students' test scores. These scores indicated that students achieved lower levels of L2 production relative to their L2 comprehension while they studied in an immersion learning environment presumed to be rich in comprehensible L2 input. Evidence for the existence of modified output and the conditions that promote and inhibit its occurrence have since been documented by Pica (1987a) and Pica et al. (1989). As yet, however, no research has examined the long-range effects of modified output on interlanguage development. Therefore, among researchers who view modification of output as simply an opportunity for learners to practice their production of language rather than to move along the path of acquisition, questions continue to be raised about the extent of its role in the learning process.

In spite of, and in some ways because of, the criticisms of the theoretical importance given to L2 comprehension, provision of feedback, and modification of interlanguage in successful SLA, researchers have been motivated to identify conditions and contexts in which these processes can occur and to link them more closely with the learner's development. Because negotiation is an activity focused on comprehension, feedback, and modified production, it has therefore served as a particularly fruitful area of research on SLA.

QUANTITATIVE AND QUALITATIVE
PERSPECTIVES ON NEGOTIATION AND SLA

Negotiation is not inevitable when learners and interlocutors engage in social interaction. Frequently, topics and referents are so mutually familiar that learners and interlocutors are confronted with few communication breakdowns in their discourse. What can also happen is that when troublesome topics or unclear referents arise, learners and interlocutors abandon them or switch to new ones (Long 1980, 1983). At other times, especially in the classroom context (as shown in Pica 1987b), learners are reluctant to signal lack of understanding of their teacher, either because the topic of the discourse has little consequence for the learner or because any indication of a lack of understanding would suggest their lack of competence or loss of attention.

Further limiting the amount of negotiation that can occur in the classroom are teachers' use of preplanned lessons and their experience with learner production. Often teachers understand everything learners say to them and pitch their L2 input at a level of complete comprehensibility. This is not unlike what happens during research interviews, as objectives of data collection dictate the topics chosen by the researcher and the course of interaction between researcher and the NNS subject of the research.

From an interactionist perspective, teacher lessons or research interviews are not an efficient means to assist language learning in the classroom or to study the processes of L2 comprehension and interlanguage modification. This is because lessons and interviews do not guarantee conditions in which learners can take an active role. In lessons and interviews, learners must comply with goals they have had no part in setting. Their opportunities to work toward collective or individual goals are blocked, as teachers and researchers control both the questions that are asked and the responses that are expected. These opportunities to negotiate meaning or exchange information are also limited since information flows in only one direction—from answer-supplying learner to question-asking teacher or researcher.

COMMUNICATION TASKS AS A BASIS
FOR NEGOTIATION

A review of current literature on task-based learning (by Pica, Kanagy, and Falodun, forthcoming) has revealed that two features of communication tasks make them superior to lessons and interviews as contexts for negotiation.[1] First, communication tasks are oriented toward mutual goals. Participants are expected to arrive at an outcome and to carry out the task with a sense of what they need to accomplish through their talk or action. A second feature of communication tasks is work or activity. Unlike lessons and interviews, communication tasks are not activities carried out on task participants. Rather, communication tasks are activities that participants themselves must carry out.

That communication tasks have been shown to stimulate negotiation has been revealed in studies comparing different kinds of tasks as well as studies comparing communication tasks with lessons and interviews. (See Pica, Kanagy, and Falodun, forthcoming, for a review of these studies, and Crookes and Rulon 1985, Doughty and Pica 1986, Duff 1986, Gass and Varonis 1985, Hawkins 1985, Long 1980, Pica et al. 1989, and Rulon and McCreary 1986, for data on some of the actual studies.) For the present paper, three types of communication tasks were used in gathering the data to be reported. They are as follows:

1. *The jigsaw task,* which was the type of task in which Fay and Tanaka engaged as described at the beginning of this paper. Jigsaw task interactants hold different portions of a totality of information, which must be exchanged and manipulated as they work convergently toward a single task goal. Based on this configuration of task features, the jigsaw task is considered the task most likely to generate opportunities for interactants to negotiate and thus work toward L2 comprehension, feedback on production, and interlanguage modification.

2. *The information-gap task,* which differs from jigsaw in its role assignments in that only one interactant holds crucial, task-relevant information and the other(s) must request this information. Information flows in one direction as the two (or more) interactants work together toward a convergent goal and single outcome. It too can bring about conditions for comprehension, feedback, and modified production, if interactants are allowed to repeat similar versions of the task, or when, in the course of the task, they alternate roles as information suppliers and requesters.

3. *The opinion-exchange task,* in which interactants are expected to work toward coming to a single opinion. However, any number of outcomes, including no outcome at all, is possible, since task interactants start out with shared access to all or some of the same information necessary for task completion. Nevertheless, this task type has been shown to promote negotiation as, for example, participants introduce each other to unfamiliar topics or unknown referents whose comprehensibility becomes a matter of mutual concern in shaping their opinions (see Pica et al. 1989 for supportive evidence).

The texts of negotiation that appear throughout this paper were generated as learners and their interlocutors worked through different types of communication tasks. As will be discussed in the next four sections, these texts reveal how negotiation provides learners with conditions of comprehension, feedback, and modified production considered essential for language learning and how negotiation might also serve as a basis for their interlanguage development. Specific features of these texts and quantitative data taken from results of statistical analyses suggest that negotiation provides learners with: (1) L2 input adjusted or modified for their comprehension needs; (2) feedback on semantic and structural features of interlanguage; (3) opportunities to adjust, manipulate, or modify semantic and structural features of their interlanguage; and (4) a source of L2 data that highlights L2 semantic and structural relationships. Each of these contributions will now be reviewed.

Negotiation for L2 Input Adjusted
or Modified for Comprehension Needs

The prominence given to the theoretical claim that comprehensible input is necessary for SLA has stimulated research on how learners come to comprehend language that they do not initially understand. Evidence has been accumulating regarding the ways in which input can be made comprehensible to the learner. Chaudron (1983, 1985), Long (1980, 1981, 1983, 1985), Gass and Varonis (1985), and Varonis and Gass (1982, 1985a, 1985b) have pioneered an impressive amount of empirical research in this area, and through individual studies on input comprehension, Blau (1982), Brown (1987), Cervantes (1983), Ellis (1985), Johnson (1981), and Kelch (1985) have supplied a wealth of descriptive data (see Chaudron and Parker 1990 and Pica 1991 for an overview).

Learners' comprehension of oral or written texts in their original state has been compared with their comprehension of versions adjusted linguistically with regard to syntactic complexity, semantic redundancy, and rate of speaking. Since, in the design of these studies, adjustments were made to the texts before giving them to the learners, but not as they read or listened to them, results identified those linguistic modifications that aided comprehension but did not reveal how negotiated input might also play a role in this process. It was the need for this latter research that prompted Pica, Doughty, and Young (1986), and Pica, Young, and Doughty (1987) to investigate input comprehension within an interactive framework and, at the same time, to research the then untested claim that negotiation between learners and interlocutors facilitates L2 comprehension.[2]

This work studied the impact on second language comprehension of two conditions of input exposure, one that allowed for negotiation, another that did not. The input consisted of a text of fifteen directions, provided through an information-gap task in which a female NS of American English asked sixteen NNSs, on an individual basis, to select items and position them on a board illustrated with an outdoor scene. The items were two-dimensional cutouts of plant, animal, and human figures, each of which shared with at least one other item a physical feature such as color, size, or shape. Illustrations on the board included figures that resembled those of the cutouts as well as landmarks such as a pond, patches of grass, a skyline, and various roadways and vehicles.

In Condition 1, eight English NNSs of low-intermediate proficiency listened to a text generated originally by English NSs, then modified linguistically, and presented to these subjects, without opportunities to interact or negotiate with the direction giver—that is, ask clarification questions, request confirmation of what they believed they heard, and have their comprehension checked by the direction giver. In Condition 2, eight NNSs, also at the level of low-intermediate proficiency, listened to the direction giver read the unmodified NS version of the text, but were allowed to interact whenever they needed, in the ways described above. The NNSs came from a variety of first language backgrounds. During the task, they sat in full view of the direction giver, worked alone behind individual screens, and were expected to rely on linguistic input in order to select items and place them appropriately. As a measure of their comprehension of the directions, subjects were given one point each for accuracy in selection and placement of the task items.

The fifteen directions used in the text for this study had a point biserial correlation coefficient of .20 or higher. The unmodified and premodified versions of this text were based on data generated as one member of a NS-NS dyad originated and conveyed directions to the other regarding item selection and placement. The premodified directions were modified linguistically (according to procedures to be described below) and then pretested on NNSs drawn from the same population as the sixteen NNSs in Conditions 1 and 2 of the experimental study. (For further details on the design of the study, see Pica, Young, and Doughty [1987].)

Portions of all three texts—that is, the NS baseline, the premodified, and the interactionally modified or negotiated versions of the directions text—are shown in Figure 1. As shown, modifications made to the NS text by the researchers in order to produce the premodified version included elaboration of content, accomplished through word and phrase repetition or rewording, and reductions in sentence length and syntactic complexity. Also shown, modifications to the NS text produced through the negotiation of the NNSs and the NS direction giver included the same kinds of elaboration of content and repetition and rephrasing of lexical and phrasal items. However, the text produced during negotiation resulted in no reduction of sentence length or complexity of the NS baseline version.

NNSs' comprehension of directions was compared in Conditions 1 and 2. Accurate comprehension of at least some of the directions was displayed by both groups, with 69 percent accuracy for subjects in Condition 1 and 88 percent accuracy for those in Condition 2; however, the comprehension of the group in Condition 2 was significantly better (t = 3.78, p < .05).

Also found were two consistent patterns with regard to negotiation and modification. First, compared to the premodified text of directions generated by the researchers for Condition 1, the text of directions negotiated by the participants in Condition 2 contained significantly more repetitions and rephrasings of direction content words (t = 2.90, p < .05). As shown in Table 1, there was an average of 7.20 of these elaborations per direction in Condition 1 versus 13.17 in Condition 2. Further, it was found that, among those directions which were understood better in Condition 2, at least 75 percent of the repetitions and rephrasings occurred during negotiation; that is, they were encoded in both the

— *Figure 1* _____

Texts of Direction Input: Syntactic Complexity and Content Repetition and Rephrasing in NS Baseline, Premodified, and Negotiated Versions

NS Baseline:

[In the center of the crossroads, [right where the three meet,] put the dog in the- in the carriage.] (2 s-nodes per T-unit)

Moving to the top right corner, place the two mushrooms with the three yellow dots in that grass patch down toward the road. (23 words, 0 repetitions of content words)

Premodified:

[Put the dog in the middle of the three roads.] (1 s-node per T-unit)

Move to the top right corner. Take the two mushrooms with the three yellow dots. Put the two mushrooms on the grass. Put the two mushrooms on the grass near the road. (32 words, 5 repetitions of content words)

Negotiated (Interactionally Modified) Input:

NS DIRECTION GIVER	NNS
Moving to the top right corner, place the two mushrooms with the three yellow dots in that grass patch down toward the road. (NS Baseline) should I repeat it?	
	mmm
OK. moving to the top right corner, place the two mushrooms with the three yellow dots in that grass patch down toward the road.	
	um what means grass patch?
a piece of grass	piece of grass, piece of grass
should I repeat it again? OK. moving to the top right corner, place the two mushrooms with the three yellow dots in that grass patch down toward the road.	
	I can't understand

OK. the top right corner of the picture place the two mush-rooms, the two mushrooms with the three yellow dots in the grass patch down towards the road	mmm mm
what's the problem? do you have a question? I can help on the top right corner of the picture in the grass patch down towards the road, place the two mushrooms	um on the—on the right? left? top . . . top right right top corner two mushrooms
OK? . . . All right.	

(122 total words [97 directions words], 53 repetitions and rephrasings)

---

direction giver's signals for the NNSs to clarify or confirm their utterances and in her checks on the NNS comprehension, or they were triggered by the NNSs' signals. Examples of this pattern have been highlighted throughout the text in Figure 2.

Conditions for Comprehension of Negotiated L2 Input

The overall finding that negotiation assisted comprehension pointed toward the design of classroom environments in which students play an active role as ne-gotiators with their teacher or classmates, so that they can seek clarification and confirmation of unfamiliar words and structures. However, this finding also raised a number of practical issues for learners whose styles of classroom participation make them reluctant to question a teacher, seek help with comprehension of content, or admit difficulty when their teacher checks their understanding as identified, for example, in studies by Politzer and McGroarty (1985); Sato (1982); Saville-Troike, McClure, and Fritz (1984). Also at issue was how to relate this finding to the results of studies by Allwright (1980), Busch (1982), Day (1984), Ellis (1985), which had shown that successful classroom language learning can occur among students less interactive than their classmates.

A follow-up study was undertaken, therefore, to understand more fully the relationships among classroom interaction, negotiation, and comprehension.[3] The impact on learners' comprehension revealed during their participation in nego-tiation suggested that less interactive, but reportedly successful, classroom lan-guage learners might somehow be benefiting from the adjusted input generated by teachers and more interactive peers. Results showing that negotiation moves

— **Table 1** ————————————————————————————————————

**Comparison of Direction Input Features of Syntactic Complexity
and Content Repetition and Rephrasing
in NS Baseline, Premodified, and Negotiated Versions**

	Content Words/ Direction	Elaboration Repetition and Rephrasing of Content Words	Syntactic Complexity S-nodes/T-unit
Baseline	16.47	.20	1.20
Premodified	33.47	7.20	1.02
Negotiated/ Interactionally Modified	51.64	13.17	1.23
Difference	18.17	5.97	0.21
t =	2.37*	2.90*	1.91
*p < .05			

served as vehicles for elaboration and repetition suggested further that perhaps *any repetitions* arising from classroom negotiation had the potential to facilitate comprehension for *all classroom participants,* not just those who directly requested clarification or confirmation of input.

The follow-up study examined comprehension on the same information-gap task used in the earlier research. Comparisons were made of three groups of NNSs, also of low-intermediate proficiency level, and also representing a variety of first language backgrounds. The direction giver was again an NS of American English, this time their teacher, a woman with many years of teaching experience. Each group was organized by the researcher to contain eight subjects, who displayed a range of classroom interaction levels. These levels were determined through a series of classroom observations during which frequency counts were made of students' signals of lack of comprehension, requests for assistance, and responses to teacher solicits. As in the first study, subjects sat in full view of the direction giver, worked alone behind individual screens, and were expected to rely on linguistic input in order to select items and place them appropriately. (For further details on the design of the study, see Pica 1991).

The first group, labeled the Negotiators, first heard each direction as a text of unmodified input. This was the same text that had been used in Condition 2 of the previous study. The Negotiators were asked to carry out the task in the same way as the previous Condition 2 subjects. They were encouraged to ask for clarification and confirm their comprehension of the directions with the direction giver. The second group, known as the Observers, carried out the same task at the same time as the Negotiators. This group was not permitted to seek assistance from their teacher but could listen to the Negotiators do this.

There was also a third group, the Listeners, who performed the task after the two other groups had done so. This group listened to the teacher read a text of directions constructed so that it contained the same content and the same amount of original and repeated input, and took the same amount of time to present as the directions that had been produced when the Negotiators and Observers carried out the task with their teacher. Through use of this text, the Listener group *heard* the same amount of elaboration and redundancy as the Negotiators and Observers but did not have direct influence on its generation. The major difference in the two conditions in which the task was carried out was that the Listeners' directions were presented without opportunities for negotiation.

It was believed that inclusion of the group of Listeners in the study would make it possible to find out whether the effect on comprehension of simply listening to repetition and rewording in itself was comparable to the effect of creating elaborated input through negotiation. Once again, comprehension of negotiated input was being compared with comprehension of premodified input. However, this time, the text of premodified input given to the Listener group was based directly on negotiated interaction between the NS direction giver and the NNS subjects rather than from researcher intuition about input comprehensibility and modification.

Portions of the Listeners' text of directions and the text of negotiated directions from which they were derived are shown in Figure 2, together with comparisons of amount of repetition and rewording, length in number of words, and amount of time from beginning to end of each direction. The text contained the following features: it had all of the elaboration and redundancy that had been generated by the Negotiators and their teacher but none of the negotiation moves that had often contained or triggered the redundancy. Also deleted from this text were management moves (such as, "Tell me when I should go on to the next direction," "excuse me," etc.), frames (such as, "right," "all right," and "ok"), acknowledgments (such as "yes," "right," "ok," "ahha," "uhuh"), and all words in hesitations and false starts except when they were repetitions of direction content words. In addition, several morphosyntactic modifications were made. Questions were changed into statements. Imperatives were deleted, except to preserve the initial encoding of each direction. Articles, pronouns, and existential *it* and *there* were also added where it was necessary to support repetitions. Finally, on a few occasions, sentences or phrases from the negotiated directions had to be reordered to provide cohesion.

— **Figure 2** ——————————————————

Texts of Negotiated Direction Input in Three Different Input Conditions

Input Conditions

1. Interactionally Modified/Negotiated Directions (self-generated)
2. Interactionally Modified/Negotiated Directions (other-generated)
3. Text of Interactionally Modified/Negotiated Directions

Representative Text of Conditions 1 and 2

(210 words, 57 repetition/rephrasing of content words, 1 minute 45 seconds duration)

NS TEACHER	NNS NEGOTIATORS (coded by number)
place the mushroom with the four yellow dots underneath the two mushrooms that are already there	16 which one?
ok? place the *mushroom*	1 what's a *mushroom*?
it's another *kind of plant*	8 a *fungus*
yeah a *fungus*	
it's a *little brown thing* . . . a *little brown thing?*	16 one? *two?*
place the *mushroom* with the *four yellow dots*	
Isaac, look for something with *four yellow dots*	1 uhuh with one?
place the *mushroom* with the *four yellow dots underneath* the *mush-rooms* that are already *there on the paper?* ok? you can see some *mushrooms on the paper*	1 excuse me, again please
place the *mushroom* with the *four yellow dots*	16 what's *dots?*
what's *dots? little round circles*	

little round yellow circles	
like *spots* ok?	
this is just *two* or one? it's one *mushroom* it has *four yellow dots*	
put the *mushroom underneath* the other *mushrooms*	
ok? got it? all right anybody who can ask a question have a question?	
another word?	
underneath the *mushrooms* that are already *there*	
underneath is one word it means *under*	
don't worry *underneath* the *mushrooms* that are already *there* ok? you got it everybody? ok, next	

little round yellow circles

like *spots* ok?

this is just *two* or one? it's one *mushroom*   it has *four yellow dots*

put the *mushroom underneath* the other *mushrooms*

ok? got it? all right anybody who can ask a question have a question?

another word?

underneath the *mushrooms* that are already *there*

underneath is one word it means *under*

don't worry *underneath* the *mushrooms* that are already *there* ok? you got it everybody? ok, next

10 I can't find

16 which one?   1 excuse me

1 *underneath* the *mushrooms*

10 *underneath? under under?*

10 *underneath?*

10 oh oh

Representative Text of Condition 3

(189 words, 57 repetition/rephrasing of content words, 1 minute 40 seconds duration)

Place the mushroom with the four yellow dots . . . underneath the two mushrooms that are already there. A *mushroom* is another kind of *plant* or a *fungus*. This is one which is a *little brown thing*. It's a *fungus* or a *little brown thing*. There are one and *two mushrooms*. Place the one *mushroom* with the *four yellow dots underneath* the *mushrooms* that are already *there*. It's something with *four yellow dots,* not with one. Place the *mushroom* with the *four yellow dots underneath* the *mushrooms* that are already *there on the paper*. Some *mushrooms* can be seen *on the paper*. Place the *mushroom* with the *four yellow dots underneath* them. *Dots* are *little round circles*. *Dots* are *little round yellow circles*. You can find them to be like *spots*. This is the one *mushroom,* not the *two*. It has *four yellow dots*. Put the *mushroom underneath* the other *mushrooms, underneath* or *under* them. *Underneath* is another word for *under*. *Underneath* is one word that means *under*. Place the *mushroom underneath* the *mushrooms* that are already *there*. Everybody should have it and be ready for the next direction.

Results of the study are shown in Figure 3. It was found that the mean comprehension score for the Negotiators was 13.25 out of 15, or 88 percent, the mean score for the eight Observers was 11.75, or 78 percent, and the mean score for the Listeners was 12.12, or 81 percent. These small differences among the groups' comprehension scores were not statistically significant. Thus, results of the study showed that, on the whole, learners were versatile enough to react to and comprehend L2 input whether they engaged in negotiation directly, observed negotiation, or listened to the text based on negotiated input.

— Figure 3

NNS Comprehension of Negotiated Direction Input in Three Different Input Conditions

	n	% Correct	Negotiators	Observers	Listeners	Negotiators plus Listeners
C	15	100				
O	14					
M		90				
P	13		x			
R						x
E	12	80			x	
H				x		
E	11					
N		70				
S	10					
I O N	9	60				
S	8					
C		50				
O	7					
R E	6	40				
S			n = 8	n = 8	n = 8	n = 16

Individual Scores

	Negotiators		Observers		Listeners	
	Sub#	Score	Sub#	Score	Sub#	Score
High	16	15	4	15	1	15
Inter-	10	15	5	15	8	15
action	7	15	6	14	5	12
Subjects	1	12	9	13	6	11
Low	8	15	3	15	7	14
Inter-	2	14	14	11	2	13
action	15	14	11	6	3	8
Subjects	13	6	12	5	4	9
Total		106/120		94/120		97/120
% Accuracy		88%		78%		81%
X/Subject		13.25		11.75		12.13

No statistically significant differences were found among comprehension scores (ANOVA: F = .59 did not exceed critical value for F for 2/18 [3.55]).

However, when these results were examined further in light of *post hoc* analyses, several noteworthy and distinctive patterns were revealed. Closer scrutiny of the data revealed that two subjects in the group of Negotiators had used no negotiation moves during the course of the task. Both had been identified originally as low classroom interactors, and one had achieved a much lower comprehension score compared to other Negotiators on the task. The two low interactors among the Negotiators who did engage in negotiation, however, scored at a level comparable to that of others in their group. Further, *post hoc* comprehension scores gathered through teacher questionnaires on all subjects indicated that those subjects who had been classified initially as high and low classroom interactors were also ranked at high and low levels of comprehension by their teachers. This information is displayed in Figure 4 on page 215.

These *post hoc* analyses revealed that for high classroom interactors as a group, the three different input conditions made very little difference in their comprehension. This suggested that for subjects who had reached a higher level of L2 comprehension than their classmates, negotiation was not the only pathway to comprehension. Indeed there were several ways of making input comprehensible to the more advanced comprehenders of the present study. This was certainly in keeping with what a number of researchers—Long (1983) in particular—have been arguing for quite some time, that negotiation of L2 input is especially important in the *early* stages of second language acquisition. And it is interesting to note that much of the work reporting the success of low interactors in the classroom, for example, that of Busch (1982), Day (1984), and Politzer and McGroarty (1985), has included relatively advanced learners in the subject samples.

Taken together, results of the study and *post hoc* analyses showed that learners could comprehend direction input as Negotiators, Observers, or Listeners to a

— **Figure 4** ————————————————

NNS Comprehension of Direction Input in Three Different Input Conditions in Relation to Actual Behavior in Input Condition

	n	% Correct
C	15	100
O		
M	14	
P		90
R	13	
E		
H	12	80
E		
N	11	
S		70
I	10	
O		
N	9	60
S	8	
C		50
O	7	
R		
E	6	40
S		

	Actual Negotiators n = 6	Actual Observers n = 10	Listeners n = 8

————————High Interactors   - - - - - - - Low Interactors

text based on negotiated input. However, at lower levels of comprehension, negotiation was the most effective means of facilitating input comprehension. Results thus suggested that opportunities for negotiation, *if taken,* facilitated comprehension of the directions about equally for high and low interactors.

Negotiation as a Resource for Additional Learning Opportunities

Research on negotiation that has sought to uncover its relationship to the learner's comprehension reflects the emphasis on comprehension that has characterized interactionist claims about SLA. Recent studies have taken a broader perspective on negotiation. This work has grown out of additional theoretical claims, such as those of Swain (1985) and Schachter (1983, 1984, 1986), and out of the need to address limitations in the interactionist perspective itself, as noted. The studies to be reviewed in the following sections have indicated that learners' participation in negotiated interaction offers them more than input adjusted to their comprehension needs. What has been revealed both in textual and quantified data of learners' negotiation with NSs is that through negotiation learners are offered L2 structural and semantic information, feedback on their interlanguage, and opportunities to adjust, manipulate, or modify their interlanguage semantically and structurally.

What kinds of studies have revealed such findings? The design of one of these studies (documented in detail in Pica et al. 1989 and Pica et al. 1991) was as follows.

Data were gathered from twenty NS-NNS dyads, arranged into same- and cross-gender pairings, and therefore consisting of five female NSs–five female NNSs, five male NSs–five male NNSs, five female NSs–five male NNSs, and five male NSs–five female NNSs. The NNSs were Japanese L1 speakers at a low-intermediate proficiency level in their learning of English L2. The NSs were native speakers of American English recruited primarily from a large, private, urban university and its surrounding community. All subjects came from similar socio-cultural backgrounds.

Four different communication tasks were used in order to provide a broad sample of the subjects' speech and patterns of interaction. In two information-gap tasks, the NNS and NS interlocutors were asked to take turns. One drew and then described an original picture; the other replicated the picture, based solely on the drawer's descriptions and comments and follow-up responses to the replicator's questions. Neither was allowed to look at the other's picture as it was being described. In a jigsaw task, the NNS and NS were required to reproduce an unseen sequence of house pictures by exchanging their own uniquely held portions of the sequence. Finally, in an opinion-exchange task, the NNSs and NSs were told to share their views on the language learning contributions of the preceding tasks.

The framework used in coding the data collected for the study attempted to identify the negotiated nature of NS and NNS speech adjustments; that is, to reveal how these adjustments can be triggered by and reflected in the form, structure, and content of what NSs and NNSs say in attempting to understand and be understood by each other during negotiation. Earlier versions of this framework had been used in a series of studies (including published versions in Pica 1987a and Pica et al. 1989), with intercoder agreement ranging from .92 to .97. In the current version of the framework, shown in the Appendix, intercoder agreements ranged from .88 to 100.

As shown in the framework, in the course of negotiation, both NNS and NS can signal a need for clarification, confirmation, or reiteration of the other's utterance. As shown in categories 2a–c (see Appendix), these signals show that the initial utterance provides a trigger for the negotiation sequence. The signals can take the form of questions, statements, phrases, or words that do not in themselves incorporate the trigger (as in 2a). They can also be repetitions of the trigger (as in 2b) or can modify the trigger semantically, morphologically, or syntactically (as in 2c). The signals in 2c3 and 4 are made by segmenting one or more constituents of the trigger, then producing them in isolation or incorporating them into a longer utterance.

NNSs and NSs can respond to these signals in a variety of ways as shown in categories 3a–g. For example, they can respond by switching to a new or related topic (3a), or by repeating their initial trigger (3b), or their interlocutor's signal (3c). They can also modify the trigger (3d) or their interlocutor's signal (3e), and do so semantically, morphologically, or syntactically. Other category 3 responses (i.e., 3f and 3g) confirm the signal or indicate an inability to respond.

To complete the negotiation, the NS or NNS can supply either an explicit signal of comprehension (4a) or a topic continuation move (4b). Whether, indeed, these latter are true indications of comprehension is an empirical question, one that requires the kinds of comprehension tests and measurements used in the research reported above on comprehension and negotiation.

Across all tasks and within the different dyad configurations in the research described above, NSs provided samples of L2 that could serve the NNSs as a resource for L2 learning. These are displayed in the texts of NS-NNS negotiation and the results described below.

Negotiation as a Source of Feedback on Interlanguage Production

As revealed in the texts of Figure 5, NSs offered different kinds of feedback to NNSs during the course of negotiation, each of which had a characteristic impact on the NNSs' follow-up response. In texts 1 and 2, for example, the NS provided feedback through the simple, open signals of *pardon* and *huh*. In text 3, feedback appeared in the form of an elaborated utterance containing the same types of semantic and structural modifications that NSs used in responding to NNS signals, namely, repetition, rephrasing, segmentation, and movement. Here, the NS modified the NNS *cross* in two ways, providing an example of its use, as a place *where people can cross,* and by using *cross* in the verb phrase, *can cross.* Except during exact imitation, feedback moves were encoded by the NS in L2 lexis and morphosyntax rather than in interlanguage form.

— *Figure 5* ————————————————————

Negotiation as a Resource for Feedback on Interlanguage and Opportunities for Interlanguage Modification

1. NS open signal–NNS response of modified interlanguage:

NS	NNS
	there is three buildings, right?
pardon?	there is three . . .
	there are three
right right I've only described one so far	

2. NS signals–NNS response of semantic and morpheme modification and segmentation

NS	NNS
	you have three . . . you have three house which is which is um . . . which is like square of uh . . . which appears sharp
huh?	is like square
huh?	the bottom of house . . . the bottom of
house . . . shape	shape is like square
is square	you have three houses . . . one is no no
not one is not square and	one is square but with a little bit a
little small house	
ok	

3. NS open signal–NNS response of semantically modified interlanguage versus NS signal that modifies NNS trigger–NNS response of acknowledgment:

NS	NNS
	so there's a cross in the center of the paper . . .
>what do you mean by cross?	traffic cross
>oh, where people can cross or traffic light	yes

Table 2[4] provides a breakdown of the frequencies and relative proportions of NS signals that contained a linguistic modification. NS signals to NNSs contained extensive feedback on their interlanguage as there were 412 modifications of NNS interlanguage among the 519 NS signals to NNSs. Of these 412 modifications, 37 percent were semantic, 30 percent contained segmentation of the NNS interlanguage, and 11 percent provided a combination of semantic modification and segmentation. NS modifications were thus focused on both meaning and form of NNS interlanguage.

— **Table 2**

Frequencies and Proportions of Interlanguage Modifications in NS Feedback Signals to NNSs
Modifications in NS Feedback Signals (n = 519)

Types of Modification	n	% of Modifications
2c1 (semantic)	151	37
2c2 (morphological)	1	0

	50	12
2c3 (movement)	50	12
2c4 (segmentation)	123	30
2c1 + 2c2	9	2
2c1 + 2c3	13	3
2c1 + 2c4	46	11
2c2 + 2c3	5	1
2c2 + 2c4	12	3
2c3 + 2c4	2	0
TOTAL	412	

NS signals were not the only means through which the NNSs were given feedback on their interlanguage. As shown in Table 3, NSs produced 32 modifications in their 569 responses to NNSs. Here, the NSs did not modify their original trigger utterance, but instead gave a version of the NNS signal, modified semantically or syntactically or through some combination thereof. This pattern, which appears in the analytical framework under the 3e category, is also revealed in Figure 6 in which the NS response of *three floors* was a modification of the NNS signal, *third floor*.

━ Table 3 ━

Frequencies and Proportions of Interlanguage Modifications in NS Responses to NNSs
Modifications in NS Responses (n = 569)

Types of Modification	n	% of Modifications
3e1 (semantic)	8	2
3e2 (morphological)	1	0
3e3 (movement)	6	2
3e4 (segmentation)	4	1
3e1 + 3e2	2	1
3e1 + 3e2 + 3e4	1	0
3e1 + 3e3	5	1
3e1 + 3e4	4	1
3e2 + 3e3	0	0
3e2 + 3e4	1	0
3e3 + 3e4	0	0
TOTAL	32	

Negotiation as a Source of Opportunities for Learners to Modify Interlanguage

As was shown in the texts of Figure 5, NS utterances of feedback during negotiation provided NNSs with opportunities to produce lexical and structural adjustments in their interlanguage. As revealed in the texts, the NNSs used the same devices of repetition, rephrasing, elaboration, segmentation, and movement in responding to NSs as NSs used in their responses to them. However, as revealed in Tables 4 and 5, NNSs modified their responses less frequently and with a greater restriction in scope.

Table 4 provides a breakdown of the frequencies and relative proportions through which feedback signals were encoded and responded to by both the NSs and the NNSs. The data in Table 4 reveal that NNSs used a response pattern similar to that of the NSs, in that they responded most frequently to NSs through trigger modification (3d) and aknowledgment of signal (3f). These constituted 35 percent and 39 percent respectively of their response types to the NSs. However, the NNS response types were distributed differently from those of the NSs. Whereas NSs modified their own trigger significantly more than they acknowledged the NNS signal (61 percent versus 23 percent, $X2 = 167$, $p < .05$), the NNSs modified their own trigger and acknowledged the NS signal about equally ($X2 = 1.20$, n.s.). As revealed in text 3 of Figure 5, NNSs tended to respond to such elaborated signals through simple acknowledgment rather than further modification of their interlanguage, whereas an open signal brought about an elaborated NNS response. Here, the NNS supplied the premodifier *traffic* in response to the NS signal, *what do you mean by cross,* but said simply *yes* in response to the NNS signal *where people can cross or traffic light.*

▬ Table 4 ▬▬▬▬▬▬▬▬▬▬▬▬▬▬▬▬▬▬▬▬▬▬▬▬▬▬▬

Frequencies and Proportions of NS and NNS Responses to Signals

Response Types	NS Responses		NNS Responses	
	n	%	n	%
3a (change topic)	33	6	27	5
3b (repeat trigger)	12	2	14	3
3c (repeat signal)	12	2	21	4
3d (modify trigger)	346	61	182	35
3e (modify signal)	31	5	41	8
3f (acknowledge)	130	23	200	39
3g (unable to respond)	5	1	34	7
TOTAL	569		519	

Thus, when NNSs modified their production in response to NS signals, it was more often in response to NS open signals (2a) than in response to other NS signal types of trigger repetition (2b) and trigger modification (2c). As shown in Table 5, when NNSs responded to NS open signals, they modified their production 60 percent of the time. On the other hand, in responding to NS signals that repeated or modified what they had initially said, the NNSs modified their responses a respective 25 percent and 32 percent of the time, using a response of acknowledgment instead. This difference between the NNS production of modified responses to NS open signals versus NS signals of repetition and modification was statistically significant ($X2 = 15.96$, $p < .05$).

— Table 5 ———————————————————————

NNS Responses in Relation to NS Signals of Feedback

NNS Responses (n = 519)	NS Signals (n = 519)					
	2a Open Signal (n = 67)		2b Repeat Trigger (n = 40)		2c Modify Trigger (n = 412)	
	n	%	n	%	n	%
3a (change topic) (n=27)	3	4	2	5	22	5
3b (repeat trigger) (n=14)	2	3	6	15	6	1
3c (repeat signal) (n=21)	0	0	0	0	21	5
3d (modify trigger) (n=182)	40	60	10	25	132	32
3e (modify signal) (n=41)	3	4	0	0	38	9
3f (acknowledge) (n=200)	9	13	20	50	171	42
3g (unable to respond) (n=34)	10	15	2	5	22	5

This pattern was quite different from that used by NSs. As shown in Table 6, NSs modified their input to all three types of NNS signals of feedback. The frequency with which they did this was greatest in response to NNS open signals, that is, modifying 74 percent of their responses to NNS open signals. However, modification was also dominant in their responses to NNS signals of repetition (54 percent of NS responses were modified) and NNS signals of modification (59 percent of NS responses were modified).

— **Table 6** ————————————————————————————

NS Responses in Relation to NNS Signals of Feedback

NS Responses (n = 569)	NNS Signals (n = 569)					
	2a Open Signal (n = 73)		2b Repeat Trigger (n = 28)		2c Modify Trigger (n = 468)	
	n	%	n	%	n	%
3a (change topic) (n=33)	6	8	3	11	24	5
3b (repeat trigger) (n=12)	6	8	2	7	4	1
3c (repeat signal) (n=12)	0	0	0	0	12	3
3d (modify trigger) (n=346)	54	74	15	54	277	59
3e (modify signal) (n=31)	2	3	0	0	29	6
3f (acknowledge) (n=130)	4	5	8	29	118	25
3g (unable to respond) (n=5)	1	1	0	0	4	1

NNS interlanguage modification through responses to NS signals consisted of semantic modification as well as segmentation and movement of constituents. As shown in Table 7, NNSs in responding to NSs produced modifications both of own trigger (3d) and of NS signal (3e) and thereby revealed that they could manipulate both their own interlanguage and linguistic features in L2 input. NNS responses to NS signals provided semantic modification and segmentation and movement of constituents in their initial input, that is, the NS utterance(s) that had triggered the NNS signal. Of a total of 223 modifications in NNS responses to NSs, 81 percent were a modified version of the NNS trigger, with 21 percent semantic modification, 35 percent segmentation, 5 percent movement, and 18 percent combination of semantic modification, segmentation, and movement.

— *Table 7* ——————————————————

Frequencies and Proportions of Interlanguage Modifications in NNS Responses to NS

Modification Types	Modifications in NNS Responses (n = 519)	
	n	**%**
3d1 (semantic)	47	21
3d2 (morphological)	0	0
3d3 (movement)	11	5
3d4 (segmentation)	79	35
3d1 + 3d2	5	2
3d1 + 3d3	13	6
3d1 + 3d2 + 3d3	2	0
3d1 + 3d4	22	10
3d1 + 3d2 + 3d3 + 3d4	1	0
3d1 + 3d3 + 3d4	1	0
3d2 + 3d4	1	0
3e1 (semantic)	10	4
3e2 (morphological)	1	0
3e3 (movement)	5	2
3e4 (segmentation)	15	7
3e1 + 3e4	10	4
TOTAL	223	

NNSs also modified the L2 input they heard, as revealed in their own signals of feedback to the NSs. As shown in Table 8, the modifications in NNS signals were primarily of a segmented variety (74 percent), although there was some semantic modification both separately (11 percent) and in combination with segmentation (9 percent). The small percentage of semantic modification reflected perhaps the somewhat limited lexical resources of the low-intermediate-level subjects who participated in the study. Nevertheless, it can be said that for at least some of their signals, the NNSs were focused on both meaning and form of the L2 input that had served as a trigger for their signal.

— *Table 8*

Frequencies and Proportions of Interlanguage Modifications in NNS Signals to NS

Modification Types	Modifications in NNS Signals (n = 569)	
	n	%
2c (modify trigger)	468	100
2c1 (semantic)	52	11
2c2 (morphological)	3	1
2c3 (movement)	10	2
2c4 (segmentation)	346	74
2c1 + 2c2	1	0
2c1 + 2c3	4	1
2c1 + 2c4	40	9
2c2 + 2c3	3	1
2c2 + 2c4	8	2
2c3 + 2c4	1	0
TOTAL	468	

Negotiation as a Source of Data on L2 Rules and Features

In their responses to learners' signals for greater clarity of input in their own signals for clarity from learners, NSs often revealed to the NNSs semantic and structural relationships about the English language. As shown in the texts of Figure 6, these relationships were revealed in two distinct aspects of linguistic modification. Semantic relationships can be seen in text 1 of Figure 6, through the NS repetition, rephrasing, and elaboration of preceding input, that is, the NS utterance(s) that had triggered the NNS signal. Here the NS substituted *easy* for *simple* in response to the learner's query about this word.

Presentation of structural relationships to the NNS can be seen in texts 2 and 3 of Figure 6, through NS segmentation and movement of units in the triggering input. In text 2, the NS extracted *above* from his original input in response to the NNS question about *buvdaplate*. In text 3, the NS moved the word *garage* from its original position as object of *got* to the subject position in a sentence that provided its definition.

— **Figure 6** ——————————————————

Negotiation as a Resource of L2 Semantic and Structural Information in NS Responses to NNSs

1. NS response that provides semantic modification of input:

NS	NNS
are you finished?	not finished yet, it's too difficult
no, it's simple	simple?
it's easy	oh

2. NS response that segments a constituent from input:

NS	NNS
with a small pat of butter on it and above the plate	hm hmm what is buvdaplate?
above	above the plate
yeah	

3. NS response both segments and moves a constituent from input:

NS	NNS
it's got a garage on it, on the side of it where you park the car inside	inside?
you know where—a garage is where you park a car inside	oh yeah

4. NS response that modifies NNS interlanguage–NNS incorporation of morpheme:

NS	NNS
	ok, you have a house which has third floor
three floors right	three floors

These texts, particularly text 3, suggest ways in which negotiation provides an opportunity for learners to be shown semantic and structural relationships about the L2. The NS reveals that the L2 can be manipulated toward different discourse foci and can highlight shifting topics, as did the examples that Prince reviews in her paper (this volume). In text 3, the NS trigger and response utterances carried the same truth value about *garage*, but each was expressed through a different discourse function. This kind of input manipulation might be highly instructive for learners, teaching them about both the formal and functional possibilities of the L2.

The frequency and proportion of NS modifications in their responses are indicated in Table 9. As shown in Table 9, there were 346 modifications to the NS trigger among the 569 NS responses. Of these 346 modifications, 37 percent were semantic, 20 percent contained segmentation, and 9 percent involved movement of constituents. Further, 35 percent of the NS modifications were combinations of semantic modification, segmentation, and constituent movement.

— Table 9 _____

Frequencies and Proportions of L2 Modifications in NS Responses to NNS

Modification Types	Modifications in NS Responses (n = 569)	
	n	%
3d1 (semantic)	126	37
3d2 (morphological)	0	0
3d3 (movement)	32	9
3d4 (segmentation)	69	20
3d1 + 3d2	3	1
3d1 + 3d3	21	6
3d1 + 3d2 + 3d3	4	1
3d1 + 3d4	76	22
3d1 + 3d2 + 3d4	2	1
3d1 + 3d3 + 3d4	9	3
3d1 + 3d3 + 3d4	2	1
3d2 + 3d3	1	0
3d3 + 3d4	1	0
TOTAL	346	

Both the quantitative analysis in Table 9 and the texts in Figure 6 revealed that the NSs supplied modified input to NNSs that was focused on the meaning and form of the L2 about which they had signaled. Information about meaning through semantic modification of input, and information about form through segmentation and movement of input constituents, were either provided separately or were combined in various ways. What could not be uncovered in the data, however, was the extent to which this information was being used by the

NNSs in adjusting their interlanguage system. Texts such as 4 in Figure 6 indicated that NNSs could incorporate modified L2 input into their interlanguage within the same data collection session. Here, for example, the NNS changed *third floor* to *three floors* after this latter was used in an NS response. Such incorporation has also been observed by Gass and Varonis (1989). However, only longitudinal studies will be able to document the extent to which these modifications are sustained in NNS production over time.

CONCLUSION

The textual outcomes of NS-NNS negotiation and the quantified data on modifications produced during negotiation suggest that this activity has much to contribute to conditions of comprehension, feedback, and modified production considered necessary for successful SLA. Further, the texts generated through negotiation offer SLA researchers a rich data base for their understanding of learning processes. The texts provide researchers with an opportunity to examine learners' experiences in attempting to comprehend unfamiliar L2 input and in responding to feedback on their production. The texts also help researchers to identify and describe the role played by the NS both in facilitating these learning processes and in providing the NNS with a source of information on L2 rules and features. Negotiation makes distinct and important contributions toward what L2 learners need to do and what L2 researchers need to know. In this way, it serves as both a process and a goal: negotiation provides learners with a context for second language development and it offers researchers a window on the acquisition process.

ENDNOTES

1. We wish to acknowledge Iffat Farrah, Jess Unger, and Zhihong Zhang for their help with an earlier phase of this project.

2. This research was supported by a grant from the University of Pennsylvania Research Foundation. This study is one component of a continuing research project on "Language Learning Through Interaction," initiated in 1983. For their assistance to us in data collection, we would like to thank Richard Young, director of the University of Pennsylvania English Language Program, the faculty and staff of the program, and the staff of the University of Pennsylvania Graduate School of Education.

3. This research was supported by grants from the Ivy League Consortium on Language Teaching and Learning and the University of Pennsylvania Research Foundation. This study is another in the research project on "Language Learning Through Interaction," initiated in 1983. Again, for

assistance in data collection, we would like to thank Richard Young, director of the University of Pennsylvania English Language Program, the faculty and staff of the program, and the staff of the University of Pennsylvania Graduate School of Education. We also would like to thank Seran Dogancay and Lorraine Hightower for their help in data transcription and typing.

4. For Table 2 and all subsequent tables, proportional figures have been rounded to the nearest hundredth.

REFERENCES

Allwright, R. 1980. "Turns, Topics and Tasks: Patterns of Participation in Language Learning and Teaching." *Discourse Analysis in Second Language Acquisition Research.* Ed. D. Larsen-Freeman. Rowley, Mass.: Newbury. 165–82.

Blau, E. 1982. "The Effect of Syntax on Readability for ESL Students in Puerto Rico." *TESOL Quarterly* 16: 517–28.

Brock, C., G. Crookes, R. Day, and M. Long. 1986. "The Differential Effects of Corrective Feedback in Native-Speaker–Non-Native Speaker Conversation." *Talking to Learn: Conversation in Second Language Acquisition.* Ed. R. Day. Rowley, Mass.: Newbury. 327–51.

Brown, G. 1987. "Investigating Listening Comprehension in Context." *Applied Linguistics* 7: 284–302.

Busch, D. 1982. "Introversion-Extraversion and the ESL Proficiency of Japanese Students." *Language Learning* 32: 109–32.

Cervantes, R. 1983. " 'Say it again, Sam': The Effect of Repetition on Dictation Scores." Term paper, University of Hawaii at Manoa. Cited in Long, M. 1985. "Input and Second Language Acquisition Theory." *Input in Second Language Acquisition.* Eds. S. Gass and C. Madden. Rowley, Mass.: Newbury. 377–93.

Chaudron, C. 1983. "Simplification of Input: Topic Reinstatements and Their Effect on L2 Learners' Recognition and Recall." *TESOL Quarterly* 17: 437–58.

———. 1985. "Intake: On Models and Methods for Discovering Learners' Processing of Input." *Studies in Second Language Acquisition* 7: 1–14.

Chaudron, C., and K. Parker. 1990. "Discourse Markedness and Structural Markedness: The Acquisition of English Noun Phrases." *Studies in Second Language Acquisition* 12(1): 43–64.

Cook, V. J. 1988. *Chomsky's Universal Grammar: An Introduction.* Oxford: Blackwell.

Corder, S. P. 1967. "The Significance of Learners' Errors." *IRAL* 5: 161–70. Reprinted in *Error Analysis and Interlanguage.* Ed. S. P. Corder. 1981. Oxford: Oxford UP.

————. 1973. "The Elicitation of Interlanguage." Special issue of *IRAL* on the occasion of B. Malmberg's sixtieth birthday. Reprinted in *Error Analysis and Interlanguage.* Ed. S. P. Corder. 1981. Oxford: Oxford UP.

Crookes, G., and K. Rulon. 1985. "Incorporation of Corrective Feedback in Native Speaker/Non-Native Speaker Conversation." Technical report no. 3. The Center for Second Language Classroom Research/Social Science Research Institute, University of Hawaii at Manoa.

Day. R. 1984. "Student Participation in the ESL Classroom or Some Imperfections in Practice." *Language Learning* 34: 69–102.

————, ed. 1986. *Talking to Learn.* Rowley, Mass.: Newbury.

Doughty, C., and T. Pica. 1986. " 'Information Gap Tasks': An Aid to Second Language Acquisition?" *TESOL Quarterly* 20(2): 305–25.

Duff, P. 1986. "Another Look at Interlanguage Talk: Taking Task to Task." *Talking to Learn: Conversation in Second Language Acquisition.* Ed. R. Day. Rowley, Mass.: Newbury. 147–81.

Ellis, R. 1985. "Teacher-Pupil Interaction in Second Language Development." *Input in Second Language Acquisition.* Eds. S. Gass and C. Madden. Rowley, Mass.: Newbury. 69–88.

Faerch, C., and G. Kasper. 1984. "On Identifying Communication Strategies in Interlanguage Production." *Strategies in Interlanguage Communication.* Eds. C. Faerch and G. Kasper. London: Longman. 210–38.

————. 1987. "The Role of Comprehension in Second Language Acquisition." *Applied Linguistics* 8: 256–74.

Garfinkel, H. 1967. *Studies in Ethnomethodology.* Englewood Cliffs: Prentice.

Gass, S., and E. Varonis. 1984. "The Effect of Familiarity on the Comprehensibility of Non-Native Speech." *Language Learning* 34: 65–89.

————. 1985. "Task Variation and Non-Native Speaker/Non-Native Speaker Negotiation of Meaning." *Input in Second Language Acquisition.* Eds. S. Gass and C. Madden. Rowley, Mass.: Newbury. 149–61.

————. 1986. "Sex Differences in Non-Native Speaker/Non-Native Speaker Interactions." *Talking to Learn: Conversation in Second Language Acquisition.* Ed. R. Day. Rowley, Mass.: Newbury. 327–51.

————. 1989. "Incorporated Repairs in NNS Discourse." *The Dynamic Interlanguage.* Ed. M. Eisenstein. New York: Plenum.

Hatch, E. 1978. "Discourse Analysis and Second Language Acquisition." *Second Language Acquisition: A Book of Readings.* Ed. E. Hatch. Rowley, Mass.: Newbury. 401–35.

Hawkins, B. 1985. "Is an 'Appropriate Response' Always so Appropriate?" *Input in Second Language Acquisition.* Eds. S. Gass and C. Madden. Rowley, Mass.: Newbury. 162–80.

Johnson, P. 1981. "Effects of Reading Comprehension on Language Complexity and Cultural Background of a Text." *TESOL Quarterly* 15: 169–81.

Kelch, K. 1985. "Modified Input as an Aid to Comprehension." *Studies in Second Language Acquisition* 7: 81–90.

Krashen, S. 1980. *Second Language Acquisition and Second Language Learning.* Oxford: Pergamon.

———. 1985. *The Input Hypothesis: Issues and Implications.* London: Longman.

Long, M. 1980. "Input, Interaction, and Second Language Acquisition." Diss. UCLA.

———. 1981. "Input, Interaction, and Second Language Acquisition." *Native Language and Foreign Language Acquisition.* Ed. H. Winitz. New York: N Y Acad. of Science.

———. 1983. "Linguistic and Conversational Adjustments to Non-Native Speakers." *Studies in Second Language Acquisition* 5(2): 177–94.

———. 1985. "Input and Second Language Acquisition Theory." *Input in Second Language Acquisition.* Eds. S. Gass and C. Madden. Rowley, Mass.: Newbury. 377–93.

Meisel, J. M., H. Clahsen, and M. Pienemann. 1981. "On Determining Developmental Stages in Natural Second Language Acquisition." *Studies in Second Language Acquisition* 3: 109–35.

Pica, T. 1987a. "Interlanguage Adjustments as an Outcome of NS-NNS Negotiated Interaction." *Language Learning* 38(1): 45–73.

———. 1987. "Second Language Acquisition, Social Interaction in the Classroom." *Applied Linguistics* 7: 1–25.

———. 1991. "Classroom Interaction, Participation, and Comprehension: Redefining Relationships." *System.*

Pica, T., and C. Doughty. 1985. "Non-Native Speaker Interaction in the ESL Classroom." *Input in Second Language Acquisition.* Eds. S. Gass and C. Madden. Rowley, Mass.: Newbury. 115–32.

Pica, T., C. Doughty, and R. Young. 1986. "Making Input Comprehensible: Do Interactional Modifications Help?" *ITL Review of Applied Linguistics* 72: 1–25.

Pica, T., L. Holliday, N. Lewis, D. Berducci, and J. Newman. 1991. "Language Learning Through Interaction: What Role Does Gender Play?" *Studies in Second Language Acquisition.*

Pica, T., L. Holliday, N. Lewis, and L. Morgenthaler. 1989. "Comprehensible Output as an Outcome of Linguistic Demands on the Learner." *Studies in Second Language Acquisition* 11(1): 63–90.

Pica, T., R. Kanagy, and J. Falodun. Forthcoming. "Choosing and Using Communication Tasks for Second Language Research and Instruction." *Task-based Learning in a Second Language.* Eds. S. Gass and G. Crookes. London: Multilingual Matters.

Pica, T., R. Young, and C. Doughty. 1987. "The Impact of Interaction on Comprehension." *TESOL Quarterly* 21(4): 737–58.

Pienemann, M. 1984. "Psychological Constraints on the Teachability of Languages." *Studies in Second Language Acquisition* 6: 186–214.

Politzer, R., and M. McGroarty. 1985. "An Exploratory Study of Learning Behaviors and Their Relationship to Gains in Linguistic and Communicative Competence." *TESOL Quarterly* 19: 103–24.

Rulon, K., and J. McCreary. 1986. "Negotiation of Content: Teacher-Fronted and Small Group Interaction." *Talking to Learn: Conversation in Second Language Acquisition.* Ed. R. Day. Rowley, Mass.: Newbury. 182–99.

Sato, C. 1982. "Ethnic Differences in ESL Classroom Interaction." *On TESOL '81.* Eds. M. Hines and W. Rutherford. Washington, D.C.: TESOL. 11–24.

Saville-Troike, M., E. McClure, and M. Fritz. 1984. "Communicative Tactics in Children's Second Language Acquisition." *Universals of Second Language Acquisition.* Eds. F. Eckman, L. Bell, and D. Nelson. Rowley, Mass.: Newbury. 60–71.

Schachter, J. 1983. "Nutritional Needs of Language Learners." *On TESOL '82: Pacific Perspectives on Language Learning and Teaching.* Eds. M. A. Clarke and J. Handscombe. Washington, D.C.: TESOL. 175–89.

———. 1984. "A Universal Input Condition." *Universals and Second Language Acquisition.* Ed. W. Rutherford. Amsterdam: John Benjamins. 167–83.

———. 1986. "Three Approaches to the Study of Input." *Language Learning* 36 (2): 211–26.

Sharwood-Smith, M. 1987. "Comprehension vs. Acquisition: Two Ways of Processing Input." *Applied Linguistics* 8: 237–55.

Swain, M. 1985. "Communicative Competence: Some Roles of Comprehensible Input and Comprehensible Output in Its Development." *Input in Second Language Acquisition.* Eds. S. Gass and C. Madden. Rowley, Mass.: Newbury. 236–44.

Varonis, E., and S. Gass. 1982. "The Comprehensibility of Non-Native Speech." *Studies in Second Language Acquisition* 4: 41–52.

———. 1985a. "Miscommunication in Native/Non-Native Conversation." *Language in Society* 14: 327–43.

———. 1985b. "Non-Native/Non-Native Conversations: A Model for the Negotiation of Meaning." *Applied Linguistics* 6: 71–90.

White, L. 1987. "Against Comprehensible Input: The Input Hypothesis and the Development of Second Language Competence." *Applied Linguistics* 9: 89–110.

APPENDIX

Framework for Coding Data on Negotiated Interaction

1. (Trigger) Utterance(s):

NS	NNS
the children are visiting their uncle for a few days	children they visit uncle few day

2. Signal directed toward form/meaning of Trigger:

2a. Question/statement/phrase/word that does not incorporate Trigger:

NS	NNS	NNS	NS
the children are visiting their uncle for a few days	>what?	children they visit uncle few day	>what?

2b. Question/statement/phrase/word that repeats Trigger without linguistic (i.e., semantic or morphosyntactic) modification:

NS	NNS	NNS	NS
the children are visiting their uncle for a few days	>the children are visiting their	children they visit uncle few day	>children they visit uncle few day? uncle for a few days?

2c. Question/statement/phrase/word that linguistically modifies all or part of Trigger:

2c1: semantically: through synonym, paraphrase, example, analogy, descriptors, and/or interpretation:

NS	NNS	NNS	NS
the children are visiting their uncle for a few days	>one week?	children they visit uncle few day	>they will stay a week?

2c2: morphologically: through addition, substitution, or deletion of inflectional morpheme(s):

NS	NNS	NNS	NS
the children are visiting their uncle for a few days	>children they visited few day?	children they visit uncle few day	>they visited for a few days?

2c3: syntactically: through segmentation, with relocation (subject to object, object to subject) (S > O, O > S), topicalization or incorporation into phrases/clauses):

NS	NNS	NNS	NS
the children are visiting their uncle for a few days	>uncle he have for few days?	children they visit uncle few days	>their uncle has the children?

2c4. syntactically: through segmentation, without relocation (S > O, O > S), topicalization, or incorporation into phrases/clauses:

NS	NNS	NNS	NS
the children are visiting their uncle for a few days	>few days?	children they visit uncle few day	>few days?

3. Follow-up response:

3a. Question/statement/phrase/word that switches to a new topic/supplies information generally related to topic, but not directed toward form/meaning of Signal:

NS	NNS	NNS	NS
the children are visiting their uncle for a few days >he lives in Florida	few days?	children they visit uncle few day >uncle he live Florida	for a few days?

3b. Statement/phrase/word that repeats Trigger without linguistic (semantic or morphosyntactic) modification:

NS	NNS	NNS	NS
the children are visiting their uncle for a few days >the children are visiting their uncle for a few days	few days?	children they visit uncle few day >children they visit uncle few day	for a few days?

3c. Statement/phrase/word that repeats Signal without linguistic (semantic or morphosyntactic) modification:

NS	NNS	NNS	NS
the children are visiting their uncle for a few days >one week	one week?	children they visit uncle few day >a week	a week?

3d. Statement/phrase/word that linguistically modifies all or part of Trigger:

3d1. semantically: through synonym, paraphrase, example, analogy, descriptors and/or interpretation:

NS	NNS	NNS	NS
the children are visiting their uncle for a few days >the children are staying with my brother for a few days	what?	children they visit uncle few day >children they stay my brother few day	what?

3d2. morphologically: through addition, substitution, or deletion of inflectional morpheme(s):

NS	NNS	NNS	NS
the children are visiting their uncle for a few days >the children have gone to visit their uncle's home for a day or two	what?	children they visit uncle few day >children they visiting uncle few days	what?

3d3. syntactically: through segmentation, with relocation (S > O, O > S), topicalization, or incorporation into phrases/clauses:

NS	NNS	NNS	NS
the children are visiting their uncle for a few days >their uncle has the children for a few days	what?	children they visit uncle few day >uncle he have children few days	what?

3d4. syntactically: through segmentation, without relocation (S > O, O > S), topicalization, or incorporation into phrases/clauses:

NS	NNS	NNS	NS
the children are visiting their uncle for a few days >for a few days	what?	children they visit uncle few day >few days	what?

3e. Statement/phrase/word that linguistically modifies Signal:

3e1. semantically: through synonym, paraphrase, example, analogy, descriptors, and/or interpretation:

NS	NNS	NNS	NS
the children are visiting their uncle for a few days >almost one week	one week?	children they visit uncle few day >almost a week	they will stay a week?

3e2. morphologically: through addition, substitution, or deletion of inflectional morpheme(s):

NS	NNS	NNS	NS
the children are visiting their uncle for a few days >no, two weeks	one week?	children they visit uncle few day >no, two weeks	they will stay a week?

    3e3. syntactically: through segmentation, with relocation (S > O, O > S), topicalization, or incorporation into phrases/clauses:

NS	NNS	NNS	NS
the children are visiting their uncle for a few days >their uncle would like them to stay a week	they stay one week?	children they visit uncle few day >uncle want them stay a week	they will stay a week?

    3e4. syntactically: through segmentation, without relocation (S > O, O > S), topicalization, or incorporation into phrases/clauses:

NS	NNS	NNS	NS
the children are visiting their uncle for a few days >one week	they stay one week?	children they visit uncle few day >a week	they will stay a week?

    3f. Confirmation or acknowledgment without linguistic modification:

NS	NNS	NNS	NS
the children are visiting their uncle for a few days >yes	one week?	children they visit uncle few day >yes	they will stay a week?

3g. Indication of difficulty or inability to respond:

NS	NNS	NNS	NS
the children are visiting their uncle for a few days >I'm sorry, I don't know how to say it better	what?	children they visit uncle few day >is difficult to say	what?

4. Comprehension signal/continuation move

4a. Comprehension signal:

NS	NNS	NNS	NS
the children are visiting their uncle for a few days almost two weeks	one week? >I see	children they visit uncle few day almost two weeks	they will stay a week? >I see

4b. Continuation move:

NS	NNS	NNS	NS
the children are visiting their uncle for a few days almost two weeks	one week? when return?	children they visit uncle few day almost two weeks	they will stay a week? >and when will they return?

— Chapter *15*

Written Texts and Cultural Readings

Janet Swaffar

University of Texas at Austin

The thesis of this paper is a simple one: cultural differences must be discovered as dialogic practices, not learned as monologic features. Cultural differences are found in mutually defining networks of practices, not inventories of practices: in patterns of behavior, not in behaviors as such. The most consistent cultural networks are located in authentic texts for listening, viewing, or reading. One working definition of authentic materials is that they were originally produced by native speakers to be read by native speakers. As artifacts of the second language's culture, such texts present the second language learner with social functions familiar in many, perhaps all, cultures. Yet at the same time they depict concrete situations that are culture specific. In other words, authentic texts offer readers case studies of fundamental human relationships, needs, and social institutions such as kinship, ritual behavior, social status, governance, or eating arrangements as they are manifested in the unfamiliar culture.*

CULTURAL MISREADINGS AND L2 COMPREHENSION

To illustrate, a marriage ritual is common to most cultures. Even where formal ceremonies seem quite similar, however, the broader significance of what is happening—its social meaning—may diverge radically from one culture to the next. Steffensen and her colleagues (1979) did a now classic study a decade ago with students from America and India. Descriptions of American and Indian weddings were read by both groups. Although the two texts were in English, recall was consistently higher for the text from each group's own culture—its C1. Differences were qualitative as well as quantitative. Consistently, connotations diverged with respect to the readers' cultural identities. Both Indians and Americans understood, for example, that the bride wore something borrowed and that the bride's parents failed to exchange gifts with the family of the groom. But these features, tagged by American readers as positive, were viewed by Indians as signs of poverty and hence regrettable. What for American readers was a typical festive occasion, was read quite differently by members of a culture for whom the bride's affluence may signal decisively her future chances for happiness.

Both passages were fairly short letters (about 700 words) that described the events. Possibly American readers who had more background might have reconstructed the Indian wedding more accurately. Alternatively, after reading additional letters about the American newlyweds and their life together, the Indian readers might have found their concerns groundless and altered their initial schemata. Other studies of foreign language (FL) reading, however, suggest that L2 students resist modifying first impressions. Unlike the self-corrections more characteristic for L1 readers, L2 readers tend to cling to their initial misapprehensions (Bernhardt 1990). Without prior orientation, FL students' faulty cultural schemata can easily result in distorted readings.

To forestall misreading, FL textbooks and syllabi now focus on cultural differences. Misreadings will, it is often assumed, be eliminated when students' thinking is directed by explicit instruction. Typically, in beginning courses, culture "capsules" fulfill this objective. Students learn about particular customs or how specific linguistic features express values or describe characteristic behaviors. What kind of culture are students learning about in such capsules? To what extent can culture be defined by feature inventories? One real danger in forestalling misreading with such instructional "correction" is that students learn to define a foreign culture in fixed typologies, static sets of features.

More extended literary texts, however, present students with implied as well as explicit statements about the L2 civilization and culture. Moreover, the cultural features in such texts are rarely fixed or univalent. For example, an East Indian bride may be as well-to-do as the groom or wealthier, yet offend her in-laws because her caste is inferior to his. The marriage may conform to economic expectations in the society (related to satisfying sustenance or survival needs) while at the same time offending social organization or kinship norms (glossed for convenience as class structures).

FIXED TYPOLOGIES
VERSUS COGNITIVE TYPOLOGIES

Worries about fixed typologies appear justified. While we know that "cultural distance" influences L2 students' attitudes toward native speakers of the L2 (Svanes 1988; Mollica 1985), virtually no research addresses the question of how students can *overcome* cultural distance. Quite possibly, teaching contrasts in values, attitudes, and behaviors results in univalent stereotyping rather than real metacultural awareness. More important, isolated features themselves are uninformative. Indian readers responded negatively to something borrowed or to an absence of exchanged gifts because these ritual features imply other features in their own culture: questions about the bride's social status or her family's ability to feed and clothe itself adequately. The feature "something borrowed" is significant not in isolation but only within the *total* fabric of a particular society.

In addition to stereotyping, a second danger exists in the inventory approach to culture. When we offer students ready-made accounts of the customary attitudes, institutions, or behaviors of a culture, they rarely learn how to interpret cultural features or to identify features on their own. For example, a detailed capsule depiction of the "typical" Central and South American *mercado* certainly presents information about shopping habits. But by itself the *mercado* is little more than a supermarket with a different ambience and the opportunity to haggle about prices. Only when students begin to see how the *mercado* contributes to behaviors and attitudes within a larger system of social behavior can its significance be "read."

Indeed, establishing cultural implications involves sorting out data about complex interrelationships—those in real life situations or those depicted in longer authentic texts, particularly literary narratives. When a literary work depicts multiple, possibly conflicting, cultural behaviors and attitudes, a challenging author creates a complex microcultural network, part of a world. Only when students learn to identify this network can they move beyond static traits (stereotypes) and into cognitive types (true cultural literacy). In other words, the *mercado* is a colorful, noisy, smelly, generally inexpensive place to buy food and other necessities (the stereotype). There is more to be learned, however. For example, a narrative's information about where stalls are located can provide readers with clues to the ways different groups dominate one another (e.g., by age, wealth, tradition, sex); details about the relationship between producer and seller (e.g., whether they belong to the same or different social groups) can suggest something about class structures. Thus the static *mercado* image of culture capsules gives way to a more dynamic network that reveals how social life and values operate. Students begin to learn how concrete details are part of a larger system.

To avoid looking only at static images or isolated features, I am urging that we ask our students to identify and re-create a more fully extended system of cultural practices in the text. These extended contexts or cultural patterns in authentic materials offer students two advantages over single feature descriptions or culture capsules. First, these materials are presented in the FL rather than English, as culture capsules often are. Second, even when cultural descriptions are presented in the FL, they provide only data for decoding (this equals that) rather than for encoding (this changes or affects something else). Decoding is limited to features already presented whereas encoding helps readers approach new aspects of the culture. The single feature description, even when presented in the L2, is removed from the larger L2 cultural nexus that ultimately makes it significant.

Stereotyped generalizations such as "French families drink wine" are hardly meaningful in themselves. They *become* meaningful when students read about how particular groups define drinking behaviors such as getting drunk. In America, where children generally consume nonalcoholic beverages at the family dinner table, drunkenness often signals macho behavior in the male peer group. In France, inebriate behavior is more typically a social blunder, a *faux pas* rather than a sign of manliness. Thus the cultural generalization "wine drinking" assumes appropriate social meaning only when linked to the way behaviors express consensus about valued or discredited behaviors within specific cultures.

Let me briefly indicate how similar generalizations might be used to encode cultural norms (i.e., uncover interrelationships) in a longer text. In literature or films, patterns emerge that reinforce the work's conflicts or consensuses—do young and old, for example, use the same mode of transportation, dress the same way for various occasions, use the same standards for speech, and recognize the same authorities when in public and in private?

Only establishing such patterns can forestall a cliché approach to culture. The links between "typical" attitudes and behaviors must be examined in specific contexts. Cultural behaviors, after all, have different implications in different social relationships or settings. Even in France, whether to tag drunkenness as manly or a social embarrassment may depend on the company one keeps (working class versus white collar). Distinctions in cultural typing change with history and locale as well. Although French families have been drinking wine together for centuries, the mode and impact of that behavior has changed over time and varies today depending on individual families, social class, or geographical region.

Consider another case where overgeneralizations can yield misleading cultural implications. Germans have had an enviable public transportation system for about one hundred years. In isolation, knowledge about public transportation in Germany is a lifeless cliché—it lacks social implications. When, however, that knowledge is linked to demographic changes or personal stories about German life-styles, FL students can begin to think about how the presence or absence of public transportation radically alters family life or public funds necessary for caring for the aged. Growing populations over sixty-five characterize most Western cultures. Cultures such as ours that rely mainly on private transportation render older members of the population dependent on others for necessities. In conjunction with a longer text about a retired person, students can assess how Germany's public transportation network provides a senior citizen with a mobility and independence unavailable to counterparts in the United States.

Seeing how such multiple cultural phenomena interrelate and change is, I suggest, the only informative way to learn about culture. And if that is true, then our instructional task is to provide two resources: first, materials rich in cultural patterns, and second, a framework enabling students to discover these patterns for themselves.

Such a framework must provide students with ways to uncover textual meaning without first hearing about the unfamiliar features they will encounter as immutable "facts." We want to forestall misreading without introducing static stereotypes. Aside from its pedagogical desirability, that framework would make the reader, not the teacher, responsible for his or her grasp of meaning. Political or ideological correctness is not at issue; cultural realities *are*. Only by identifying cultural patterns from extended clues can students encounter cultures on something like natives' terms; prejudging those clues will impede learning alternative cultural realities.

As a consequence, the FL class must focus on helping each person use prior capabilities and background to uncover new ideas and information in an L2 text. Students must learn to base their readings on what the text says rather than on their own preconceptions about what it should say. A cultural reading can take place only when students can distinguish textually conveyed messages from their own preconceptions. To differentiate between textual messages and their own culturally situated opinions and assumptions, students need to be careful and consistent.

A FRAMEWORK
FOR CULTURAL READING

The basis for a consistent approach, an accountability mode for "cultural reading," implies what J. Hillis Miller (this volume) calls discernment of patterns: a text's narrative point of view, structure, content, and context (textual macrodetails), and its realization in the patterns of word- and sentence-level discourse markers, semantics, and syntax (textual mirodetails).

Patterns in these text features reveal culture-specific information. Any narrative art from any culture will deal with some of the primary functions found across cultures. For any ethnographic group, questions can be raised about some fundamental aspects of human life and social organization: for example, governance, how survival needs are met, distinctions among people and their significance for the division of labor and the distribution of wealth, the forms of etiquette regulating social relations. Such categories form a grid of cultural universals or invariants to be realized in culturally specific variants, depending on where and when the text was created.

Cross-cultural variations are defined differently, depending on the anthropological approach (e.g., Geertz 1973). No particular anthropological theory is required, however. What FL students need are strategies to identify basic relationships that characterize all human communities as they are represented in texts. The list on page 243 was constructed by Katherine Arens in discussion with the author and identifies features commonly represented in literature.

To establish specific examples for the abstract structures, students will need to apply a simple test. They must ask themselves, "What do these features reveal about the belief systems of the culture? What behaviors result in profit or loss for the individuals in this cultural system? What is considered good or bad, worthy or unworthy?" In short, it is at this point that the common definition of culture as behaviors, attitudes, and values assumes a cognitive shape. Behaviors,

Invariant/Abstract Structures	Variant/Specific Examples
Enjoyment/pain	what activities constitute pleasure or pain
Rituals	what behaviors are appropriate
Governance	who decides what will be done
Manners/etiquette	appropriate and inappropriate behaviors
Class structures	what makes a class; who decides
Dominance/legitimacy	what characteristics put people in charge
Sustenance/survival needs	what is considered necessary for what class

attitudes, and values are not equivalent features. Instead, they represent a system of signs whose significance can be assessed only through rigorous separation and ordered analysis. Behaviors are, after all, value free until measured by the censure or approbation of society. To avoid prejudgment, the reader must scrupulously link attitudes expressed in a text toward behaviors depicted in that text. Only this process reveals the value systems within a given text.

By ascertaining what behaviors in a novel, story, or film characterize the abstract structures listed above, and how those behaviors are judged by others in that work, students can uncover the way unfamiliar cultural features affect one another. For example, the fact that students equate a movie's noble heroine with their own value scale is probably unavoidable. Students can more profitably ascertain what the "noble" features are, what characters in the movie find them valuable, and whether those same types of people would identify nobility or ignobility in the same way. The important result is less a "correct" reading than careful reading/real-life comparison.

Only by discovering differences themselves can students learn to recognize how such differences operate as pieces of a larger system. One Western's noble savage (*Dances with Wolves*) is another's marauding half-breed (*Lonesome Dove*). As Sander Gilman illustrates, "[M]ore complicated texts provide more complicated representations of difference" (1985: 27). Texts that challenge a dominant societal image explode stereotypes. Hence such texts must first alter the reader's stereotypical associations with a given image—that reader's preexisting mental *gestalt* of "good" and "bad" behavior when, for example, the word *patriarch* occurs.

To confront their own stereotypes, readers must examine how individual behaviors and institutional arrangements are judged by the characters in the text and by implied authorial voices, comparing such textually indicated judgments and attitudes with their own. Students will have their own views about a behavior like wine drinking or an institution like public transportation. Only after they discover that their views are not shared by characters or groups in the text can students reflect about the basis for different perspectives. What behavioral networks are implied by the way the text's characters think, act, and react? Is wine drinking connected to cultural constructions of masculinity? Do men of all ages and walks of life engage in insobriety or is drunkenness a token of masculinity only among young men or men in particular social circles? Which publics use subways and trains? Most business people or virtually none? Only blue collar workers or a high percentage of the elderly and school children as well? Of necessity, such patterns emerge at the macro- or plot level. Their distinctive features are, however, often elaborated at the discourse and sentence levels.

Applying Cultural Reading as an Interpretive Tool

Apply the check list in the aforementioned chart to a book or movie whose plot and characters are relatively familiar. Jane Austen's *Pride and Prejudice* offers a well-known cameo portrait of English landed gentry at the turn of the nineteenth century. As such it provides a picture of a culture foreign to us in time and locale. Applying these variant/invariant criteria, students would emerge with a matrix such as the following:

Abstract Social Function	Specific Manifestation
Enjoyment	dinners, card playing, balls, conversation
Pain	not being invited or admired
Rituals	acceptable behavior follows strict social rules
Governance	men decide, women complain and manipulate
Manners/etiquette	breeding reveals "real" class
Class structures	noble birth, wealth and leisure, breeding
Dominance/legitimacy	breeding, enforced by legitimacy of title and bloodline
Sustenance/survival needs	provided by others, presupposed independent wealth

Students can substantiate their assertions with textual events. Thus, an example of governance problems arises in Mr. Bennet's visit to Mr. Bingley. The narrator makes clear that only after such a visit can Mr. Bennet's five daughters be properly introduced to this eligible young man. Men decide who will meet whom. The issue of dominance, on the other hand, is equally clear. Implicitly,

Mrs. Bennet's ceaseless complaints prompt the visit. Mr. Bennet acts to please his insistent, nagging wife. Later in the novel, the motive behind Mr. Bennet's fateful decision to let Lydia visit Brighton is expressly stated when he tells Elizabeth, "We'll have no peace . . . if Lydia does not go to Brighton" (Austen 1940: 246). Thus, consistently, while men decide, those decisions are rarely unilateral. Women have input. If the man in question is weak or indifferent, that input will be decisive. The patriarchal social order governs, but women may dominate weak men via manipulation.

After these various assertions have been documented in the text, an inventory reveals conventional English life in this particular time and place. At this juncture students can apply the belief system test. Does any figure modify his or her beliefs about class structure, governance, and the like? Clearly, at least one major figure does. When Elizabeth challenges Darcy's claim to superiority, he shifts to the hierarchy of values she believes in, accepting breeding over blood. He changes his attitudes about the relationship between class and social conduct. What he had heretofore considered "good manners" is no longer the purview of the landed gentry. Elizabeth has shown him that, within his class, etiquette has become an empty social form. Rather than making a statement about blood lineage, good manners reveal true class—or at least reveal those gentlefolk with integrity and breeding.

If *Pride and Prejudice* were no more than light entertainment, such an inventory would suffice. Popular literature, after all, reaffirms a particular cultural myth—pretty women get their man, hard work pays off, breeding tells. The belief systems in popular novels may vary with individual behavior, but their social conventions stay intact. The work signals no major cultural shifts.

More demanding literature *will* signal changes in social conventions.[1] What is involved in the distinction between popular culture and a literature viewed as of greater merit or as canonical? I am suggesting that popular literature presents stereotypical structures that dominate the daily mental life of a given culture. Demanding literature, in contrast, explodes stereotypes by creating disequilibrium among social norms. Gilman distinguishes between "reflected" and "unreflected" stereotypes (27). In this paper I assume that demanding literature challenges cultural norms and, in this sense, enables the reader to reflect about cultural stereotypes discredited or rendered implausible in a given work. The Prague School suggests that challenging literature takes everyday language or behavior and "foregrounds" it—that is, forces the reader to rethink accepted norms (Mukarovsky 1964). Part of the reason popular literature sells well is because it confirms accepted social conventions for native readers.

A demanding text, however, will challenge the substance of one or more conventions and thereby reveal cultural flaws or instability—readers may be discomfited. Individual deviations in behavior assume larger significance as indices for social change. Precisely Darcy's and Elizabeth's ability to see alternatives to the status quo suggests where larger public or cultural consensus in their society hides underlying social conflict and forces for change, where the stated may not be the real.

Thus we can read the cultural messages in popular literature to confirm a culture's myths, its desired image for itself—its self-stereotyping. We can read so-called classic literature to assess where the real and apparent cultural images diverge—to glimpse the cultural ruptures beneath surface forms.

To discern these ruptures, the reader must locate tensions between individual and cultural expectations. In other words, the reader must ask whether cultural consensus about individual behavior is present or absent. This consensus or lack thereof emerges from three tests for social acceptability:

1. Do discrepancies exist between what is allowable in public and in private spheres?
2. Do strict differences exist between what men and women can do?
3. What behaviors result in economic or social profit and loss?

Let us apply these tests to normed and non-normed behavior in *Pride and Prejudice*. First, the public and private spheres are not isolated: each affects the other. Personal decisions result in public approbation or disgrace. Unless Wickham marries her, Lydia effectively ruins her sisters' chances for marrying well. Similarly, Wickham must malign Darcy publicly to avoid revealing his personal defects. The second test, whether men and women maintain their social roles, seems stable: fathers, wealthy uncles, and suitors rescue daughters, nieces, and sweethearts while mothers, aunts, and sisters wait at home. Women maneuver and manipulate in the private sphere; men make public decisions as legitimate governors.

Of the three tests for stability, only one seems to be malleable. Only in the profit and loss category does a shift occur: the absolute dominance of blood gives way to the primacy of good breeding. When Elizabeth rejects Darcy's suit with the accusation that he is proud to an ungentlemanly degree, Darcy, instead of rejecting Elizabeth in kind, reviews his own value scheme and falls, as apparently was said then, even more violently in love. A man who has declared Elizabeth beneath his station in life is nonetheless influenced by her judgment. In judging the dominant individual by her own standards, not his, Elizabeth, a woman of less estate, takes Darcy's legitimacy into her hands.

The right Darcy concedes to Elizabeth to criticize behavior of her social superiors reveals Darcy's broader public definition for acceptable behavior—transcending formal definitions of social legitimacy. The standards operative in polite society, even polite society that is financially and genealogically inferior, matter more to him than being defined by his own social class. Significantly, this private decision becomes public dictum as well. Darcy's friends and servants take his word as gospel and accept his match. Even his aunt ultimately capitulates. Society supports his decision to acknowledge that more appropriate norms exist outside the pale of birth. In accepting Elizabeth's standard Darcy also accepts an aunt and uncle from the merchant class and even a mother-in-law totally lacking in acquired good manners. Elizabeth's propriety and ability ennoble her. Darcy's judgment heralds far-reaching changes that would eventually lead to a Disraeli and knighthood for many of England's state-schooled entrepreneurs.

If read in this way, Jane Austen's first novel foreshadows patterns in social acceptability in Dickens, Thackeray, and Trollope unlike those of France or Germany. In England unlike the continent, class-bound social standards tend to resist change on the basis of economic dominance alone. Only if the class immediately below the socially dominant one can exhibit equal or superior manners, intelligence, or talents, is it entitled to be acknowledged. A middle-class protagonist in a Dickens novel can, by virtue of breeding rather than birth but not by wealth alone, become the universally respected Lord Mayor of London.

Moreover, this concern for propriety as the hallmark for social acceptability remains a prominent theme in English culture to this day, furnishing variant versions from Oscar Wilde to John Le Carré, from *Chariots of Fire* to Monty Python. This trope continues into the televised *Upstairs, Downstairs,* where, because she is a duke's daughter, Lord and Lady Bellamy are a social mismatch. His political skills, however, overcome their social disparity and the two forge a union acknowledged in England's most exalted circles.

Pedagogical Implications

This paper began with the claim that when a reader relates social practices systematically, cultural networks emerge. These networks can best be identified in authentic texts for listening, viewing, or reading. Pedagogically speaking, at what point in time can FL readers discover such networks for themselves? At present, most beginning courses for adults provide students with virtually no exposure to longer texts. I think that is a mistake. If we provided first-year students with a library of popular literature, literature without a pretense to high culture, they could read it for cultural clichés. They would recognize parallels to familiar harlequin romances or detective fiction. They would not understand every word, but reading to identify a text's cultural conventions, they could grasp the tropes in that text and their implied stereotypes.

Would that be a superficial reading? If the text in question were *Madame Bovary, Pride and Prejudice,* or *Wilhelm Meister,* canon literature that challenges societal norms, the answer is probably yes. First-year students would lack the vocabulary and background to grasp subtleties in carefully wrought narrative and complex social conventions. For popular literature, however, if reading simply to confirm how cultural structures manifest themselves in behaviors associated with governance, legitimacy, etiquette, or entertainment, adult FL students possess enough schemata in Western best-sellers and box office hits to experience success.

Because behaviors are manifested in episodes in a longer text, students who read popular works to identify cultural networks are directed toward the plot or macro-level. A blatantly predictable text need not be read at more than the macrolevel. My reader may, at this point, argue that such reading is therefore without educational value. To such objections I counter with the following pedagogical arguments.

First, with regard to psycholinguistic evidence, our best indications from L1 research suggest that in vocabulary building, extensive reading makes the difference. We have insufficient information about L2 readers to know whether the same is true for them. In the span of five years of study with four to five contact hours weekly, learners of English as a foreign language in India and Indonesia have only a 2,000 word vocabulary (Nation 1990: 12). However, 2,000 to 3,000 words are assumed sufficient "for general usefulness in English."[2] Nation estimates, however, that students need a vocabulary of at least 3,000 *headwords* (words belonging to a particular root—*own,* adjective; *own,* verb; *ownership,* noun, etc.) to read unsimplified texts (119). Theoretically, then, readers with high motivation, familiar schemata, and passive vocabulary of between 2,000 to 3,000 words may read to encode texts in a manner not unlike those reading in a first language and acquire incidental vocabulary while so doing.

Whether as preparation for content learning or as further FL study, students must have extensive exposure to language yet not be overwhelmed by that exposure. Moreover, if it is conducted in their interest areas, students find extensive reading informative and enjoyable. The format for cultural readings suggested in this paper enables comprehensible input because it demands no more than macro-level understanding. Even students with meager vocabularies can read popular texts for patterns in behavior—consistencies in textual actions, events, or outcomes. While more confirmation is needed, there are already some indications that when reading enables comprehensible input at the macro-level, vocabulary acquisition takes place (Saragi, Nation, and Meister 1978).

Second, from an interpretive standpoint, reading for cultural meanings in relatively predictable texts prepares students for more sophisticated analyses with more challenging texts. Once networks for typical cultural images can be readily identified, their deviation or non-normative variants are more likely to be recognized. Indeed, such comparisons are useful. Given prior familiarity with predictable cultural networks, students have less difficulty linking ruptures in individual cultural patterns to shifts in the network as a whole. They have developed a set of tactics for analysis.

Thus when figures in an episode interrupt one another, students trained in cultural reading have learned to note the social class, gender, or age of the interrupter and the interrupted (see Tannen, this volume). They have learned to attend to whether such patterns occur consistently in other episodes. Students can now engage in predicting patterns and synthesizing newly confirmed patterns with those noted previously.

When readers predict what behaviors and reactions are likely to occur, they engage in *protention.* The cognitive processes through which the reader adds new behaviors and reactions to the cultural network Iser calls *retention* (1981: 110–112). Conducted as suggested in this paper, reading can render explicit the implied relationships between socially allowable and disallowable practices. Those readers who collate isolated features into patterns of larger social networks read literature as case studies in culture. They uncover the hidden rules for variant and invariant behaviors. To use Iser's term, such readers *concretize* a text's cultural implications. In his word:

At this point the role of the reader starts to become more concrete. He [/she] now has to occupy certain standpoints, so that his relation to the text, hitherto undefined, takes on a degree of determinacy. The negation of specific elements of the repertoire had shown him that something was to be formulated which was outlined but concealed by the text. The gradual progress of this formulation draws the reader into the text but also away from his own habitual disposition, so that he finds himself impelled more and more to make a choice between standpoints. [This incongruity] . . . can generally only be removed through the emergence of a third dimension, which is perceived as the meaning of the text (1981: 218).

ENDNOTES

*Thanks to Katherine Arens for helping me think through the premises described here, and to Heidi Byrnes for feedback and detailed editorial suggestions.

1. In my oral presentation at the conference on text and context, I used the German term "trivial literature" (*Trivialliteratur*) to refer to popular texts. I am indebted to Elinor Ochs for pointing out the inappropriateness of this term in English and to other participants who suggested useful substitute terminology.

2. Since other standard work in the field suggests that about 81,000 of 86,000 words occur only 10 percent of the time in a range of passages assessed (Carroll, Davies, and Richman 1971), 5,000 words may suffice to facilitate comprehension. While 2,000 words is seriously short of native speaker counts, the gap is not as large as was once thought. Nation (1990) points out that while the estimates vary widely for English (with some earlier estimates as high as 120,000 words), recent research "suggests around 20,000 words for undergraduates are most likely to be correct" (11).

REFERENCES

Austen, J. 1940. *Pride and Prejudice.* New York: Heritage.

Bernhardt, E. 1990. "A Model of L2 Text Reconstruction: The Recall of Literary Text by Learners of German." *Issues in L2: Theory as Practice/Practice as Theory.* Eds. L. Bailey and A. LaBarca. Norwood, N.J.: Ablex. 21–43.

Carroll, J., P. Davies, and B. Richman. 1971. *Word Frequency Book.* New York: American Heritage.

Geertz, C. 1973. *The Interpretation of Cultures.* New York: Basic.

Gilman, S. 1985. *Difference and Pathology: Stereotypes of Sexuality, Race, and Madness.* Ithaca: Cornell UP.

Iser, W. 1981. *The Act of Reading*. Baltimore: John Hopkins UP.

Mollica, A. 1985. "Student Exchanges: Getting to Know One Another." *Canadian Modern Language Review* 41: 697–722.

Mukarovsky, J. 1964. "Standard Language and Poetic Language." *A Prague School Reader*. Ed. Paul L. Garvin. Washington, D.C.: Georgetown UP. 17–30.

Nation, I. S. P. 1990. *Teaching and Learning Vocabulary*. Rowley, Mass.: Newbury.

Saragi, T., I. S. P. Nation, and G. F. Meister. 1978. "Vocabulary Learning and Reading." *System* 6: 72–78.

Steffensen, M. S., Chitra Joag-Dev, and R. C. Anderson. 1979. "A Cross-cultural Perspective on Reading Comprehension." *Reading Research Quarterly* 15: 10–29.

Svanes, B. 1988. "Attitudes and 'Cultural Distance' in Second Language Acquisition." *Applied Linguistics* 9: 357–71.

— Chapter *16*

In and Around the Foreign Language Classroom

Barbara F. Freed

Carnegie Mellon University

Elizabeth B. Bernhardt

Ohio State University

INTRODUCTION

We would like to lead our discussion of contexts of learning in a slightly different direction from that of the preceding chapters. We might begin by asking you to visualize the more or less typical American college or university foreign language classroom.[1] While your fantasies or images may vary somewhat from person to person, the immediate vision is probably fairly consistent: one instructor, more or less fluent in the use of the target language, and some fifteen to twenty-five students with varying backgrounds, varying degrees of motivation, aptitude, and experience who for one reason or another are joined together in a four-walled learning environment. The physical characteristics of this setting may vary from one defined merely by a blackboard and traditional instructional materials to a setting enriched by a wide variety of high-tech learning devices. This more or less self-contained learning community spends some fifty minutes together, three to five times a week, focused on the general goal of "learning a foreign language."

There are, of course, variations of this theme. These variations may depend, for example, on the training, skills, and talents of the instructor. Some instructors take advantage of local foreign language resources to bring students out of their assigned classroom. The variations also depend on the flexibility, resources, and innovativeness of the institution. Some high schools offer brief exchange programs for their students; more and more colleges and universities are encouraging study-abroad or work-abroad experiences (Carlson et al. 1990; Freed 1991b). In addition, students' goals, expectations, and backgrounds may stimulate some variation. When many students have study-abroad experience or special interests in specific facets of a foreign culture, accommodations can be made for them, particularly in the curriculum of small liberal arts colleges. Nonetheless, these variations are the exception, not the norm. A highly restricted learning environment represents the standard setting for learning a foreign language within the American university context.

This paper will consider contexts of learning such as these and will examine their potential links to second language acquisition research. In this discussion as elsewhere (Freed 1991a), no distinction will be made between second and foreign language acquisition except to acknowledge that the context of learning represents one of several variables that play a role in the acquisition of non-mother tongues. The notion of "context of learning" itself will be expanded to include not just students in various types of instructional settings, in and around the foreign language classroom, but also the general educational system as it exists within the American sociopolitical context, with all its associated values and concomitant constraints.

Liston and Zeichner (1990) have noted the necessity of acknowledging and accounting for this larger context in education. They argue:

> It is simply impossible to isolate classroom life from the school's institutional dynamics, the ever-present tensions within the community, and the larger social forces. . . . In order to act effectively we have to recognize the influence of the social context. In order to bring about a desired state of affairs, we have to examine the societal structures in which students live and teachers work. (612)

This discussion will therefore examine a variety of broader social and institutional contexts that shape the instruction and ultimately the learning of foreign languages within the American system of higher education.

THE AMERICAN CONTEXT OF LEARNING

In order to explicate the context of foreign language instruction in the United States in the last decade of the twentieth century, one must first consider the beginning decades of the twentieth century. Only with an understanding of the social history of America can one capture the spirit that has brought about what we currently term "foreign language instruction."

America has frequently been criticized not only for its staunch monolingualism, but also for its failure to preserve ethnic languages and to foster ethnic cultural identity. Advocacy of cultural and linguistic homogeneity was widespread at the turn of the century. For example, Teddy Roosevelt argued in 1910 that there was no role in the United States for "hyphenated Americans" and he adopted an active policy of "Americanization" (Krug 1976). Krug comments:

> Most educators and teachers profoundly believed in the sacred mission of Americanization and had an abiding faith in the ability of the American environment and of American education to transform human nature. (102)

Criticisms of this melting pot ideology are well-founded but they need to be put in the proper perspective. During the great immigration waves of the first decade of this century, this country had to provide an education for the large masses who reached its shores. Schools had to be opened overnight to provide for the millions of children and adults who for the first time in their lives could begin to realize a knowledge beyond that which would sustain them until the next day. The only way this kind of mass education could work was through a *lingua franca* that provided basic knowledge in reading, writing, and arithmetic. Seen through the eyes of contemporary foreign language educators, this education through one language might seem to have focused unduly on the delivery of factual information, too little on critical thinking. But again these were the constraints imposed by the need to provide, quickly and efficiently, large masses of illiterate or semiliterate immigrants with basic literacy skills.

Our task in this paper is to explicate these facts in greater detail, trying to be historically accurate, without being either apologetic or anachronistically critical. We have organized our discussion around the points alluded to above: first, America's monolingual yet multi-ethnic heritage; second, our structure/fact-oriented system of public education; and, third, the effect of these legacies on foreign language teacher education as well as on the language delivery system.

America's Monolingual yet Multi-Ethnic Heritage

In a recent article, Ferguson and Huebner have identified the overall dominance of English in American life as the most salient part of the language situation in the United States. In the course of their discussion they emphasize what we all know only too well: "English is the *de facto* national language of the U.S.; its status is maintained by powerful social pressures and non-English speaking immigrant groups have generally experienced relatively rapid attrition of mother tongue competence and corresponding shift to English" (1989: 1). This situation carries with it obvious and powerful prejudices not only against the need for Americans to learn second languages, but also against the use of other languages and diverging cultural values and practices. Despite recent acknowledgment and growing concern for the economic, political, and cultural limitations imposed by this set of values, the American monolingual perspective remains the prevailing belief system and context in which foreign language instruction takes place. Considering the English Only movement as well as the number of states that have adopted or proposed legislation to declare English the official language (di Pietro 1988: 2), it would not be an exaggeration to state that the social context of the United States is largely responsible for the marginal role foreign language learning plays in our society. Granted, there has been some increased enthusiasm for the learning and teaching of foreign languages in the past decade; yet this enthusiasm is colored by what Kramsch (forthcoming) terms "conflicting trends [that] currently coexist: the push for greater assimilation of immigrants, and the push to make Americans proficient in foreign languages."

In contrast to Europe, in fact to most of the world, where the learning and use of second and often third languages is begun at a young age and taken for granted, the importance of foreign language learning has never been incorporated into the American value system. Di Pietro (1988) reminds us that the early colonies were rather tolerant toward non-English speakers because of the need for immigrants from a variety of nations to "populate the frontiers" (5), adding that concerns about non-English speakers were raised only when there were questions regarding "control of national matters" (6). But di Pietro notes that this attitude did not last much beyond the first hundred years of the United States. He continues:

> Negative feelings toward German, Polish, and the Scandinavian languages were especially strong during and after the First World War. It was around this time that local ordinances were passed forbidding the use of German. One state governor went so far as to ban the use of all languages other than English on the telephone and in public places. (6)

Developments in education and psychology also contributed to the negative attitude toward non-Anglo languages and cultures. Kamin (1977) reports that screening tests for "feeblemindedness" conducted in the 1920s "established" that 83 percent of the Jews, 80 percent of the Hungarians, 79 percent of the Italians, and 87 percent of the Russians fit into the feebleminded category. Thomson and Sharp (1988) argue that this type of "finding"

> directly contributed to Congress passing the Johnson-Lodge Immigration Act of 1924, which effectively established national origin quotas as permanent immigration policy discriminating against southern and eastern Europeans. There is thus considerable evidence to indicate that in America, eugenic concerns received sufficient prominence from these social changes to have a marked impact on attitudes and policy making at the highest level. (263)

It is this century-long societal and ultimately institutional attitude that mitigates against the learning of foreign languages in the United States. Young Americans have been taught to believe both in ethnic and cultural integration as a value and in the rights of the individual. Social studies educators argue that this state of affairs is a potential paradox, referring to neither monolithic integration nor ethnocentric pluralism, but rather to a kind of pluralistic integration. Patrick (1986) comments:

> Pluralistic integration embodies majority rule with minority rights and thereby is most compatible with western theories of political democracy—derived from the Enlightenment—and with the American civic tradition. Pluralistic integration has a justifiable claim on the curriculum, because . . . it is more congruent with social reality and more compatible with the U.S. civic tradition. (175)

The end result of these teachings is a society that more or less accepts ethnic plurality, but that demands integration through a common language.

There are two indirect consequences of such an attitude. First, the vast majority of foreign language programs do not, indeed cannot, bring students to advanced levels of proficiency. It is not difficult to find adults who announce with embarrassed pride that they never learned to say anything in the foreign language they studied for several years. Sadly, it is also not uncommon to hear language teachers admit that "the only way you can really learn to speak the language is by spending time abroad." Clearly, when teachers essentially admit that they cannot teach what they have been charged with teaching, their public is reluctant to hold them in much esteem.

Closely associated with these attitudes is the fact that funding for foreign language learning research and instruction has remained at a minimal level. It is true that in recent years the United States Department of Education has provided notable support for foreign language education, and the National Endowment for the Humanities has increased its commitment to foreign languages, especially the less commonly taught languages. By establishing National Language Resource Centers, federal policy is now taking a more favorable stance toward foreign language education. However, up to now, the limited monies have been used to support more short-term than long-term projects. Jarvis (1991) characterizes these efforts as follows:

> The meager amounts that were provided were often utilized for short-term, glamorous-appearing goals, such as the development of model programs that others would presumably emulate. There appeared to be little patience for the quest for long-term isolated insight, which, when combined with other such insights, might improve language teaching early in the twenty-first century. . . . Another consequence of the paucity of funding is the very small number of long-term research programs discernible in the literature. (297–98)

The situation described above reflects community attitudes and expectations that are inherent in our sociopolitical context. They all contribute to what Valdman has aptly labeled "the highly specific context of foreign language instruction in this country" (1991: 184).

Structure/Fact-Oriented Public Education

American education has traditionally been characterized by a behaviorist orientation to teaching and learning: an orientation that stresses conformity and that is often seen as the servant of the economy rather than of the individual; as the "practical application of knowledge," rather than as "knowledge" itself (Hirsch 1987). As noted earlier, this tradition evolved from the numerous social forces at work in the nineteenth century.

The most crucial of these was the role played by the common school, defined as "a school under state control, teaching a common body of knowledge to students from different social backgrounds" (Spring 1986: 74). The intention of such schooling was to decrease hostility between and among ethnic groups and to foster political and social harmony. These intentions were shared by liberals who were interested in helping lower social classes become economically viable; they were shared by conservatives who were fearful of an uprising from those same lower social classes. The result, however, of providing schooling to all, regardless of background or ability, was a system that focused on information that could be grasped by all.

Simultaneously, large industries were beginning to evolve. The concern of these businesses was to have a healthy workforce that had enough skills to succeed in the workplace. This constituency, too, wanted fact-oriented laborers who were intent on doing a good job—not philosophizing about it or bemoaning their condition in life. Both of these forces helped to form the American public school system as we now know it.

This model of schooling has had its critics. Aronowitz and Giroux (1988) call it "the factory model of schooling." Freire (1970) describes the assembly-line nature of the model most graphically:

> Education thus becomes an act of depositing, in which students are the depositories and the teacher is the depositor. Instead of communicating, the teacher issues communiques and makes deposits which the students patiently receive, memorize, and repeat. This is the "banking" concept of education. (58)

Such an orientation carries with it a related focus on product above process and, in the case of language, an almost exclusive focus on language as an object. This phenomenon has created in foreign language classrooms, at both the secondary and the college level, a tightly organized system of curricular organization. This system has been described by Kramsch as one that relates learning to "the ability of learners to display items of academically defined, and thus socially acceptable, knowledge, to match this knowledge with pre-established norms, to equate it with numbers of chapters in a textbook or items on a syllabus" (1990: 31; see also Graman 1988: 443). It is a system that values achievement or mastery over proficiency or competence and tends to measure learning by time served— as Brod once observed, "perhaps an appropriate way to measure criminal justice, but not, it seems, to measure learning" (cited in Freed 1981).

The curricular organization of the modern university has also worked against creating optimal contexts for foreign language learning. Various aspects of language study have traditionally been spread throughout the university curriculum, removing language teaching and learning from the fundamental disciplines with which they are associated: linguistics, psychology, anthropology (see Stern 1983 for a fuller discussion). Not only does such a system separate language teaching, language learning, and language learning research from the disciplines with which they are most intimately related, but it creates an infrastructure that devalues both language teaching and ultimately language learning (see also Lange 1990c). This situation has led to a fragmentation that disrupts, retards, and occasionally distorts language teaching and language learning research.

We do not need to rehearse the history of foreign language teaching in this country. Suffice it to say that despite the considerable, if sometimes misunderstood, emphasis on communicative orientations to instruction within the last fifteen years, and regardless of the increasing attention to the classroom as a social context (Kramsch 1990: 31), there remains a preoccupation with structural approaches to instruction: approaches that stress well-formed speech and insist on presenting one linguistic item at a time in building block fashion (Long 1991: 4). In fact, in an examination of the second language curriculum from a banking model of education, Graman (1988) argues that "the main objective of most university foreign language programs is not to foster second language acquisition, but rather to keep the program and the teaching assistants uniform and orderly" (443). In summary, it seems that we continue to perpetuate a decontextualized view of language, regardless of increasing numbers of textbooks that offer often superficial attempts at situational and contextualized language learning exercises. We have not yet arrived at the point where language learning is understood to be more than just acquiring a tool or skill for conveying content but also a means for shaping that content.

Exacerbating these concerns are the powerful influences of the publishing industry. As in all other commercial endeavors in the market place authors are encouraged to produce what will sell well. Few are the publishing houses or authors willing to meet the challenges and take the risks of publishing texts and materials that reflect our growing understanding of second language acquisition research and its relationship to the classroom. Lange (1990b) comments:

> The real curriculum is not necessarily determined from speculative deliberations by academics or by practical requirements of classroom teachers. It is determined more by publishers and textbook authors than curricular theorists, curriculum supervisors, and teachers. In simple terms, we have handed the design of elementary, secondary, and college curricula to commercial interests that have determined both the content and direction of language problems. (104)

Graman (1988) makes a similar point, noting that foreign language textbooks are "almost always banking, rather than dialogic, in nature" (443–44).

As Liston and Zeichner (1990) reminded us above, all schooling is situated within a societal and institutional context. In this regard, there is nothing novel about the system of foreign language education in the United States. It parallels other content areas within the larger educational context. This is a context that demands measurable accountability and efficiency—both quantitative, "banking" concepts. As such the foreign language system is not a victim of these concepts; it is a part of the system that perpetuates them.

Foreign Language Teacher Education

Our system of foreign language teacher education, too, reflects the underlying structure of our educational system: one that rewards integration and that reflects an input-output or factory model of schooling. For example, we speak more in terms of teacher training than true teacher education. Recent literature on second language teacher education has taken up precisely this theme. Richards (1990) notes that the concept of teacher training is linked to a "methods-based view of teaching" (218). He continues:

> The history of our profession in the last hundred years has done much to support the impression that improvements in language teaching will come about as a result of improvements in the quality of methods, and that ultimately the perfect method will be developed. Some breakthrough in linguistic theory or in second language acquisition research will eventually unlock the secrets of second language learning, and these can then be incorporated into a supermethod that will solve the language teaching problem once and for all. (218–19)

Richards continues his comments by arguing that the training concept is mechanized in nature and presupposes that teachers are "technicians" (220). "Trained teachers" fulfill the commands of others and are given no and take no responsibility for their decisions; that is, they are perceived essentially as intellectual factory workers.

Juxtaposed to the training perspective on teaching is the development perspective. Richards and Nunan (1990) as well as Lange (1990a) have discussed this view at length. The concept of development implies a reflective practitioner who uses an arsenal of information to make decisions about interactions with students. Lange (1990a) outlines the information sources from which developing foreign language practitioners must make decisions: a competence in the second language; a knowledge of traditions of teaching in second language acquisition; research findings; clinical experience; discussions of theory; and understandings of evaluation processes (248–49). Lange concludes that teacher development "describes a process of continual intellectual, experiential, and attitudinal growth of teachers" (250). The extent to which this more contemporary view of teacher education has found its way into foreign language teacher education programs is most unclear.

At the secondary preparation level we have a potpourri of systems for teacher education. In some cases those who carry the responsibility for certifying teachers are housed in language departments; in other cases in colleges of education; in the case of very small institutions, local secondary teachers in collaboration with college faculty shoulder much of the responsibility (Schrier 1989). What is most clear is that the relationship between language teaching and the language learning disciplines is uneven. As Liston and Zeichner (1990) observe, a general statement about the nature of any educational endeavor is bound to be unsound: the context in which the institution sits, by and large, determines a particular model. Schrier (1990; 1991, personal commmunication) notes:

> In large institutions of over 20,000 undergraduates, 50 percent of the foreign language student's coursework is in the major and 30 percent is in the professional education area (based on the average B.A. of 124 semester hours). In institutions of less than 5,000 undergraduates, 50 percent of the coursework is in the foreign language major, and 25 percent of the coursework is in professional education work (based on the average B.A. of 180 quarter hours).

It is important to note that about half of the professional education coursework consists of student teaching or internship hours. In other words, much of the professional education is garnered under the supervision of practicing secondary school teachers. One general statement about the state of the "training" of secondary school teachers is that they receive the vast majority of their direction about becoming foreign language teachers from their time spent in college foreign language classes and in secondary school foreign language classes. They spend little time intellectualizing and reflecting on the process.

In training our teachers just as in teaching our students we tend to inculcate a shortsighted view of language learning. We promulgate different methods in the mistaken belief that they actually make a difference and with the conviction that our teachers will actually distinguish in practice between the tenets of these so-called different methods (Swaffar, Arens, and Morgan 1982). We leave teachers little time to think about why and how they might deliver instruction. We remind them that they must survive Monday morning and that the students must "learn to like" the foreign language or the enrollment might suffer. We instill in teachers the same model of economics that appears elsewhere throughout the educational system.

Many of these same issues persist at the university level where the situation is somewhat different but not much better. At this level we must begin by asking, "Who are our language teachers?" At the secondary level we have some information about who our teachers are, how they were trained, what the expectations are for public school certification. At the university level we have far less information. Our teachers may be first-year graduate student teaching assistants who have been entrusted, sometimes with no training at all, with the awesome responsibility of imparting an understanding of another culture, another consciousness. They also may be part-time lecturers or professors of literature or literary theory who do not want to teach language at all and who, as the disparaging statement goes, have not managed to publish their way out of teaching. Or they may be talented, dedicated, frequently published and well-informed senior professors who continue to teach languages and instill in their students a love for language and language learning.

The deficiencies in the language teachers' professional education are exacerbated by problems in the content area. The content area education of teachers, which forms the bulk of their coursework, has two major shortcomings. First, an appreciation for the richness, complexity, and variation of language and language use, for example, is rarely developed in students. Notable exceptions are at institutions that have undergone or are currently undergoing curriculum reform such as Loyola and Carnegie-Mellon universities. Herbert Simon (1990 personal communication) has long maintained, and we are inclined to agree with him, that students who study a foreign language should also learn about language learning and language learning research. This type of study would serve to enrich their understanding of what knowing a second language means. We find instead a continued emphasis on language as the object of study itself, an emphasis that promotes a piecemeal incremental approach to learning with an input-output product orientation.

Second, in our language programs we fail to bring our students to high levels of competence. This is hardly new information: Carroll (1967) told us more than two decades ago that foreign language majors did not graduate with more than a beginning level of oral proficiency. This situation does not seem to have changed much. ESL teachers are in a similar position. Wong Fillmore (this volume) tells us that one-third of all ESL teachers are interlanguage speakers. We can only guess at the percentage of currently employed foreign language teachers who are interlanguage speakers. We fail to bring our foreign language students to an acceptable level of oral proficiency (language majors as well as graduate students who are future members of the professoriate); concomitantly, we provide no provisions for professional development. We forget the language loss research and expect practicing teachers to maintain the level of proficiency with which they exited their foreign language program without any financial assistance or support from the profession they have chosen (Hammadou and Bernhardt 1987).

Teacher education is complex and varied. The many facets of it must be examined and reconceptualized within the biases and understandings of American education. It is the responsibility of all members of the profession to aid in this reconceptualization.

THE RELATIONSHIP TO SECOND LANGUAGE ACQUISITION

Given this review of some, if not all, of the uncontested realities of the macro-context of foreign language learning in this country, we must ask what the relationship is, or even can be, between SLA research and the larger institutional setting. Consider for example the nature of some of this research. There are, for example, studies such as those described in this volume by Ellis in his chapter addressing the nature of simplified input, the role of interactional modifications, the use of questions, the use of the learner's L1, and learner participation. Other SLA researchers, too numerous to cite here, analyzed the impact of various language teaching methodologies, the question of focus on form versus focus on content, the role of instruction, the development of interlanguages, and the usefulness of error correction (for reviews of much of this work see Freed 1991, for example). SLA research has also addressed questions that relate to learner age, the role of the first language, and language transfer, as well as Chomskyan notions of universal grammar and parameter setting in the acquisition of second languages (see, for example, Gass and Schachter 1989). Research has also considered the contrast between acquisition in tutored or classroom environments and in the untutored or natural environment, particularly analyses of developmental stages in SLA (see Chaudron 1988; VanPatten and Lee 1990). Some recent work has focused on second language acquisition in immersion and study-abroad environments. Much SLA research has also been concerned with various theories or models of second language learning (see Ellis 1986; Klein 1986; McLaughlin 1987, as examples).

Certainly in the narrower context of the individual language classroom, SLA research can help inform our teaching just as teaching can help inform our research. SLA research continues to bring us new insights about the process of language acquisition as it develops and is affected by numerous variables in and out of the classroom. Ellis (this volume), Pica (1991), and others attempt to relate this research to the improved design and delivery of second and foreign language teaching. But on a more global level we must ask how SLA research can be helpful in facilitating language acquisition and language learning within the expectations and demands of the American educational and sociopolitical context.

It has become commonplace to either reject out of hand any implications for teaching from SLA or linguistic theory and research or to disclaim the applications because they have been misunderstood, misconstrued, compromised, or ignored. These judgments may sometimes be accurate but they are also too simplistic.

All of the research findings have implications for foreign language teaching. Certainly concepts of language development so well documented in interlanguage research give us reason to reevaluate and rethink our expectations of students and programs. Research on interactional modifications in classrooms based on perceptions of proficiency also forces us to understand students not in a generic sense, but as individuals. Yet, given the constraints of the American educational system mentioned above, we must conclude that the relationship between SLA research and foreign language teaching in academic contexts can only be an indirect one at present. Lightbown (1985) made the point several years ago:

> Language acquisition research can offer no formula, no recipes, but it is an essential component of teacher education, because it can give teachers appropriate expectations for themselves and their students. (183)

Like Lightbown, we believe that SLA research can change the focus from teacher training to teacher education; but we believe that it will achieve its potential impact only as the social context for foreign language learning changes. How can interlanguage research ever be applicable in a structuralist system of education? How can interaction research be valid in a system that does not permit teachers to be independent decision makers?

SLA research must, of course, maintain its focus on the cognitive processes involved in learning languages; but it must include context-specific socio-attitudinal questions as well. This type of research has been dealt with extensively in the Canadian context, but it has been virtually ignored with respect to American foreign language students in classroom settings. As a profession we must ask among other things: How can we motivate a monolingual population that sits in an unspoken multicultural setting to learn second languages? And then: What can we do to facilitate that learning? How can the institutional/instructional context be molded to accommodate what we know about SLA? How can we adapt what we know to the expectations and attitudes regarding the learning of second languages? We submit that this is a large demand and one that fundamentally requires social change.

Hymes has reminded us for years that understanding the functions of language in the classroom is a special case of the general study of language in its social context. He repeatedly points out that the key to understanding language in context is to start not with language but with context, and to systematically relate the two (language and context) within a single model (1972: xix). This is no less true for understanding the foreign language classroom than the first language classroom.

Hymes insists as well on the necessity of knowing what goes on outside the school setting for understanding what goes on inside (1972: xi–lvii). In this case, understanding some of what goes on outside the foreign language classroom setting clarifies the limitations and constraints imposed on foreign language acquisition by the realities of the institutional, instructional, and sociocultural context.

CONCLUSION

As Ferguson and Huebner have pointed out, foreign language instruction and SLA research can be interpreted and understood only "as a result of historical process and [in] response to current needs and values" (1989: 1). Thus, it may be difficult if not impossible to reconcile the potential applications of research on language learning in various settings in and around the foreign language classroom, with the broader context in which language learning takes place.

We must strive nonetheless to find a way to adapt and utilize what we know and are continuing to learn about foreign language learning with the realities of the educational setting. At the institutional level this can be done by continuing to fight for changes in foreign language teaching legislation, administration, and policy. We must continue to insist on more time, more flexible scheduling, and greater interdisciplinary links. We must identify and establish more innovative programs that integrate language learning into discipline specific courses and across the university curriculum, despite the bureaucratic headaches and hassles this causes for administrators. We must rethink the educational curriculum for foreign language students at the undergraduate and graduate level and create more comprehensive foreign language education programs. We must work toward the introduction of international programs and toward the introduction of international dimensions in all courses on our campuses. We must secure for students the opportunity to engage in informal out-of-class contacts that complement what takes place within the classroom. We must guarantee that language education is well articulated and incorporates a wide range of activities along the oral-literate continuum. Indeed, some excellent institutions are meeting these challenges: St. Olaf College, Northfield, Minnesota; Earlham College, Richmond, Indiana; Brown University, Providence, Rhode Island; and the University of Rhode Island, Kingston, Rhode Island. These universities have been actively implementing content-based courses and are dedicated to language across the curriculum (for a description of one such program, see Jurasek 1988). Yet, a handful of innovative universities is not enough in a country that boasts thousands of colleges and universities.

Beyond confronting our institutions of higher education, we must at the national level confront American society and political institutions at large. As d'Anglejan remarked in a penetrating article on language learning in and out of the classroom: "There is something alarming in the growth of the second language educational establishment in contemporary North American society. It suggests that we are placing on the shoulders of educators a responsibility which should be shared to a much greater extent by society in general" (233). An awesome task but who if not we should assume it? Only by assuming these responsibilities will we be able to incorporate the insights brought to us by SLA research and adjust what happens within the classroom context to the greater realities of what happens outside the classroom.

ENDNOTE

1. Throughout this chapter, the terms *America* and *American* refer exclusively to the United States of America.

REFERENCES

Aronowitz, S., and H. A. Giroux. 1988. "Schooling and Literacy in the Age of Broken Dreams." *Harvard Education Review* 58: 172–94.

Carlson, J., B. Burn, U. Yachimowicz, and J. Useem 1990. *Study Abroad: The Experience of American Undergraduates in Western Europe and the United States.* Westport, Conn.: Greenwood P.

Carroll, J. B. 1967. *The Foreign Language Attainments of Language Majors in the Senior Year: A Survey Conducted in U.S. Colleges and Universities.* Cambridge, Mass.: Harvard Grad. School of Ed.

Chaudron, C. 1988. *Second Language Classrooms.* Cambridge: Cambridge UP.

D'Anglejan, A. 1978. "Language Learning in and out of the Classroom." *Understanding Second and Foreign Language Learning.* Ed. J. C. Richards. Rowley, Mass.: Newbury. 218–37

di Pietro, R. 1988. "U.S. English: Filling a Need?" Paper presented at the Fifteenth Annual LACUS Forum, Michigan State University, East Lansing, Mich.

Ellis, R. 1986. *Understanding Second Language Acquisition.* Oxford: Oxford UP.

Ferguson, C., and T. Huebner. 1989. *Foreign Language Instruction and Second Language Acquisition Research in the United States.* Occasional Paper No. 2. Washington, D.C.: National Foreign Language Center.

Freed, B. 1981. "Establishing Proficiency Based Language Requirements." *ADFL Bulletin* 13: 2. 6–12.

———. 1991a. "Current Realities and Future Prospects in Foreign Language Acquisition Research." *Foreign Language Acquisition Research and the Classroom.* Ed. B. Freed. Lexington, Mass.: Heath. 3–27.

———. 1991b. "Report on Survey of Current Evaluation Practices in Assessing the Linguistic Impact of Study Abroad." Paper presented at the Annual Meeting of the American Association of Applied Linguistics, March 23, New York, N.Y.

Freire, P. 1970. *Pedagogy of the Oppressed.* New York: Continuum.

Gass, S. M., and J. Schachter, eds. 1989. *Linguistic Perspectives on Second Language Acquisition.* Cambridge: Cambridge UP.

Graman, T. 1988. "Education for Humanization: Applying Paulo Freire's Pedagogy to Learning a Second Language." *Harvard Educational Review* 58: 433–48.

Hammadou, J., and E. Bernhardt. 1987. "On Being and Becoming a Foreign Language Teacher." *Theory into Practice* 26(3): 301–6.

Hirsch, E. D., Jr. 1987. *Cultural Literacy: What Every American Needs to Know.* Boston: Houghton.

Hymes, D. 1972. "Introduction." *Functions of Language in the Classroom.* Eds. C. Cazden, V. John, and D. Hymes. New York: Teachers College Press. xi–lvii.

Jarvis, G. A. 1991. "Research on Teaching Methodology: Its Evolution and Prospects." *Foreign Language Acquisition Research and the Classroom.* Ed. B. Freed. Lexington, Mass.: Heath. 295–306.

Jurasek, R. 1988. "Integrating Foreign Languages into the College Curriculum." *Modern Language Journal* 72: 52–8.

Kamin, L. J. 1977. *The Science and Politics of IQ.* New York: Wiley.

Klein, W. 1986. *Second Language Acquisition.* Cambridge: Cambridge UP.

Kramsch, C. 1990. "What Is Foreign Language Learning Research?" *Second Language Acquisition—Foreign Language Learning.* Eds. B. VanPatten and J. F. Lee. Clevedon, U.K.: Multilingual Matters. 27–33.

———. Forthcoming. "Foreign Languages and International Education in the United States." Eds. C. Gnutzmann, F. Königs, and W. Pfeiffer. *Fremdsprachenunterricht im internationalen Vergleich: Perspektive 2000.* Tübingen: Gunter Narr.

Krug, M. M. 1976. *The Melting Pot of the Ethnics: Education of the Immigrants, 1880–1914.* Bloomington, Ind.: Phi Delta Kappa Ed. Foundation.

Lange, D. L. 1990a. "A Blueprint for a Teacher Development Program." *Second Language Teacher Education.* Eds. J. C. Richards and D. Nunan. Cambridge: Cambridge UP. 245–68.

———. 1990b. "Sketching the Crisis and Exploring Different Perspectives in the Foreign Language Curriculum." *New Perspectives and New Directions in Foreign Language Education.* Ed. D. W. Birckbichler. Lincolnwood, Ill.: National Textbook. 77–109.

———. 1990c. "A Content-Analysis of the MLA Draft Statement on Language Study in the United States." Presentation at the Modern Language Association Annual Meeting, December 28, Chicago.

Lightbown, P. 1985. "Great Expectations: Second-language Acquisition Research and Classroom Teaching." *Applied Linguistics* 6: 173–89.

Liston, D. P., and K. M. Zeichner. 1990. "Teacher Education and the Social Context of Schooling: Issues for Curriculum Development." *American Educational Research Journal* 26(4): 610–36.

Long, M. 1991. "Focus on Form: A Design Feature in Language Teaching Methodology." *Foreign Language Research in a Cross-Cultural Perspective.* Eds. K. de Bot, R. Ginsberg, and C. Kramsch. Amsterdam: John Benjamins.

McLaughlin, B. 1987. *Theories of Second Language Learning.* London: Arnold.

Patrick, J. J. 1986. "Immigration in the Curriculum." *Social Education* 50(3): 172–76.

Pica, T. 1991. "Foreign Language Classrooms: Making Them Research-ready and Research-able." *Foreign Language Acquisition Research and the Classroom.* Ed. B. Freed. Lexington, Mass.: Heath. 393–412.

Richards, J. C. 1990. "The Dilemma of Teacher Education in Second Language Teaching." *Second Language Teacher Education.* Eds. J. C. Richards and D. Nunan. Cambridge: Cambridge UP. 3–15.

Richards, J. C., and D. Nunan, eds. 1990. *Second Language Teacher Education.* Cambridge: Cambridge UP.

Schrier, L. L. 1989. "A Survey of Foreign Language Teacher Preparation Patterns and Procedures in Small, Private Colleges and Universities in the United States." Diss. Ohio State U.

———. 1990. "The Effects of the Foreign Language Curriculum on the Development of Language Teachers in the United States." Presentation at the Modern Language Association Annual Meeting, December 28, Chicago.

Spring, J. 1986. *The American School 1642–1985.* New York: Longman.

Stern, H. H. 1983. *Fundamental Concepts of Language Teaching.* Oxford: Oxford UP.

Swaffar, J. K., K. Arens, and M. Morgan. 1982. "Teacher Classroom Practices: Redefining Method as Task Hierarchy." *Modern Language Journal* 66: 24–33.

Thomson, G. O. B., and S. Sharp. 1988. "History of Mental Testing." *Educational Research, Methodology and Measurement: An International Handbook.* Ed. J. P. Keeves. New York: Pergamon. 261–67.

Valdman, A. 1991. "Some Comparative Reflections on Foreign Language Learning: Research in Europe and the United States." *Foreign Language Acquisition Research and the Classroom.* Ed. B. Freed. Lexington, Mass.: Heath. 170–87.

VanPatten, B., and J. F. Lee, eds. 1990. *Second Language Acquisition—Foreign Language Learning.* Clevedon, U.K.: Multilingual Matters.

Section V

Conclusion

— Chapter *17* _____

Conversational Epilogue

Claire Kramsch
University of California at Berkeley

Sally McConnell-Ginet
Cornell University

In the following conversational epilogue we would like to give the readers a flavor of the intellectual excitement generated at the conference from which this volume developed and of the type of dialogue that took place across disciplines and across cultures. In addition to the cast of characters identified in the table of contents and the preface, there are some unidentified voices heard in these conversations, most of which belong to language teachers who attended the conference.

ON CREATING CONTEXTS OF COMMUNICATION

What implications do the papers in the first section have for language teachers within an academic environment? The anxiety of the teacher caught between academic constraints and contextual multiplicity is well captured by Sandra Savignon in her opening statement. She quotes from the diary of a language teacher in training:

> SAVIGNON   "I believe in the essential value of a communicative approach, but still wrestle with the demons of my own education. I look wistfully upon drills in other textbooks and recall with fondness pattern drills in my own high school Spanish class and the pleasure I took in executing them well. There is also something to be said for the power that one must feel, much like a drill sergeant running the hapless students through their paces as you sadistically change pronouns and verbs and objects at will. I exaggerate, but the pull of the old while I struggle with the new reminds me of when I quit smoking. I knew it was bad for me and believed fully in the future without it, but, boy, it was hard to leave it behind."

The subsequent conversation among Elinor Ochs, Courtney Cazden, and Lily Wong Fillmore not only makes the feeling of intimacy created by conversational cooperation one of the major topics in this first session, but it also demonstrates what they preach.

CAZDEN The activities in which different groups in the classroom decide on interpretations of texts to the point of scripting them lead to terrific discussions with virtually everybody participating because everybody has to defend their interpretation and answer questions from other people about why they scripted the way they did. . . . So that there is both an engagement with texts and a very genuine stimulus for discussions. . . . Where you are dealing with texts that come from another culture, these activities also offer the possibility of coming to terms or at least approaching cross-cultural and cross-linguistic differences in text structure.

OCHS The kind of work that everyone has demonstrated today indicates that the interface between acquiring a language and acquiring culture is not so much looking at the content of language for what constitutes cultural knowledge or cultural competence, but looking at the way in which people are actually using language as a vehicle for gaining entry into one's culture. . . . We're constantly moving into culture even within the same physical community. There are communities within communities, and we're constantly having this process of learning. . . .

One of the most important aspects of it has to do with intimacy and what intimacy can gain you. Postulating hypotheses, defending, challenging, and so on, is a very important part of many cultures. It certainly has a privileged place in this society. You can't get access to certain kinds of communities of practice unless you're able to engage in those kinds of skills. As such, I think that creating intimate social contexts is an important thing to try to replicate in settings like school settings. The work that Courtney [Cazden] was speaking to in her presentation was in many ways trying to achieve exactly that. By having students read something and students then comment on it, it was trying to create a community, trying to decrease social distance, increase solidarity and a feeling of bonding with one another for that period of time. That sense of trust and sharedness allows for other kinds of language practices to be enacted.

WONG FILLMORE What Elinor [Ochs] has just said triggered something in my mind about these children like Lam losing or apparently giving up their mother tongue well before they have learned English . . . and, believe me, they give it up and they forget it. . . . As children give up their languages and the parents can't keep up with them because they're not learning English as quickly, what you have is a real loss of intimacy. And the kinds of socialization that Elinor has talked about—socialization in values, beliefs, attitudes, ways of doing things—get, if not destroyed, then certainly weakened. Gerda Bekalis, chief spokesman for the U.S. English people, said it's necessary to sacrifice a generation of people who aren't quite connected with their families and their roots, but I don't think so. I'd rather have a Mrs. F with my kids than someone else who's got no connections.

If interaction is important to language learning, the question is: What type of interaction? Do students learn to talk only by talking? Ochs shows that we have to differentiate among speakers, addressees, bystanders, eavesdroppers, all of whom play a variety of roles in classroom conversation.

OCHS   Another aspect of these language practices is the importance of multi-party interactions in socialization. It seems to me that many of the problems that have been addressed in classroom research as exemplified by Lily's [Wong Fillmore] and Albert's [Valdman] presentations have to do with the fact that students are placed primarily in the role of addressees. In the work on family interaction you see that children are very much placed in a variety of what Goffman called "footings," where they are secondary audiences, overhearers, unratified participants. They pick up information in a lot of different ways; something like overlap or ways of producing contingent queries in French get you socialized by engaging in interactions in which you may not be the direct addressee, but where you are participating (silently) and watching what happens. So, changing the footings of students seems to me a very important element in learning of all kinds.

According to Valdman, there are many features of speech students can and should only observe, not produce themselves.

VALDMAN   I believe that, in addition to using the language, students should have the opportunity to observe the authentic use of language. Today, with the availability of video, it's inexcusable not to have students witness intimate interactions such as those Elinor described. . . . I also believe that particularly at advanced levels we should have varied roles so that it should not only be student-student interaction or teacher-student interaction, but one should bring in resource persons. . . . It would be useful to stage interactions where you bring in two native-speaker peers of the students interacting in real communication on some important and current topic. These could be videotaped and then you could have the resource persons interact with students. . . .

The role of observation, listening, and reading as one kind of exposure to authentic language will be addressed again in the third conversation, p. 282. Non-authentic texts such as dialogues and drills, and non-native-speaker teachers like Mrs. F., when seen from the point of view of their appropriateness for creating contexts of communication, pose the vexing problem of creating group cohesion at the expense of linguistic authenticity. The question of authenticity is confronted directly in the conversation immediately following. The perspectives vary according to whether we see the learners as: children learning English in the U.S. (Wong Fillmore), adults learning foreign languages in academic settings (Valdman), or novices and experts in problem-solving situations (Ochs).

WONG FILLMORE   The instances of classrooms where the kids have absolute free access to one another, to interact as freely as they wish, ended up with children not learning English particularly well. There were those who wanted to identify even at five or six years of age, and those kids generally did better. Some kids . . . made use of a variety of sources of input and they were able to get along further than most of the other children. . . . But structuring a class strictly by peer teaching or do-it-yourself or giving children a whole lot of assignments to work at at their desks with ditto pages are not great ideas for language development in these kinds of settings. What you really need are teacher-structured discussions where there is a native speaker around to provide the kind of support and modeling and corrective feedback of the right kind.

VALDMAN   Many students come back from a year's experience [abroad] without having made significant progress. And this is because these years abroad are totally unstructured. Students do not have opportunities for these intimate contacts, for the real use of language in negotiating meaning, for example, trying to get problems solved.

Is Mrs. F likely to improve her accent and syntax?

WONG FILLMORE   Over ten years she hasn't improved much that I can tell; it's really a very stable system for her. And yet, she is very, very fluent. How did I myself achieve a more or less native-like command of English? I learned English when I was eight with no previous exposure to it; but I was in a small town where the Chinese children in the schools didn't outnumber the English speakers. Also, I had the privilege of playing with kids from Oklahoma, Texas, Arkansas who gave me a very rich kind of southern twang that I had to get rid of as well. But the main thing was that for a number of years there was nothing I wanted to be more than just like the round eyes with the big noses. And I worked at it. Now can Mrs. F and others like her do it? Yes, I think so, if she worked at it, if it was really important to her, if she wanted to talk like other people around her. But I don't think she wants to.

Can student-student interactions be dangerous and lead to a fossilized interlanguage?

VALDMAN   I don't believe so. There obviously will be interlinguistic features, but I believe that these can be eventually and progressively eliminated. . . . I think that student-student interactions are very important if students are to eventually develop what I call minimal communicability. And of course these are not authentic interactions, they are simulated. But nonetheless, I think that we should encourage them. . . .

What are the advantages and disadvantages of using undergraduates with an incorrect knowledge of the language to do drills, like in the Rassias method, where drills are supposed to encourage correctness?

VALDMAN   Some teachers believe that if students show significant interlinguistic features, then they should drill and eventually they will eliminate the problem. But that's a pure act of faith. I was myself a firm believer of this, until I progressively gave it up because I did not see any demonstration that drills will eventually lead to more accurate production. And when I was referring in my earlier remarks about complementing student-student interactions with other activities which lead the students closer to the selected norm, I did not mean that these activities ought to be anything that resembles pattern drills.

So should we abandon drills because they are inauthentic language?

OCHS   This issue of authenticity can go several ways. What we haven't addressed here is the authenticity of the foreign language classroom and the socialization of students into that kind of community of practice. A drill is one of the practices in this community, but there are others. There are multiple cultures in the foreign language classroom. In a drill, students are learning how to be experts in one kind of culture, as an entity unto itself, which can be authentic with respect to that community.

Also there are many things which we do in the classroom that don't directly foster language acquisition but foster the kind of intimacy and sense of group community that Elinor was talking about. Drilling is one of those activities.

VALDMAN   I agree. One of the functions of drills is to wake up and speed up rhythm. Drills create a certain type of social climate, or if you have an unruly class, if you want to get some discipline, fine, why not? But the teacher should recognize the function that it serves.

SAVIGNON   But the intonational contours of these drills have nothing whatsoever to do with the way these phrases would be uttered in any kind of outside-of-the-classroom context! They are completely misleading if you want students to comprehend spoken texts, where the intonational contours are very important to understand intentions and functions in conversation.

CAZDEN   There has been some research in the South Pacific where you have a similar situation of children learning English who get very little chance to hear English spoken by a native speaker, and the teachers are like Mrs. F. The English of these kids was far more improved by hearing the teacher read and by reading themselves with a lot of books available than by the pattern drills that had been the prevailing English language teaching methodology. Also far more should be done with the reading of plays. You can read them again and again and different kids can play different roles. So you have reason for doing repeated readings, and that is very good input for mental language systems.

How about dialogues? Thousands of students memorize thousands of dialogues in the hope that in real life the other person will say at least one line. What are the current views on the use of dialogues for language learning?

VALDMAN   If you look at current textbooks, you'll find that they're getting away more and more from twenty-to-thirty-line dialogues with incredibly complex sentences. What you'll find are mini-dialogues of about three or four lines that tend to be more authentic though they are not actually ever uttered by native speakers. Nonetheless, I would claim they are authentic. We have to make a distinction between what is actual data and what is authentic. For example, one of my friends who's done a TV course confessed that he was unable to have a butcher actually show what a butcher does. As soon as you put a butcher in front of a TV camera, he acts the way he thinks a butcher should act. So he had to get actors who were much more authentic, because they had observed butchers. Likewise, students can gain a lot by observing those rules of language use which have not yet been codified and thus are not found in our textbooks.

Why has the implementation of proficiency-oriented ideas lagged so often behind the proficiency goals?

VALDMAN The proficiency movement has invested too much time and money in speaking tests instead of looking at skills in which students can show much greater development, namely listening comprehension and reading. In last week's *Newsweek's* special issue on education, there was a statement by a former president of the MLA in which she tried to describe to journalists the full proficiency test and the ACTFL scales. She said: "Novices are word people, they simply reproduce words and phrases. Intermediates are sentence people. Advanced are paragraph people." The reason we are not more advanced in communicative language teaching today is because the people involved in the proficiency movement really did not know what proficiency is. First they stayed at the sentence level with discrete grammatical features. Then they discovered that there is such a thing as paragraphs, so now they look at shifters, like *quoi, eh bien,* and so forth in French. They view the development of proficiency as an additive process. But this is not going to lead us very far, because the relationship between grammar and a system of pragmatics is much more complex. We need to go beyond this type of very simplistic one-to-one relationship. If the proficiency movement had been involved in looking at rhetoric and text analysis, we could have by now some very good testing instruments for reading and listening comprehension and I think we would be much further along in genuine communication-oriented language teaching.

The difference between learning a foreign language in a classroom setting and in a natural communicative setting becomes apparent when one looks at prosodic features of speech and how learners tend to impose the prosody of their L1 on the L2, when they haven't had enough exposure to authentic L2 discourse.

To what extent do discourse functions determine syntax? Is it not the case that syntax is determined by the rules of prosody?

PRINCE First, we have to distinguish languages with strong constraints on what they can do with their prosody. I'm thinking particularly of Romance languages where you can't just move the tonic stress around the sentence depending on what you're talking about. In such cases, perhaps the prosody constraints can drive the syntax. I'm thinking of Professor Valdman's observation that you cannot use the inversion question form in French for an echo question. So the equivalent of "What's your name, William? *What's* your name?" in French has to be "Vous vous appelez comment?" And that may just follow from the fact that you couldn't say in French for intonation reasons "*Comment* vous appelez-vous?" as you can in English. That aside, English and Yiddish are both languages that can move stress fairly freely, so I don't think there is any way we can say that intonation would drive the syntax in English or Yiddish. In both cases the prosody follows what you want to say. So, in both the Yiddish Movement case in English [ed. Yinglish] and the Focus Movement case in English, the initial constituent is the focal constituent, the new information, that gets the tonic stress. There are differences in the stress that the rest of the sentence gets. In the Standard English Focus Movement, the rest is salient in the discourse context, and therefore tends to get very destressed. So in: "They bought a dog, *Fido* they named it," *they named it* is destressed because it's supposed to be on your mind. "What did they name it?—*Fido* they named it." In the English cases, as in Yiddish, it simply has to be plausible. The speaker is not expecting to hear or necessarily to be thinking about that, and so it's less stressed than the initial constituent, but it's not as destressed as it would be if it were taken to be absolutely salient. So let's take a minimal pair as an example of Standard English Focus Movement. If someone says: "He wants a Lincoln?—No a *Caddy* he wants," that's standard. I'm changing the value of the make attribute on the car. Contrast that with English "A *Caddy* he *wants*," where there is a little more stress on the *wants*, but I don't think that's a dialectal difference. This is because the fact that he wants something is not taken to be salient in the context. So, in the cases that I talked about I don't think the prosody drives the system.

Do foreign language students tend to maintain L1 prosody in L2?

PRINCE   Twenty-six years ago I taught French, and as I recall, they did.

How close are we to actually having a grammar of enunciation that we could systematically teach?

VALDMAN   The level of research in syntax and pragmatics is still very limited, and it would be risky to try to write sociopragmatic rules when we do not yet have abundant data. We cannot write absolute rules. But this does not prevent us from having third- and fourth-year French students and teacher trainees observe and analyze what native speakers actually do. They can see, for example, that the four constructions (*Tu vas où? Où vas-tu? Où tu vas? Où est-ce que tu vas?*) are not synonymous, that native speakers do not freely go from one to the other, that there are some constraints that they might themselves try to work out in the absence of textbooks. . . .

OCHS   This speaks in favor of making teacher and students into ethnographers. We can learn from ethnomethodologists that there are very many aspects of language use that are below the level of conscious awareness. They can be made conscious by pointing out the linguistic resources and discovering together the interactional work that these linguistic structures do.

ON NEGOTIATING MEANING ACROSS CULTURES

If the first conversation had to do mostly with authenticity of language use and the psychological effects of interaction in the classroom, the second one tries to grapple with the production and reception of meaning of spoken and written texts in cross-cultural contexts. Here again the moderator, Nicolas Shumway, states the problem in paradoxical terms:

> SHUMWAY   Can foreign language students actually be taught how to read and not to misread? Professor Miller seems to say that meaning is ultimately inaccessible. I tell my graduate students, who came to Yale to study literature and not language teaching methodology: "Look. It is perfectly fine for you to speculate endlessly about the elusiveness of meaning in your literature classes, to say that meaning doesn't really exist, that everything is simply a movement from one abyss to another. But, in beginning Spanish, meaning exists."

In his response, J. Hillis Miller makes the important distinction between reference and meaning. Words always say more than what they refer to, and that is what makes translation and, indeed, teaching meaning in a foreign language so difficult. The problem is not teaching meaning, but knowing when and how to complexify the students' views about what meaning is.

> MILLER   I'm not against meaning. I think there's too much. I think it's a matter of meaning being very hard to carry over. Nor did I say that words only refer to other words. The three possibilities of meaning in the Goethe text are not chosen among, they're not arranged hierarchically. There is no possibility of simply abandoning the notion of reference or meaning, those being two different things. The example of the Hölderlin translation of Sophocles is an extreme one, but it's worth recognizing what happens when you say, "Well, I'll be really faithful to the original because he is a very great poet." Such translations are almost unreadable, but they are very, very instructive.

In the face of such multiplicity of meanings, what should the foreign language teacher do? Janet Swaffar suggests using popular texts, or "Trivialliteratur," because the meanings or values they convey are culturally straightforward and expressed in simple syntax. This suggestion raises questions, as the following conversation shows, where the participants try to tease out the various facets of reading to learn versus learning to read.

> SWAFFAR   First there is a pedagogic concern here. I want to get the students to read. Students don't learn enough vocabulary because we don't give them sufficient contexts. In general in the course of a second semester, they read only 100–150 glossed pages. For them to read more, I have to give them things to read that they will enjoy reading because they are immediately comprehensible. So I have my students read up to fifty pages of trivial literature for one class preparation. They're not going to understand everything, obviously, but trivial texts belong to an international culture. So even if they don't grasp the discourse function of certain syntactic usages, that won't interfere with their fundamental grasp of what's going on, because the context is familiar to them.

What do you mean exactly by "trivial texts"?

SWAFFAR   I mean texts that confirm a culture's myth of itself, its self-stereotype. I'm thinking of the difference between *Dallas,* the TV show, and maybe a movie like *Giant* or *Hud,* where the whole notion of the myth of the West is put into question. Or take, for example, soap operas. Students will watch a soap opera but they won't watch *Wilhelm Meister* on a television program. Or they will watch *Das Boot,* but they're not necessarily going to see *The Tin Drum.*

We're talking about different genres, and they have different kinds of complexities about them. What about conversational texts? Would they be trivial texts? Triviality doesn't seem to be a property of the text, but rather a property of something you might do with the text.

SWAFFAR   I was trying to make a pedagogical distinction, and I would agree that ultimately no text is trivial. I am really attempting to do two things at once: have students talk about the language of the text and negotiate what pieces of the text constitute what types of systems of signifiers. We read various kinds of literature to assess where the real and apparent cultural images diverge. Certain types of works of the more popular kind have a more univalent typology. They are not extended discourses that look at ruptures in the society, but rather they confirm the same images over and over again. They present systems of beliefs that people have and that they want to see recognized or realized and reaffirmed. Our students need to look at these beliefs and analyze them.

Whether they are trivial or not, popular texts in the foreign language can be a good source of information about the culture. But beyond information, where does reading for meaning, or critical reading, come in?

SWAFFAR   I am first interested in getting them to read. And they really enjoy, for example, reading about our culture, about what is written in French or Spanish about Americans. You can deconstruct that, as it were, in terms of what kinds of prejudices these texts convey. Reporters in a German magazine describing, for instance, the situation in Detroit, ask why there is no revolution in the United States. Their cultural tolerance to the type of poverty we have in some of our larger cities is very different from ours. And it is very useful to point out that difference in cultural tolerance. It is important to start out with the C1 in the L2. There's nothing wrong with using the second language to talk about your own culture, on the contrary. But I would agree that students need to be critical of all kinds of literature, and they need to recognize which literatures really take on the norms of the society and question them, both at the linguistic and at the semiotic levels.

How can students grasp the typology of unfamiliar contexts?

SWAFFAR   My approach is to give them first the comfort of familiar contexts where they are able to negotiate, to play jigsaw with the various categories I suggested ("Here's where governance is taking place, this is where legitimacy is being questioned"). Once that critical language is in place, then you can read more challenging literature and discover the subtleties, at the micro-level Professor Miller is talking about.

Shouldn't we be suspicious of the type of micro-analysis Professor Miller engaged in with respect to the word Bild *in Goethe's novel, inasmuch as it does not present the big picture?*

> MILLER   Sure. You should always be suspicious of all micro-examples. On the other hand, the big picture depends on the small details in the act of translation and in the act of reading. For me, it's the parable of Pooh and the honey pot, which he's going to use as a bait for the Heffalump. Pooh wonders whether it's honey all the way down. After all, somebody may have put cheese in the bottom. I think it would be well to be properly skeptical about a single example and wonder if there might not be some cheese elsewhere in that novel.

This debate about the deconstruction of texts in language classes shows the fundamental dilemma of language pedagogy. On the one hand, it might be necessary to take texts that are culturally familiar to the students so that they will be motivated to read and increase their vocabulary. On the other hand, if we don't want to perpetuate stereotypes, we need to defamiliarize these texts by deconstructing the very cultural context that made them attractive to the students in the first place. How and when both activities should take place are major questions facing the language teacher. The issue touches not only the teaching of literary texts, but that of conversation as well, as Miller points out in the following.

> MILLER   The opposition between daily life and literature is a very problematic one. We're all the time in daily life re-creating a world of our own out of the ordinary, trivial language that we use. So I don't see literature as being all that different from daily life, or one kind of literature being distinguishable from another on those grounds. The question of triviality, however, is an important one, and I want to respond to it in relation to what Professor Shumway said about those poor graduate students who have to teach beginning Spanish to make a living. As was said earlier, the most ordinary language is not trivial. At the very beginning of language instruction you encounter problems which are the same problems that you encounter twelve years later when the people have total near-native mastery of the language. And to pretend that that's not the case, that you begin with simple sentences which there's no problem translating, seems to me a mistake, because it's condescending to the students and it's not true. It's a lie. The graduate students' knowledge of theory has to be capitalized on. This is an important point, because so many of the graduate students who teach beginning languages are there to do something else. The knowledge they have of theory and of literature, of reading, can and should be made use of, not erased, even though that may be very difficult. In the teaching of English composition, it's the same kind of problem. I find fascinating the question of the links you can make between literary theory at the most abstract and apparently far out direction, and the teaching of composition at the other end. In the area of English composition and the teaching of English as a second language, this is a frontier

area at this point. What appears to be at the very beginning and what's at the highest level of advanced graduate work come back together again. I'd like to make a plea for that as an important feature that brings me together with those of you who are interested in language at work as language teachers.

SAVIGNON   The problem is that language teaching itself is perceived as a trivial task. We can change that if we can make our graduate students who are teaching the introductory courses aware of the nature of language, interpretation, and negotiation of meaning in language learning.

An interesting aspect of this debate is that it touches the core of the educational dilemma we described in our introduction. Whereas scholars engaged in literary or linguistic theory can plausibly claim to be accountable only to their fields, language teachers must be held accountable to the social order. The more research brings to the fore the complexity of human communication, the more it raises questions about the ability of language teachers to teach what students need to know about the social order. Savignon's remark above reminds us how easy it is for scholars engaged in theory to trivialize the efforts of the practitioners. And yet the language teacher ultimately represents the very *raison d'être* of academia.

We can see some additional facets of this dilemma in the following conversation among Deborah Tannen, Pete Becker, Muriel Saville-Troike, and Eleanor Jorden. The moderator, Vijay Gambhir, speaking for language teachers, formulates the issue with a noticeable urgency.

GAMBHIR   Is it feasible or even desirable to teach this sociolinguistic competence—diglossia, code switching, code mixing, conversational styles, discourse functions—within a university instructional setting where we meet with our students for no more than three to five hours per week? The problem is particularly acute in the case of the languages of pluralistic societies like India, where we switch language, we switch cultures all the time.

TANNEN   I don't think such things can be taught per se. If we tried, for example, to teach a foreign culture's patterns of power and solidarity, we would violate the basic principle of contextual relativity I was talking about. These patterns vary according to who is talking and in what situation, and you can't codify this. What you can do is make the students aware of these conversational dynamics by making them observers of conversations throughout the semester.

SAVILLE-TROIKE   The situation of the foreign language learner is quite similar to that of the monolingual American Indians who have adopted English as their only language, but who have refused to violate the values and beliefs they learned in their native language socialization. I have a student from Japan who bows a lot to me and to other professors. The other day, one of her professors told her that she shouldn't bow in English or to American professors, because that wasn't considered appropriate. This professor was trying to teach her a sociolinguistic rule in English. She was crushed. "I know Americans don't bow," she said, "but that's my culture, and if I don't do that, I'm not being respectful and I won't be a good person." The sociolinguistic rules can be talked about, but it should be left to the learners' own decision to adopt them or not for productive use.

JORDEN   I agree, but without forcing the person to change her ways, I think it's extremely important to explain to her how the average American reads that particular signal. The person can then make her own decision. In one ESL class, for example, Japanese students were asked to introduce themselves by their first name. So they said, "My name is Taro" and so on; but then suddenly one man, the oldest in the class, said, "I will be called Mr. Tanaka." The teacher was very upset and asked me what to do about it. And I told her, of course it's all right for him to be called Mr. Tanaka, but he must know how Americans are going to react to someone in this culture who says: "Don't call me by my first name, call me only Mr. Tanaka."

The teaching of sociolinguistic competence: Not feasible? Not even desirable? Only something to be observed, a knowledge to be acquired, not a behavior to be adopted? The conversation related above seems to put in question the very concept of the classroom as the appropriate setting for teaching language as cultural practice.

BECKER   If we concentrated more on programs to get our students overseas and less on faculty salaries and classrooms, that might help. It's much better to send a student of Javanese to Java than to make them suffer through this inter-language that we pour on them in America. After years of torturing students, I came upon a different way of teaching which harked back to my field experience in Burma. There were two requirements in my class: students had to memorize a Burmese, Indonesian, or Malay proverb every day, to stock up their memory of the culture. They also had to play a song from that culture over and over, fifteen times. Listen to it fifteen times with some translation and then you can hear the song and hear all the words without them being translated, then you're done. There was no grammar instruction per se. What we call the structures and the grammar were just there in the songs along with the words. It seems to me a part of the torture to try and separate them.

Don't you think what's being put on trial here is the concept of the classroom?

JORDEN   I hope not! I think a great deal can be accomplished in the classroom. Students who go to Japan without some knowledge of what to look for and how to learn come back with all kinds of problems. If you send a beginner to Japan knowing no Japanese and he utters his first word, the first thing he hears is, "Your Japanese is marvelous." And the worse it gets, the more he gets praise. Now thanks to video technology we can introduce them to the culture before they go to Japan so they can understand better what's going on.

What do you mean by culture? The kind of timing Professor Tannen talked about is very difficult to teach. Are there any overt markers, for example, that make inter-ruptions acceptable, like "Well, excuse me, but . . ." or "That's pretty interesting, but I wonder if . . ." that we could teach?

TANNEN   The overt markers would be just the tip of the iceberg. For instance, there are always some people who will say, "Well, what really was going on is that the other people were rude," meaning "They haven't used the right marker." The obvious thing to say would have been, "Excuse me, I wouldn't normally interrupt you but . . . ." For some people, it would be condescending to go into a whole story, when obviously all you should do is to say it. And to other people, it would be rude no matter how you excused the interruption. So I think it's good to notice such markers, but they're just the most noticeable part of a very complex system. What we want to teach students is not how to use markers, but how to appreciate their variable meanings. What we want to teach them is a respect for diversity.

I am a French teacher with a multiethnic class. Americans always eat in class, Scandinavians take off their shoes, Germans knit, and Japanese never say a word. Do you have any advice for the frustrated instructor?

TANNEN   I would say: Talk about it.

ON SHAPING CONTEXTS OF LEARNING

This third conversation takes a closer look at the relationship between interaction and learning, specifically in instructional settings. The moderator, James Noblitt, sets the tone for a provocative conversation.

NOBLITT   If we actually look at the context in which we try to teach foreign languages and this great banquet of things that [is needed] for intelligent language learning, we might be putting in place a vision that far outstrips our ability to deliver in the time given to us. How do we know that the students are learning anything? They can learn the grammar perfectly and still not be able to order wine. Now we hear that they can order wine, but they can't understand the grammar. Maybe that's an artifact of not having time to do everything.

The most important questions addressed in this section are: What type of interaction best promotes acquisition of the forms of the language? and What is the relationship between negotiation of meaning and language learning? Research seems to show that the more varied the models of input and the opportunities for interaction, the more contexts of use the students will be exposed to and the more they will be able to develop natural modes of speaking. Feedback appears to be the most useful when given not in advance of fluency, but rather, at the time when the need arises in communication.

If we wish to retain fluency as an important goal, what specific pedagogical strategies would you support?

LIGHTBOWN   There are many different contexts in which students can develop fluency. It is clear from my experience observing language classrooms that people develop fluency through experience, by encountering fluent language. However, what really surprised me with these children in the comprehension-based program was the amount of text that they were able to produce on the basis of no experience in speaking, but only experience in hearing and reading texts. When we first came in and said, "Okay, now tell us about this picture that we're showing you," they produced quite lengthy texts, whereas the students who came from the audiolingual interactive classes tended to produce very limited, short texts, usually using the verb *be* and no lexical verbs. They would describe the picture by saying, "It's a boy, it's a bicycle, it's a swing, it's a tree," whereas the children from the comprehension-based program would say, "There's some children, they're playing on a swing." They would give them names: "Mary is on her bicycle, and John is riding the something or other." They had experience in extended texts, in stories, that went on beyond question-answer, question-answer. Part of teaching fluency is giving students an opportunity to hear fluent language instead of this choppy kind of interaction that we see in a lot of foreign language classrooms.

The students in the intensive programs that I talked about also have developed fluency through lots of group and pair work. When teachers did bring some attention to form, it did not seem to cause negative reactions on the part of the students. They appeared to appreciate the fact that the teacher was trying to help them say what they were attempting to say. So this corrective feedback offered by the teacher on a limited number of points was not contrary to the development of fluency, nor did it seem to diminish the students' motivation. As was said earlier about dialogues, practicing correct forms even if they are sometimes lengthy texts, doesn't necessarily lead to the kind of fluency that we would like to see. It is the gradual building up of the learner's own system that will lead to the fluency that we seek. Once they have developed some fluency, punctual, corrective feedback can be very helpful.

Students need to be exposed to models of natural fluency so that their interlanguage can take its course, but at the same time they need to be corrected, that is, their interlanguage needs to be destabilized. Do you see a contradiction there?

PICA   I don't see any contradiction. We know that languages aren't learned all at once. As Rod Ellis has pointed out, the developmental sequence is very similar in all learners, but the rate of acquisition is different, depending on the various inputs, the various models that destabilize the interlanguage system. Interlanguage is a dynamic system, so for us, the question is: How do we catch it and push it so that it goes in the direction of more target-like use.

What role do you see reading playing in the development of oral fluency?

LIGHTBOWN   In the comprehension-based program I was talking about, the students read very simple texts, and their English is still at a very basic level. But nevertheless they supply grammatical markers in their oral speech. Even though they don't supply them in all of the obligatory contexts, they still have observed that those markers are there and occasionally they will use them, whereas students from the audiolingual classes hardly use them at all when they speak freely. The importance of the written text is very great. In the intensive classes that I described in the other context, five hours a day, five days a week for five months, these students almost never see a written text. I'm convinced that that is a major gap in the development of foreign language in the elementary school particularly. One of the things that we're experimenting with now is bringing what we've observed in the comprehension-based programs into the experimental programs to expose the students to much more written texts as well as to oral texts.

Another way of developing fluency in a foreign language is to have students interact with other speakers of the language. Do these need to be native speakers?

PICA   As Rod Ellis has shown, there are many ways in which classrooms can be acquisition-rich environments. If we think about the conditions for comprehension of input in language acquisition, certainly there is no reason to think that learners can't be sources of comprehensible input for other learners. They can give each other access to meaning. They can also give each other opportunities to modify their production, manipulate it structurally. However, correct feedback or negative input is not necessarily given by other learners. The big question is: To what extent is understanding meaning in the foreign language a resource for the acquisition of syntax? One could argue that if in the process of negotiation you try to understand someone, you manipulate structures and you extract segments, and if these segments that they extract teach the learners about word order and phrase structure, then maybe that's good. But if they try and do this among themselves, maybe they're going to teach each other first language word order. This is an area that needs research, and I have just started on a project involving learner-learner interaction using the same framework I've been using for native and non-native speakers.

Does this put in question the privileged role of comprehensible input in language acquisition?

PICA   For a long time, standard theory in second language research was that comprehensible input fueled the acquisition process. Interaction and negotiation have been studied as a source of comprehensible input. However, people like Merrill Swain and now Lily Wong Fillmore have shown us that there is more to it, that there are people who are perfectly fluent, who understand everything, and yet who are not using the syntactic system of the second language. So we need to go further and examine these conditions to see in what way they are a source of data for syntax. Even nativists are saying that it is not just a matter of exposure.

What role do you see for native speakers in the foreign language classroom?

PICA   In the ideal world, we would like to have as many native speakers in the classroom as possible. With younger children in public schools, we need more opportunities for native speakers to want to come back to public schools. In the city of Philadelphia, you can't tell the difference between a second language class, a bilingual class, and a mainstream class because all the children have backgrounds where they have a different language at home than in their classrooms. So if more and more urban schools can be balanced in some way so that we have a lot of native-speaking children and children who come to school speaking a different language, we will have more opportunities for them to get this kind of input.

Do the adult native speakers need to be trained people?

PICA   We've done some work with native speakers just about off the street who haven't had any experience teaching, but when we put them in a classroom they act just like teachers! They don't negotiate (even teachers don't negotiate); they elicit the questions, they provide the feedback, take charge, guessing what students are trying to say to them. So when communication breaks down, students wind up thinking: "Oh, it must be me." I'd like to turn your question around and say: How can we train the teachers to behave less like teachers and more like native speakers? One way we're getting around it is through these jigsaw tasks. There, teacher and students have equal access to the information, both work toward a goal. Teachers don't ask the kinds of questions to which they already know the answer. Everyone is equal, everyone has to begin to understand each other in order to complete the task.

Pica shows quite clearly in her paper how these learning tasks can be structured so that their goals are similar to those of natural conversations. This theme is precisely the one that Ralph Ginsberg had picked up in his paper (unfortunately, unavailable for inclusion in this volume). He had argued that the "cognitive apprenticeship" provided by such tasks is transferable to real life outside the classroom. The discussion that follows gives an interesting example of how cross-disciplinary conversations can be the source of misunderstandings. In this case, the term "goal" used by Pica and Ginsberg means something else than what foreign language teachers generally understand by that term.

Your point about goal similarity and knowledge transfer is very important, but what do you do when you have a whole lot of different students with different goals and with only one thing in common, namely a level of proficiency on a test?

GINSBERG   The question is a valid one. However, I was not talking necessarily about people's motivations, but rather about the goal structure of particular activities they had to engage in, comparing the tasks that have to be done in the classroom with the tasks that have to be done in real life.

Would you negotiate goals up front with your class before you start? Is that something that can be agreed on beforehand?

GINSBERG   This probably doesn't answer that question, but I feel we want to avoid the radical disjunction between what people are learning in the classroom and what they learn out of the classroom. We want to structure instructional settings in such a way that the proper scaffolding is presented for transfer of skills to real settings. This is what I meant by the term "cognitive apprenticeship." I don't think we get at the psychological issue by negotiating the goal of transfer with the students themselves.

I wonder if students in a university setting are that clear as to what their goals are. Many students find themselves in classes without having really asked themselves precisely what their goals are. Could we make students actually think about what they would like to get out of this particular course?

Should we not look at motivation from a pedagogical and a sociopolitical perspective?

FREED   I'm not sure what we have to gain by learning more about what the motivational questions are. One thing that has impressed me in the work of Robert Gardner is his remark that sometimes the very fact of having a positive learning experience in learning a language begins to change attitudes. So one of the things we need to work on is creating more positive opportunities for learning and beginning them at earlier ages for longer times.

One of the noteworthy features of this conversation is that the two definitions of goals coexist over the first four turns-at-talk, prompting the speakers to talk at cross-purposes: for one, "goal" is a cognitive concept referring to the orientation of task structure; for the other, "goal" is an affective concept, representing the feelings that prompt students to even tackle the task. Foreign language education is so used to thinking only about the latter that participants have difficulty even talking about the former. Freed's remark, that motivation is intrinsic to learning, and that learning breeds its own rewards, so to speak, echoes the first conversation in which Ochs insisted that intimacy is not the condition but the reward for family conversations. This view of motivation runs contrary to what many teachers consider to be "motivating" and that is often of the noncognitive type. Freed's remark gives prominence once again to the fact that language as cognitive activity is the source not only of affective satisfaction and pleasure, but of social bonding as well. However, the insistence of the language teachers on addressing the issue of psychological motivation brings to light one of the major underlying issues in any such discussion, namely the tremendous social and political pressure placed on foreign language teachers by the growth of anglocentrism and the low value attached to literacy in the United States.

SHUMWAY   One of our great cultural myths is that of the melting pot. So we love examples of people who have melted, and we think it's wonderful that children of immigrants cannot talk to their grandparents any more.

But this goes on in many countries, not only in the United States! Look at Japan, China. The United States has a rather isolated geographical position and until the twentieth century was slightly out of touch with the rest of the world in ways many other countries were not out of touch with each other. In Israel, in the Soviet Union, it's the same thing. And doesn't French education promulgate the same monolingual attitude?

VALDMAN   I think our record in respect to teaching minority ethnic languages is much better than that of the French. The French revolutionaries in 1793 discovered that only one-sixth of the entire population at that time was capable of speaking French moderately well. So they asked the southern French speakers to sacrifice their language, which was deemed up to then the proper language, on the altar of the revolution.

Shouldn't the language teaching profession assume its responsibility for the changes that are needed for adequate instruction?

FREED   One beginning has been made with "language across the curriculum" programs or content-based instruction. These are efforts [not to limit] language [to] departments of language and literature, but to integrate foreign languages into other disciplines as well, so that students can read primary source texts in the foreign language in their history and social studies courses. We also need to rethink our undergraduate major. Currently it is rare that a major in German, French, or Spanish is made to think about language in any of the ways that we are thinking about [language] here.

It is our hope that continuing conversations like these may ultimately transform the contexts of language education.